Critical Acclaim for The Learning Paradox

"Every day the future keeps coming at us whether we like it or not. *The Learning Paradox* provides individuals and organizations with the keys to unlock the right attitude and the mechanism for developing the necessary skills to go out and meet the future with confidence."
– Kenneth Clarke, Chairman, Royal LePage

"*The Learning Paradox* allows us to internalize points and understand completely through meaningful, real-world anecdotes."
– Nick Truyens, Vice President, Finance, LEGO, USA

"*The Learning Paradox* is a manual for today's business leaders – a template for future strategy and decisions. Continual learning should be the basis of every leader's agenda. The ultimate test is staying green and growing."
– Bill Williams, CEO, TEC (an international organization of CEOs)

"In an era of rapid change and uncertainty, job security has quickly become a thing of the past. *The Learning Paradox* is a must-read."
– Arthur R. Soler, President, Cadbury Chocolate Canada

"*The Learning Paradox* provided insight and focused on the future by teaching us that we are ultimately responsible for managing our careers."
– Mark Sheinfeld, Senior Vice President, SHL Systemhouse (an MCI Company)

"*The Learning Paradox* forces you to think. Every leader and aspiring executive should read it."
– Rick Broadhead, Co-author, *Canadian Internet Handbook*

A crisply focused and well-written outline of what individuals, organizations and leaders must do to thrive in the chaotic changes of our time. Jim's central theme – learning, changing and coping with uncertainty are the only sources of security – should be emblazoned on every pay stub and financial statement."
– Jim Clemmer, Author, *Pathways to Performance*

"The power of *The Learning Paradox* is in its breadth and conciseness. Mr Harris has a strong grasp of the issues and the interplay of forces in today's business and working environment, and this is conveyed with clear language and effective examples."
– D'Arcy Mackenzie, Manager, National Education & Development, Ernst & Young

THE LEARNING PARADOX

*To my mother, Suzanne Harris whose love and support
encouraged me to pursue a life of learning,
and in memory of my father, Bob Harris.*

*To my brother and sister, Ian Harris and Cathy Harris,
with whom I have grown in love and life.*

*And to Aubie Graham, Thomas Berry, and Lee-Anne McAlear, who are
my greatest inspiration and teachers.*

Strategic Advantage Mission Statement

*We work to change the world
by changing ourselves and by helping our clients change.*

Strategic Advantage is a learning and teaching organization. We study emerging trends and technologies and their potential impact on businesses. We are committed to advancing the understanding and practice of cutting-edge leadership and assist our clients – individuals and organizations – to achieve the greatest possible security within a dynamic and changing marketplace.

JIM HARRIS

THE LEARNING PARADOX

GAINING SUCCESS & SECURITY IN A WORLD OF CHANGE

CAPSTONE

First published 1998 by Macmillan, Canada. This edition published by:

Capstone Publishing Ltd (A John Wiley & Sons Co.)
8 Newtec Place
Magdalen Road
Oxford OX4 1RE
United Kingdom
http://www.capstoneideas.com

British Library Cataloguing in Publication Data

A CIP catalogue record for this book is available from the British Library

ISBN 1-84112-189-4

The Learning Paradox is available on audio and videotape. See last page for order details. In North America fax in your order to (416) 467-0333 or call 1-800-491-6000 or visit www.jimharris.com. Email comments to: info@jimharris.com.

Grateful acknowledgement is made for permission to reprint excerpts from the following works:

The Digital Economy: Promise and Peril in the Age of Networked Intelligence. Copyright © Don Tapscott 1996. Page 77. Reprinted by permission from McGraw-Hill Companies.

Shifting Gears: Thriving in the New Economy. Copyright © Nuala Beck 1992. Reprinted by permission of HarperCollins Publishers. Published by HarperCollins Publishers.

Paradigm Shift: The New Promise of Information Technology. Copyright © Don Tapscott and Art Caston 1993. Page 129. Reprinted by permission of McGraw-Hill Companies.

Moments of Truth. Copyright © Jan Carlzon 1987. Ballinger Publishing Company. Pages 232–233. Reprinted with permission of Jan Carlzon and HarperCollins Publishers.

Diagrams on pages 93 and 111 by Key Consulting Group in Calgary. Copyright © 2001. Reprinted with permission.

Microsoft Secrets: How the World's Most Powerful Software Company Creates Technology, by Michael A. Cusumano and Richard W. Selby. Copyright © Michael Cusumano and Richard W. Selby 1995. Page 146. Reprinted with permission of The Free Press, a Division of Simon & Schuster, Inc.

Reprinted by permission of *Harvard Business Review*. "Factors affecting job attitudes as reported in 12 investigations. From "One more time: how do you motivate employees?" by Frederick Herzberg, *Harvard Business Review*. January/February 1968. Copyright © the President and Fellows of Harvard College, all rights reserved.

"eLearning Hype Cycle Diagram" by Gartner. Copyright © 2000. Reprinted with permission.

How to Succeed with People. Copyright © 1971 Stephen R. Covey. Page 23. Reprinted with permission of Deseret Book Company.

Typeset by Forewords, Oxford (www.forewords.co.uk)

Printed and bound by T.J. International, Padstow, Cornwall

This book is printed on acid-free paper

Contents

GETTING THE MOST OUT OF THIS BOOK

Right now, before you begin the book, I want you to rip out this page. Yes, you understood me correctly, I said rip out this page. If you are in a bookstore, please pay for the book first.

Go ahead. I give you permission to release all your inhibitions and rip this page right out of the book! If you have been raised to respect books and this is a horrible thought, you can do it secretively while no one is watching. That's okay. But just do it.[1]

MAKE YOUR MARK

Now that you have ripped out the page, this book really belongs to you. Many readers are hesitant to mark books. They have been taught for years that it's evil and wrong. However, I encourage you to highlight the text, make notes in the margin and earmark the pages. I guarantee you will get more out of the book. You will have deeper insights and you will have a lasting reference of the points that you feel are of most value.

CHAPTER 1

Shift from Satisfaction to Security

Here's a simple fact: 80 percent of the technology we will use in our day to day lives in just 10 years hasn't even been invented yet! Some people don't believe this when they first hear it, but think about this: Netscape didn't exist prior to 1994 – and e-commerce is now estimated to grow to $6.78 trillion by 2004![1] So in less than one decade the web will have had the most profound impact on human society of any technology. Amazon.com, founded in June 1995, had $2.6 billion of sales in 2000, becoming the third largest bookseller in the world by sales! Here are some predictions:

- Long distance rates will fall to 3 cents a minute by 2005 and it will be free by 2007.
- E-commerce will save organizations $1.25 trillion by 2002!
- 30 percent of all long distance phone calls will be carried across the Internet for free by 2005 using VoIP (Voice over Internet Protocol).
- Microsoft assumes that the average size of a hard disk today will be the amount of RAM on a "average" PC in seven years. In 2001, the average hard disk on a new PC was 80 gigabytes – imagine having 80 gigs of RAM on an "average" PC in 2008.
- Internet security will be based on biometric data – finger prints, voice prints, retinal scans – eliminating the need to remember dozens of passwords for different applications, increasing security, thereby increasing web based transactions.
- In 10 years time a standard PC will be 100 times more powerful than an average PC today.
- New programs will allow average PC users to collaboratively access idle computational power across the Net. I predict by 2010 an average 10-

> Give a man a fish and you feed him for a day; teach him how to fish and you feed him for a lifetime.
> *Lao Tzu, philosopher*

year-old will be able to access more computational power than exists on the planet in 2001.

- We will have full screen, full motion video-conferencing on desktops by 2003 for free across the web. It will be the same quality as watching TV (30 frames a second); in 2001 it was still jerky and small frame.

The rapid increase in the power of computing and the explosion of the web will profoundly affecting the way all organizations work. People often ask, "Why would we need such powerful computers? What would we use them for?" Applications will be fundamentally different:

- Voice recognition will be integrated into most computer applications. I use *Dragon NaturallySpeaking* – a software program that allows my computer to take dictation at 160 words per minute with 99 percent accuracy! I simply wear a microphone headset and chat away. I predict that the Graphical User Interface (GUI) will give way to AUI – the Audio User Interface – and like Jean Luc Picard, of *Star Trek*, that by 2010 we will predominantly interact with computers by talking to them.
- By 2010 we will have real time, instantaneous international translation – so you will be able to speak to your computer in English, and someone in Japan will watch your mouth moving but will hear Japanese.

With so much change how can individuals create job security? How can organizations keep their market share?

Job security today is based on learning, changing and accepting uncertainty. Paradoxically these are what we as adults fear the most! We have moved from a knowledge-based to a learning-based economy. This is the theme of *The Learning Paradox*.

IMPLICATIONS FOR BUSINESSES

The rapid rise in power and sophistication of computers is spurring a revolution in business and will fundamentally change the way all organizations work. Consider for instance, that airlines rely on high-margin business fliers to remain profitable. By 2003, we will be able to videoconference, with full screen, full motion (TV quality of 30 frames per second), from our desktops with anyone else across the Internet for free. What happens when executives who hate to be away from their families so much decide to take fewer business trips because they can videoconference face-to-face from their desktop – and collectively their travel falls by 30 percent? What will happen to airline profitability? Airline rationalization? Do you think airline executives in their strategic planning sessions consider other airlines as their competition – or do they consider cable and phone companies that are selling high-speed access to the Internet as their competitors? Are they planning for a future that involves full motion video conferencing?

Now I don't think that the airlines are going to all go out of business because of video conferencing, but right now a return business class ticket from New York to Los Angeles is over $2,000. You have to sell a lot more $299 trips to Mexico for every business class ticket that is taken out of the mix. If I were an airline executive I'd be keeping a very clean balance sheet – so that when the eventual rationalization comes along I will be able to buy a lot of planes really cheaply as other airlines have to sell off planes to stay afloat.

With long distance rates falling to 3 cents a minute, what will the cash flow future of telecommunication companies (telcos) look like? In 1994 telcos received on average 27 cents for every minute of long distance traffic. Using VPNs – Virtual Private Networks – which send data across the Internet for free, the telcos' largest customers' long-distance rates have plummeted to less than a cent a minute. What will happen to telcos when half of all long distance corporate calls travel across the Internet as data? What will happen to telcos when cable companies begin carrying voice traffic across their cable network? Do the telcos have a future? I believe so, but to thrive, their businesses will have to look substantially different than they do today. They will have to add new products and new services.

Some people have not realized how profound an effect the web will have on commerce. Dell Computer began selling computers across the web in 1996.

Dell is now selling $50 million dollars of computers over the web every day. Annualized that's a run rate of $18.3 billion a year – and that is just for one company. In an interview, Michael Dell said that an Internet order is basically a no cost transaction – the only thing that would be cheaper would be mental telepathy – that is where you just think you want a Dell and two weeks later it arrives at the office!

In 1999, Compaq fired Eckquart Pfeiffer. The reason? Since 1996 Dell has grown at twice to four times the industry average – year over year! Dell has continued to take share from competitors. In fact, International Data Corporation IDC now estimates that direct PC sales will exceed indirect sales in 2001.

QUESTIONS FOR ORGANIZATIONS

- Amid such rapid change what value do rigid job descriptions have?
- What will possibly offer people a sense of job security?
- What new skills will be required for individuals to thrive in the new millennium?
- How amid such change can organizations attract and retain the best people?

The Learning Paradox will answer these questions and many more.

GAINING COMFORT FROM DISCOMFORT

When I address conferences and seminars, I ask participants to write their names as fast as they can three times. Then I ask them to switch hands with the pen or pencil and repeat the exercise.

At this point there is usually a lot of laughter. When I ask how it feels to write with the "other" hand, I get comments like, "Awkward!" "Frustrating!" "Clumsy!" One man said, "When I was writing the first time, I felt like a lawyer; the second time like a doctor."

Next I ask, "How would you feel if I told you that you had to write with your other hand for the entire first day back at the office?" Typical answers are, "I'd take the day off!" "Stressed!" "Anxious!"Then I ask, "How about if you had to write with the other hand for the entire next week?" Responses include, "I'd take holidays!" "Do you expect me to keep serving the same number of customers?" "I'd dictate!" "I'd delegate!" "I'd start typing!" "My productivity would plummet." Finally I ask, "What if I told you, that you had to write with the other hand for the rest of your life?" People typically are resistant: "I can hardly wait to retire!" "What's in it for me?" "Why?" "Who are you to say?" Some are accepting: "Well, I guess I'd learn." Most of us are addicted to feeling competent. We are uncomfortable when we feel incompetent. We like the feeling of knowing. If you can become comfortable with the discomfort you feel when learning new skills – if you can become accustomed to the discomfort that change brings, then you will never have to worry about job security for the rest of your life!

JOB SECURITY

What created security in the past? If you wanted job security what kind of company did you want to work for? What were the characteristics of a secure position? Just for fun, I ask audience to put their answers in words beginning with the letter "s". Typically, people suggest the following categories:

SIZE OF ORGANIZATION   Security was a function of the size of the organization you worked for. If you landed a job with IBM or the government and worked hard, you never had to worry about the future.

SHARE OF MARKET   If you worked for a corporate leader with dominant market share – Coca-Cola, Procter & Gamble or monopolies such as utility companies – you were more secure.

STABILITY OF INDUSTRY/COMPANY   If you had a job in a stable company in a stable industry such as insurance or banking, you had a job for life.

SALARY AND BENEFITS   Many people worked for companies that offered good pay and benefits. If you were loyal, worked hard and didn't question authority, you could depend on regular salary increases. Upon retirement you could count on the company pension plan.

STATUS OF POSITION　The higher up you were in the corporate hierarchy, the more secure you were.

SERVICE　The longer you worked for a company, the more secure you were. After 40 years you could expect to retire with a gold watch awarded to you at the president's annual dinner.

SENIORITY　Unions created security. Once you got into a closed shop, you were home free. The stronger the union, the more secure your job.

SPECIALIZED KNOWLEDGE　If you had a PhD, MBA or specialized knowledge, you were more secure.

SPECIALIZED FUNCTION　If you had a specialized function – mainframe guru, for example – you were more secure because the organization depended on you.

Over the years, I have had some funny answers:

SEX　"What do you mean? Gender – i.e. men got ahead of women faster? The glass ceiling – the invisible barrier that prevents equality in the most senior ranks of Fortune 500 companies? Sometimes this was what the participant meant, other times it wasn't.

SON OR DAUGHTER　of the owner.

SUCK UP　As long as you told the boss what he wanted to hear you were secure.

An answer that took me by surprise was "plants." "What do you mean?" I asked, "manufacturing plants, production plants?"

"No, green plants." Her father worked in an office where if you had a green plant in your office you had "arrived." It was a signal in the culture. Plants represented security!

THE NEW RULES

I argue that everything that used to create job security in the past – size, share, stability, seniority, etc. – Now creates insecurity:

SIZE IBM once prided itself on offering employees lifetime security. But between 1989 and 1995, IBM laid off 200,000 people – half of its world-wide workforce. In fact, large companies have been the largest net job losers! Layoffs by large organizations have been dramatic:

Company	Date	Announced layoffs
General Motors	December 1991	74,000
Sears, Roebuck & Co.	January 1993	50,000
Boeing	February 1993	28,000
IBM[2]	July 1993	60,000
Delta Airlines	April 1994	15,000
Digital Equipment	May 1994	20,000
AT & T	January 1996	40,000
Nortel Networks	January 2001	15,000
Daimler Chrysler	April 2001	35,000
Ericsson	April 2001	15,300

General Motors, Coca-Cola, AT&T and many others have downsized dramatically. Most of these job losses were due to changes within huge corporations that were once considered immune to market forces. Clearly, they aren't offering the security they used to.

> Loyalty is the absence of a better value alternative.
> *Dave Nichol, creator, President's Choice Products*

SHARE In 1997, *Fortune* magazine proclaimed that Coca-Cola was America's most admired company and that "brands rule."[3] However, not even Coke has been immune to crushing market shifts. Coca-Cola has been hurt badly by private-label pop bottlers, most noticeably Cott. Wal-Mart annually sells over a billion cans of *Sam's Choice* pop produced by Cott. In Canada, Cott has cornered 26 percent of all supermarket pop sales.[4] Coke's profit has been so eroded that the company closed its Canadian head office in 1995 and now runs the Canadian operations out of Atlanta. Despite *Fortune*'s claims, any company that is selling a billion of anything is taking market share away from some other company. Private-label sales are putting brand loyalty to the test. Market share is less secure than ever. Competition is coming from unexpected sources and from small, cost-effective and highly focused companies.

STABILITY   The less your industry has changed in the past 30 years, the more it is at risk of being blind-sided by competition from an unexpected sector. A study by Royal Dutch Shell found that between 1979 and 1994, 40 percent of *Fortune 500* companies ceased to exist. Some were acquired or merged while others simply failed to keep up with the changing times and lost their leadership positions. Many people believe that a particular industry provides security. Consider the insurance field. Nothing really changed in insurance between 1960 and 1990. But all of a sudden, banks began selling insurance and large insurance companies began selling direct. Everything has changed. With technology enabling the birth of new businesses and making others obsolete overnight, the longer your industry has been stable, the sooner it is likely to suffer a shake-up.

SALARY AND BENEFITS   A common belief was that if you worked for the government you just had to show up every day, have a pulse and you would automatically get a cost of living allowance increase every year. At one seminar a man yelled out, "a pulse was optional." But today – we don't get increases just for showing up. Today it is performance that counts. The philosophy in past was paternalistic – the government or a large corporation would take care of my pension, the health care system would take care of my health and the company would look after my career. But increasingly we are recognizing we have to be self-reliant. As Judith Bardwick points out in *Danger in the Comfort Zone*,[5] entitlement – the notion that salaries and annual raises are a right as a result of showing up for work, rather than rewards for productivity – is rapidly disappearing. Increasingly, compensation at all organizational levels is based on performance. Expectations about pensions are also changing. Many Western governments are heavily in debt and employees are realizing that they must save for their own retirement. No longer can employees depend on the government or their employer to provide financial security in old age.

STATUS   The higher you go, the thinner the air gets! Downsizing, delayering, reorganization, restructuring and reengineering have undermined the security of having a title. Often, the more senior you are, the more insecure you are because of ever-increasing performance expectations.

SERVICE If you have been in the same position for 30 years and have learned no new skills I argue you are more likely to get a pink slip than a gold watch. The longer you've been in your position without learning new skills or accepting new responsibilities, the more you risk relying on obsolete skills that will give you a false sense of security. In the past, people who worked for several companies or held many different positions were viewed with suspicion. They were considered unreliable, unable to hold a steady job. Now the opposite is true. If you stay at the same job all of your life, people will wonder what's wrong with you. Research shows that on average, today's workers will hold 10 different positions in three different fields over their work life.

SENIORITY The traditional union model of seniority no longer offers the job security that it once did. In fact, it creates insecurity! Unions must be challenged to change along with the organization. Gary Hamel asks the question, "Who has the skills that will help the organization transform itself for the future? The 18-year-old who surfs the Web every night, or the 55-year-old union member who doesn't know how to turn on the computer?" Based on seniority (last in, first out) in a downsizing situation, who will the union push out of the organization? The 18-year-old. In other words, seniority will increase organizational *insecurity* by shedding employees who possess the new skills necessary to help create a viable organization for the future. Traditional seniority over the long term increases the insecurity of all members because it does not ensure that members are continuously learning, undergoing cross-functional job training, rotating positions and hiring people from outside the company – bringing new skills and perspectives. Over time organizations that fail to keep up with change will perish, resulting in all employees losing their jobs. Old-style unions typically oppose cross-functional job sharing and training. Which member is more secure – one who has only worked in a narrow job description for 25 years or one who has worked in four different positions over eight years? In fact, I question the validity of job descriptions today. Products and services, markets and competitors are changing so rapidly that rigid, negotiated job descriptions only ensure that an organization will be unable to change rapidly, which over the long term will increase the likelihood of its demise. New unions are embracing flexible work and new work arrangements, thereby creating greater security for their members. Today job security is based on learning, changing and accepting uncertainty. And yet what we fear most as adults is learning, changing and uncertainty. I call it *The Learning Paradox* – because our job security is based on the very things that we fear the most.

LEARNING PARADOX

Individuals who go through the learning paradox over and over again develop greater comfort with ambiguity and uncertainty. They no longer fear the unknown. They develop faith in their abilities to learn. The feelings of discomfort that learning and changing brings never goes away but the tolerance for accepting them increases. And the excitement that learning and changing brings sure beats boredom and apathy! In general, people are more excited when they are encouraged to fully engage their broad range of talents. As soon as they have mastered a task, completed a project or finished a training course, employees should be given a new challenge. Of course, no one deserves to be thrown into the deep end of the pool. Tasks should be carefully set in a series of stages to match abilities, and challenges should be based on the principle that peoples' reach should exceed their grasp. Our future will increasingly depend on our ability to learn and change. Yet what we fear most is the sense of discomfort we feel when learning and changing. At times, we lack the confidence that we will ever learn the new skill. Or we fear failing in front of colleagues. We are impatient with ourselves, expecting to learn a new skill the first time we try. Other times we are embarrassed to ask for help, or don't know whom to turn to. We try to figure it out ourselves and after repeated false starts or after it has taken too much time, we give up in frustration. If this is a recurrent pattern, we may eventually doubt our abilities. This is the learning paradox. The good news is that there are ways to overcome it. Becoming comfortable with being

> Good questions are better than good answers.
> *David Hurst, author*

uncomfortable is at the root of the new security. This is the essence of learning-based security.

QUESTIONS, NOT ANSWERS, CREATE SECURITY

This book is meant to challenge you to think differently. Today, many business-book readers are searching for solutions to the complex challenges their organizations face. Instead of looking for answers, I challenge you to wrestle with the questions that this book raises. The "answers" that work for one company, if applied in another, may create disastrous results. A strategy that creates exceptional success today may cause failure in the future. Answers aren't the answer. Instead, we must question the questions.

Instead of simply seeking solutions to perceived problems, successful individuals and organizations question the way they *see* problems. In other words, they question the questions. The way questions are posed predetermines the range of potential answers. By continually posing questions from different perspectives, successful individuals and organizations can more closely strike at the root cause of their problems.

In this book you will read many case studies that explain how the best organizations are continually reconfiguring their systems and structures to provide new value to customers by launching new products and services.

> If you can keep your head when all about you are losing theirs, it's just possible that you haven't grasped the situation.
> *Jean Kerr, American playwright*

Dogma breeds blindness. Leaders of the most successful companies live amid the questions instead of believing that they have all the answers. When new answers don't mesh with their current perspective, they explore the new ideas rather than dismiss them.

But in these rapidly changing times people are uneasy and uncertain about what will happen to their jobs, their departments or even their company. They are under stress at work and anxious about the future. They yearn for stability, security, peace and tranquility – for simpler lives and jobs. I have experienced this strong desire myself. People have been beaten up by management theory and the latest fads. They are fatigued and burned out. They want "the magic bullet." People want prescription lists.

"Don't talk about principles," they plead. "Just give us the seven steps, the 42 critical success factors, the 17 fatal flaws, the 19 implementation techniques." "Just give me the programmatic, formulaic, simple solution I can slap on my organizer." What they are really saying is, "Help me." "Make the pain go away. Now!" "Tell me what to do." "Make it easy for me." "I don't want to wrestle with it."

But formulaic, simple solutions are not only illusory, but dangerous. Don't accept any simple formula that a consultant suggests without testing and validating it from your experience and within your corporate culture.

Attempting to find answers without considering the differences between organizations – markets, capital intensity, maturity, competition, strategic direction – would be comparable to my taking medicine prescribed by your doctor for you. I may have some of the same symptoms, but the cause, the ailment itself or possibly my reaction to the medicine might be quite different.[6]

> The road to success is always under construction.
> *Sam Geist, professional speaker*

Albert Einstein was holding an exam for his university students when a teaching assistant rushed up to him and said, "Dr. Einstein, there's been a terrible mistake. This exam is exactly the same as last year's! All the questions are the same!"

"Don't worry!" replied Einstein. "This year the correct answers are all different."

The questions for business this year are the same, but the answers are different. How do we better serve our customers? Will we add more value by introducing new and better products and services? How can we increase margins? Increase customer delight? Increase employees' growth and development? Shorten cycle times? Better align stakeholder interests? Eliminate non-value-added activity? Create new products and services as new technology and practices enable new relationships with customers, suppliers and employees? Create, anticipate or at least respond quickly to new market trends as they emerge?

Even the best organizations cannot become complacent if they expect to remain market leaders. I predict that the courier industry's document volumes will continue to fall with the exponential growth of email and the ability to send formatted documents over the Internet. In 1997, the volume of email in North America for the first time surpassed the number of letters carried by the US Postal Service.[8] In 2000, an average of 9.7 billion non-spam email messages were sent every day, worldwide.[9]

Microsoft was blind-sided by Netscape. Wal-Mart may one day be threatened by virtual retailing. In other words, even the most successful companies and industries must remain eternally vigilant, continually questioning their assumptions. Furthermore, what works for one organization may not work for another.

Therefore, the examples in this book are intended to provoke you to think differently and create the strategies, systems and structures that are best for your customers, your employees, your department and your organization. People like the security of knowing the answers, but today we must live and work amid questions because everything is changing.

Do not swallow whole any theory set forth in this book. Think about it! Debate it! Challenge it! Ultimately, decide what will and won't work for your organization. (This book is written for people at every level in an organization. If you don't feel that you can change the organization, substitute division or department. Today everyone in an organization is required to assume responsibility for adding more value for customers.)

I believe that most organizations already have people with the talent, knowledge and skills required to solve all their problems. The challenge for organizations is how to draw out employees' full potential with an exciting, compelling vision of the future.

After co-authoring *The 100 Best Companies to Work For in Canada*, I began giving seminars and speaking at conferences on corporate strategies for survival and success. In 1990, participants most frequently asked, "What makes an organization one of the best companies to work for?" Today they want to know, "How can I gain a sense of control over my career and my life?" "How can I count on being able to support my family?" Executives are asking, "How can we encourage employees to constantly change?" "How can we create a culture where fear does not rule?" In short, everyone is looking for security.

> There is no such thing as a secure job anymore. There are only secure people.
> *Warner Woodley, CEO, Mainstream Access*

Drawing on case studies of some of the best companies, including Microsoft, Wal-Mart, Intel, FedEx, Hewitt Associates, Sun Microsystems and Progressive Insurance, this book outlines how organizations and employees can best guarantee their long-term security in an environment of rapid change. The determinants of success and security are not what they used to be.

A JOB FOR LIFE

People have a deep yearning for meaningful and challenging work. Yet, it is staggering that 73 percent of North American employees report that they do not find their work exciting.[10] Given that we spend one-third of our adult lives at work, this is a terrible tragedy. Despite this yearning, the times are such that people today aren't concerned about having a good job. They consider themselves fortunate to have any job. Downsizing, rightsizing, reengineering and outsourcing have made people shift their concern from workplace satisfaction to workplace security.

THE OLD RULES

In her book *When Giants Learn to Dance*, Rosabeth Moss Kanter, the former editor of *Harvard Business Review*, says the old, unwritten social contract was based on loyalty in return for security. People worked for one company for most of their lives and at the end of their careers received a gold watch. The implicit message was: Work hard, do what you're told, don't question authority and in return, you'll be secure. We all knew the rules of the game.

SPECIALIZED KNOWLEDGE   We are more educated than ever before. Knowledge has become a commodity in the global village – more widely available than ever. Why hire a North American graduate for $30,000 a year when an equivalently educated person in China is available for $1,200? Even specialized knowledge over time becomes a commodity. During the 1950s, 56 North American schools offered Master of Business Administration (MBA) degrees, turning out a few thousand graduates annually. Today there are more than 325 accredited MBA programs in the United States alone.[11] According to the US Department of Education, 228,000 students graduated with bachelor's degrees in business in 1997 and another 98,000 graduated with master's degrees in business.[12]

In times of rapid change, knowledge depreciates in value just as quickly as computers and software technologies. Knowledge counts, but the right attitude and a commitment to lifelong learning is more important. A PhD could simply mean you know a lot about old stuff. Stephen Covey, author of *The Seven Habits of Highly Effective People*,[13] points out:

> Education's main value does not lie in getting knowledge, much of which will be obsolete sooner or later. It certainly doesn't lie in credits earned or degrees conferred. These may open doors of opportunity but only real competence will keep them open. In fact, in our rapidly changing world there is no "future," no economic security in any job or situation. The only real economic security lies within the person, in his competence and power to produce.
>
> Education's main value lies in learning how to continually learn, how to think and to communicate, how to appreciate and to produce, how to adapt to changing realities without sacrificing changeless values. Result? An inner confidence in the basic ability to cope successfully with whatever life brings.

SPECIALIZED FUNCTION Assembly-line workers, bank tellers, typesetters, telephone operators, receptionists and even mainframe programmers – every time you turn around, another job function is being threatened. If your job is being replaced by technology or restructuring, how can you feel secure? Specialized knowledge, while still important, no longer provides the long-term security it once did.

SOCIAL CONTRACT The old social contract of working hard and never questioning authority in return for security is dangerous. When markets were homogeneous and stable, consumers predictable and brand loyalty certain, the social contract could operate. Today, however, many of the best and brightest employees refuse to work 50, 60, 70, 80+ hours per week. People want "balanced" lives. Do we live to work or work to live? The social costs of workaholism are well documented. Working hard needs to be redefined as adding more value through creativity and innovation rather than working longer hours. In many corporate cultures it is still a status symbol to work long hours. In the future, I predict it will be a status symbol to hold a significant position of leadership, perform exceptionally and work only 40 hours a week! Finally, the old theory "Never question those in positions of authority" creates insecurity. To thrive today, organizations must promote open, honest and vigorous internal debate. Employees should be encouraged to challenge decisions they believe are wrong. None of us knows what the future holds. No individual has all the insight into which new products or services will be winners, or can say definitively how they should be designed, implemented and delivered. Creating new value for customers requires a corporate culture in which open, honest debate can occur and where employees can challenge management decisions without fear of recrimination. Serving the hierarchy must be subordinated to serving the customer. One executive coined the phrase "the egoless corporation" to emphasize how today no individual has a monopoly on insight. Organizations need to draw upon the full intellectual talents of all employees. The sign of an excellent place to work is one in which there is healthy, vigorous, open debate.

SPEED Complacency kills. Even in rapidly expanding industries there is little job security. Computer software is the fastest-growing industry sector worldwide, growing by 30 percent compounded annually between 1980 and 1995 in real terms. Yet, even in this explosive industry there is no security. *Information Week* annually ranks the top 50 independent software companies in the world. More than half the computer companies on the 1990 list did not appear on the 1995 list! Some were sold, others fell behind and a few went belly-up. In short, even the vaunted computer market is uncertain.[14]

> By identifying the new learning with heresy, you make orthodoxy synonymous with ignorance.
> *Desiderius Erasmus, Dutch scholar*

CHANGE: THE KEY FACTOR IN TODAY'S ECONOMY

Companies in all industries are susceptible to complacency and arrogance. Of the top 100 US retail discounters in business in 1976, only 24 existed in 1994! What happened to them? Wal-Mart happened! In 1983, Wal-Mart's 641 stores had sales of $4.8 billion.[15] By 2001, Wal-Mart had become the world's largest retailer with over 4,190 stores and sales of

$223 billion. Old retailers with complacent attitudes are easy prey for a formidable giant like Wal-Mart.

Who or what brought all this dramatic and painful change upon us? We did! As consumers, we are driving the change. As consumers, we are more knowledgeable than ever, and we are exercising our freedom of choice.

"Value consciousness" is rapidly replacing brand loyalty as the driving force behind purchasing decisions. If you provide better value for your customers, you win their loyalty. With consumers demanding value, and technology making it possible to serve needs faster and more economically, no wonder everything is in a state of flux! Every sector of our society is being affected – governments at all levels, health care, business, not-for-profit organizations, social programs, arts and culture. There are no exemptions. The change is sweeping and dramatic:

- In 1980, who could have predicted that a black political prisoner would become president of South Africa and end apartheid; or that the Cold War would end and the Soviet Union would dissolve; or that the Berlin Wall would crumble, broken apart by people with their bare hands?

> In 1993, large US firms announced nearly 600,000 layoffs – 25 percent more than in 1992 and nearly 10 percent above 1991 levels.
> *Gary Hamel and C.K. Prahalad, authors*

- Who could have predicted in 1975 that: Microsoft's value would be 12 times greater than that of General Motors in 2001? And with its spare cash on hand Microsoft could buy GM outright?

- In Canada, it is surprising to find that more people work in the computer industry (equipment, semiconductors and services) than in the auto, auto parts, steel, mining and petroleum refining industries combined!

- Why are some banks still busy building branches? Do they think that banks of the future will have more to do with bricks and mortar than keystrokes and mouse clicks? Who could have thought you would one day be able to get a checking account or a Visa card from your stockbroker? Charles Schwab's clients can also trade stocks, mutual funds and other financial products 24 hours a day from their personal computer.

- Who could have imagined that in the 1980s, General Electric would make more money from its financing operations than from making appliances in the 1990s; or that American Airlines' parent company,

AMR, would make more money from its competitors through its Sabre reservation system than by flying its airplanes?

CREATING SECURITY IN THE MIDST OF CHANGE

If work security no longer comes from traditional sources, how can individuals find fulfillment and peace of mind? In a sea of change, how can we create stability? I believe that there are three main sources of security today. They are:

- Our ability to learn continually.
- Our ability to change (personally and organizationally).
- Our ability to cope with uncertainty.

Paradoxically, these are what we fear most as adults.

CREATING SECURITY FOR THE FUTURE

Eighty percent of the technology we will use in our day-to-day lives in the next 10 years has yet to be invented! If you find this hard to believe, think about how quickly technology is changing. The web – created by the release of Mosaic in 1993 or Netscape in 1994 – has profoundly changed the world. Ecommerce is now estimated to grow to 6.78 trillion by 2004.

So how can I take a course today that will prepare me for the future? I can't unless in the course I learn how to learn, think about how I think, become more creative about creativity and deepen my understanding of teamwork in order to become a better team player. This is "meta" learning – conscious learning about the underlying processes of learning, thinking, creativity and teamwork.

> The ability to learn faster than your competitors may be the only sustainable competitive advantage.
> *Aire de Geus, author*

Security for individuals is based on becoming self-reflective and self-correcting. Similarly, security for organizations is based on putting in place processes that guarantee self-reflection and self-correction at the individual and organizational levels.

THE LEARNING PARADOX

A paradox is an apparent contradiction. This book will examine many paradoxes: To create security, we must accept the insecurity that uncertainty brings. To feel comfortable about our future, we must accept the discomfort of learning new skills. Stability of market share or peace of mind comes only from changing. The more tightly leaders cling to control, the more out of control their organizations will be. The more power leaders give away, the more power they will have.

The challenges we face in these dramatically changing times can be overwhelming. When an organization falls on tough times, employees need support and encouragement. Unfortunately, unless the leaders are exceptionally courageous, principled and centered, tough times are when people receive the least amount of help and support.

The things that once created security now create insecurity. Yet, paradoxically, we will only add to our burden of insecurity unless we overcome our fear of acquiring new skills and knowledge. The secret of creating a sense of security and stability lies in confronting the barriers in our minds that stop us from learning and changing. Fear and uncertainty stop us, not our ability to learn.

> Change is inevitable, except in a vending machine.
> *Anonymous*

Individuals can create their own security on the road ahead by living a life of learning. Leaders are responsible for ensuring that processes are in place to guarantee organizational learning. Nothing is more important, rewarding, enriching and enjoyable than growing as a result of seeing and acting differently. Life is learning. Learning is life.

Reflection:

What is the key learning/insight for me in this chapter?

Action:

What one action shall I take tomorrow to move learning into action? And over time repeat, to move action into habit?

CHAPTER 2

The Learning Paradox

True wisdom involves the head, the heart and the hand. Imagine that you are the parent of a child who is learning to walk. She takes her first tentative step, wobbles and falls. You'd probably pick her up, give her a big hug, encourage her to try again and praise her. "Honey, grab the video camera! She walked! Call Granny!"

> True wisdom involves the head, the heart and the hand.
> *Thomas Berry, theologian*

No parent would ever stand over the child, lean down and at the top of one's voice yell, "I have seen many first steps in my time. That was the worst first step I've ever seen!" No parent would ridicule her for trying. Her setbacks would be treated with love and encouragement and enthusiasm.

No matter what our age, when we are learning and growing we will stumble and fall periodically. If we are always beating ourselves up or being beaten up by others for making mistakes, we will learn more slowly. Children who are punished every time they fall will grow up to be insecure. If we are perfectionists by nature, we often set unattainable goals and beat ourselves up when we fail to reach them. Even when we come close, we are not happy. Inwardly, we will always be punishing ourselves for making mistakes even though it is impossible to learn anything new without failures.

Rather than spurring us on to greater heights, perfectionism stunts growth and satisfaction. As a Chinese proverb states:

> Wisdom comes from good judgment
> Good judgment comes from experience
> Experience comes from mistakes
> Mistakes come from bad judgment.

After reading this, a friend shared the following, saying:

> To live but not to learn is not to live
> To learn but not to understand is not to learn
> To understand but not to do is not to understand.[1]

A father once approached me after a presentation and said, "My son is learning to walk. He doesn't want to learn just for the sake of walking, he wants to learn to walk because it is the fastest way of getting from here to there. Walking is the only way he will be able to get toys for himself." This was a powerful insight. Is that not why we want to learn as adults? Because we want to get from here to there. We want to have richer relationships in our personal lives. We want our organizations to grow and gain market share, increase margins and add new value for customers. We are required to learn and change because we want to get from here to there.

LEARNING IS CENTRAL TO LIFE; FEAR IS PART OF LEARNING

Consultant and speaker Martin Rutte often talks about how he learned to dive.[2] Rutte was in his forties when he decided to take up diving. Before he knew it, he found himself standing at the end of a one-meter diving board with his instructor on the sideline.

One meter might not seem very high, but keep in mind that Martin's eyes are two meters above the board and when he looked down he didn't see the water but rather the bottom of the pool, another five meters below the surface. So, peering into the pool, Martin saw a drop of eight meters. He was frozen with fear. In fact, for such a period that a long line of little kids formed behind him. And their attitude was, "C'mon, mister, jump!" "We don't have all day!" "Just do it!" Rutte was terrified. He looked at the instructor and asked, "When does the fear go away?"

Her answer, "Never!"

When will the fear end? Never.

When Rutte became comfortable with jumping off the one-meter board, his instructor pushed him back into his discomfort zone, challenging him to learn how to dive. Once he mastered diving, she challenged him to learn a forward flip. Then a one-and-a-half flip. Once he mastered every dive on the one-meter board, where did she send him? To the three-meter board. And then the terror really set in! There will always be new dives and higher diving boards to awaken your fear. If you are always learning and growing as a human being, if organizations are committed to always providing new value for their customers, always pushing the envelope, the fear will never disappear.

The fear abates once you have mastered a new skill. But we human beings soon become bored and need to challenge ourselves again. As we go through the process of facing fear and overcoming it time and time again, we increase our tolerance for discomfort, ambiguity and uncertainty. We develop courage and faith in our abilities to face and overcome the unknown.

> A man's reach should exceed his grasp.
> *Robert Browning, poet*

Fear of failure is a part of learning and growing. Once you accept that, you will get better at dealing with and overcoming it.

We need to treat ourselves as we would treat a child who is learning to walk. Similarly, we must treat other people who are learning with patience and understanding. If we beat up others when they fail, we justify their resistance to change and reinforce their fears.

But just because we are respectful of ourselves and others doesn't mean we should ignore the need for results and tough decisions. It is the difference between acceptance and complacency. I am complacent when I know a problem exists but am either too frightened or lazy to act or ask for help. By contrast, I need acceptance once I have honestly done everything in my power to correct a situation.

A man told a story that had a powerful effect on me. His son was born with deformed legs. Every week for the first year of his child's life, the man took him to the hospital where doctors would twist the child's legs and set them in a temporary cast. The little boy would scream in pain. The father had to witness his son's torment. He worried terribly, "What is my son thinking of me? What kind of father does he think I am?" But the man didn't relent and every week took his son back to the hospital. Eventually the child began to fear driving in the car because he knew it meant going to these appointments, but the father's resolve didn't waver.

Today, the boy can walk and run as well as any healthy child because his father set aside his own feelings to do what had to be done. Compassion and love were at the core of his actions.

At times, managers must be demanding to get results. But whatever actions are required, they must be undertaken with care. We must always look to the work culture in which we are asking people to function before we point fingers, make demands or take disciplinary action. Is the culture built on blame, or does it accept that stumbling and falling are part of learning? Are people given the freedom they need to be accountable? Are they given the necessary training and education to help them overcome the challenges they are expected to overcome? Unless employees are treated fairly in the first place, it is almost impossible to solve long-term problems.

Many once-sound organizations are undergoing the wrenching pain of reengineering. The term was first popularized by Michael Hammer in the 1990 *Harvard Business Review* article "Reengineering Work: Don't Automate, Obliterate,"[3] in which he celebrated Ford Motor's decision to cut 75 percent of its 400-person accounts payable staff. Ford's internal processes had become inefficient, overstaffed and unnecessarily expensive. By comparison, Mazda's accounts payable staff totaled five. Why the huge disparity?

Organizations that must reengineer typically have not kept pace with the times. Consequently their competitors, their customers and the whole market have passed them by. The result is a desperate catch-up effort in which employees lose their jobs. Ironically, unwillingness to change, develop options and question operating systems had caused the costly build-up in the first place.

Michael Hammer is confused by resistance to reengineering. For instance, in a *Fortune* article he is quoted saying, "Human beings' innate resistance to change is the most perplexing, annoying, distressing and confusing part of reengineering."[4] What is hard to understand? Imagine that I arrive at your organization and say, "I have a wonderful new management theory. It simply requires you to terminate three out of four colleagues and may require you to fire yourself." It would be natural for people to oppose it. Hammer uses terms such as "nuke" and "obliterate," and refers to "breaking legs." Does this language tend to increase or decrease fear? Does Hammer's theory show sensitivity towards people? It is, after all, people who make organizations work.

A rigid management style that stifles learning, creativity and change is like a cancer-causing habit. After smoking two packs of cigarettes a day for 40 years, a smoker gets cancer and then goes to a specialist to be cured. Reengineering is the supposed surgical cure to intervene and "fix" the company. But often it's too late to deal with the root problem.

By contrast, Peter Senge, in his book *Fifth Discipline: The Art & Practice of the Learning Organization*, advocates preventive medicine by creating "learning organizations." Like adopting a healthy lifestyle, lifelong learning creates personal and corporate security. This path may sound simple, but it is not easy. Everyone knows exercise is good, but too few people work out regularly. Knowledge (theory) is one thing, application (practice) is another.

More books have been written on management and leadership in the last two decades than in the last century combined. Do we really need more knowledge? Or do we need to better practice what we already know? I believe we need to focus on application.

We live in the information age. In fact, far more information is available today than an individual can assimilate in a lifetime. Here are a few examples:

"The volume of electronic information on our desks increases by 20 percent each year; the volume of paper by eight percent."
– Declan Treacy, *Conquering the Information Mountain*

"Fifty percent of managers frequently cannot cope with the volume of information they receive."
– P. Waddington, *Dying for Information?* Reuters

"Forty-three percent of managers believe that important decisions are delayed/adversely affected by too much information."
– P. Waddington, *Dying for Information?* Reuters

What we need is wisdom. Below are four definitions:

DATA   These would be daily sales figures, the average sale. But these statistics have little value. We are drowning in data.

INFORMATION   gives meaning to data by explaining its relevance, thus allowing for interpretation and determining of importance. Patterns in data are recognized.

KNOWLEDGE is the assembly of information, often from disparate sources to create new understandings.

WISDOM is the application of knowledge to create new value.

For instance, imagine that in 1980 an airline examined its passenger records. Millions of records (data) were analyzed. Patterns (information) became apparent. For example, certain passengers were flying frequently. Further study revealed that these frequent fliers were the most profitable customer segment (information). This led an analyst to ask, "How can we ensure the loyalty of this small segment that comprises the bulk of our profits?" (knowledge) How can we better understand the behavior and profile of customers in this segment? (knowledge) What program can we implement to guarantee the loyalty of this segment, which is the most profitable? (knowledge)

Airlines designed frequent flier programs to ensure that their most frequent fliers remained loyal. (wisdom) American Airlines was the first airline to co-brand a credit card giving one frequent flier air mile for every dollar a customer spent on the card. (wisdom) This program was based on the insight that frequent fliers have high disposable incomes and therefore are a good target market for a prestige credit card.

This example shows how knowledge combines disparate pieces of information to create new understandings of customers or markets. Finally, wisdom is having the courage to act on the knowledge and implement the programs. Because the programs will not be implemented perfectly on the first attempt, patience and courage are required

> I can't read my way into
> physical fitness.
> *Jim Harris*

to venture through the uncertainty and persevere until new value is created and the market responds.

Knowledge is not even enough today. I could be a world authority on balance, having read all the books on the subject and even having taught a course at Harvard on the workings of the inner ear, but if I can't ride a bicycle while a seven-year-old can, who has more wisdom? Knowledge without application is worthless.

While knowledge can be acquired by reading and reflection, wisdom is only acquired through practice, self-reflection and self-correction. Some companies are very open to sharing their strategic plan with suppliers and customers and are seemingly unafraid that this information could get into the hands of competitors. Knowledge of competitors' plans gives little strategic advantage. The key is in execution. Intel, I am certain, plans to design and produce faster, more powerful generations of computer chips. As Intel's competitors already know, this knowledge isn't much help.

The key to all wisdom is execution. It is not enough to know what we should do, the key is to have the courage and stamina to carry it out.

LEARNING AS PLAY; LIFE AS CHALLENGE

Many children today play video games. Parents describe their kids as "intense," "challenged," "excited" and "obsessed" when they receive a new game. A mother once commented that her son was "deaf" while a father said, "Unable to mow the lawn!"

Do kids read the manual before they begin? As one mother put it, "I'm the one who reads the manual." Children show no fear while learning.

> The purpose of life after all is to live it, to taste experience to the utmost, to reach out eagerly and without fear for newer and richer experiences.
> *Eleanor Roosevelt,*
> *First Lady*

Have you seen or heard of any courses such as Sega Dreamcast for Advanced Users? Or Nintendo 101? Or have you seen that bestseller Sega for Dummies? Of course not. After one presentation, a woman came up to me and said, "You mentioned those Dummies books in your talk – I just want to let you know that they are *way too advanced*! What I want is a computer book for real, bloody idiots!" So how do kids learn? By doing. By trial and error. How many times are kids willing to make mistakes? As many as it takes to learn.

To play a video game, a child must develop certain competencies at Level One. Once mastered, the child moves on to Level Two, where new challenges require the development of new skills. As soon as these are acquired, the child progresses to Level Three, which presents more complex challenges requiring even higher levels of skill. To keep a child's attention, game designers make each level more difficult. One tactic is to require players to develop skills that are the opposite of those needed at a lower level. That is, the very moves that allowed them to escape the challenges of Level One cause their character to die at Level Three. Unless they can unlearn what made them successful at Level One and learn new skills, they will not progress. As much as we need to learn, we also have to unlearn.

How else do kids learn? Their peers. Absolutely. I once had a father come up to me in a break and tell me, "my son went into his grade four class last week and said, 'A dozen doughnuts for anyone who can show me how to get to level six of the game from level five!'"

Each time a new challenge is overcome, a new problem presents itself. At every stage the child is challenged to learn new skills. At seminars, I ask the audience, "What happens once the child has mastered all six levels?" They answer, "They show all their friends." "They stop playing." "They chuck the game." "They trade it or sell it."

> The significant problems we face cannot be solved at the same level of thinking we were at when we created them.
> Albert Einstein, physicist

This reveals a simple but powerful insight: Challenge is one of the greatest human motivators. This is the second aspect of the learning paradox: (the first aspect is that our future security is based on what we fear most – learning, changing and accepting uncertainty.) Facing our fear provides our deepest sense of satisfaction.

I challenge you to think of some time in your life when you were the proudest. Upon reflection, I am sure that you will find it was when you undertook some challenge you didn't know how to overcome. But through hard work, trial and error, perseverance and networking with colleagues you whipped it. You got the "YES!" high-five feeling that kids get when they master all levels of the video game.

Learning a video game is a powerful metaphor for change in a business. Whether new or established, organizations require progressively different competencies. At every stage of growth, new problems are encountered that will limit development unless they are overcome.

With a new business, capital is often the first limiting factor. So the entrepreneur works out of his basement, puts in sweat equity, buys second-hand furniture and equipment and generally keeps costs to the bone. So what's the next challenge? Time. Yes the entrepreneur is doing everything – accounts receivable, payable, product development, customer service, shipping, logistics, and post office mail runs. So as cash flow increases, the entrepreneur hires some people. But because cash flow is tight, he hires very inexperienced people because the wages are low. That gives rise to the need for training. So the entrepreneur invests in training, to the point where employees are now worth $17 an hour, but because the entrepreneur is cheap he is paying only $13 an hour. What happens? They leave – you know, the only thing worse than training people and having them leave is not training them and having them stay! So the entrepreneur learns he must not only invest in people, but pay fair market wages. After that, it may be necessary to focus on marketing. From the founder's basement, the company may be forced to lease office space, hire more staff, introduce benefit programs, acquire more equipment and so on and so on. Every level of development presents a new set of challenges.

> The chief object of education is not to learn things but to unlearn things.
> *G.K. Chesterton, novelist*

Imagine, for example, that a manufacturer launches a new product with an aggressive advertising campaign in an effort to increase market share. The campaign is so successful that demand exceeds the company's production capacity. This results in long delivery delays for customers. The company must increase production capacity, maintain sufficient inventory levels and more accurately forecast market demand.

As soon as one limiting factor is addressed, a new one will arise. Suppose the company responds to increasing demand by hastily building new production facilities and rushing products to market. What suffers? Quality. So now the answer is an ISO 9000 certification. A half million dollars later the organization is certified but has introduced all sorts of paperwork. What's the new problem? Winning back customers who defected because of delays and poor quality products. The company may respond by lowering prices in an attempt to win back disgruntled customers.

But now there is a new problem. When the new production line was built, the company required additional volume to cover costs. Rather than have the line sit idle, sales reps were given incentives to increase volume, even with low-margin business, thereby amortizing the cost of the new line. This strategy lowered the per-unit cost of production. Compensation systems were designed to reward sales reps based on volume. The results were so successful that after a few years the company experienced another capacity crunch. Peak volumes were again losing the company business.

The solution to one problem has now become a new problem. Now that the line is at full capacity, the company needs a new strategy: drop the high-volume, low-margin business and concentrate on the lower-volume, high-margins and niche markets.

As the business booms and profit margins rise, the sector becomes more attractive to competitors. Competition may become the primary problem. As soon as this problem is addressed, another one will crop up, guaranteed.

Once any limiting factor is overcome, a new limiting factor will arise. Put another way, solving any problem will, over time, create a new problem in any business. The problems will not necessarily be linked, but they will always emerge. There will always be problems and challenges in business.

As in the video game, as businesses graduate to higher and higher levels, the problems become more and more complex. The problems challenge us to think in new ways – ways that were not previously required and that may in fact be the opposite of those that worked at lower levels. The interaction of the various forces may also be less apparent.

So why is this important? Because people have a deep yearning for the answer. They think – if I could just get this marketing problem solved and win more market share, then all my problems would go away. And no sooner is the marketing problem solved than now we have to focus on production? I thought marketing would solve all our problems. Inevitably people are refocused on the new challenge – "Okay if we can just get production under control – then everything will be great." You see we are unaware that our real problem is our mindset of thinking that one strategy, system, product or service will solve, all our problems. Instead we need to focus on building our tolerance for ambiguity, complexity — becoming more flexible, creative and willing to continually change.

> Our aim must be to make our successive mistakes as quickly as possible.
> *Karl Popper, philosopher*

At the very start of a business, the entrepreneur is involved in every decision. That's what created success (Level One). But now that the company has grown to 100 people (Level 17), the entrepreneur's involvement in every decision is the problem. Have you ever noticed that bottlenecks are always at the top of the bottle? In other words, what made the company thrive at Level One could cause the company to fail at Level Three. So, as much as we need to create learning organizations, we also need to foster unlearning organizations. To progress and develop, we must also be prepared to unlearn or let go of practices that may have been key to our past success!

To grow and change, an entrepreneur must accept that his or her greatest strengths from yesterday could become his or her greatest weaknesses today. When a snake sheds its skin, it gives up its tough, old armor for a soft but flexible covering. The old skin wasn't working but the new skin isn't working either. The snake must live through the vulnerable time – similar to writing with the other hand. Even in our personal lives, we must be prepared to evaluate old attitudes and replace them, if necessary, with ones that work better in the present. This will ultimately make our lives happier and more fulfilling.

The business "video game" ends only if the company ends. As a company continues to grow, the systems and structures become more elaborate, more complex and more cumbersome. Sometimes, these systems prevent the organization from being able to respond effectively to change – bureaucracy chokes the lifeblood out of the organization. The company has come full circle. It needs to be more entrepreneurial, not in the old style when the entrepreneur did the accounting on the back of envelopes, but in a way that focuses on the customer and strategic growth, and allows for flexibility with enough checks and balances to avoid fatal mistakes.

> Bottlenecks are always at the top of the bottle.
> *Lou Pritchett*

LIFE IS DIFFICULT

I often encounter a disturbing assumption in my consulting work. Clients will say, "If we just do this reengineering or this quality thing or this customer focus approach, then all our problems will be resolved." The assumption is that we just need to solve this one thing and everything will be all right. What a dangerous notion! As we have seen, no sooner is one bottleneck overcome than another presents itself. Will any business ever be easy and problem free? Never! When will the challenge end? Never!

M. Scott Peck begins *The Road Less Traveled* with the first of the four noble truths of Buddhism:

Life is difficult. This is a great truth, one of the greatest truths. It is a great truth because once we truly see this truth, we transcend it. Once we truly know that life is difficult – once we truly understand and accept it – then life is no longer difficult. Because once accepted, the fact that life is difficult no longer matters.[5]

Corporate life is difficult. The search for simple solutions to problems is futile. Not only does the belief in a single, simple solution lead to continual disappointment and more problems, it limits our vision and confines our thinking. We need to rise above the problem/solution dynamic if we are to see the larger world of possibilities. No consultant or program can "save" us.

In reference to total quality management (TQM), I often hear, "Quality is not working!" According to reports, three-quarters of quality initiatives in North America fail. *Information Week* reports that two-thirds of reengineering initiatives fail. According to Arthur D. Little Inc., only 16 percent of companies are satisfied with the results.[6] That's like saying 70 percent of all screwdrivers are failing. To blame the tools is to miss the point. It is how tools are used that determines how successful they are at solving problems. Quality, reengineering and customer focus are just tools. They are processes, not the answers. The way in which these programs are *implemented* over the long term determines their success or failure.

> The art of progress is to preserve order amid change and change amid order.
> A.N. Whitehead, mathematician

The truth is, problems are central to the human condition. We need to increase our tolerance for the discomfort, ambiguity and failure that learning and changing bring. Only by facing up to what we fear most will we be able to learn, grow and make our work rewarding, stimulating and secure.

LEARNING AS A CHILD

Like other business people, I have been influenced by such thinkers as, W. Edwards Deming, Peter Senge and Stephen Covey, whose work provides powerful tools for analyzing and implementing change. Yet in my work with executives over the years, I have been constantly amazed at how few companies are able to make necessary changes, even with so much theory, so many examples and good suggestions at their disposal.

We often know what needs to be done, but we still aren't able to do enough. What forces are holding us back?

Let's get back to the child who is learning to walk. We would be surprised if, after falling a few times, she suddenly gave up as if she thought, "Hey, this walking stuff is just too painful. I'm going to give up right now and save myself from more bumps and bruises." That sounds ridiculous and yet how many times do adults give up too quickly? We must get back that childlike love of learning, letting go of our insecurities and ego that hold us back through fear of stumbling and falling.

The best companies have a high tolerance for mistakes. Why? Without risk, innovation is impossible. Risk-taking and mistakes go hand in hand. Corporations that get results take extra pains to create environments that encourage acting on ideas, taking risks and making mistakes.

Once we truly accept the need for change and undertake to create a working environment where change is encouraged, risk-taking rewarded and mistakes expected, learning becomes fun, joyous and exciting.

Think again about kids with their video games. What emotional state are children in when they open a new game? They are thrilled, engaged. They have mastered four levels before breakfast and are already asking for the next version. It's pure fun. Yet it's challenging, and parents hear enough groans to know that mistakes are being made.

> Nothing in life is to be feared. It is only to be understood.
> *Marie Curie, scientist*

If you have a daughter, think back to when she was two years old. Whenever you come home she runs up to you and throws her arms around your legs. You call her "my little Princess," and she thinks you are wonderful. She makes your heart melt. But two-year-olds are a real challenge. It has been difficult for you. You have had to learn to be firm and yet compassionate. You can't negotiate with a two-year-old or she'll run your life. So you have worked hard to develop this fantastic relationship with her. However, you remain frozen in time. You don't change as a parent, and two years pass. She is now four but you treat her the same as when she was two. After all, you had perfected the relationship and it worked. How is the relationship going – is it stronger or weaker? Someone once said, "She has you wrapped around her little finger."

She is now 10 years old and you treat her exactly as you did when she was four. How is the relationship now – happy or tense? Your daughter is now 16 and you treat her as you did when she was 10. What's your relationship like? I get answers like, "What relationship?" "She isn't talking to me." "She has left home." "She's joined a biker gang." "Got a tattoo." "She's pregnant and you're about to become a grandparent."

This is very difficult for both of you. You are both continually venturing into the future, uncertain of how to behave, uncertain of how to create a meaningful relationship. You never had a two-year-old before. You don't know how to treat her. You were always questioning yourself, "Is she getting to bed at the right time? Is she spending enough time with other kids? Is she watching too much TV? Are my expectations too high? Am I too permissive? What is the right balance?" You are learning at every stage of the child's development. And no sooner do you start to feel that everything is under control because you have perfected the relationship at a certain age, than she grows and new challenges arise. The relationship is characterized by periods of stability and then instability when you feel out of control again. At every stage of this growing relationship you must continually question yourself and work through the dynamics of the evolving, uncertain future. You must continually learn, change and accept uncertainty. When she is going through adolescence is a particularly difficult time. After all, we have all read those national surveys in magazines showing that kids today are having sex at 13 and 14 – not my little Princess!

> In this world nothing can be said to be certain, except death and taxes.
> *Benjamin Franklin, inventor*

And it's equally difficult for your daughter. She is facing new situations, new peer pressure. She is starting to date and her parents are acting strange. Everyone is struggling, learning and changing together. Everyone must accept the uncertainty that the future brings.

Life is funny. It tends to be circular. Despite your discomfort with her emerging sexuality, you have to begin modifying the parent-child relationship to a peer-to-psuedo-peer relationship. You can't treat her like a full peer, but you can't treat her like a child either. The success of the relationship will depend on how well you make that transition. And the degree of compassion and understanding that you show her in this difficult time is likely the degree of compassion she will show you when the roles are reversed and at 80 with Alzheimer's Disease, you become the child and she the parent.

Security is not in doing what you did well in the past. Your security lies in letting go of the past and creating new relationships. All of life is learning.

If you married your childhood sweetheart when you were both 19 and your relationship is still the same 30 years later, what is your relationship like? We all intuitively know that learning and changing offer us security, yet we resist them. Ultimately, we have to accept the uncertainty that life brings because we cannot know the future.

> Everything is in a constant state of change. Nothing ever stays the same.
> *Heracleitus, Greek philosopher*

A grandfather told me of spending time with his grandson as he learned to ride a bicycle. It was his first day without the training wheels and he fell, scraping his knees. Crying, the grandson came back saying, "I don't want to ride a bike ever again."

It broke the grandfather's heart. He would have gladly taken the fall and the pain for his grandson but he couldn't. Pain is part of the process of learning.

"Yes, you do, son. Only you just don't know it. The day I learned to ride my bike was one of the most exciting days for me. Instead of just walking a few blocks from my house, all of a sudden I could ride 15 miles from home! It opened a whole new world to me."

When we stop learning we limit our horizons. Too often we focus on the scraped knee and not the excitement, the wonder, the new worlds that await us on the other side of learning.

The consequences of our mistakes become more serious as we grow older. The child learning to walk will only fall about a foot. When learning to ride a bike, knees can be scraped at 10 miles an hour. CEOs are in the same boat. When a company is entering a new market, everyone is on a learning curve. However, the stakes are higher and the consequences of an error could cost 500 people their jobs.

The fear never goes away. Continual growth in the context of the learning paradox requires that we increase our emotional muscle, our ability to accept uncertainty and discomfort. We must increase such character strengths as patience, compassion and courage. There must be a tolerance for, and acceptance of, learning and the mistakes that it, by definition, brings. Leaders work to ensure that the mistakes are non-fatal.

Corporations can create and benefit from cultures that encourage the joy of learning and change. Only by rising to the challenges of our changing times and working through the learning paradox will we gain security and prosperity.

TO SUMMARIZE...

- Security today depends on the ability to learn and change.
- We become better at overcoming fears associated with the unknown by continually taking on new challenges.
- Mistakes are part of the learning process. We must accept that we and others will make mistakes.
- Security lies in change. Changing will ensure an organization remains viable and that people remain employed.

Reflection:

What is the key learning/insight for me in this chapter?

Action:

What one action shall I take tomorrow to move learning into action? And over time repeat, to move action into habit?

CHAPTER 3

The Business of Paradigms

Any time a word appears in the Dilbert cartoon strip, I become very wary of it. Paradigm has become a buzzword. It's become a cliché and is often misused. As a result, many people don't understand the power or importance of paradigms. What exactly is a paradigm? A simple story illustrates the concept. Imagine yourself in the following situation:[1]

You have a stopover at Heathrow International Airport in London, England, and you're very hungry because you weren't served breakfast on your morning flight. You go to one of the airport shops, buy a package of Walker's shortbread cookies and put them into your carry-on luggage.

You venture back into the airport, which is very noisy and crowded. Exhausted, you finally find a seat. After a minute of your stomach growling, you reach down into your bag and pull out your package of cookies.

What is unnerving about the situation is that the man next to you is literally staring at the cookies – his eyes are riveted on your package! As you open the package and take out the first cookie, his eyes follow your hand to your mouth. Then, without saying a word, he reaches for the package and grabs a cookie!

> The eye cannot see itself.
> *Anonymous*

You're shocked! You're speechless. You are in England, so you think, "How would the English react?" The answer comes to you, "Keep a stiff upper lip, pretend the situation is not happening and say nothing." Not knowing how to react, you impulsively go for another cookie. He grabs another. And so it goes.

How would you describe this man to your spouse or to a colleague at work? "What an aggressive jerk!" "Maybe they didn't serve breakfast on his flight, either." Once, an audience member said, "He's obviously with the government – he's used to taking 50 percent!"

What would you do? The best answer I've ever heard is, "I'd lick all the cookies." A woman once said, "I'd shoot him." (She was American.)

With all the reserve of a Brit, you continue to ignore the situation and do nothing. You take a cookie. He grabs the next.

Finally, it's down to one cookie. He reaches over, grabs the last cookie, breaks it in half, gives you half and eats half himself.

In a great indignant huff, you gather up your belongings and forfeit your seat, anything to get away from this cookie snatcher.

You're terribly upset. Your stomach is churning. You decide to go back to the shop to get some Alka-Seltzer and more cookies.

You pay for your new purchases and open your carry-on luggage to drop them in. And what do you see? Your unopened package of cookies! Suddenly you realize that you accidentally reached down into *his* luggage and were eating *his* package of cookies! You were the cookie thief!

> We do not see the world as it is, we see it as we are.
> Stephen R. Covey, author

Now, how would you describe this man to your spouse or to a colleague at work? The person you branded a villain just a moment ago suddenly becomes a saint – so tolerant, so generous. Your perceptions shift instantly. You have experienced a paradigm shift.

A paradigm is the way we see a situation. It's a mental model, a map. Paradigms encompass our beliefs, values and attitudes towards life and people. All our thoughts, all our actions flow from our paradigms. It's like a pair of glasses that alter our perception of what we see.

Getting back to the cookie debacle, imagine that you hadn't experienced the paradigm shift when you purchased another package of cookies. In other words, while walking through the airport, your original package of cookies had jiggled its way to the bottom of your bag. When you opened the bag at the shop, you didn't see your original package of cookies and put the new package on top, unaware that you now had two packages of cookies in your carry-on luggage. So now you can get back into the frame of mind that this jerk was eating your cookies. Reinvest yourself emotionally. Now, I don't know about you, but for me there is nothing more enjoyable than self-righteous, indignant, justified anger!

You board your plane, and can you believe who they've seated beside you? The cookie snatcher!

They are about to serve lunch. What's your attitude towards him? "You come near my lunch, and I'll stab you!"

Look at how the paradigm colors our interpretations. If he is smiling when they're serving lunch, how would you read his behavior? He's gloating about stealing my cookies. He thinks it's funny and he's plotting to steal my lunch. What if he is frowning? How would you interpret that? "Bloody well right, you should feel guilty for eating my cookies!"

You see, whatever he does, we will find evidence in his behavior to justify our paradigm. The frightening thing about paradigms is that we are not even conscious of them. Paradigms are like a pair of glasses we have become so accustomed to, we are not even aware that they bias our perception of the underlying reality. We assume we are objective. Only by changing our paradigms can we profoundly change.

If we want to transform our organizations, reinvent government, create a new society or make our own lives happier, we must change ourselves first by questioning our own belief systems, our own paradigms. Paradigms are primary. Notice how your behavior and attitude changed instantly when the paradigm shifted in the airport. Changing the way we see ourselves, our organizations and our world offers the greatest hope for personal and professional success.

In Christopher Columbus' day, most people believed that the earth was flat and that if you sailed too far, you would fall off the edge. People who held this view never sailed far out into the ocean; they always kept land in sight. Their actions were entirely logical given their paradigm.

But Columbus saw the world differently. He saw it as being round and believed that by sailing West he could get East to India. His actions flowed out of his paradigm.

The interesting thing to note is that reality remained constant. The world didn't change. The earth remained as it had been for five billion years. What changed history was the way Columbus saw the world. As a result of seeing the world differently, he behaved differently. As a result of behaving differently, he achieved different results.

A paradigm is like a map. Why? Because it is not the actual territory, it is a mental model, a visual representation of the underlying territory. The paradigm is primary. Working with a better map will make more difference than working harder and longer hours with a bad map.

Today, individuals and organizations can create their future by "seeing" new products and services that do not exist and then working to bring them to market. Creating value where none exists today requires an active paradigm shift, which makes real that which exists only in our imaginations. For instance, our need for the telephone existed before Alexander Graham Bell discovered it. It's just that consumers of his time didn't know they needed phones. Similarly, the principles of physics required to enable the invention of the phone existed before Bell stumbled upon them. Bell had to actively uncover them.

By contrast, creating a more accurate map of what already exists is a passive paradigm shift, because the underlying territory is already visible. So Columbus' confirmation of the world being round was a passive paradigm shift.

Our imagination and the creation of new value shape the future. Customers will overwhelmingly respond when businesses delight them by meeting and exceeding their needs. The most successful organizations work to meet needs that their customers may not even be aware that they have. The challenge for businesses is to uncover these needs or anticipate them and then work to meet them. Businesses must constantly revise and update their maps in a dynamic, ever-changing business environment.

In *Paradigms: The Business of Discovering the Future*, Joel Arthur Barker relates the classic business paradigm shift.[2] In 1968, the Swiss had more than 65 percent of the worldwide market share of watch sales and over 80 percent of the profits. By 1981, their sales had collapsed to a 10 percent share and profits fell to less than a 20 percent share. A staggering 50,000 of the 62,000 Swiss watchmakers lost their jobs in two years. What happened? The world changed because of a paradigm shift in the way watches work.

> One does not discover new lands without consenting to lose sight of the shore for a very long time.
> *André Gide, novelist*

The crisis was entirely preventable. In 1967, researchers at the Swiss industry research center in Neuchâtel, Switzerland, invented the electronic quartz movement. This revolutionary watch had no mainspring, didn't need bearings, had no gears and was electronic and battery powered. Swiss manufacturers rejected it outright because it did not fit their paradigm of what a watch was. They believed the discovery was so worthless that they let their researchers show the invention at the 1967 World Watch Congress. Seiko took one look and the rest is history. Seiko and other Japanese companies now have about 33 percent of worldwide watch sales and an equivalent share of profits.

Facing bankruptcy, the Swiss watch manufacturers banded together in

1983 to form the Swatch Group. They saw an opening in the market for a low-cost, stylish watch and produced the Swatch watch, a fashion accessory of the eighties and nineties. In 2000, the Swatch Group of companies accounted for 25 percent of all watch manufacturing in the world.[3]

When we are most successful we are most at risk of becoming complacent and ignoring the potential risks and benefits of paradigm shifts. The watch story is fascinating, not only because it highlights how precarious market share is, but also because it demonstrates the enormous potential power contained within new ways of perceiving the world. The Japanese conquest of the international watch industry began when they recognized a paradigm shift. From that point on, competitors could only play catch-up; the world market had already changed its preference. As the Japanese expression goes: there are only three things that matter: market share, market share, market share.

Remember the simple observation that 80 percent of the technology we will use in our day-to-day lives in just 10 years has yet to be invented! Think about how quickly technology is changing and how much it's affecting our lives. By the year 2005 most people will not deal with a bank that does not offer its customers online access to their accounts. This will have wider implications than the shift to 24-hour ATM banking. Each technological change can dramatically alter our lives. Each innovation brings a future vision into the present.

Gordon Moore, co-founder of Intel, devised Moore's Law.[4] It states that the computing power of microchips will double every two years while staying at roughly the same price point. Moore's prediction has held true, even though it was made in 1965.

This compounded annual growth in microprocessor power has forced high-tech companies to adopt non-traditional management methods and structures because the rate of change in the industry is so fast. High-tech leaders such as Sun Microsystems live on the "bleeding edge." Ninety-five percent of Sun's revenues come from products introduced in the last 18 months![5]

These facts have profound implications for all organizations. To begin with, the policies and procedures that made companies successful in the past may produce failure in the future. Many historical practices and structures run counter to the new reality.

For instance, businesses used to have five and ten year strategic plans.

The speed at which change is occurring within markets has rendered such planning obsolete. IBM's 1989 five-year plan was off by 200,000 employees! Between 1989 and 1995, "Big Blue," which once prided itself on lifetime job security, laid off half of its workforce. Long-term strategic planning as we knew it is dead. Strategic planning in the past assumed that things would basically be the same as they were in the past, but with a 10 percent annual growth in sales. This can no longer be the case. Now, strategic planning must assume that the future will look radically different than the present and past.

In these turbulent times, how can we cope? How can individuals and organizations create security? Only by serving as paradigm innovators, continually questioning personal and organizational paradigms. Amid the dramatic and sudden shifts that characterize our modern world, how can we plan for the future? Only by creating it!

This is at the core of the learning paradox. Security can come only by accepting the uncertainty of an unfolding future.

TO SHIFT OR NOT TO SHIFT . . . THAT IS THE QUESTION

Imagine that you are appointed vice president of marketing and sales for a company that is a market leader. Here's the chart of your annual sales in your new position after just two years:

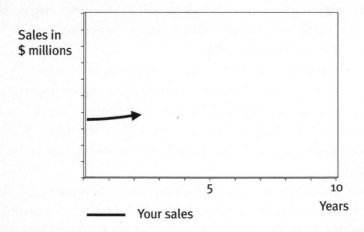

You are justifiably proud of your record. After just a few years in the position you look back on your sales and see how they have been growing

10 to 15 percent a year! Your product enjoys 75 percent of the market share. That's dominance! You are at the peak of your career and are featured on the cover of *Marketing* magazine as executive of the year.

After a few years, a small competitor introduces a product that is panned by the media. Customers also view it as a flop and sales of the product go nowhere. Do you pay any attention to it? Probably not. In hindsight, your decision is justified because your sales rise to the highest levels ever while your competitor's sales languish:

> Planning by its very nature defines and preserves categories. Creativity by its very nature creates categories or rearranges established ones. That is why strategic planning can neither provide creativity, nor deal with it when it emerges by other means.
> *Henry Mintzberg, author*

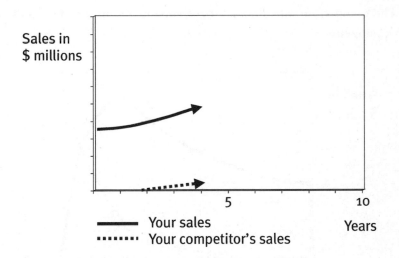

A couple of years later, the competitor introduces an updated version of the product and again it receives bad reviews. Customers don't really respond. The competitor's sales increase but only marginally. Why worry: 10 percent growth on top of nothing is still nothing. Would you focus on this product? Most say they would ignore it. Your sales continue rising, reaching record-breaking heights. Visions of the value of your stock options dance in your dreams. Your company and the industry have never seen such growth. You now enjoy 75 percent of worldwide market share! You are at the top of your game.

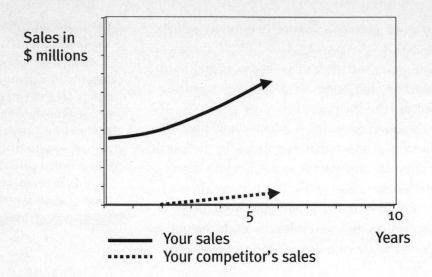

The competitor introduces a new version of the product and this is what happens:

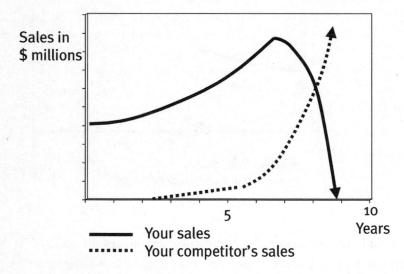

I hate it when that happens!

This is an actual case study. You were the vice president of marketing and sales for *Lotus 1-2-3* for *DOS*. You enjoyed 75 percent of market share. In November 1983, a tiny company, Microsoft, announced that it would develop a new graphical user interface (GUI – pronounced "gooey"). Working with *DOS* was difficult; you had to use long, hard-to-remember commands. The system was "user-vicious,"[6] counter-intuitive and difficult to learn. The Macintosh, by contrast, used visual symbols called icons.[7]

In November 1985, Microsoft released *Windows* Version 1.01. It was awkward, sluggish and user-vicious. It was widely seen as a marketing flop and taken up only by computer programmers and "techies." Microsoft stood behind its initiative, continuing to develop *Windows*. Version 2.0 was released in November 1987 with improved features and sales increased slightly.

With the continued success of *MS-DOS* (Microsoft Disk Operating System, the operating system for 90 percent of the world's personal computers in the 1980s and early 1990s), Microsoft was able to fund the development of *Windows*.

> Faced with the choice between changing one's mind and proving that there is no need to do so, almost everybody gets busy on the proof.
> *John Kenneth Galbraith, economist*

Microsoft had faith in the eventual success of *Windows* and during the early years was the only vendor developing and offering applications for this new environment: a word processor, a graphics package and a spreadsheet. Because market analysts and software makers were pessimistic about *Windows'* future, very few of Microsoft's competitors developed *Windows* products.

Following the release of Version 2.0, Microsoft again invested in improving *Windows*. Version 3.0 was released in May 1990 and took off, with sales exceeding even Microsoft's wildest projections. As the only software vendor with a variety of *Windows* applications, Microsoft was well positioned to benefit. Microsoft's early lead and the quality of its products have given the company dominant market share in most of the major mass-market business applications, especially the large spreadsheet and word processing categories.

Bill Gates, CEO of Microsoft, noted in October 1993:

At the time that *Windows* came out, our competitors in applications paused. And in doing that, it took them a long time to come out with their first *Windows* version that many people would have deemed adequate. And it's only recently that they either have come out with or are about to come out with decent *Windows* versions. So we've had all that time to continue to move ahead and lengthen our lead.[8]

By the time Microsoft released of Version 3.1 in April 1992, *Windows* was recognized as a major force in the computer world. The upgrade immediately began selling 1.5 million copies a month and by the end of 1994 was selling over two million copies a month – 66,000 copies a day! With the corresponding revenue flowing into Microsoft, the company began stretching its tentacles into every software market imaginable. By the end of 2001, *Windows,* in one form or another, was installed on approximately 700 million computers worldwide and by 2005, over 200 million new PCs will be sold every year, and barring a major shake-up in the PC industry, over 90 percent will have a form of *Windows!*[9]

In 1993, sales of *Windows* applications such as word processors, spreadsheets and graphics programs surpassed DOS software sales. The personal computer (PC) world had undergone a fundamental paradigm shift.

DOS ruled the PC world from 1981 to 1993. Lotus became synonymous with spreadsheets; *Lotus 1-2-3* enjoyed a market share of over 75 percent! As vice president of marketing and sales for *Lotus 1-2-3 for DOS*, would you invest millions to develop spreadsheets for a new environment – Windows – that was experiencing little success?

> Lord grant that we may always be right, for thou knowest we will never change our minds.
> *Scottish proverb*

From 1985 on, you knew about this terrible operating system called *Windows*. You felt that Microsoft had no chance of ever becoming a successful spreadsheet competitor. After all, your sales had been steadily increasing. But all of a sudden in 1990, *Windows* became a sales phenomenon. Still, you didn't really worry. After all, standard *DOS* sales had been steadily increasing for the past few years and projections showed a rosy future!

But your concern grew as *Windows 3.0* continued to sell at a terrific rate. You had no *Windows* products and you knew it would take over two years to develop a proper application for this new operating system. What to do?

Lotus began the two-and-a-half year development cycle to bring out *Lotus 1-2-3 for Windows*. By 1993, Microsoft had captured 56 percent of the spreadsheet market, dominated by *Windows* application sales. *Windows* had become the dominant operating system for personal computers.

It wasn't just Lotus that was blind to the shift. Almost all *DOS* software developers missed the boat, including *WordPerfect*, the program that had the dominant market share in the word processing category. Most successful *Windows* software developers – companies that have sold more than one million copies of their programs – began developing software after 1990! In other words, they saw the opportunity because they were new to software development, they were not entrenched in the old *DOS* paradigm.

The *DOS*-to-*Windows* shift did not happen overnight; it emerged slowly over more than five years, from the release of Version 1.01 until Version 3.0 became the best-selling operating system.

> Take care of what is difficult while it is easy and deal with what will become big while it is still small.
> *Lao Tzu, philosopher*

The success of *Windows* reminds me of a type of timber bamboo called *Phyllostachys vivax*. You plant the bamboo and in the first year it produces a one-inch shoot. A year later the shoot is still only one inch tall. You begin to worry, "Does it have enough sunshine? Has there been enough rain?" In the third year, the shoot is still only one inch tall. The fourth year it's the same! You wonder, "Did I buy a genetically deficient bamboo?"

In the fifth year the bamboo grows 90 feet in just six weeks. The question is, did the timber bamboo take six weeks or five years to grow 90 feet? The answer is five years. Most of the time was spent laying the root system that would support the stunning growth. The same is true in this Microsoft example.

As VP for Lotus, your stock options were plummeting in value. You felt ill whenever you saw Bill Gates on the cover of a magazine. If only you could have seen the future, it would have been different. However, you could now rest easy – at least your *Windows* spreadsheet was out on the market.

Microsoft had less than 10 percent of the spreadsheet market before the introduction of *Windows 3.0* in 1990. By 1993 it had soared to 56 percent! But Microsoft was still not complacent. The company began bundling its *Windows* applications – *Word* (word processor), *Excel* (spreadsheet), *PowerPoint* (graphic presentation), *Mail* (email client) and *Access* (database) – as an application "suite" called *Office*. Microsoft priced *Office* at slightly more than the price of one stand-alone application. Suites integrate the stand-alone applications. Instead of each application having its own spellchecker, they share common code.

Just when Microsoft's competitors were releasing good *Windows* applications, the ground rules changed *again*. Now they had to make word processing, spreadsheet and database software, and then integrate and sell them at roughly the price point of a single application! Applications suites, for both technical and pricing reasons, have virtually eliminated the sale of individual applications. Microsoft now dominates the suite category with over 80 percent of unit shipment market share and over 90 percent of the revenue. So from 1990–1997 Microsoft went from less than 10 percent market share of all spreadsheet sales to over 87 percent through the sale of Microsoft *Office*[10] As Chris Peters, former vice president of *Office*, notes:

Everything we've ever done won't matter three years from now. In terms of products, the amount of computing power that will become available in the next five years will be equal to all the computing power ever made before. What it basically means is that you always have to be jumping well ahead. If you internalize that exponential growth, everyone else thinks that the thing will be like last year only a little different, which of course is true for a very short period of time. When you look at the industry in a two-year chunk, it does look very linear and you have to step back and find out that it's always exponentially growing. And then, when you do that, you do make bigger bets and a little bit different kind of bets.

I think it's the underlying principle for Microsoft. I think it's something that Bill Gates always understood and internalized, that you [must] radically change things and really have big plans. A classic example is that, *DOS* was doing great. [We could have said,] 'Let's just come out with this new version of *DOS*. Why make *Windows?*' And, 'Well, *Windows* takes up so much more hardware and computing power.' In a sense, [though, an innovation like] *Office* makes the individual apps obsolete. Just when our competitors are trying to be good in *Windows* [applications], now they have to make a good word processor and a good spreadsheet and a good database. You have to be that kind of software company now.[11]

In planning for the future, Microsoft looks at the exponential change in the computer industry and makes nonlinear assumptions. For instance, what will an average PC look like in seven years? Where you feel the market is moving will profoundly influence the bets you place today. Microsoft assumes that the size of the average hard disk of a new personal computer today will be the amount of RAM (random access memory) of an average new computer in seven years! In 2001 the average size for the hard disk of a new computer was 80 gigabytes. Imagine 80 gigs of RAM on a new PC by 2008! All sorts of new applications become possible. Powerful voice-recognition applications allowing you to dictate letters to your computer, become feasible. Full-motion videoconferencing becomes possible.

> In times of rapid change, experience could be your worst enemy.
> J. Paul Getty, US oil billionaire

By 2009, applications will look fundamentally different than they do in 2003. Therefore, strategic planning needs to be radically different than it is today. It needs to assume the future will bring radical discontinuity.

The *DOS*-to-*Windows* shift will, I predict, repeat itself with *Windows XP Professional*. *Windows XP Professional* is Microsoft's high-end operating system that has replaced the NT line of operating systems. It is more robust than *Windows 98* or *Windows ME* and it allows inexpensive microprocessors such as Pentiums to be harnessed together like a team of workhorses to deliver significantly more power. Microsoft has been investing a great deal of revenue in *Windows XP Professional*.

Harnessing the power of multiple processors is the wave of the future. If, as a result of *Windows XP Professional* fewer companies buy mainframes, hasn't a software maker become the main competition to mainframe vendors?

Windows XP Professional sales may be slow when it hits the market towards the end of 2001, but Microsoft is not in any market it enters for the short run. The pattern was the same with the launch of *Windows 2000 Professional* in February 2000. The company continued to invest in *Windows 2000 Professional* by launching Service Pack 1 in August 2000 to address problems with the system. *Windows 2000 Professional* sales hit the one million mark in March 2000.

Windows XP will, over time, dramatically change the high-end operating system market, threatening *Unix* just as the shift occurred to *Windows* from *DOS*. The pattern is a predictably slow initial adoption, with

Microsoft continually investing in the new operating system. Eventually, a critical mass of sales will be established and then the product will take off. This doesn't mean that *Unix* is dead, it's just they will not experience the growth they would have had, had Microsoft not entered the market.

As Joel Arthur Barker says, "When a paradigm shifts, everyone goes back to zero." In other words, success in the old paradigm will not guarantee success in the new. In fact, success in the past actually tends to inhibit success in the future because organizations seem to be inherently incapable of seeing things in new ways. If leaders in an organization cannot see the market differently, they will not seize emerging opportunities and avoid potential problems. They will not create any urgency around the need to change. Organizations that are slow to change will lose market share to more agile competitors that can quickly seize opportunities. Organizations that are incapable of seeing new paradigms as they emerge become victims of paradigm rigor mortis.

> Success has ruined
> many a man.
> *Benjamin Franklin,*
> *inventor and statesman*

SHIFTS FROM SLOW TO SWIFT

Imagine a pond that starts with one lily pad and the number of plants doubles every day until the pond would be entirely covered by lilies after 30 days.

However, one day before the entire pond is covered, half the water would still be open. On Day 28, two days before the lilies completely cover the pond, three-quarters of the pond would be open water. On Day 27, a full seven-eighths of the water would be open. And on Day 26, more than 90 percent of the water would be open.

By Day 26, you have noticed the arithmetical progression. You have studied the situation, become alarmed and begin to go around yelling, "Beware, beware, the pond is about to be covered over with lilies." But people look at you as if you're crazy. "What are you talking about?" they ask. "Can't you see that 94 percent of the water is open?"

It is hard to be a paradigm shifter. The shift from *DOS* to *Windows* is like the pond being overtaken by lilies. *Lotus 1-2-3* and *WordPerfect* were overrun.

Imagine that you are a programmer at Lotus and see the emerging pattern of Microsoft *Windows* growth. You start making noises. You want to develop *Windows*-based products. But at the time, 1989, Lotus is making significant net profits of almost $68 million, principally from sales of *DOS*-based *Lotus 1-2-3*. *Windows* Version 2.0 is a dog. So a few more lilies appear on the water's surface. You yell a bit louder and people still think you're being an alarmist. By the time people finally wake up, the pond has been overgrown with lilies.

> History is the ability to select from the many lies that which most closely resembles the truth.
> *Herodotus, Greek historian*

The more successful a company is, the more is at stake. Today, the longevity of successful companies is surprisingly low. The average life span of large companies is less than 40 years. In more recent studies the trend has been shown to continue. In 1994, a staggering 40 percent of the Fortune 500 of 1979 had ceased to exist. To succeed in the long term, organizations must continually reinvent themselves.

In a learning-based organization it is everyone's business to question and challenge the paradigms that are shaping their work. The leaders, though, are ultimately responsible for creating an environment where innovation and change are possible, valued and encouraged.

TO SUMMARIZE ...

- Paradigms are ways of perceiving. They govern our attitudes and actions.
- In today's business world, paradigms are constantly shifting. Sometimes, the change is imperceptibly slow, but sometimes sudden.
- The only secure individuals and organizations are those with the ability to anticipate and discern paradigm shifts.
- Paradigm shifters are market makers.
- Leaders create their own paradigms consistent with their vision, and shift existing paradigms to keep their organizations in a leadership position.

Reflection:

What are the paradigms in my department, organization, industry and even my own responsibilities that I don't question.

CHAPTER 4

Leaders are Paradigm Innovators

As we enter a new millennium, the greatest challenge has become problem-seeing, not problem-solving. Business leaders and managers are generally excellent problem solvers. But we have to become more adept at anticipating problems and perceiving opportunities to stay ahead of the competition and exceed customer expectations.

> A leader is a dealer in hope.
> *Napoleon Bonaparte,*
> *French emperor*

To create new products and services, executives and others in organizations must perceive opportunities. The highest margins lie in creating as yet unrealized value for the customer.

If we are all apple vendors in a small town, what price can we get for our apples? What is the nature of the market? In such a market, how do you win market share?

It's a dog-eat-dog, price-driven, commodity market. What the competition does affects us powerfully. To survive we might differentiate ourselves by polishing the apples or by spending more on advertising. While important, these approaches add to our cost. Unless we can raise our prices, we are squeezing our own margins.

In commodity markets, competitors who offer the lowest price win. This is Wal-Mart's strategy – always striving to increase operational efficiency and lower prices. Wal-Mart wants to maintain the perception that it offers the lowest prices.

Price-sensitive market share is the easiest to win, but also the easiest to lose. If your competitors lower their prices tomorrow, you instantly lose customers.

Back to our story of fruit vendors in the small town. If only one vendor sells oranges, what price can be commanded? Whatever the market will bear. Margins are high. The orange vendor isn't concerned about what competitors are doing with apples because of the monopoly on oranges.

Leaders who continually question business paradigms and create new value for their customers create *effective monopolies* for a period in which they can enjoy high margins. As competitors catch up, the market leader must be prepared to introduce new products and services that will make their original product obsolete. This keeps them at the front of the market.

At a seminar a CEO observed, "What you're saying is, if we were our own competitors, knowing what we know about our own weaknesses and strengths, we must always be trying to beat ourselves." He was right. Organizations must continuously compete against themselves and reinvent themselves to remain market leaders.

THE CHANGING NATURE OF LEADERSHIP

How we perceive leadership is changing significantly. A marching band is the perfect metaphor for the way organizations used to be. There was one leader and everyone else marched in lock-step conformity.

As products and services became more complex, specialization was required. An orchestra became a better metaphor. A series of specialists and a conductor selected the music, assigned the solos and controlled the tempo. The new model is more like a jazz band. A group of highly specialized, talented players improvise together. No one individual is in charge. Leadership "flows" from one player to the next. They celebrate one another's talents and successes. They play best when they let each other shine in the spotlight for some time. And no one individual controls the play. In this scenario, leadership is demonstrated in the bringing together of the jazz players, ensuring that the group works well together, and perhaps managing the finances and logistical challenges facing the group so that the players can do what they do best – play.

> Maturity is the ability to delay gratification.
> M. Scott Peck, author

In today's dynamic, changing market, strategic planning is a bit like trying to fly a plane while building it.

FUTURE CHALLENGE

Think about what your industry will be like in five years. Do you think competition will have increased or decreased? Will customers be more, or less sophisticated? Will competition in high-margin niches be increasing or decreasing? Will price-based competition be increasing or decreasing? Will competitors be coming from non-traditional areas, or will you be competing against the same competitors you have faced for ages? How about people? Will the best and the brightest employees be easier or harder to retain? Will there be increased or decreased pressure to integrate more tightly with suppliers to shorten cycle times? Will you be able to do exactly what you are doing now, only work a little bit harder or longer or with a more positive attitude and gain market share, increase customer satisfaction and create higher margins? We all know that our organizations must change. Change is inevitable; either organizations change or their market share will.

THE CHALLENGE OF LEADERSHIP

People often envy leaders. I was speaking with a group of 200 managers from a large national bank. They were complaining about all the problems they faced, including how unresponsive the organization was to their needs. So I asked them, "The higher you rise in an organization, do more or fewer people bring you problems? Are the problems harder or easier to deal with? Does the weight of responsibility grow or diminish? Are the timelines for implementing solutions longer or shorter? Are the consequences of decisions more, or less difficult to anticipate? Are the factors affecting the decisions more, or less numerous? Are the solutions more, or less complex? Do the problems require deeper or simpler analysis? In working with people who bring you problems, do you require more, or less patience?"

The higher you rise in an organization, the greater your tolerance for challenge, pain and complexity must be, the greater your willingness has to be to embrace the learning paradox. The higher you go, the greater the weight you carry; therefore, the deeper your analytical abilities and the greater your patience and perseverance must be. And yet many people equate leadership with perks and prestige. Remember, the higher you go, the thinner the air gets. So at the end of this line of questioning to the group of 200 managers I said, "Remember, you chose to be leaders."

BENEFITS VS. BEST LEADERSHIP

It seems every business book you pick up today is about leadership. It's definitely one of the hot topics. Larry Wilson, the founder of both Wilson Learning and Pecos River, and the author of *Play to Win* and *Stop Selling, Start Partnering* and the coauthor of *The One Minute Sales Manager*, does a fascinating exercise with seminar participants around leadership.[1]

First Larry asks workshop participants "What are the benefits of being a leader? If you were to stop people in the street and interview them on what are the benefits of being a leader, what would they say? Why do you think most people want to be leaders? Answers typically include: power, more money, executive perks, first class travel, having the resources of the organization at your disposal, control, prestige, recognition, having others listen to you, being able to enact your vision, being able to set direction for the organization. Basically it boils down to power, control, money, prestige and being served.

Larry grouped these answers into three categories:

1. The most popular was power.
2. The second was control – the ability to exercise their vision and deploy resources to achieve that vision.
3. And the third broke down to a number of things such as status, recognition, pay – which he summarized as to be served.

Larry calls these the ego needs.

Larry then would say:

I want to put forward a definition that true leadership is when people follow someone not because we *have to* but because we *want to*. What leaders in your life have you been attracted to? The assignment that evening for each individual was:

"Think of some instance where you followed someone because you wanted to not because had to – a parent, teacher, boss, someone who had written a book. The experience should have had a profound effect on you in some way – it was a defining moment in your life. And then describe the situation.

I phrase the question slightly differently, asking participants to think about the most "magical" experience they have had with a leader and what was it that made that experience so special? The interaction with the leader could have been in business in community a volunteer organization religious organization of family.

Here are Larry's comments:

Invariably people answer: "He/she saw something in me – some potential that I hadn't seen in myself."

"She helped me discover something I didn't know."

The most extraordinary experiences people relayed were when leaders empowered the people involved! "The leader's role was to help me find my true self.

The second thing that people invariably listed as the second aspect of transformational experiences with leaders was that they were stuck in a rut. "I couldn't see a way out. The leader helped me see options and possibilities. Instead of controlling me this was the exact opposite – the effect of their role was to set me free.

And the third – to serve. They helped me remove barriers; they spent time with me to coach me. They believed in me. The sum total of all of these is that they served me. The true nature of leadership is to help other people find power, set them free, to help them become who they are truly meant to be. To help them learn, to grow, to develop.

Here we collectively think the benefits of leadership are power, control and to be served, and the best experiences we have ever had with leaders – we experienced the opposite – these leaders empowered us, gave us freedom, invested in our vision, and served us. The exact opposite. It is the concept of servant leadership.

In other words, what we define as exceptional and magical leadership is 180 degrees the opposite of what most people perceive as the benefits of being a leader. This raised the whole concept of servant leadership, the concept made popular through the extensive writing of the late Robert Greenleaf.

HOW DO LEADERS STAY AHEAD?

Leaders must continually question the viability of their products and services to ensure that their organization is not succumbing to complacency and, over time, mediocrity. Complacency kills. It's the only corporate disease that prevents you from knowing that you have it. Continually questioning helps individuals and organizations to deepen their understanding of potential market shifts, helping the organization to formulate and embrace new paradigms. Here are some examples:

WHO DOES THE WORK? I was in Florida in the early 1990s to give a talk and discovered that I had forgotten to take any US currency. There I was in the sunshine state with only Canadian cash, which my American friends call *Monopoly* money. I went to a bank I have never heard of – the First National Bank of Florida – stuck my bankcard into the automatic banking machine (ATM) and on a Sunday night withdrew US dollars from my Canadian account. Now think about what banking used to be like in 1980: Monday to Friday, 10:00 a.m. to 3:00 p.m., only at my local branch. Today, banking is anywhere, anytime and in any currency. The technology has dissolved what were once barriers to banking, enabling a radically different relationship between banks and customers. It's not about efficiency, but radically new relationships.

WHO DOES THE WORK? I, the customer, am doing the work, not a teller. Not only that, but I paid one dollar for the honor and privilege of doing the work myself. And I was profoundly grateful to the bank for allowing me the opportunity. Now that's a paradigm shift!

If we limit ourselves to seeing only our employees doing work, then self-serve gas stations and banking machines would be impossible to imagine. We must look beyond traditional employee-driven workplaces and consider introducing new technologies and perhaps outsourcing some functions to the customer so we can remain focused on what we do best.

FedEx introduced *PowerShip* in 1987, giving its 1,000 largest customers a free terminal to automatically fill in waybills and keep track of packages and shipping volumes. Before 1987, people had to write out the waybills by hand, then call the courier to order the pick-up. The courier took the packages and waybills. Back at FedEx someone had to key in the information. You would receive the bill in the mail, but if you caught an error, you would have to call FedEx and another invoice would be issued. You would approve it, send it to accounts payable where the information was keyed in to your system and payment was sent through the mail.

> You can't dig a hole in a new place by digging the same hole deeper.
> *Edward de Bono, author*

PowerShip software, now called *FedEx Ship Manager Workstation*, automates the whole process, automatically filling in your shipping information. And when you have keyed in a customer once, they are on a quick-pick list. So the software eliminates most of the time it used to take to complete the waybill. The system orders the pick-up online, FedEx's system generates an invoice that interfaces with your online accounts payable system and through electronic funds transfer sends payment back to FedEx. The whole process is instantaneous.

These 1,000 largest clients represented 30 percent of FedEx's total package volume. The program was so successful that FedEx launched a spin-off program called *FedEx Ship* (now called *FedEx Ship Manager software*) in 1995. Now businesses of any size that have the software can order online pick-ups. Over 2.6 million FedEx customers use these two systems daily.[2] Finally, FedEx allows customers to log on to its web site, key in their waybill number and find out in real time exactly where their package is. As a result of these three initiatives, FedEx has not had to hire an additional 20,000 staff as package volumes grow or to sort and file over two billion pieces of paper a year![3] Similarly, FedEx saved the cost of having to print over 2 billion forms. Over 700,000 package tracking inquiries a day are answered online by customers themselves, more than twice as many as are answered by FedEx's own customer service agents over the phone. And who is doing the work? The customers. And the customers are profoundly grateful because from their perspective it eliminates unnecessary administrative work, too.

WHAT BUSINESS ARE WE IN?   Any business that defines itself in terms of its product or service is ultimately doomed because products and services are constantly becoming outdated. During the late 1800s and early 1900s in the northern part of North America we kept our food cold in iceboxes. Numerous companies went out to the rivers and streams in the winter. Using saws, teams of men cut large blocks out of the ice, leveraged them up onto the horse-drawn sleighs and dragged them to barns where they were insulated in hay. During the summer, small blocks of ice were chipped off and delivered door-to-door using horse- drawn carriages.

> There are three kinds of organizations: those that run into brick walls; those that see the brick walls coming and swerve to avoid them; and those that are out in front and are busy building walls for their competitors.
> *James Champy, author*

Think about the core competencies required for the ice-block company: working with saws, working with horses, first aid would probably be good, there would be a barn acquisition department, a door-to-door sales force and an accounting department. And how would the company spend its research and development (R&D) budget? Most likely on trying to find better ways of cutting ice, insulating materials and breeding horses that work better in cold weather.

But when refrigeration came along none of the companies that survived in the ice age made it in the refrigeration paradigm. Why? Well, look at the core competencies required in the new paradigm: handling Freon gas, manufacturing and servicing compression motors, mass manufacturing, and retail and wholesale distribution. The only competency that would remain the same would be accounting.

Why is it so difficult for organizations to change? Because in the icebox paradigm, if you were a good saw handler you became head of the saw department, the employee who handled horses best became head of horses, the best barn buyer became head buyer. However, none of these skills was required in the new paradigm. In other words, the strengths of the organization – its people, its R&D – were the weaknesses in the new paradigm.

We need to separate *form* from *function*. Banking is essential but banks are not. The function of banking is essential but the current form is not. Banking in the future will have more to do with mouse clicks and software than with bricks and mortar.

An organization focused on meeting its customers' underlying needs in the best way possible is more likely to have the courage and freedom needed to continuously reinvent itself, its products and its services. Ultimately, all organizations should exist to serve the needs of their customers. Many customers' needs will remain unarticulated until an innovative individual or organization discovers them and creates products and services to meet those as yet unrealized needs.

But don't throw the baby out with the bath water. Paradigm shifts happen over time. Organizations should not stop what they are doing and focus exclusively on a new way of doing business. Instead, they must make the transition from old paradigm to new one gradually as demand for the new product or service grows. For example, we still have radios. It is just that radios no longer occupy the dominant position in providing family entertainment at home. So a radio manufacturer in the 1930s would not give up radio production. But to create security in the future, it would have to be constantly searching for new applications for radios; for example, car radios and portable radios. As television emerged as a new and growing medium, the company's long-term security would be guaranteed by making the move to manufacturing televisions.

WHERE DO WE SERVE THE CUSTOMER?   Traditional wisdom in retailing teaches that only three things matter – location, location, location. But when I order a shirt from Land's End or L.L. Bean, I don't know if I am talking to a customer service representative in Texas, Florida or Michigan. When the shirt arrives by courier the next day, I don't know where the manufacturer or warehouse is located. Similarly, banking can be done with ease wherever there is an ATM.

If the owners of a mechanic's garage were to define their business in terms of physical location, then it would be impossible for them to conceive of 24-hour, roadside service anywhere in North America, dispatched from an entrepreneur's basement to tow-truck contractors across the continent. Technology has redefined the workplace.

Similarly, where does work occur? One physical location? Or any location where employees and associates are working?

WHEN DO WE SERVE OUR CUSTOMERS?   Many customers today have expectations of being served 24×365. We now have 24 hour supermarkets, drug stores, restaurants and technical support.

When is it best for people to work? Most organizations have a nine-to-five mentality. People are expected to be physically present at work during those hours. Why? Because our work paradigm comes from the textile mills in England in the 1700's. People were called "hands" to the industrial process. Employees had to be physically present on the production line during their shift because production was physical. But today, what are we interested in – people's brawn or their brains?

Many computer programmers and other creative people often do their best work late at night. If their organization demands their presence from nine to five, they grudgingly show up by 9:00 in the morning, but they probably aren't productive until 11:30 or so – after they've had 15 cups of coffee – because they were up until 3:00 a.m. working on their pet programming project. In such cases, where does energy, enthusiasm and creativity go – into day jobs or late-night, pet projects?

If organizations want creativity, they must give employees the latitude to work under the conditions that most foster creativity for them. Some people may be most creative listening to music, while others may be late-night workers.

Why shouldn't computer programmers do most of their work during the hours when they are most creative? I am often asked, "If employees worked at home, how would we know that they were working?" New information technology (IT) systems allow us to overcome barriers of time and distance. If the issue is trust and a company wants to have time clocks, log-on and log-off times can be recorded and keyboard activity measured. But I would ask in return, "How do you know how hard your employees work during office hours?" More important than measuring log-on and log-off times or the number of keystrokes is measuring results. Manage by results, not methods. Organizations want new, high-margin products and services, increased sales, higher productivity, shorter cycle times, higher quality and increased customer satisfaction and retention. If you can achieve these things, it doesn't matter where or when employees do the work.

HOW DO WE SERVE OUR CUSTOMERS? Do we serve them based on our rules, policies and procedures that are designed for our benefit? Or do we design policies from customers' perspectives?

An insurance firm studied its internal processes and discovered that, on average, it took eight weeks from the time one of its clients suffered an accident until they received their claim payment in the mail. Imagine that you suffered a car accident. You would call your insurance broker, who would call the insurance company. A case manager would be assigned to your file. The file would then go to the claims adjuster, who would talk to your garage mechanic. Then the file would come back to the case manager, who would have to receive the police report before finally approving the file and sending it off to accounts payable until, finally, you receive your payment. Ya!

Paper-based, time-intensive process

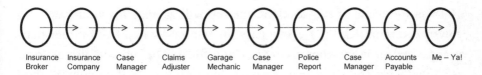

| Insurance Broker | Insurance Company | Case Manager | Claims Adjuster | Garage Mechanic | Case Manager | Police Report | Case Manager | Accounts Payable | Me – Ya! |

The company found that, throughout this time-intensive, paperbound, linear process, the amount of time actually spent working on the average case by all staff totaled only eight hours! The rest of the time, the file was either in someone's in-box or out-box, or in transit between boxes.

Here is how one insurance company reengineered. The claims service objective of Progressive Insurance's Immediate Response is to provide policyholders with fast, fair, caring and personal service when they need it.

Progressive reengineered its processes in 1992 because of CEO Peter Lewis' vision of reducing the human trauma and economic costs of auto accidents. Lewis believes insurance companies abuse customers: "They get dealt with adversarially and slowly. I said, 'Why don't we just stop that? Why don't we start dealing with them nicely?' It would be a revolution in the business."[4]

Lewis wanted to restructure insurance processes so that Progressive could help customers when they need it most – when they're in accidents.

The first problem was that people are so flustered when they get into an accident they can't remember the name of their insurance company, let alone the phone number. Focus group studies show that people will carry "Gold Cards" in their wallets. So Progressive gave all its policyholders a "Gold Card" with a toll-free, 1-800 number that is staffed 24 hours a day, seven days a week. With the prevalence of cellular phones today, policyholders are now calling from the scene of the accident. Progressive staff work to help in any way they can. Company claims adjusters don't sit in the office, they rove around North America in marked company vehicles. The operator can dispatch the nearest available claims representative to the accident scene. At times they have arrived before 911-dispatched vehicles! Bit of a worry! Just wait until we have lawyers on wheels!

The claims reps are focused on assisting you. Their first concern is to make sure no one is hurt. They have a cellular phone that you can use to call your family or friends to let them know you will be late. They have a digital cassette recorder to interview witnesses and a digital camera to take photos in case the accident ends up in court.

From the scene of the accident, the rep will arrange for your car to be towed and repaired. Progressive pays for the services up front rather than you paying for it and then trying to claim for it. The rep will also arrange for a rental car and will drive you over to pick it up. Or, if you prefer, they will drive you to where you need to go and have the rental car dropped off at your home.

Some clients prefer the cash to fixing their vehicle. Using specialized software and a notebook computer, the claims rep can estimate the damage and issue payment of up to $2,000 to the policyholder on the spot.

Progressive representatives contact 80 percent of all accident victims less than nine hours after learning of the accident. Adjusters inspect 70 percent of damaged vehicles within one day and wrap up most collision damage claims within one week.

The benefits for the policyholder are obvious: the insurance company becomes a personal valet, a problem solver during the time of greatest need and stress. Progressive becomes an ally. It's one-stop shopping. It's help when the client needs help.

From Progressive's point of view the benefits are also obvious: faster claims processing, less paperwork, fewer people involved, significantly higher customer satisfaction and strategic advantage in the marketplace. The company knows that when people are dealt with quickly and fairly it reduces the involvement of lawyers, and of the overall amount paid out by the company, more goes to policyholders rather than to pay legal fees.

Progressive has been one of the fastest-growing insurance companies, going from the forty-third largest US insurer of private passenger autos in 1980 to the fourth largest in 2001. It has also been very profitable, with a 22.3 percent annual compounded rate of return between 1971 and 2000 (the comparable Standard & Poor's 500 rate was 9.8 percent in the same period). Progressive is able to insure risky drivers that no other insurance firm will accept because its overheads are so low.

BEST OF THE BAD

Progressive looked at the database of drivers who are typically thought of as bad risks by insurance companies – drivers with bad records such as driving while under the influence of alcohol, reckless driving charges or numerous accidents. If the average driver pays a premium of X, all insurance companies charged this group of bad drivers $4X$ premiums. Progressive's analysts who set the rate for premiums began to ask, "What possible changes in lifestyle would lead us to assess these drivers' risk profiles differently, despite their past bad records?" The analysts decided that if you had your first child it would likely change your sense of responsibility and therefore your driving pattern. So Progressive went into the database, found all new parents who were bad drivers and offered them a premium of $3X$, which was better than any other insurer in the market. By looking differently at these customers they skimmed a very lucrative category of customer.

It's not just reengineering an old process, it's radically redefining the relationship between the company and the customer.

As a policyholder, which insurance firm would you choose – one that pays in eight weeks but has given the customer service agents training, teaching them to smile while talking to customers over the phone because their happiness is conveyed through their voice, or one that is capable of paying on the spot?

How could Progressive continue to challenge existing paradigms? Imagine that the company places a small microchip/transmitter under the hood of insured cars that would emit a radio signal if a car was in a collision at over 15 miles an hour. The signal would be picked up through a land-based cellular or radio network and relayed to an orbiting satellite. Using geographic location software, the satellite would determine the location of the accident, call the client on a cellular phone and, if necessary, dispatch the nearest claims adjuster. If the impact occurred at greater than, say 45 miles per hour, the system could be designed to call 911 services. Imagine a near-fatal crash on a little-traveled road late at night. You swerve to avoid a deer, roll your car and crash into a telephone pole. You are unconscious, and without immediate medical help will die, but your insurance firm saves your life! Sound too far off? New Lincoln Continental cars come with such a system:

> . . . Our roadside service . . . goes 10,000 miles into space with a satellite. It's the Remote Emergency Satellite Cellular Unit we call RESCU. Simply push a button and global positioning satellites will determine your location. Your position is then relayed to the Lincoln Security Response Center, which will dispatch assistance and keep you informed via your hands-free cellular phone. Both of these systems are part of Lincoln Continental's Personal Security Package with RESCU.[5]

These features are now available on many lower priced cars. For example, General Motors' *OnStar* system can notify emergency personnel in the event of an accident, provide roadside assistance, and stolen vehicle tracking. For an additional fee, *OnStar* users can access an operator that will provide information about construction-free driving routes, hotel and dinner reservations. General Motors factory-installs the system in 32 of its 54 US models and had one million subscribers in 2001 and expects to have over 4 million in 2003.[6] The subscription fee for this service ranges from $200 to $400 per year. This means that in 2001, the *OnStar* system represented a $200 to $400 million-revenue stream.

How we deliver products or services to our customers is significant. For example, how is corporate training delivered? Until 1995 it was usually delivered in person. I used to organize executive development conferences that cost $1,000 per person for two days. Executives, who came from across North America, would easily spend another $1,500 on flights, hotel rooms and meals. The travel cost more than the course!

In 2001, Stephen Covey charged $75,000 per day to speak. Few companies or seminar promoters can afford this fee. Today it's possible to participate in a live Stephen Covey seminar in the comfort of your boardroom or auditorium by satellite or videoconferencing system for just $2,500!

When I turn up to see Stephen Covey live, I am usually in the audience with 1,000 other people. From the back of the room I'm not watching

Stephen, I'm watching a projected image on a large screen. So if I'm watching Stephen on TV at the live site, I find little difference in watching him at a remote location by satellite or videoconferencing. Instead of paying $350 to $500 for registration, I pay as little as $50! Any participant at any remote location can pose questions by telephone and interact with the presenter.

Business education no longer has to be expensive and exclusive to executives. It can be made available to thousands of employees, allowing for consistency of training and the development of a common language across a whole organization. You can afford to have the world's leading business thinkers – Edward de Bono, Stephen Covey, Peter Senge and many others – presenting live in your boardroom!

Individuals and organizations must question how they conduct business. Companies must not define themselves by their policies or procedures.

WHY ARE WE IN BUSINESS?

Over the years the primary purpose of business has shifted. In the past, the purpose was to produce the best possible profit or dividends per share. In other words, the purpose of business was to serve the shareholder(s). In the 1980s the popular focus turned to customer satisfaction, the theory being that if you take care of your customer the bottom line will take care of itself. Taking this progression one step further, my research into the best companies showed that success is also dependent upon having excited, satisfied employees (internal customers) who, in turn, are motivated to serve the (external) customer. We need to

> A journey of a thousand miles begins with a single step.
> *Lao Tzu, philosopher*

continue expanding our concept of why we are in business. It is ultimately to serve the needs of all stakeholders. Stephen Covey has a simple definition of stakeholder. He asks, "Who would be hurt if your business failed?" Anyone who would be hurt is a stakeholder. Ultimately, the most successful businesses follow an inspiring mission to serve all stakeholders.

Paradigm shifts in the past happened slowly over a long period of time. For instance, the shift from horse-drawn carriage to car took two decades. This was due to the time it took Ford to develop and refine the assembly line, but more importantly the lack of infrastructure to support and promote car sales. On unpaved roads car travel was bumpy and slow. Paving happened slowly as automobile travel became more common and drivers demanded better roads from governments. The shift from *DOS* to *Windows*, by contrast, took eight years, primarily due to the time it took to refine the software. Today, however, with easy-to-use software and powerful microprocessors, the information technology infrastructure is in place to enable fast-and-furious paradigm shifts. For instance, new technology allows PC users to make long-distance phone calls over the Internet without paying long-distance charges. Companies such as HotTelephone provide free long distance calling from a PC to another PC, or from a PC to a land-based phone. In 1999 only one percent of all phone traffic in North America was carried over the Internet, but by 2003 this is expected to rise to 17 percent and by 2005 to 30 percent.[7] How will this affect phone companies that rely on long-distance charges to supply most of their profit? To date, phone companies have downplayed the significance of this technology, ignoring its potential threat.

PARADIGM SHIFTING DIFFERS FROM REENGINEERING

Reengineering was the hot management theory in North America from 1991 to 1996. Reengineering focuses on how to make existing processes more efficient, but does not create new products, services or markets. Reengineering is necessary but insufficient to ensure thriving in the future. Businesses can better their bottom line by increasing revenue (numerator) and/or cutting costs (denominator). As Hamel and Prahalad point out:[8]

> ROI [Return on Investment] or RONA [Return on Net Assets] . . . has two components, a numerator – net income – and a denominator – investment, net assets, or capital employed. (In a service industry a more appropriate denominator may be headcount). Managers know that raising net income is likely to be a harder slog than cutting assets and headcount. To grow the numerator, top management must have a point of view about where the new opportunities lie, must be able to anticipate changing customer needs, must have invested preemptively in building new competencies and so on. So under intense pressure for

a quick ROI improvement, executives reach for the lever that will bring the quickest, surest improvements in ROI – the denominator. To cut the denominator, management doesn't need much more than a red pencil. Thus the obsession with denominators.

In fact, the United States and Britain have produced an entire generation of denominator managers. They can downsize, declutter, delayer and divest better than any managers in the world.

> I can't tell you what the future will look like, but I can tell you it won't look like the present or the past.
> *Jim Harris*

Adding to the numerator creates greater long-term security because inventing new, high-margin goods and services creates new markets and distances the competition. Cutting costs is the focus for mature industries and commodity, price-driven businesses, where competition is fierce and markets are limited. Few people can see the future – focusing on the top line requires creativity, ingenuity and innovation. It requires trial-and-error testing to discover or uncover new value that customers may not even be able to articulate. The numerator mindset focuses on what everyone (including competitors) can already see. It's not an *either/or*; business must focus on *both*. To summarize:

$$\frac{N}{D} = \frac{+\text{Value}}{-\text{Costs}} = \frac{\text{Harder}}{\text{Easier}} = \frac{\text{Long term security}}{\text{Short term security}} = \frac{\text{Effective}}{\text{Efficient}} = \frac{\text{Invisible}}{\text{Visible}} = \frac{\text{Anticipate}}{\text{Control}}$$

PARADIGM SHIFTS ARE NOT BLACK OR WHITE

People often see issues as black or white. Paradigm shifts often take time to become apparent. For instance, the *DOS*-to-*Windows* shift occurred from 1985 to 1993. In hindsight the shift would seem sudden. Looking back from 1992 or 1993 it would seem that the market would have shifted in just a year or two. However, the early warning signals of the impending shift were there for years before. These subtle early warning signals are often imperceptible to leaders. Not only are the indications small but, more important, they are outside their realm of experience.

This blindness plagues even the best companies. How did Netscape blind-side Microsoft? Bill Gates is supposedly the brightest guy in the computer industry. How could he have initially missed the trend to the World Wide Web? No one is immune to missing the paradigm shifts.

Billions of electronic mail messages are now being sent daily. In fact, emails now far exceeds the number of letters carried by the US Postal Service! (See Chapter 11.) This along with the exponential growth of the World Wide Web has dramatically eroded the anticipated growth in the courier market for letters and documents. Does this mean that the Internet is killing FedEx's markets? Yes, in some ways it is. But FedEx is thriving because it is reconfiguring its operation to take advantage of the new opportunities the Web provides, such as product fulfillment.

Paradigm shifts simultaneously offer peril and promise. While FedEx has not experienced the anticipated growth in documents, it has significantly saved administrative expenses by integrating the Web into all of its business as discussed above. However, to use new technologies only to cut costs is to miss half the equation. FedEx is adding new value for customers at fedex.com. For instance, it offers a portfolio of services, called eOffice Manager, that provides global shipping and document management services that can be easily accessed primarily through fedex.com. One of those, Global Trade Manager, offers a comprehensive document determination service for more than 12,000 commodity items. The service provides all recommended import and export documents, shipping advisories and prohibited shipment notices for an ever growing list of countries: US, Canada, Puerto Rico, UK, Hong Kong, Singapore, Japan, Taiwan and Australia.

Every company will be blind-sided at some point. The real challenge is whether:

1. An organization can anticipate shifts and reconfigure its operations to provide new goods or services.
2. An organization that does not proactively create shifts recognizes and responds to them as they are occurring, taking advantage of the new opportunities.
3. When an organization has missed a shift, executives have the humility to admit it and then the courage to re-orient the corporate strategy to the new reality.

When these shifts occur, the new way may not eliminate the old. Some people dismiss these "paradigm shifts" as being unrealistic. Some have challenged me, saying, "The Internet will not completely eliminate branch banking." I agree. ATMs haven't eliminated tellers. For some transactions customers will use a teller, some an ATM, and for others the web. Some customers will never use the Internet to bank. But over time, more and more customers will use the new media.

New ways of looking at business require leaders to question every aspect of their operations. The policies, systems, structures, products and services that produced success in the past may produce failure in the future. Leaders at all levels of an organization have to unlearn what made them successful in the past in order to learn what will make them successful in the future. Leaders have to learn, change and accept uncertainty. This is the essence of the learning paradox.

What are the early warning signs of an impending shift? Customers' classic frustrations are a good predictor of potential shifts. For instance, the *DOS*-to-*Windows* shift could have been predicted because of the difficulty in learning *DOS*. People who had never owned a computer before were able to boot up a Mac, open a word processor, type and print off a letter all within the first five minutes of owning the computer. But the same process was painful and user-vicious for IBM-compatible PC owners in the *DOS* era. It wasn't until the introduction of *Windows 3.0* that PCs began to approach the user-friendliness of Macs.

I can tell when there has been a power failure in someone's home because the VCR will be flashing "12:00." Resetting the time is a major project for most people. The manual must be found, the instructions read and numerous attempts must be made before the consumer emerges victorious. It seems that you need to have a PhD in engineering before you can figure out how to program your VCR. This is an early warning signal that a software company needs to develop an easier-to-use, faster-to-learn, more intuitive interface, thereby creating a paradigm shift in the VCR market.

Leadership Begins with Humility[9]

"An amazing invention, but who would ever want to use one?"
– US President Rutherford Hayes, after participating in a trial telephone call between Washington and Philadelphia in 1876.

"Everything that can be invented has been invented."
– Charles H. Duell, Commissioner, US Office of Patents, urging President William McKinley to abolish his office, 1899.

"Sensible and responsible women do not want to vote."
– US President Grover Cleveland, 1905.

"Horses are here to stay. The automobile is only a novelty, a fad."
– President, Michigan Savings Bank, 1903, advising Ford's lawyer not to invest in Ford Motor. Disregarding the advice, he invested $5,000 and later sold the stock for $12.5 million.

"There is no likelihood man can ever tap the power of the atom."
– Robert Millikan, Nobel Prize winner in physics, 1920.

"Who the hell wants to hear actors talk?"
– Harry Warner, Warner Brothers, 1927.

"I think there is a world market for about five computers."
– Thomas J. Watson, Chairman, IBM, 1943.

> I never go to where the puck is. I go to where it is going to be.
> *Wayne Gretzky, hockey player*

"Television won't hold on to any market it captures after the first six months. People will soon tire of staring at a box every night."
– Darryl F. Zanuck, head of 20th Century Fox, commenting on the effect television would have on the film industry in 1946.

"640K is enough for anyone."
– Bill Gates, Chairman, Microsoft, 1981.

"There is no reason for any individual to have a computer in their home."
– Ken Olsen, president, Digital Equipment, 1977 (Digital Equipment is now owned by Compaq).

EXECUTE WITHIN PARADIGMS – INNOVATE BEYOND THEM

Stephen Covey highlights the difference between leadership and management in a simple story.[10] Imagine trying to cut a swath through the Amazon rain forest. Management would be working with the front-line machete wielders, putting on motivational seminars, providing training in sharpening and machete-wielding techniques, holding scheduling optimization courses for production managers and conflict resolution classes for angry machete wielders – a dangerous vocation at the best of times.

But what would leadership involve? Climbing to the top of the highest tree in the forest, judging the lay of the land, getting the big picture and asking questions like, "Are we heading in the right direction? Are we even in the right forest?" Leadership might involve having to yell down, "We're in the wrong forest!"

What might be management's response? "Shut up, we're making progress!"

At times leadership is dangerous, especially if management, in its enthusiasm for progress, accidentally cuts down the tree the leader has climbed!

Leadership deals with vision, direction – the big picture – and requires ongoing evaluation of existing paradigms. It focuses on effectiveness. Management, on the other hand, deals with execution and focuses on efficiency. Managers deal with existing problems. Leaders work to identify new problems and opportunities.

In *Managing in Turbulent Times*, Peter Drucker says that in periods of change and upheaval the most important managerial skill is the ability to anticipate. Unfortunately, most organizations and professions are deeply into management (efficiency) without ever questioning whether they're even in the right forest (effectiveness).

Imagine you are working for a company that is making horse-drawn buggies in 1900. The company launches a total quality management (TQM) program so that its products meet quality standards of six defects per million buggies. It has also embarked on a continuous improvement program to reward employees for productivity-enhancing suggestions so that, over time, production costs fall, allowing the company to lower the price of buggies. Furthermore, the company takes the executive team through an outdoor team-building exercise in which they have to fall backwards off a wall into the arms of their colleagues, which succeeds in increasing trust within the organization.

Perhaps the company has also embarked on a new focus on customers, asking past buyers whether they prefer blue leather seats or black leather seats and which would influence their buying decision? It has involved staff in customer service training that stresses the need for a pleasant approach. And the marketing department is busily thinking up such slogans as, "Buy a buggy – get a whip free."

These sound like good management strategies. The company is clearly working to increase the efficiency of existing processes. But none of these efforts will be effective because the industry is doomed by the automotive industry. By 1910 an irreversible paradigm shift will become apparent and it will be too late for a business without strong leadership to survive. Most of the buggy companies will go bankrupt. Paradigms are primary, efficiency is secondary.

LEADERSHIP, VISION AND MISSION

Imagine that you win the lottery and decide to build your dream home. What's the first thing you'll do? People in my seminars have answered, "Buy the land." "Hire an architect." "Pinch myself to make sure it really happened." "Deposit the money in the bank."

"Why hire an architect?" I ask. Answers include, "To structure our concepts." "So that we take an idea of what a dream home is and make it a reality, really plan it out." "So that we can measure the progress during construction."

A woman once answered, "So I won't get divorced!" She meant that while she had one concept of a dream home, her husband had another. An architect would act as a referee and make sure the overall concept and the details of the design had been agreed to before construction.

Leaders are the architects of business. In the world of shifting paradigms, leadership has become more complex and more necessary. But unlike a house whose blueprints are static, businesses are involved in a dynamic, ever-changing environment. While the mission (Why are we in business?) will tend to remain constant, the vision or direction (Where are we going?), will be continually changing over time. Therefore, everyone in the organization needs to be involved in creating the corporate blueprints of where the organization is headed.

Blueprints allow the clients, builders, trades workers and architect to visualize the end goal before construction begins.

Imagine arriving on the job site with no blueprints and saying to the workers, "Hey, you guys, I'm not paying you to stand around here drinking coffee and smoking cigarettes. Get cracking, build this baby!" How effective would that be?

How many people on the job site should have access to the blueprints? Everyone! Imagine that the master architect would not let anyone see the blueprints and only verbally told the supervisor what the various wings of the dream home looked like. What kind of dream home would you have? Visitors would likely comment, "My, what eclectic taste you have. This wing is Tudor in style, that one is Japanese and the one over there is distinctly Spanish."

Without seeing the blueprints, every supervisor would assume a common vision while in fact working toward an individual goal. The result would be nobody's dream home!

One of the exciting promises of new technology is that you will be able to visit an architect's office and strap on a helmet and visor connected to a computer. Using virtual reality, you will be able to tour conceptual houses. A three-dimensional blueprint will allow you walk through every room in your dream house, experiencing it. As a result, the final blueprint will be a closer reflection of your ideas, needs and desires.

Designing a building is not only a top-down process. It's also bottom-up. There is one master set of blueprints and then subsets of the master plan. For instance, the plumber has plumbing blueprints and the electricians have electrical wiring diagrams. Multiple blueprints can exist as long as they are in harmony or alignment. In the planning process, the plumber could go to the master architect and suggest moving the bathroom on the ground floor from one location to another to install the plumbing more easily, thus saving thousands of dollars. The architect would then have to check with the owners and redesign the plan.

Plans are not static. They can and must evolve with everyone's input. By encouraging input, you create an empowered work team in which individual ideas matter and everyone is encouraged to question and challenge assumptions. Paradoxically, a house that people have spent more time planning will meet high standards and will take less time to build because it has fewer mistakes and needs less rework. Worker satisfaction on the job site will definitely be higher, too.

Empowering employees is not a one-shot deal. Some people have a negative view of empowerment that stems from the experience of being given carte-blanche responsibility and then being criticized or fired for not meeting expectations. Empowerment is not abdication. Leaders must create an environment in which people are willing to take risks and act with autonomy. Individuals earn autonomy over time as their competence increases. This brings us back to the learning paradox. By definition, people will make mistakes while they are learning, yet many organizations that demand innovation don't tolerate mistakes. Leaders must ensure that the mistakes are not fatal; first, by including everyone in planning so there is ownership and understanding of the mission, and second, by monitoring progress. The goal is to create a learning environment. Of course, the company shouldn't bet its whole future on just one product or service. During times of rapid change, security is actually achieved through a diversity of strategies. For instance, Microsoft has *Windows 95, Windows 98, Windows NT, Windows ME, Windows 2000, Windows XP,* single applications, *Microsoft Office XP, MSN, Encarta,* games and home applications divisions, and Microsoft and NBC have created MSNBC. The company is constantly innovating and working to find new opportunities.

CREDIBILITY

Many leaders believe that they will lose credibility if they make a mistake or make a decision and then don't stick with it. They see changing their mind as a sign of weakness. The unspoken assumption that this is based on is that leaders are in control. They are all-knowing.

Imagine the president of a company standing in front of employees and saying, "Today I am going to present to you my vision of the future. But I have been caught off guard – blindsided out of left field so many times before that I am certain that this vision will change. And even if it is accurate I have no idea of how we are going to get there. I have to admit, I often feel uncertain about whether our strategy is correct. I feel uncomfortable placing bets on new technology I don't fully understand – and isn't all this exciting?" Does this inspire faith? Is this reassuring? Is this what people want to hear?

The president could easily add, "But what I do know is that if we work together as a team, we will ultimately be successful."

But it is the truth. The environment is changing so quickly that no leader can have all the answers. Bill Gates' Microsoft was blind-sided by Netscape. The emperor has no clothes. Leaders are only human. A healthy, creative environment is one in which everyone, including the leader, is allowed to make mistakes, take responsibility for them, learn as quickly as possible and move on. Leaders who have the humility to recognize when they are wrong and the courage to admit it to engender loyalty and respect from employees and create greater organizational security.

LEADERS STAY ON COURSE

It is inevitable that any project or organization will stray from its course, even with excellent leadership. How should we feel when we deviate from our mission? Imagine you are sailing on the ocean in the middle of thick fog. How often do you look at the compass? Constantly.

The average airplane is off course 98 percent of the time. Changing wind currents are always altering the flight path. As a result, the pilot or autopilot is constantly making small corrections to bring the plane back on course. There's no sense of guilt or shame involved. The pilot doesn't say, "I've been off course for Cincinnati 98 percent of the time. I'm a bad, bad pilot. I feel so guilty. In fact, I feel so bad that I've decided to give up the course and head for Buffalo instead! Besides, I like chicken wings."

> People like the security of knowing the answers. What you're really saying is that today we have to live and work amid questions – because everything is changing.
> *Barbara Marshall, human resource professional*

I am off course with my personal mission much of the time. I shouldn't, however, beat myself up and give up the goal.

We need to adopt the same attitude when discussing a corporate mission. Rather than blaming, how do we come back to the mission? What should we do from first principles, given this situation? Leadership requires tremendous patience, especially when listening to criticism about the company's direction from employees.

Listening is the first step to converting criticism into constructive suggestions, fresh ideas and renewed creativity. Listening is essential for creating and fostering a positive environment.

I am often asked, "What is the one thing that all the best companies to work for have in common?" In a word, I would say, "respect." The best companies respect people as individuals. This means that people have faith that if they have a problem they will be able to raise it and find a solution. Having a culture that is open and honest is essential if an organization is to auto-correct when it is off course. Only by listening to new ideas – some of which may initially sound crazy – can an organization create new products, services and markets. Sometimes it is only when we are lost that we discover new places.

> Sometimes the best places are discovered when one is lost.
> Judy Bell, labor relations consultant

Imagine the pilot, after noticing that he is far off course, begins to feel terribly guilty. Eventually his depression is so great that he begins to take Prozac so he won't feel bad. Or he covers up the compass so he won't have to look at it. When I get depressed about something, usually my conscience – my personal compass – communicates with me to let me know that I am off course. But I shouldn't kill the messenger by medicating the symptom. I need to search for the deeper root cause.

The key to success for both individuals and organizations is to practice self-reflection and self-correction, for we are all blind when it comes to the future. Whenever I am in a hall with a tall ceiling, I ask the audience, "Imagine a pillar stretching from the floor to the ceiling that represents all knowledge in the universe. Both knowledge that we have uncovered as a human race and knowledge we have yet to discover. Where would all collective human knowledge fall as a percentage of all knowledge, close to the top, bottom or middle of the pillar?" Inevitably people respond, "Close to the bottom."

"Okay, let's take all human knowledge, that little section close to the bottom and stretch it out until it represents a pillar from floor to ceiling. Where would my knowledge or your knowledge as an individual fall as a percentage of all human knowledge, close to the top, bottom or middle?" Most people answer, "Close to the bottom."

I only know a tiny fraction of a tiny fraction. Am I not, therefore, a child of the universe? I need to have the same compassion for myself as I would for a child learning to walk. I must practice compassion and toler-ance with myself because by definition I will make many mistakes – both personally and in business – if I am trying to add new value for my family or my customers. Because I will make mistakes I need to practice self-reflection and self-correction.

LEADERS WORK ON CONTEXT

Leaders work on the quality of relationships. It is the relationship that governs, organizes, entices and excites performance. The gardener doesn't grow the plant, the plant grows itself. The gardener (the business leader) works on the context – tilling the soil, planting the seeds, weeding and watering. As in a Zen paradox, the leader does nothing but is responsible for everything.

In *Leadership and the New Science: Learning About Organization from an Orderly Universe*, Margaret Wheatley uses quantum physics as a meta-phor for organizational leadership. Among the atomic particles, which one is in charge? None, they are governed by laws of physics, organizing principles. The electrons, neutrons, photons and other particles naturally fall into their respective patterns. It is the same with an organization. If there is a strong, commonly shared mission and vision, it will organize the activities.

Every business is founded on relationships – relationships with custom-ers, employees, suppliers, shareholders and the community. Businesses operate within a web of relation-ships. Shifts in the nature of these relationships change the nature of business. Business leaders must be careful to foster relationships that will benefit their organiza-tion.

> The sage is like a little child . . . so return to the beginning, become a child again.
> *Lao Tzu, philosopher*

Old-style union management relations often operate within a win–lose paradigm and are characteristic of a low- trust corpo-rate culture. Imagine that two criminals jump ship at night while being taken to an island prison such as Alcatraz. It is a great strategy until they both realize that neither of them can survive. But there's a catch: they're handcuffed together. In order to get a breath of air, Convict A pushes the other's head under the water so he can hold his head high and take a huge breath. That's a win–lose situation (A wins; B loses). On surfacing, Convict B, sputtering and gasping, knows that he needs a good, deep breath so he pushes Convict A's head under. That's a lose-win situation (A loses; B wins). This goes back and forth until one of them is too tired to keep going and drowns. As Convict B begins sinking, Convict A is dragged down with him. This is the ultimate lose–lose situation! In interdependent relationships, Win–Lose and Lose–Win eventually move to Lose–Lose.

In interdependent relationships, only win–win agreements are sustainable. Win–win relationships take a great deal of time to cultivate.

> The universe is full of magical things patiently waiting for our wits to grow sharper.
> *Eden Phillpots, Victorian poet*

Unionized organizations wanting to remain viable in an increasingly competitive international marketplace have no alternative but to alter the win–lose paradigm. No union wants to see its members out of work. When historically adversarial union–management opponents get together to discuss new security, their objectives are basically the same. Both groups want to ensure the longevity of the organization. Both want satisfied, empowered and challenged employees. Both want greater financial security. Reaching these objectives requires an entirely new approach, an entirely new relationship.

Think about a marriage. When the relationship is strong, is the marriage contract what keeps you together? No. If the relationship is poor, will the contract keep you together? No. So what is more important, the relationship or the contract?

Long-term success requires a commitment to continually question the prevailing industry wisdom, and a long-term focus on developing strong relationships based on mutual gain. Using the gardening metaphor: in the absence of a gardener the weeds will grow the fastest, but they are easy to pull out, they have no strong, deep, sustaining root systems. By contrast,

> It takes a long time to grow young.
> *Pablo Picasso, artist*

trees – or Chinese bamboo – take many years to show growth but once rooted is very difficult to remove. Gardening is an active, not passive, experience. So it is with corporate leadership. In any organization, without active leadership bad practices will cause dissatisfaction and tension (weeds in a garden). Leadership by definition is active and requires creating organizational systems and structures that proactively work to bring out the best in all employees.

LEADERS OPTIMIZE THE WHOLE

The leader's role is to optimize the whole organization. At times this will require "sub-optimizing" certain departments. On the surface this seems counter-intuitive. Within any organization this leads to tension because the natural inclination of people is to optimize their departmental function.

For instance, the accountants buy the best accounting software to address their needs, the marketers buy the best marketing software, the MIS (management information system) team buys the best MIS software, the executives get the best executive information system and the shipping department buys the best logistical software. Each department is fully optimized, but the company ends up with many islands of information technology that may not be able to communicate with one another. Information can't flow seamlessly through the organization and as a result customers' needs can't be dealt with quickly. The organization cannot respond adequately in a dynamic, changing environment. But the costs of poor performance – for example, loss of market share to more nimble competitors – do not show up as any one department's fault. Instead, how the organization works as a whole is the responsibility of the leader.

Each department must keep in mind that it exists to serve the organization as a whole. Departmental decisions must be made within the context of what is best for the whole organization.

> A man can know even less about God, than an ant can know of the contents of the British Museum.
> *Carl Jung, psychologist*

In the above example, the company should standardize using one software package that meets 80 percent of the accounting department's needs, 80 percent of the marketing department's needs, 80 percent of the MIS department's needs and 80 percent of the executives' needs. Each department can then customize the software to obtain the remaining 20 percent of its required functionality, still allowing data to flow seamlessly through the organization. The leader should ensure that the entire organization is optimized first, and then the departments can further optimize their functions within the new systems and structures.

If the purchasing manager receives a bonus based on how low a price is paid for goods and services, the organization is optimizing one departmental function at the expense of other departments. So the purchasing manager this month buys computers from IBM on special, next month its Compaq and the month after it's Dell. The purchasing manger is rewarded, but in the meantime the cost to support the PC network is exploding because the IT department has 15 different types of PCs to support. A purchasing manager who buys cheaper equipment is rewarded, but when the computer network breaks down and the company can't ship the product, the IT department is blamed. The savings accruing to purchasing may be small compared with the costs for network support, the MIS team or the training professionals. The root of the problem, as we will see in the next chapter, is a faulty system. In this case it is a compensation system that rewards the purchasing manager for attaining the lowest possible purchase price for computers. However, the hard cost of the computer is like the tip of the iceberg, representing 18 percent of the total cost of ownership. The vast balance is training, ensuring system compatibility, software, repairs, maintenance and ease of use.

> Human relationships are the key to all commerce.
> *Robyn Allan, management consultant*

Often individual departments, in their quest for quality in their particular field, lose sight of the fact that the real goal is the quality of the ultimate product. Software developers have many competing goals to balance: as few bugs as possible, increased functionality, ease of use, speed of the software, simple code and getting to market before the competition. Many of these are opposing goals. The more features developers include, the longer the software takes to reach the market and the greater the chance of being beaten by the competition; the more features (more code), the more bugs; the more code, the slower the software runs – but if there are not enough new, compelling features, few users will upgrade. The tricky part of leadership is to find a balance that results in the most marketable, timely product that users desire.

PARADIGM SHIFTS EQUAL GROWTH

Today, powerful forces are at work fundamentally changing the way every organization operates. Relationships on all levels are changing – business–customer relationships, employer–employee relationships and even the nature of competition. Both individuals and organizations need the tools and skills to meet new challenges and create paradigm shifts. Leaders who work to understand and accept the nature and effect of these forces and who change accordingly stand an excellent chance of advancing the success of their organizations. The financial rewards that stem from acting proactively in all these areas are astonishing, as we will see in case study after case study. By bringing an enterprise into alignment with these shifts, the organization can benefit from the changes and experience growth.

Growth and success in any organization is only achieved through teams. The switch from a hierarchy to a team-based organization can be painful for everyone, but once teams are established and begin to function, a natural balance is found, barriers to decision-making are removed and the whole organization begins to focus on the big picture.

The next chapter discusses the changing nature of leadership. Leaders work to change organizational systems and structures to create greater alignment and to enable the organization's vision to come to fruition. Chapter 6 outlines a process for creating a common vision, where employees across the organization not only understand the vision, but are committed to and excited by it. The process involves, excites and galvanizes employees, drawing out their best ideas and greatest commitment from people.

> Nothing inspires genius like a tight budget.
> *Sign at the California State Finance Dept*

TO SUMMARIZE . . .

- Leaders must continually assess their organization's direction and question personal, organizational and industrial paradigms.
- A "blueprint" is essential. All parties involved with a project should have input into its development.
- Leaders cultivate win–win relationships, both inside and outside the organization.

Reflection:

When was the last time that I questioned the industry wisdom, the "way we have always done it," or how I see problems?

Action:

What one action shall I take tomorrow to move learning into action? And over time repeat, to move action into habits?

CHAPTER 5

Creating Sustainable Enterprises

Each organization – its systems, structures and the results it experiences – is a product of individual interactions. A business is nothing more than a web of relationships between the business and its customers, employees, suppliers, shareholders, the community and governments.

CHANGE BEGINS WITH SELF

I attend over 50 conferences a year and everywhere I go I hear people talking about how we need to change. Individuals need to change, organizations need to change, society as a whole needs to change. With so much discussion, why then is there so little change relative to the rhetoric? And why does change take so long to implement?

These questions haunted me and prompted me to search for answers. Despite powerful and growing literature on change, what is holding us back?

Organizations are nothing more than a collection of individuals. If the individuals in the organization are incapable of changing, the organization as a whole will not change. So fundamentally, change begins with the individual.

We can't change the world if we can't change ourselves. If we can't change ourselves, we will not be able to bring about change on a grander scale. Many people want to save the planet, end poverty or fix government, but few want to wash the dishes after dinner. If we make the world a better place, the best thing we can do is make ourselves better people. The "Serenity Prayer" reads:

God grant me the serenity
To accept the things I cannot change,
The courage to change the things I can
And the wisdom to know the difference.[1]

First, it is important to determine what we have the power to change, both individually and organizationally. For instance, I can't change the government's pattern of deficit spending, but I can change my own pattern of credit-card usage. I can't change my partner's habits, but I can change my reactions, thereby contributing more positively to our relationship. I can't change the government's tax credit system for research and development, but I can influence how my organization focuses its R&D efforts.

Second, we need to identify the changes we would like to make to ourselves, and then set out on the long and winding road to find the answers and support needed to change.

THERE IS NO OBJECTIVE REALITY

Werner Heisenberg (1901–1976), the nuclear physicist, noticed that in laboratory experiments atomic particles often behaved differently than he predicted. This led him to postulate the Uncertainty Principle, which shattered the notion of objective reality and the relationship between observer and observed. Heisenberg discovered that the very act of observing the atomic particle influenced its behavior. Until Heisenberg, cause and effect had been thought of as a linear, one-way street:

CAUSE ·············▶ EFFECT

Instead, Heisenberg discovered that the relationship is circular – effect influences cause just as cause influences effect:

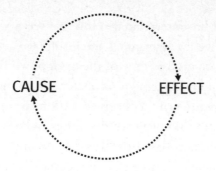

CAUSE AND EFFECT

When scientists observe an atomic particle, they change its behavior.

How we see determines *what* we see. In other words, as our perceptions – or our paradigms – change, the object we observe changes. As you will recall, in the cookie story (Chapter 3), our beliefs led us to assume that the strange man in the airport was stealing our cookies. Initially, we saw the other person as a thief, but by the end of the story, the man had become a generous and charitable chap.

WHAT WE FOCUS ON TENDS TO IMPROVE

An experiment conducted by Elton Mayo in 1927 at the Western Electric's Hawthorne plant in Illinois examined working conditions and their effect on factory personnel. Before the experiment began, the workers were introduced to the concept and informed that their productivity would be measured in relation to various factors. A base level for the workers' performance was determined. The lights in the factory were turned up and productivity increased. The lights were turned up further and production increased again. A pattern was emerging. Mayo then turned the lights down, but to his surprise production continued to increase.

Known as the Hawthorne Effect, the experiment revealed that what we focus on will tend to improve. Nobody had ever paid attention to the factory personnel before. The researcher's attention influenced the workers' performance. The observer influences the observed.

Cause and effect are interrelated. How we see a situation determines what we do. What we do determines the results we get. We need to focus on the way we see situations. Some of the most powerful breakthroughs in science, medicine and management have come from individuals who were willing to assume that their preconceived notions were wrong.

We need to question the way we do things (who, what, where, when, how and why). The interrelated nature of cause and effect underpins the "Be–Do–Have" principle. Who we are as people – our paradigms, our values (be) – determines what we see in the world and how we interpret it. Who we are and what we believe determines what actions we will take (do). Our actions determine the results we experience (have). Being is the foundation of Be–Do–Have.

BE ············▶ DO ············▶ HAVE

In North America, happiness for many people is a function of what they have or do. Many people think, "If I win the lottery, I will *have* a million dollars and be able to *have* a Mercedes-Benz and *do* things like go on expensive vacations. Then I will *be* happy." Or if I *have* a partner who looks a certain way or children who are angelic, I will *be* happy. My internal state of being (happiness, security, self-esteem and sense of fulfillment) is a function of external circumstances – doing and having.

This outside-in approach inherently creates insecurity. If my security comes from people, places or things, and circumstances change, I lose my security. At a luncheon once, a woman at my table, when asked how she was feeling, replied, "Not too well, I just had a double mastectomy." Not the kind of lunch conversation you'd expect. Her candid answer got me thinking – how would I feel if I lost an arm, an eye or a leg and ask, "Who am I? Am I more than my body?"

If I derive my security from external factors and these are taken away from me (I don't get the promotion, I lose my job, my spouse dies or the house burns down), then I lose my security, happiness and sense of self-worth. Grieving is normal, but defining our existence by externals is dangerous. Lasting security, stability and happiness can only be a function of being – who I am, what values I believe in.

Expanding and adapting this model to organizations, it might look like this:

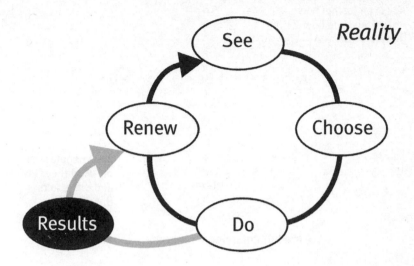

Our personal reality, our *being*, shapes what we see, our choices and our actions. Ultimately, it determines our results. Analyzing those results is the first step to renewing our basic beliefs and the cycle of choosing and acting that these beliefs initiate.

Let's say we *see* employees as being untrustworthy, we will tend to set up (*choose*) policies and procedures that convey to staff that they're not trusted. We will act accordingly (*do*). This lack of trust and respect undermines motivation and breeds contempt and subversive behavior (*results*). Our original view is then confirmed, reinforcing belief systems that maintain our paradigm (*see*, again).

> Life is a grindstone. Whether it grinds us down or polishes us depends on you.
>
> *L. Thomas Holdcroft,*
> *author*

How can we break this all too typical self-fulfilling cycle? If we really want to create change, we need to work at renewing our personal paradigms, challenging our assumptions about the results we achieve, and the causes behind these. We need to exercise our freedom to imagine other possibilities and see causes and effects in new ways that can lead to different choices.

Learning organizations and the executives leading them are continually working at the level of seeing and choosing. Focusing on the marketplace,

Focus on being

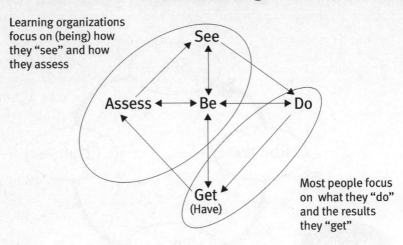

Learning organizations focus on (being) how they "see" and how they assess

Most people focus on what they "do" and the results they "get"

We are human beings not human doings

they work hard to perceive and anticipate emerging opportunities, potential problems and new competitors. Leaders are always assessing their results and how they explain them. Just because a company had its most profitable year is no reason to become complacent. In fact, the more profitable the company, the more competition it will attract. Therefore, the more successful, the more vigilant leaders must become about subtle but potentially major problems and opportunities. The challenge of renewal is to design systems and structures that encourage people to see the changing needs and frustrations of customers and create products or services to solve them.

RATIONALIZING THE PRESENT

Most organizations are locked into paradigms of the past. Too much time is spent explaining and rationalizing why we do things the way we do. In fact, most policies and procedures exist for this purpose. We use rules to explain to customers why we can't serve them the way they want to be served. We limit the freedom and decision-making ability of employees.

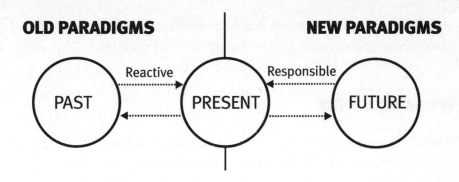

THE FUTURE IS OUR REASON FOR BEING

What we need to do is to spend more time looking to the future. We need to delight customers by providing for needs that they have not yet articulated (Chapter 9). By working with the future in mind, we can take a more objective look at how we're functioning in the present. We can ensure that we are setting the stage for future success. This is a proactive approach.

The past gives us a sense of our history. The present is our opportunity to act. The future, however, gives us inspiration and vision. As the expression goes, "If we do not dream, we have no power to act."

Inevitably, organizations that are locked into old thinking eventually perish. The definition of insanity is: "doing the same thing over and over again and expecting different results," as Alcoholics Anonymous points out. And yet, most organizations are caught in this trap. Their efforts, rather than being driven by the future, are rooted in the past and present. They are focused predominantly on doing, not on being. They lack the self-reflection and self-correction required to bring themselves to think differently.

> If a ship misses the harbor it is seldom the harbor's fault.
> *Dr Janet Lapp, professional speaker*

Anticipating the future is transformational. We can get a glimpse of destiny, both on an individual and an organizational level. Western culture tends to place too much emphasis on doing; otherwise, why would there be such demand for time management? We are all trying to do more with less. But too much focus on doing and not enough on dreaming negates the power of the future. The real value of any manager, states Peter Drucker, is being able to anticipate. Leaders who anticipate trends are able to conceive a future different from the current reality. Then they can make the different choices necessary to change their organizations.

LEVERAGED ACTIVITY

Pareto's Law states that 80 percent of results come from 20 percent of effort, and the remaining 20 percent of results come from the remaining 80 percent of effort.[2] The goal in organizations, then, is to focus on high-leverage activities. In North America we work at a frenetic pace, often losing sight of what are the most important issues. What is most important is not always apparent. As W. Edwards Deming said: 94 percent of the problems in organizations are due to bad systems and structures. So the key to leadership is working to improve systems and structures.

A supertanker that is three football fields long is moving at 35 miles per hour through the ocean carrying hundreds of thousands of tons of cargo. Think of the momentum.

Peter Senge, in *The Fifth Discipline*, asks the rhetorical question: If the captain of the ship decides to turn the ship, who has the most control – the captain who gives the order, the helmsman who turns the wheel or the engineer in the boiler room who runs the engines? It's a trick question. The answer is, "The architect who designed the ship!"

The efforts of the seaman, engineer and even the captain all focus on doing. But the designer's efforts focus on basic structure – the paradigm that determines the possible movement of the ship. What the captain, seaman or engineer can do is constrained by the limitations imposed by the designer. They all work within the existing systems and structures of the supertanker.

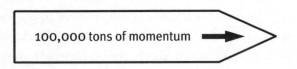

Now imagine a different structure. Instead of one supertanker carrying 100,000 tons, the cargo is divided among 100 smaller ships, each carrying 1,000 tons, working as a fleet.

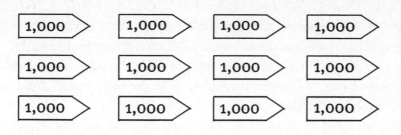

The supertanker is a metaphor for the command-and-control structure of many old organizations. This model emerged from the military and the church. Organizations based on it are hierarchical, top-down, inflexible and bureaucratic. These characteristics make them constitutionally incapable of responding rapidly to a dynamic, changing environment. Such organizations are based on the unspoken assumption that one person or an elite group at the top does all the important thinking and everyone else carries out orders. How many people have power in the supertanker model? One (the captain), perhaps two or three others (the first mate and second mate).

> If you fail to plan, you plan to fail.
> *Anonymous*

By contrast, the fleet is a metaphor for the new organization, where employees captain their own ships. I do not believe that leadership is the purview of one individual or an elite group of individuals. We are all called upon to be leaders – in our families, in our communities, in our society and in the workplace. In the new paradigm, the organization needs and calls upon the full intellectual power of all people.

W. Edwards Deming, recognized as the founder of the quality movement, believed that systems and structures determine the performance of an organization. The organizational architect determines the performance of an organization. Deming believed that 94 percent of problems in organizations are due to bad systems and structures, not bad people. People are basically good and have good intentions. The systems and structures generate unproductive actions. Even the way an organization hires people is a system and structure.

Rosabeth Moss Kanter, former editor of the *Harvard Business Review*, said, "To be successful in the future, organizations will have to focus on the four Fs: fast, focused, flexible and friendly." Applying the four Fs to the supertanker and the fleet highlights significant differences between the two structures:

FAST   Which structure, the supertanker or the fleet, can get up to speed faster? Which can slow down sooner? Which can turn more swiftly?

After the audience had answered "the fleet" to all three questions, a man yelled out, "Assuming they all turn at the same time!" "And in the same direction!" added a woman.

Yes, we need empowerment, but empowerment without alignment is downright dangerous. Alignment, the ability to coordinate the activities of motivated, empowered, knowledgeable and competent individuals captaining their own ships, is the responsibility of the senior leaders of an organization.

> Organizations will have to be flexible, fast, focused and friendly to succeed in the future.
> *Rosabeth Moss Kanter, former editor, Harvard Business Review*

FOCUSED   Which of the two structures, supertanker or fleet, is more focused? This is a trick question. People invariably answer that the supertanker is more focused. Yes, at first it appears more focused. But it is mono focus. Which structure can have more foci?

In nature, security is diversity. There are thousands of varieties of wheat. It is only modern farming techniques that have focused on having a single strain of wheat that is susceptible to blight and therefore requires large inputs of insecticides. Nature's more elegant solution is to have a number of varieties, each with different properties. If there is ever a blight, not all strains will be affected.

In business, diverse strategies within the same set of core competencies will have a greater chance of creating lasting success. Microsoft doesn't have one strategy – there is *DOS*, *Windows 3.x*, *Windows 95*, *Windows 98*, *Windows NT*, *Windows 2000*, *Windows XP*, single applications, *Microsoft Office*, *Microsoft Network* (*MSN*), *MSNBC*, home products division, products such as Microsoft *Mouse* and *Natural* keyboard, games, *Encarta*. There is not just a single monolithic focus, there are many foci.

> Power isn't given, it is taken.
> *Pat Robinson, health care professional*

Edward de Bono – the world's leading thinker on creativity – cites the case of a species of hawk with excellent eyesight that only preys upon mice. Another type of hawk has bad eyesight and can't distinguish between mice and other small creatures. This species will prey upon mice, baby rabbits, small gophers and so on. If the mice population is devastated by a disease, which hawk species is better off? Who has perfect eyesight when it comes to the future?

If the supertanker hits an iceberg, ripping a hole in the first three panels of the bow, what happens to the ship? By contrast, if the fleet hits an iceberg, what happens? The first three ships sink, but as they do they radio back to the fleet and warn of the impending danger. Then a few ships stop and pick up their comrades while the rest of the fleet navigates around the iceberg.

The issue of focus also applies to the creation of strategy and tactics. At a conference, Gary Hamel, co-author of *Competing for the Future*, related an experience of consulting to a large multinational firm. He was working with a group of the top 20 executives – who all happened to be silver-haired men. He asked them, "How many of you have worked for the company more than 20 years?" Everyone raised their hand. "How many of you came up through sales and marketing?" All but two raised their hand. It was a very market-driven company. "How many of you have worked for five years or more outside of North America?" Only two people had any significant international experience, and it was a transnational firm. You know what used to happen in the 16th century when there was too much inbreeding in royalty!

> Don't ask a barber if you need a haircut.
> *Daniel Greenberg, author*

Hamel's point is that organizations need genetic diversity. Mono focus, having only one way of thinking, creates insecurity when the future is unfolding rapidly. Organizations tend to weed out genetic diversity, as people often feel uncomfortable facing sustained challenges to their assumptions.

FLEXIBLE Which of the two structures has more flexibility? There can be only one direction, one strategy and one set of tactics with the supertanker. But the fleet can apply a variety of directions, strategies and tactics. A few ships can be sent on a strategic sortie to explore a new market, develop new products and return. If the venture is successful, the organization can dedicate more resources to the new direction. This type of exploration is essential to create new value for customers and to ensure long-term security for an organization. Microsoft's initial success was due to its sales of *MS-DOS* and *DOS* applications, but the company now receives less than one percent of its revenues from these sources. In a rapidly shifting marketplace, organizations need to be continually exploring new, high-margin markets that in some cases may eliminate the need for their current core products and services.

Search behavior is more important than brilliance. Dave Nichol, when he worked at Loblaw to create *President's Choice* products, spent his time travelling around the world eating at the best restaurants and visiting the best retailers. Sam Walton, the founder of Wal-Mart, was infamous for always carrying a notebook to jot down ideas when he visited competing stores.

> What most companies want is homogeneity. They want 150 trumpets playing in unison. But homogeneous teams have blind spots; they move like a herd and often in the wrong direction. What's needed instead is complexity, the team as a jazz band that both harmonizes and improvises.
> *Dave Marsing, vice president, Intel*

FRIENDLY Which of the two structures is friendlier? Would you prefer to be a hired hand on the supertanker, always being told what to do, or the captain of your own ship? Remember, 73 percent of North American employees report that they do not find their work exciting.[3] This is because organizations generally underutilize employees' talents.

Many people feel that power is zero-sum gain. That is, if one person in an organization has more power, others by definition will have less, because power, like a pie, is fixed in size. Power is only limited by an organization's systems and structures.

How many people have power on the supertanker? One, perhaps a few. How many people have power in the fleet? At least 100. The captain of the supertanker becomes an admiral in the new structure. Promotion or demotion? The structure of the fleet unleashes over 100 times more power than the supertanker.

In the old command-and-control paradigm, only one leader had to have full knowledge of the organization's mission, vision, strategy and tactics. In the new model, all 100 captains must know the fleet's overall mission, vision, strategy and tactics. When power increases exponentially, so must communication. The fleet doesn't require twice as much communication but 100 times more! Everyone needs to know where the fleet is going, what its purpose is and how to contribute to its overall goals.

> If you would hit the mark, you must aim a little above it.
> *Henry Wadsworth Longfellow, poet*

Effective communication has never been more important than today. In an empowered organization, everyone has a role to play in creating an exciting and compelling vision of the future.

In seminars people often say, "we have too much communication – we're overloaded with emails." Don't confuse quantity of communication with quality. There's no question that most people are burdened by too many unnecessary emails. (Visit www.jimharris.com for an article on strategies to reduce unnecessary email.)

> In an age of perpetual change, it's no longer just the big who devour the small, but rather the quick who eat the slow.
> *Richard Searns, president, Key Resource Group*

In most organizations, if there is loss of market share, what is the typical response? Downsize. Using the analogy of the supertanker, this would be equivalent to firing all the engineers on the ship. The organization still has the same problem but fewer people to cope with the workload. The structures and systems remain the same. If losses continue, what happens next? More layoffs. In the short term, productivity may increase as the crew, fearful of losing their jobs, scramble to get in and out of port as quickly as possible. But over time they will tire, burn out or quit and productivity will nosedive. Often, the response is to cut even deeper. The crew is smaller, but the ship has not changed. Downsizing in many organizations is like amputation before diagnosis.

Such downsizing is futile when it does not question an organization's design at its most fundamental levels. We need to rethink the organization. This is what looking to the future rather than to the past is all about. We need to be drawn to what we and our organizations can become rather than focusing on where we have been or where we are now. Unfortunately, most organizations need to experience acute pain before they are willing to rethink their systems and structures. They behave like an individual stoically suffering through a toothache for years rather than facing a visit to the dentist.

Only when the pain of staying the same is greater than the perceived pain of changing do many organizations begin to take actions required for change.

CREATING A SUSTAINABLE ENTERPRISE

While they are naturally concerned for day to day success, leaders must also continually ask, "will we succeed in the future? How will we survive and thrive tomorrow?" A sustainable enterprise needs to meet the challenge of today while maintaining and enhancing the capacity to meet new challenges. (An enterprise is simply any firm or business – public and not-for-profit organizations or private companies. An enterprise can also describe a team, department or project group.)

> Even if you're on the right track, you'll get run over if you just sit there.
> *Mark Twain, author*

Any enterprise is involved with many stakeholders, all with expectations and perspectives that must be considered. Sustainability for any organization means striking a dynamic balance among all these individual and collective interests.

Stephen Covey's definition of a stakeholder is anyone who is hurt if an enterprise fails. Shareholders, customers, staff, suppliers and communities are all affected by the actions of our businesses, and we should not underestimate the responsibility to all of them.

Stakeholders can include the industry in which a business operates, the populations around it, the natural environment, the families of employees, the government, the tax collector and researchers who advance our base of knowledge.

There are no guarantees that an organization will last forever. Change is constant. But all stakeholders, are interested in seeing the business thrive if it can continue to generate value for them and further opportunity. Harnessing the power of happy stakeholders can produce extraordinary and sustained results.

"OUTSIDE-IN" DIAGNOSIS

Every enterprise operates within a unique environment. The challenges presented by paradigm shifts that we will discuss in Chapters 7 to 13 (the new economy, valuing people, eLearning, keeping customers, real time information systems, the Internet and the environment) are increasingly complex. More than ever, organizations must be prepared to continuously redefine their products and services, and rethink their internal practices. Doing this involves:

- Identifying the organization's key stakeholders

- Defining the value that will satisfy and even delight them
- Planning, building and maintaining the capacity to produce stakeholder value. This includes developing individual capability of performers, creating a sense of partnership among them, engaging a sense of stewardship for goals and results and designing aligned systems and structures that support productivity.
- Anticipating and responding effectively to challenges and opportunities presented as the business environment changes

"Outside-in" thinking takes into consideration the bigger picture and how the organization can create a brighter and more fulfilling future for all it's stakeholders.

CUSTOMERS

Our customers' interest is the value of our service and the quality of our products. Successful businesses anticipate then exceed the expectaions of their customers. These organizations seek to create customer delight and ongoing loyalty. Such companies are continuously improving and developing products and services that deliver better value to customers than in the past (Chapter 9). Customer retention rates are positive indicators of sustainability, as are growing sales revenue, increasing market share and high market valuation relative to the the industry.

INVESTORS

The investors' interest is the economic success of the enterprise. They are concerned for profit, lack of waste, and wise financing. The fundamentals of financial accountability – revenues, expenses, cash flow, profitability, productivity of assets and return on investment – are indicators of business success. These words have found their place even in the language of government and not-for-profit organizations. Investors, taxpayers, contributors, lenders and financiers expect any organization to be accountable and responsible for ensuring that the enterprise can survive and thrive within specific limits of debt, return and risk. Continuing investor enthusiasm is crucial to sustainability.

If we are to become captains of our own ships, we must understand such basic rules of business as the need to maintain a positive cash flow. Most bankruptcies are caused by poor cash flow. Even an organization with a large net worth can go bankrupt if a positive cash flow is not sustained.

PERFORMERS AND SUPPLIERS

The people who work for an organization have a stake as well. Call it a satisfying work life. They are looking for such tangibles as pay and benefits, hours of work, and safe attractive work spaces, and intangibles like meaningful work, recognition, respect and collegiality. What sustainable organizations receive in return is full engagment of the competence, commitment, creativity and common sense that every performer brings to work each day. Job satisfaction and productivity are inextricably linked even though the conditions of satisfaction can vary from person to person.

A simple thing like recognition – taking note of employees' contributions – has a tremendous impact. Dale Carnegie in *How to Win Friends and Influence People* notes that parents who do not feed their children for six days will be charged with criminal negligence. Yet many of us go for six days without praising our children, our spouses, our colleagues or our bosses, even though praise is food for the soul!

Sustainable organizations pay attention to such things as employee attitude surveys, turnover rates, competitive compensation surveys, job security, atmosphere, communication and personal development – in other words, pays attention to its people, and ensures that they are challenged and happy.

COMMUNITIES

An organization exists within many communities: local, national, global, ethnic, environmental and special interests of all kinds. Their stake is the expectation of social responsibility on the part of the enterprise. Communities are often protected by laws and regulatory agencies. Being a socially responsible corporate citizen means being a positive influence while operating within the laws of the land. Meeting the reasonable expectations of this group of stakeholders brings many rewards, including greater political influence, a more relaxed regulatory environment, supportive community relations and ultimately, customer loyalty. Enterprises that establish good reputations with the public at large, also may be seen as desirable employers, allowing them to continue to recruit the capable performers they need to renew their success.

> Too many executives are quick to hire and slow to fire.
> Peter Buchanan, management consultant

Acknowledging all these stakeholders – communities, performers and customers, as well as investors, reminds us that the bottom line is important, but it is not everything. Many organizations experience the mixed consequences of making economic gains while service levels and workforce loyalty suffer. Others discover the far-reaching ill effects of compromising communities or the environment while stressing productivity and profit. And of course there are examples where enterprises that stress customer satisfaction and employee happiness fail when they become economically compromised.

What is needed for sustainability is a holistic view of success and management that can hold a broad view, recognizing that every part is essential to the health of the whole. With creativity and an openness to new possibilities, improved results in one area do not have to come at the expense of another.

SUSTAINING CAPACITY

Capacity is what gets the job done in any successful enterprise. It is the net result of a complex interplay of abilities, processes and relationships, built upon a foundation of capable individuals. In an organization, individuals need to build relationships based on the values of interdependence and collaboration. The work to be done must be apportioned and accepted with a sense of responsibility and accountability by individuals or teams. Systems, structures and strategies must be aligned with the efforts of performers in ways that support and enhance accomplishment. All stakeholders can enhance capacity as well, choosing to remain involved with the enterprise and provide incentives for success.

INDIVIDUAL CAPABILITY

The competence and commitment of individuals – their capablity to create results – is at the heart of organizational capacity.

Organizational behavior is rooted in individual behavior. People are the "programmers" of organizational performance, all the other elements are "programs." Their skills, experience and creativity, their commitment to learn and grow, to serve, to be responsible, to reach for high standards are all critical for sustained success.

Individuals who see the "big picture" and want to contribute to making it better should be sought and valued. Do we hire the best and brightest people? A hiring system can be built that will bring the right kind of people to work in the organization. Microsoft, for example, hires only two to three percent of all its applicants. The rigorous screening process (up to seven interviews) means that the company can attract the best and the brightest minds.

As external change occurs, and the organization responds, people will need to change. Sustainability depends on individuals being willing to develop their competence as new technologies, processes and practices are introduced. Sustainability also depends on maintaining commitment through the periods of uncertainty and turmoil.

Empowerment will only work if we delegate tasks to people capable of doing the work. When assigning responsibilities, managers can help staff to extend themselves by challenging them while ensuring they have the necessary resources, coaching and support to succeed. Is there sufficient training and education? Are they provided with the equipment they need? Do systems and structures ensure that managers will be demanding on results while being compassionate with people? Do we assign tasks to individuals and teams so that they are challenged (stretched) but not overwhelmed? Do we spend enough time in self-reflection and self-correction? On a personal level? In teams? As managers and leaders? As an organization as a whole? Do we have the means to share the learning throughout the organization? Is our infrastructure in alignment with our mission and vision?

Very few companies address one of the subtler but important capability issues – ensuring that all employees understand how the business works financially. Most of the time this is left to managers and accountants and financial executives. Yet how can employees behave responsibly with respect to the bottom line if they don't know any details about how the company makes money, what the cost structures are, how to read and interpret key financial indicators, and how to recognize how one department's actions influence another's? Companies benefit when every employee, on a rudimentary level, knows how to read a quarterly report and understand cash flow, operating and capital expenses. Businesses with profit sharing, gain sharing and employee stock-ownership plans naturally engender much greater interest in understanding and influencing the bottom line.

Imagine that you have never been bowling before – and one night a group of people from work go bowling. But before you bowl your first ball, your boss, runs down to the far end of the bowling lane and drops a curtain so no one can see what pins they have knocked over. You throw your first ball and while your score comes up on the monitor – you can't tell why you did well or not. And you don't know how to knock over the remaining pins with your next ball because you can't see where they are.

Sound ludicrous? Well, isn't that the way most organizations work? Most organizations won't reveal to employees figures such as the cost structure, and profit per item. And yet they exhort people to increase profit. But how can you increase profit when you don't know how to optimize the cost structure – because no one will let you see the figures.

Now think about some of the strategies that organizations employ to increase profitablity. Bring in motivational speakers to pump up the troops – but the company won't lift the curtain. Or send teams out to do rope courses to build trust among employees. Or empower people. Or launch at TQM initiative. While all of these things are good – without giving people access to real figures how can they make substantial improvements? It's like bowling with a curtain hiding the pins. How can people play the game if they don't know the rules or how to keep score?

Jack Stack and John Case have each written books on open book management, which involves teaching employees how the business works, sharing financials and rewarding them for improving profitability.

Executives, because they deal with financials all the time, often overlook the fact that average employees don't understand the financial concepts. For example, does everyone in your organization understand why cash flow is crucial? This business principle can be illustrated with a simple example. Say you buy a house for $300,000. After several years of paying the monthly mortgage, you own 50 percent of the house ($150,000). In other words, you have 50 percent equity. If you now miss six mortgage payments in a row, what happens to the house? The bank repossesses it. In this case, cash flow is more important than equity. You may get some money back from the bank, but you have lost control of your house and have to find another place to live. As easy as this example may be, do we use it (and others) to check that all our staff understand financial principles that apply to their company?

PARTNERING RELATIONSHIPS

We are not only individuals. We live in an interdependent reality. None of us can do our best work without some reliance on the efforts of others. Our successes are intertwined. My work might not even begin unless and until yours is done. I may not be able to finish without the contributions of several people. Sometimes one person is just not enough; only the combined strength of a team can make the right result. So we need to work together; we need to have working relationships.

Like all relationhips, trust is the glue that holds performers in an organization together. In the workplace, trust comes from understanding the strengths and limitations of individuals, from providing them with a clear understanding of expectations but still allowing them to make decisions and exercise their creativity. Trust at work is the confidence that others have your interests at heart, as well as their own - that they are your partners, not competitors or adversaries.

Without trust and respect, communication is strained, small problems fester into large ones and attempts to work together are sabotaged by apprehension, conflict and self-protection. Mistrust produces breakdowns, draining energy away from production.

Trust provides the foundation for partnership, collaboration and coordination at the work level so that joint efforts can succeed. Trust allows us to positively influence others and is an essential ingredient in sustaining leadership.

WORK AS STEWARDSHIP

With capable individuals able to work in partnership, an organization's capacity to perform then depends on people, individually and in teams, acting out of a sense of responsibility and accountability for their work. In a culture of trust, capable people will feel a sense of ownership and will come to believe that their contribution matters.

Traditionally, organizations have emphasized control and management of performance rather than empowerment and release of energy and potential. This has typically produced, in employees, compliance, dependence and indifference toward organizational results. Control strategies are expensive, drain energy from workers, stifle creativity and innovation, and contribute to low levels of morale and productivity. Especially when organizations can no longer offer secure employment to balance off the loss of autonomy. These conditions are not sustainable.

Stewardship implies acting almost like an owner of the enterprise. It means caring to do a job, and do it well, because it matters to me, because I have a personal and professional stake in succeeding, and because I have freely chosen to accept responsibility for achieving results. For stewardship to exist, leaders must help employees understand how they can benefit by aligning their efforts with the company's mission and by committing to certain performance expectations. And leaders must be prepared to empower others, or stewardship will never happen.

Many organizations have concerns about empowerment. Perhaps it seems like abdication of management or leadership. This is not what empowerment is about. No one would have their dream home built by simply telling a contractor to go ahead without planning the design. That is abdication. But after ensuring that the contractor shares our vision and clear goals, and is capable and responsible, we should happily let him or her get on about the work and report routinely on how it is going, alerting us to problems or decisions that require discussion. Empowerment works when both parties are disciplined in developing a clear, mutually understood vision of the end result, conditions and guidelines. This may require more patience or courage than keeping direct control, but the results are usually worth it.

INFRASTRUCTURE

Any organization requires a number of systems and processes to take care of crucial routines, ensure basic fundamental activites can be completed and enable coordination of work and results. For example, there may be a production system, a sales system, a distribution system, and a transportation sytem. A system for paying employees, for purchasing, for paying bills. There are systems and processes for communication, for storing, retrieving, and sharing information, and for making decisions. There are organizational structures and policies and strategies that attempt to keep our efforts aligned with our goals and with the efforts of others.

All of these components of infrastructure must be effective and efficient on their own if they are to be truly useful. We have all experienced supposedly helpful systems that were overly bureaucratic, cumbersome, unreliable, or that did as much harm as good. But effective and efficient on their own is not enough. Each component must also be compatible with the rest of the infrastructure and with the goals of the enterprise, the needs of performers, and the work they are doing. In other words, aligned with the vision of the enterprise and the strategies it is pursuing.

At one seminar a CEO asked why CEOs are compensated on quarterly stock performance when investors and other stakeholders are ultimately interested in long-term performance. Why not award CEO bonuses based on a five-year rolling average of the stock price? It was an enlightening example of misalignment. Why must an organization focus on quarterly results to the detriment of long-term, sustainable success? Look no further than the CEO incentive system. Poorly aligned systems and structures can, and will, compromise performance.

Strategy describes our approach to achieving the vision. It defines the connection between organizational capacity and the reality of the environment. Structures and systems support strategy. As environmental forces change, infrastructure must adapt. This can be difficult. When people

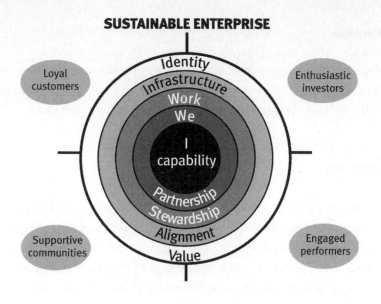

don't understand the changes around them or don't identify with a new vision, they hold on to old, comfortable, strategies, structures and systems. They resist change, perhaps passively, but ultimately at their own expense nevertheless.

Sustainability requires that an enterprise respects the realities of it's stakeholders and it's own capacity to meet their expectations. The vision of the future that the enterprise develops is not for it alone. It is for sharing with all stakeholders and for engaging them in an ongoing interchange of value. The identity we are accorded by our customers, investors, performers and communities is their version of our vision.

The "Sustainable Enterprise" model reminds us of the relationship between our organizations and our stakeholders, and expresses graphically the notion that our capacity to generate value for them is an inside-out process. Just as no stakeholder group can be safely ignored for long, developing capacity at any level is necessary but insufficient. Outer layers of capacity are built upon the inner ones; all levels are needed for continuing success; efforts for change that are targeted at only one level can be hindered or undone by forces at levels we have neglected. Building sustainable enterprises requires a comprehensive and coordinated approach to change and growth.

LEADERSHIP

Sustainable enterprises require strong leadership throughout the organization. People at all levels must be encouraged to step up to the challenge. Leaders have two vital functions – pathfinding and empowering.

PATHFINDING

Pathfinding leadership involves "outside-in" thinking. This means learning about the needs and expectations of all stakeholders, examining and understanding the environment the organization must respond to, and forecasting the challenges and opportunities ahead. Pathfinding is also about raising consciousness of stakeholder demands and environmental realities throughout the organization. Pathfinding leaders strive to build commitment everywhere in the enterprise for a shared, positive, comprehensive vision of success and a sustainable future.

EMPOWERING

Empowering leaders build capacity in the enterpise. They nurture the conditions that allow every team and every member of the organization to make a unique positive contribution. This is an "inside-out" process, a spiral of growth. It starts with nurturing individual capability and partnering relationships and progresses to establishing stewardship for work and ensuring aligned, supportive infrastructure. The empowering leader's first challenge is personal - to be an effective model of what is expected from everyone. The second challenge is interpersonal - to be a partner, to serve others, to coach and develop others, to enable everyone to contribute fully to a shared vision of the future.

CREATING COMMON VISION

The next chapter will present a process to create a common, compelling vision of the future.

TO SUMMARIZE . . .

Sustainable enterprises address the needs and expectations of all stakeholders – customers, investors, performers and communities.

Sustainable enterprises generate capacity at five levels – individual capability, partnering relationships, stewardship for work, alignment of infrastructure, and shared vision.

- Successful leaders always work to sharpen their perception of the future, and anticipate opportunities and competitive threats. They focus on the future, not the past.
- Systems and structure determine performance; leaders are the architects of their organizations and create appropriate systems and structures.
- Creating an empowered, aligned culture unleashes exponentially more power in the organization, but requires exponentially more communication.

Reflection:

What is the key learning/insight for me in this chapter?

Action:

What one action shall I take tomorrow to move learning into action? And over time repeat, to move action into habit?

CHAPTER 6

Creating Value

Leaders are responsible for creating the environment in which employees work. Creating a positive, motivating work environment is challenging. How do leaders:

- Build a positive, motivating vision of the future while experiencing the wrenching, demoralizing effect of reorganization or change?
- Focus people on the challenges facing the organization when they are so focused on their personal concerns?
- Align people with a strategy when they seem so cynical and lacking in trust toward those who developed it?
- Create, innovate and continuously improve while maintaining the atmosphere of stability and security that people need?
- Maintain control, yet allow people the freedom to do what they need to be effective and satisfied in their work?
- Be "hard" (demanding, insistent, challenging) on performance while being "soft" (empathetic, supportive, compassionate) with people?
- Generate teamwork and collaboration among people who have been competing and in conflict for years?
- Create learning organizations when people are so reluctant to take risks and be open about their mistakes?
- Deal with overwhelming workloads while reallocating staff to new initiatives?
- Encourage people to take responsibility for their careers and lives when they feel like victims of uncontrollable circumstances?
- Develop leaders who are powerful without having to diminish the power of others?
- Generate confidence in leadership when the leaders themselves are unsure of what will happen in the future?

This chapter will provide a concrete method for leaders and organizations to solve some of these classic dilemmas. The process is founded on having faith that individuals can solve their own problems (plants grow themselves).

Communication is much misunderstood. The fleet of ships (Chapter 5) does not require twice as much communication as the supertanker but exponentially more. Every captain must understand the mission, vision, strategy and tactics of the entire fleet. Each captain has responsibility, accountability and authority. Each has the power to act.

CREATING A COMMON VISION

What is a "fast" car? Ferrari? Porsche? Lamborghini? To one person it may be a Mercedes-Benz on the Autobahn at 160 miles per hour with such a smooth ride that the coffee in the cup holder doesn't jiggle. To another it might be driving in a Corvette at 50 miles per hour with the top down during the summer. To a third it may be driving an Indy Pace Car on the racetrack.

The only way that I can find out what "fast" means to someone else is to enter into a discussion. It is only through involvement that I create understanding.

Even such a simple concept as "fast car" can generate a wide array of understandings. Think of how a vague corporate mission or vision statement could create different understandings. For instance, most mission statements involve serving the customer; however, what if serving a particular customer requires a financial loss? All organizations exist to make a profit. In this situation what should be done? There is no right or wrong answer. Only by discussing the case study will people in the culture come to understand what the mission means.

One of my clients has a goal of achieving 15 percent revenues from entirely new products and services within 12 months. I asked, "How will people accomplish the goal when everyone has to work from line items that lock them into existing activities?"

If managers are expected to create new products and services they will have to engage in activities that they are not currently engaged in. So managers must increase the top line (revenue) or cut costs through efficiency to free up at least 15 percent of their budget to dedicate to researching and developing new products and services. In most organizations, however, any expenditure outside of existing line items must be approved. In this sense the budget locks managers into the current way of doing business. Line items cannot predict future staffing, product and service inputs. Instead of being the master of managers, the budget should be their servant. The better managers are at increasing revenue or cutting costs, the more freedom they should have to act without requiring multiple approvals.

Budgeting, as practiced in most organizations, dictates *how* the organization will work. But what is more important, the method by which the end is achieved or the actual achievement of the result? In dictating the *how*, the budgeting process often denies people the flexibility required to achieve the ends.

Budgeting, in fact, puts the cart before the horse. Before budgeting, everyone in an organization needs to know where the organization is going (vision) and why the organization exists (mission). Once everyone in the organization has a deep understanding of the mission and vision, budgeting will be an easier, speedier process. The budget, then, is a guideline, a rough outline of the best prediction of where the organization will allocate resources to achieve its vision over the next year. The budget is the servant, not the master.

In *Reinventing Government*, Osborne and Gaebler point out that:

> Most organizations are not driven by their missions but by their rules and budgets. They have a rule for everything that could conceivably go wrong and a line item for every subcategory of spending in every unit of every department. The glue that holds bureaucracies together, in other words, is like epoxy: It comes in two separate tubes. One holds rules, the other line items. Mix them together and you get cement.[1]

While the mission and vision of an organization are different, the process outlined below to achieve consensus for either within an organization is the same. In the example below, I will refer to vision. The same process could be used to facilitate the creation of an organization's mission.

Many executive teams believe that their employees understand their organization's vision. This is because the executive team has been deeply involved in the process of developing it. However, front-line employees often don't understand their organization's vision. They haven't grasped what its implications are for them, for their department or for their future.

Even people who believe in the vision and are committed to it may have entirely different understandings of its implications! How can that be?

Back to "fast car." What is a fast car? It could be many things. But I only understand what a fast car is to you when I am in dialogue with you. So a CEO can present his or her vision of the future, but employees may not understand it, agree with it or be willing to commit to it. Trying to force a vision on an organization is like trying to push a string. It's far more effective to pull it. It's far better to have employees understand, agree with and be committed to and excited by the vision of their organization than having the executive team continually try to sell it.

How can a CEO pull the vision through the organization? By involving people in the process of developing, refining and clarifying it. Here is a simple principle: no involvement, no commitment. Paradoxically, the more a CEO holds on to control, the more out of control the organization is. The more a CEO empowers, the more power there is in the organization.

For most organizations, creating a vision of the future is a one-way, top-down process. The assumption is that the CEO or executive team has better predictive powers; therefore, charting the organization's course is left to them.

There is no doubt that the executive team has special talents. The organization needs to create the best vision possible. Just because this group cannot control the whole process doesn't mean that they should be excluded. In fact, the executive team, in most cases, will have many of the most important and richest insights and contributions to make to the process. Letting go of controlling the process, however, doesn't mean abdicating responsibility for the overall operations of the organization. The executive team will guide the process throughout the organization.

CO-CREATING MISSION AND VISION: PARALLEL PROCESSING

Normally, in a strategic planning session involving the top 20 executives in an organization, one person is speaking and 19 are listening. It is like having a 20-cylinder engine but using only one cylinder at a time. How can more creativity and power be released through the planning process? How can an organization generate more commitment to change in its employees?

The following process works well in creating a common mission or a common vision for a group. We will use the example of vision here. For an executive team of 20, I break up the group into 10 pairs. Each pair discusses its vision of the future in five years until it reaches consensus. The hallmark of a good vision is one that is exciting and compelling, a future that people will gladly work toward.

As each pair concludes its discussion, it brings its written vision to the front of the room where I am working with a typist. The typist keys the visions into a computer that is projecting them onto a large screen so that everyone in the room can read them. Once the last group is finished, each pair presents its vision to the group. This allows a synergistic, cross-fertilization of ideas. No matter how brilliant each pair is no one will have perceived all the areas where the organization can seize opportunities to develop new markets in the future. The presentations get everyone thinking creatively.

The groups are not allowed to comment positively or negatively on the other visions. They only listen. This creates an atmosphere of respect where individuals feel able to share ideas that may be "off the wall."

I then break up the pairs and form new groups. This is very important to note. If you keep the same pair together, they will likely not come up with anything new in Round Two. Before beginning the next round, each person receives a hard copy listing all 10 visions from Round One. This serves as the input for the new discussion.

If we were taking a full day to develop the vision, the group would be formed into new pairs. If we were developing a vision in only half a day, I would compress the process, forming seven groups of three people or five groups of four people for Round Two.

Again, once each group has reached consensus, its vision is posted using the overhead projector. When all groups are finished they present their vision to the entire group. A fascinating dynamic occurs: the visions move closer together.

The process is then repeated for Round Three with four groups of five people, ensuring that the groups comprise people who haven't yet worked together. Round Four might be three groups of seven people and Round Five, two groups of ten people.

What staggers me each time I facilitate this process with an executive team is that the vision is almost exactly the same for the final two groups of people. The wording may be slightly different and one group may have four main points and the other three, but the two visions will be roughly the same. Executives are blown away!

> Where there is no vision, the people will perish.
> Proverbs 29:18

The final discussion is as a large group working out the final wording of the vision.

When there are strong disagreements, these need to be aired, discussed and debated. If it boils down to two protagonists, I ask each to fully air his or her views and why he or she feels the future will follow that path. Once both views have been fully aired we go back into the groups and resume parallel processing. In this way the focus is taken off the individuals and is brought back to the ideas. The groups wrestle with the question as to which view of the future is more likely to unfold. The groups not caught in an either/or approach often identify third alternatives that take into account aspects of both views.

In the traditional way of developing a vision with a large group – where one person speaks at a time – the force of a personality, power of a position or tenacity of an individual can sway the group. But in this process an individual initially can only influence one out of ten groups. The power, personality or position of one individual doesn't have as great an influence on the whole group. The compelling nature of the ideas rules. At the end of Round One an individual can influence only one of the nine visions. The individual is then forced back into discussion with two, three or four other individuals and his or her opinions are continually challenged.

> If you do not know where you are going, then any road will take you there.
> The Koran

Even more important is that the entire group has been discussing the vision in parallel. In a normal meeting of 20 people only one person is talking at a time and 19 are listening. So at the end of a four-hour meeting there has been four hours of talking. In the parallel process there has been over 20 hours of discussion, the equivalent of a three-day meeting! But even more important, there has been a cross-fertilization of ideas. People have been excited, galvanized by the process.

Round #	# of groups	People per group	Time (mins)	Total # people	Av. time talking (mins)	Total time per round (mins)
1	10	2	30	20	15	300
2	10	2	30	20	15	300
3	7	3	30	20	10	200
4	5	4	30	20	7.5	150
5	4	5	30	20	6	120
6	3	7	30	20	4.3	86
7	2	10	30	20	3	60
				Total time talking (minutes)		**1216**

This first stage – reaching consensus on the vision of the future – is the most exciting part of the process. The second step is to identify the barriers that will prevent the organization, in its current state, from achieving the vision. Again, we go through the same process until we have an agreed hierarchy of restraining forces. For instance, the organization may not have the information technology infrastructure to achieve the vision. Employees may require more training. The organization may have to develop new core competencies.

The amount of time spent on each round will vary depending on how quickly the groups reach consensus or how divisive the issues are.

Once the process has created consensus on the major problems facing the organization, the group then goes through the same process a third time to develop action plans to overcome the top three limiting factors. Again, each round varies in time depending on how long the team wants to dedicate to creating a common vision of the future. It can range from a one- to three-day process.

> If you don't know what you stand for, the marketplace is an expensive place to find out.
> *Adam Smith, economist*

At the end of the strategic planning session, the group of 20 people has a widely shared, commonly understood vision of the future – one that everyone agrees with and is committed to. Additionally, the group has agreed upon a hierarchy of limiting factors that will prevent the realization of this vision. Finally, the group has developed a series of action plans to overcome these obstacles. The executive team is motivated, excited and ready to take on the world.

However, the rank and file of the organization has not had the same galvanizing experience. So the next step is to take this process to the front-line staff. Executive committee members are now responsible for facilitating the same process in their respective departments, perhaps with the assistance of the human resources department. In this way ideas from front-line people bubble up and influence the overall vision of the organization.

Two-step vision development

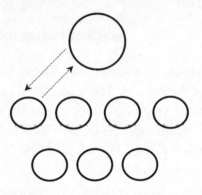

A colleague of mine, Robyn Allan, asks, "What was Thomas Edison's greatest discovery?" Answers that immediately spring to mind are the light bulb and phonograph. She answers, "The discipline and process of discovery."[2] In other words, the methodology of uncovering new knowledge.

Edison patented 1,093 inventions in his life, including the typewriter and phonograph. He credited hard work for his success, as he had to experiment with 6,000 different materials for the filament in his light bulb before finding one that worked.[3] He used to say that, "Genius is one percent inspiration and 99 percent perspiration."

Similarly, Allan asks, "What was Henry Ford's greatest invention?" Her answer is, "Not the Model T, but the process of breaking manufacturing down into its component parts and creating the assembly line. Ford said that if his car didn't sell he would simply find something else that people wanted and manufacture it."

Edison was disciplined in his approach to creativity. He was self-reflective and self-correcting. He kept journals about his insights that run into the thousands of pages. Similarly, Ford was conscious of how he saw production, realizing that his contribution was not the product (the car) but the process of manufacturing. Today security comes from being self-reflective and self-correcting. The process outlined above is a disciplined approach that brings out the best ideas that people have.

How can an organization create a five-year plan? How can people have any sense of what to do in the organization? Why is this process so important?

The process of reinventing the organization on the basis of a rich, widely shared vision of the future is not an easy, linear process. It is messy, circuitous, disorganized and chaotic. In hindsight a discovery makes perfect sense but in foresight it is impossible to see. Otherwise, someone would have already seen it!

Gary Hamel has a dry wit. We were both speakers at a conference in 1995. He launched into a line of questioning that I would paraphrase as, "Who is closest to the future, the 65-year-old who doesn't know how to turn on a computer or the 18-year-old who surfs the World Wide Web every day? Who does all the strategic planning? Who is most disenfranchised from the planning process? Is it any wonder organizations get incremental change?"

First, I do not want to be ageist. I don't believe the saying "You can't teach an old dog new tricks." Having gray hair or no hair doesn't prohibit learning. I look at Andy Grove, Chairman of Intel, who was born in 1937, and Gordon Moore, the chairman emeritus, who was born in 1929. These two gray-haired, balding individuals have been leading the microchip industry and changing the world. Gray hair coupled with attitude, discipline and practice is a potent force. In fact, the most dangerous dogs are old dogs that learn new tricks because they can take you by surprise! Gray hair is hardly a barrier to learning, and youth does not always spell cutting-edge brilliance. But it makes sense that a company's culture benefits from a blend of ages, cultural backgrounds and expertise. Remember Hamel's story about genetic diversity at the boardroom level.

While it is common to stand in awe of the 18-year-old computer whiz, don't confuse technical competence with business wisdom. The 18-year-old who knows how to surf the Web wouldn't be asked to design the organization's strategic plan. That would be like going to someone who knows how to run the photocopier and asking, "What will the future bring?" And then betting the company's future on the answer. Companies need to marry the new technical skills of the 18-year-old with the deep business wisdom of the 65-year-old. It's not either/or, it's and. If an organization's CEO is not on the cutting edge of learning the new technologies firsthand, what systems and structures exist within the organization to ensure that those developing the new technical competencies are briefing the senior team that does all the strategic planning?

> Don't be afraid of opposition. Remember that a kite rises against the wind, not with it.
> *Hamilton Mabie,*
> *newspaper editorialist*

Strategic planning in the past assumed that a group of very bright individuals could figure out the market and then write a plan for others to implement. The underlying assumptions were that you just need bright people at the top and if you study the market long enough you will create the perfect plan.

However, these assumptions are fatally flawed. Not even the brightest people can predict the future. Remember the quotations from the experts (Chapter 4), or the fact that Bill Gates was blind-sided by Netscape.

The second assumption has a danger of leading to analysis paralysis. Is it likely that a child's first step will be perfect? Why do adults assume that we will get things right the first time, when scraping our knees is part of the learning process?

The same is true of strategic planning. If an executive team studies the market until they identify the perfect product or service and the perfect strategy, and then calculates how to perfectly reorient their organization to produce the product or provide the service, they will wake up one morning to find that a competitor has stolen the market before they have begun implementation. This is analysis paralysis. In today's rapidly changing marketplace, by the time you have figured out the perfect product, service and implementation plan and then executed it, market requirements have changed. At the heart of the analytic model is a desire for control. But remember the paradox: the more in control an executive team is, the more out of control the organization. Where leaders exercise control is by working on the context of the organization, creating the systems and structures in which employees work. People are then free to be creative within that framework. Leaders cannot control creativity. Controlling creativity is an oxymoron.[4]

A best guess approach is to take the best guess at what will work, do it,

Future vision

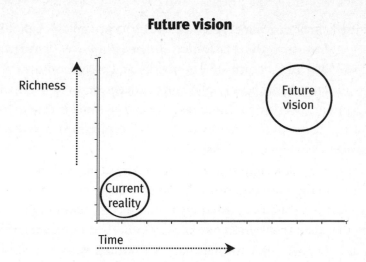

learn from the mistakes, and then refine the implementation. It's Think–Do–Fix rather than a Think–Think–Think–but–Do–Nothing approach. Inherently there is a bias for action and a recognition that the only way we learn and understand as human beings is by doing. It's the difference between head knowledge (knowing what needs to be done) and hand knowledge (practical experience). In the long run a best guess approach will succeed.

In real life it is very difficult for adults to accept that we achieve a high score in a game and then our performance falls. No one can post a new high score in a game every day. Advances are followed by the return to old levels of performance. But over time performance improves.

Future vision

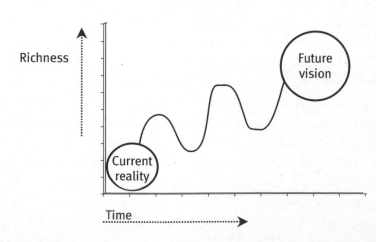

Golf is all about discipline. After a bad shot, a pro golfer can't afford to get angry and frustrated and beat him- or herself up over it. After a great shot a pro golfer cannot afford to get cocky and complacent. After every shot the pro must have the discipline and concentration to make the next shot exceptional. Consistency and discipline. The same is true of an individual learning to play a new game or a corporation playing in the marketplace. Consistency and discipline.

The nature of leadership today (Chapter 4), is that leaders are gardeners, creating in their organizations the optimal environment for growth. A leader's most important contribution to the success of an organization is ensuring that the organization has in place processes that guarantee innovation and creativity by ensuring that the learning is shared throughout the organization.

The process outlined above guarantees that the organization is able to evolve and respond quickly in the rapidly changing business environment.

THE HEAD, THE HAND, THE HEART

Change for an individual comes about by involving the head, the hand and the heart. Everywhere I go, people talk about the need to change. Clearly, people know that they have to change (head knowledge). However, many fear change (heart). They dislike the feelings of fear, frustration and inadequacy that they experience when learning. Their fear may be so strong that it paralyzes them, preventing them from taking action (hand).

> We are more likely to act our way into feeling than feel our way into acting.
> *William James,*
> *psychologist*

Many business people believe that if employees within their organization just had more knowledge (head) they would be able to change the practices within their organization (hand). They believe they can think their way into new action. But I cannot read my way into physical fitness no matter how much I would like to. I don't mean to disparage head knowledge – changes in thinking can lead to new behavior.

New action leads to new learning, feeling and thinking. It is an organic process. A child will not become an Olympic hurdler on the first day of learning to walk. So think and start small. Learn from mistakes. As competence increases, the risks that an individual is willing to take increase.

Similarly, a team working to develop new products and services in an emerging market develops experience and practical insight as the market emerges and becomes more clearly defined. In this way individuals and teams act their way into right thinking. Insight flows out of experience. The more the team goes through the learning paradox, the greater their emotional courage becomes to face uncertainty, fear and ambiguity. The greater the experience (hand) of developing new markets, the greater the courage and faith (heart) and the more willing (head) the individuals, teams and organizations are to embrace new markets even when the new ventures appear risky. It's not either/or, we need all three: the head, hand and heart.

COMMUNICATION: PUSH/PULL

Ravi Vijh[5] is a consultant who advises North American organizations wanting to enter international agreements. He was helping a North American company negotiate an agreement with a Middle Eastern company. The English contract was translated into Arabic and the Arab executives were aghast by what it proposed. Ravi told them, "Don't worry, translations create misunderstandings." He hired another translator to translate the Arabic back into English. Then the North American executives were shocked, saying, "We didn't mean that." So they went through a process of clarifying what they had intended to convey to their prospective Middle Eastern partners.

This went back and forth, with new translators frequently brought into the process until the misunderstandings were eliminated and both parties understood the contract and all of its details and implications. This is a powerful story because we often assume that we understand each other when we speak the same language. If we applied the same diligence when working out mutual understandings in a win–win relationship, we would have fewer problems at the back end.

It is a sign of a healthy corporate culture when any employee feels comfortable approaching his or her team leader with problems.

CREATING FUTURE SECURITY

Companies must continually add value to their core products or services to create future security. No customer writes to an airline president to say, "Thank you for the flight from New York to Paris. We landed safely and I am deeply grateful." We've come to expect the service. So airlines must differentiate themselves on items further and further from their core business of flying and landing planes.

> The idea is there, locked inside. All you have to do is remove the excess stone.
> *Michelangelo, painter and sculptor*

A company must begin at the core of its business and add value. If the core business is faulty, adding value won't matter. If planes crash frequently, it really doesn't matter how good the airline cuisine is.

Customers today expect more than customers did a century ago, ten years ago or even last year. Any successful product or service goes through a predictable life cycle. When first introduced, the product or service is unique and offers competitive advantage to its creator. Margins are high. There is no competition. As others begin to mimic the product or service, it becomes a value-added service. Margins begin to compress as competition increases. Eventually, customers come to expect the product or service. If you don't offer this product or service you will lose customers. Competition is intense and margins are tight. At this stage, the product or service tends to become a price-driven commodity. Operational efficiency – working on the denominator – becomes key.

What was unique four years ago has become value-added today, and it will join the core service offerings tomorrow. The banks that had automated tellers in 1980 were on the leading edge. But today, I would not use a bank that did not have widespread distribution of ATMs and that was not connected to the Interac or CIRRUS network.

VALUE VORTEX

Companies create a value vortex by continually adding radical new value to their core products or services. A value vortex is like a whirlpool that sucks new value to the center. The process is swift and fundamentally redefines the market. Companies that adopt a value vortex philosophy

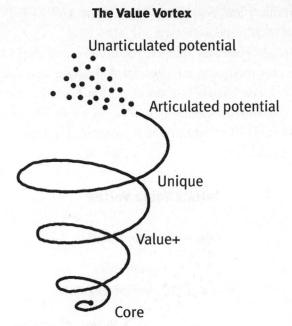

The Value Vortex

Unarticulated potential

Articulated potential

Unique

Value+

Core

continually throw their competitors off balance, expand rapidly and enjoy higher margins than their competitors.

By definition every problem you solve will create another problem (Chapter 2). In the PC industry, every bottleneck that is solved exposes another bottleneck. In such a rapidly changing industry, leading-edge companies are continually creating innovative solutions to the bottlenecks that PC users encounter.

For instance, in the early 1990s one of the slowest aspects of personal computers was the way in which graphics were displayed on the monitor. While the average central processing unit (CPU) ran at 33 MHz and was a 32-bit chip, the motherboard bus that carried the graphics information to the monitor ran at 8 MHz and was only 8 bit. It was like having a Ferrari engine in a farm tractor. The brains of the computer could think quickly but the body couldn't keep up. Consumers could buy computers with fast CPUs but had to wait while their monitor refreshed the screen.

As a result, a number of companies created graphic accelerators (special PC cards) to speed up system graphics. These companies expanded and became very successful. But Intel began making motherboards for its chips to ensure that bottlenecks such as the slow graphics bus were eliminated. The companies doing a booming business on graphics accelerators had to find new products and services as their value was sucked into the core products that Intel provides today.

In other words, the value that PC consumers used to get by buying separate add-ons for their computer was brought right into the core product, the CPU and motherboard. The net effect has been that Intel has doubled the average amount of money it makes on every PC sold, from under $100 in 1985 to $150 - $300 in 2001. An Intel chip represents 15 percent of the cost of a PC.

Intel's Value Vortex

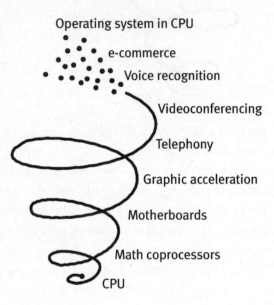

Operating system in CPU
e-commerce
Voice recognition
Videoconferencing
Telephony
Graphic acceleration
Motherboards
Math coprocessors
CPU

In Fall 2000, Intel launched the Pentium 4 chip, its fastest chip yet at 1.5 GHz. This chip features NetBurst technology that makes it easier to download and play video and music files over the Internet. Faster processing power means that real-time streaming video and audio will function better than it ever has before and that means that as videoconferencing over the Internet becomes widespread, a whole new category of consumers will begin to purchase PCs. It also gives compelling reasons for individuals and organizations with older computers to buy newer ones.

Companies that practice the value vortex are always rapidly bringing high value into the core of their products or services, thereby creating an effective monopoly and continually redefining the nature of the market.

What will airlines that rely on high-margin business fliers to remain profitable do when executives reduce their traveling because they can videoconference from their desktop? (For executives, the real cost of traveling is time away from their families.) This is an example of how the practice of value vortex radically redefines competition and the market. When videoconferencing becomes widely practiced, Intel innovation may threaten the profitability of airlines. With serious reductions in high-margin business travelers, tremendous consolidation may occur in the airline industry.

Microsoft aggressively pursues the value vortex. Microsoft's new versions of *Windows* create opportunities for other software companies to develop niche markets. For instance, Norton (owned by Symantec) sells utilities for *Windows*. *Defrag*, a disk-decrementing utility,[6] is one of the most popular features. It was the reason many users bought *Norton Utilities*. *Windows 3.11*, when it was released in 1993, included the utility within the operating system.

With the release of *Window 3.11*, Microsoft added peer-to-peer networking capabilities into its operating system. Until then, Novell had dominated the market for networking software. Novell's specialized software runs computer networks. Called *NetWare*, it was the software that large companies purchased to run complex networks. Microsoft included rudimentary networking software in *Windows 3.11*, allowing PCs to communicate with each other.

Windows 3.11 was inferior to Novell's software. However, by practicing the value vortex philosophy, Microsoft selects only the most important features from competitive products to bring into its core products. Pareto's Law applies to software: 80 percent of the excitement that mass-market consumers have for software comes from 20 percent of the features. Microsoft product managers work to identify the features that will compel the largest number of customers to upgrade to a new software release or to switch to Microsoft products.

Microsoft keeps adding functionality (or building value) into its programs. New value can be identified by many sources. In addition to focusing on successful competitors' products, Microsoft creates value proactively through a number of strategies. In usability labs, development teams study users as they work on PCs trying to complete certain tasks without assistance. By studying the problems that users have, developers work to make the software more intuitive so that users can more easily figure out how to use features on their own without calling Microsoft's help desk.

The help desk has input into new releases that are being planned by listing the features that generate the most help calls. Given that each call to the help desk costs Microsoft between $15 and $30, there is a strong incentive for improving features that users have the most difficulty with. Finally, the development team creates new features on their own to add value to the software.

Once the list of new features is identified and ranked in terms of hierarchy of importance, the Microsoft development team begins writing code. In the case of competitive products Microsoft may license code from a competitor. This was the case with Symantec, where Microsoft licensed the defragmentation utility.

By only focusing on the most popular competitive features and continually incorporating them into software releases, Microsoft gains market share. At the core of the philosophy is a commitment to progress rather than perfection. Microsoft identifies the most important features that most software buyers want and incorporates most of the functionality of those features – leaving its competitors to compete over niches.

OUTER REACHES OF THE VALUE VORTEX

The greatest security, the highest margin, the most excitement and the greatest customer delight lie in the far reaches of the value vortex. This represents products and services that do not exist yet and they fall into two categories: those that customers can articulate and those they can't. Some customers will be able to tell you what it is they want, but that no company in the marketplace is meeting their need. This offers great opportunity and the focus groups and market research can help refine the product because prospective customers can talk about what it is they want. The furthest away is unarticulated, potential products. Here, customers cannot even tell you what it is they want. I argue that tremendous opportunity exists at this level. For instance, our need for the personal computer existed before Steven Jobs invented it. Also, the laws of physics that would enable the invention of semiconductors existed before engineers uncovered them. Customers just didn't know that they needed personal computers. Think of the president of Digital Equipment's comment, "There is no need for anyone to have a PC in their home." This shows that executives or consumers, even when a new invention is presented to them, may not see its value until they begin to use it and incorporate it into their lives.

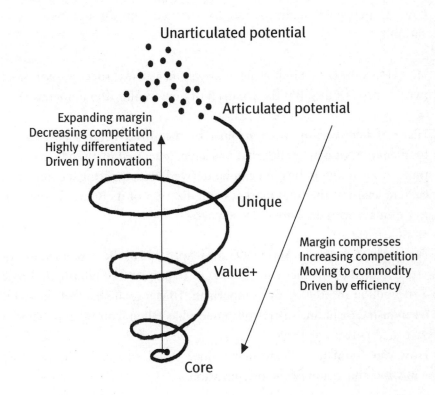

As you struggle with constant change, keep in mind the good news: Organizations that continually create unique products and services that delight customers continually create high-margin business and future security. As products and services move from the outer rings to the core, competition increases and margins compress. At the outer fringes companies enjoy no competitors and have high margins. The core, with its many competitors, demands operational efficiency. Organizations that continually reinvent their products and services live in the outer ring.

TRUE MEASURE OF SUCCESS

As Gary Hamel notes in a *Fortune* cover story on strategy,

> In a survey of 550 US CEOs, 38 percent said that industry newcomers – non-traditional competitors – had taken the best advantage of change over the past 10 years. When asked how the newcomers had succeeded, 62 percent said they had profoundly changed the rules of the game. Only 31 percent thought the newcomers had won through better execution.[7]

Hamel proposes a fascinating way of measuring success, not sales growth or profitability, but the creation of new wealth (the numerator).

> Share of new wealth creation must be measured with respect to the total amount of new wealth that has been generated in an industry over time. . . . A rough indication can be derived by comparing a company's current share of the total market capitalization of its relevant competitive domain with its share a decade ago.[8]

For instance, between April 1995 and April 1996, the capitalization of Internet-related companies rose from zero to almost $10 billion[9] and rose to $507 billion in 2000[10]. By comparison, IBM's total share of the computer industry, including office equipment, has fallen from 45.9 percent in 1988 to 7.2 percent in 1999.[11]

How can companies create new value? What will drive the process? The mission and vision of the organization.

MISSION AS A WAY OF BEING

Johnson & Johnson (J&J) was founded in 1886 as a medical supply company. Robert Wood Johnson, the son of the founder and chairman from 1938 to 1963, was responsible for shaping the company's philosophy and culture. He believed that large, ponderous organizations were ineffective and that small, autonomous units were inherently superior. In 1943, Johnson formalized his beliefs on corporate and social responsibility in the company credo. In 1979, then-CEO James Burke perceived some degree of tokenism regarding the Credo. He described his actions:

> People like my predecessor believed the Credo with a passion, but the operating unit managers were not universally committed to it. There seemed to be a growing attitude that it was there but that nobody had to do anything about it. So I called a meeting of some 20 key executives and challenged them. I said, "Here's the Credo. If we're not going to live by it, let's tear it off the wall. If you want to change it, tell us how to change it. We either ought to commit to it or get rid of it.
>
> The meeting was a turn-on because we were challenging people's own personal values. By the end of the session, the managers had gained a great deal of understanding about and enthusiasm for the belief in the Credo. Subsequently, Dave Clare and I have met with small groups of J&J managers all over the world to challenge the Credo.
>
> Now, I don't really think that you can impose conviction or beliefs on someone else.[12]

The strongest evidence of the Credo's power was in the company's response to the Tylenol crisis. In 1982, seven people died after taking Tylenol capsules that had been tampered with and laced with cyanide. Even though the poisoning was limited to the Chicago area, J&J took immediate action and withdrew all Tylenol capsules from the US market at an estimated cost of $100 million. The company developed tamper-evident caps; reintroduced Tylenol and consumer confidence was not only restored but grew to new heights.

In 2001 Johnson & Johnson, with $29.1 billion in sales, was the world's largest manufacturer of health care products serving the consumer, pharmaceutical and professional markets. J&J has about 98,500 employees and more than 190 operating companies selling products in over 175 countries.

J&J organizes each business around a given market and a given set of customers. So how does such a diverse organization of over 190 operating companies work in unison? What organizes all of the activities? The J&J Credo is printed on the next page.

In her book *Leadership and the New Science: Learning About Organization from an Orderly Universe*, Margaret Wheatley asks the reader to

Credo

We believe our first responsibility is to the doctors, nurses and patients, to mothers and all others who use our products and services.
In meeting their needs everything we do must be of high quality. We must constantly strive to reduce our costs in order to maintain reasonable prices. Customers' orders must be serviced promptly and accurately. Our suppliers and distributors must have an opportunity to make a fair profit.

We are responsible to our employees, the men and women who work with us throughout the world. Everyone must be considered as an individual. We must respect their dignity and recognize their merit. They must have a sense of security in their jobs. Compensation must be fair and adequate, and working conditions clean, orderly and safe. We must be mindful of ways to help our employees fulfill their family responsibilities. Employees must feel free to make suggestions and complaints. There must be equal opportunity for employment, development and advancement for those qualified. We must provide competent management, and their actions must be just and ethical.

We are responsible to the communities in which we live and work and to the world community as well. We must be good citizens – support good works and charities and bear our fair share of taxes. We must encourage civic improvements and better health and education. We must maintain in good order the property we are privileged to use, protecting the environment and natural resources.

Our final responsibility is to our stockholders. Business must make sound profit. We must experiment with new ideas. Research must be carried on, innovative programs developed and mistakes paid for. New equipment must be purchased, new facilities provided and new products launched. Reserves must be created to provide for adverse times. When we operate according to these principles, the stockholders should realize a fair return.

Johnson & Johnson Family of Companies

think about an atom and all its parts: the proton, neutrons, and electrons. And she asks, which part is in charge? The answer is none. So where does leadership come from? The laws of physics. What organizes the behavior of 170 different companies within J&J? The Credo and the vision of each separate operating company.

BEGINNING THE CHANGE PROCESS

I am often asked, "If a company has not changed for many years, how should executives lead their organizations through change?" Begin by involving people in developing the mission and vision of the organization. There is far more understanding (head knowledge) of the need to change in any organization than most people realize. People need to have a strong understanding of where they are going, why they must go there and how they will get there.

Pareto's analysis applies to the willingness of people to change an organization that has not been involved in change. In a stable organization 20 percent of employees will rapidly embrace change, the bulk of employees will adapt a wait-and-see attitude and 20 percent will oppose change. Begin with individuals who are excited and committed to change.

Work with this group of committed people to create early, quick, small victories. Continue to build upon them. As momentum grows, employees

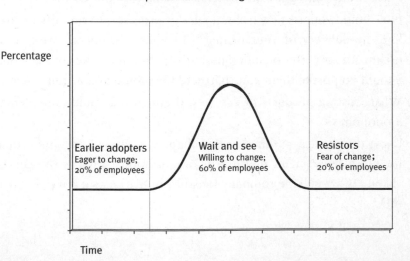

Receptiveness to change in stable cultures

Percentage

Earlier adopters
Eager to change;
20% of employees

Wait and see
Willing to change;
60% of employees

Resistors
Fear of change;
20% of employees

Time

who took the wait-and-see attitude will see the success and get involved. Once the bulk of this middle group has embraced the change initiatives, the final group will have a choice: join the new culture or leave. People have an inherent capacity for growth and learning, but after years of no change, don't expect employees to change overnight. Change takes time, patience and perseverance.

TO SUMMARIZE . . .

- Top-down strategic planning is dead. Strategic planning now requires the involvement and input of everyone in the organization. People at every level must begin to think strategically to create new products, services and markets.
- The more tightly a CEO or team leader holds on to control of developing the vision/mission, the more out of control the organization/ department. The more that people can challenge, clarify and refine the vision, the greater their commitment to and understanding of it.
- There will be reverses in performance. Individuals (and most organizations) will not post high scores every day.
- Planning should not be academic but be action based.

WORKSHOP QUESTIONS AND ACTIVITIES:

- How could you significantly increase value for your customers?
- How could you use new technologies or processes to simplify or streamline the delivery of your products to your customers? Are any other organizations better qualified to do this? Will they take your customers? Should you make them your partner? Or should you acquire them?
- What existing products or services, if enhanced, could create effective monopolies?
- Using the process outlined in this chapter, prepare a mission statement for your department, division or organization. What is the corporate vision? What will the company look like in five years if it is to be successful?

Reflection:

- Is there any difference between my understanding of the mission/vision of my department/organization and that of others?
- What is the key learning/insight for me in this chapter?

Action:

What one action shall I take tomorrow to move learning into action? And over time repeat, to move action into habit?

Shifting to the New Realities

Each of the following chapters explores new ways of perceiving an aspect of the business environment. Adopting these new paradigms will fundamentally change the way leaders perceive the market, threats and potential opportunities. The chapters are designed to provoke discussion within organizations, divisions and departments. At the end of each are a series of questions designed to stimulate discussion within your team after everyone has read the chapter. The shifts are:

- The rise of the new economy (Chapter 7).
- The importance of people and development (Chapter 8).
- eLearning (Chapter 9)
- Focus on customer retention and delight (Chapter 10).
- Information technology (Chapter 11).
- The Internet as the key to future commerce (Chapter 12).
- The environmental imperative (Chapter 13).

Everyone in an organization must ask how these shifts challenge existing policies, systems, structures, products and services, and what opportunities they create. By continually scanning the horizon and questioning assumptions, leaders can help build a new security for all stakeholders in the organization.

Email your feedback to jim@jimharris.com. Suggest new case studies, information or improvements to the text. If your suggestions result in changes to a subsequent edition of the book, I will send you a complimentary audiotape.

CHAPTER 7

The New Economy

History is a series of rolling waves of change, wrote Alvin Toffler in *The Third Wave*.[1] The first wave occurred when the agricultural revolution transformed hunter-gatherer tribes into agrarian societies. In 8000 BC nomadic tribes began to settle. Societies grew as farming sustained larger populations. Arts and culture flourished as survival no longer consumed every waking minute. The city-state evolved. In short, everything about life changed.

The second wave swept through Europe at the end of the 17th century, when the industrial revolution unleashed a dramatic new era of mechanical production. While human labor alone fueled the first wave, gas, oil and coal drove the second. The state began to assume many of the traditional functions of the family: health care, education and social security.

The third wave began in 1955 when for the first time in history white-collar workers outnumbered blue-collar workers. We entered the information era of the knowledge-based economy where employees are valued for their brains, not their brawn.

This brings the learning paradox into sharp focus. Much of today's management theory is still based on the industrial, or second wave, systems and structures. Progressive companies have adopted third-wave management theory, where value is first created in the mental realm and then in the physical realm. This has forced business leaders to *unlearn* principles that were successful in the past in order to *learn* new strategies for the new era. Starting from zero is sometimes an advantage. Imagine having to unlearn a bad golf swing.

During the industrial revolution workers were known as "hands" because that was what people contributed to production. Workers had to be physically present on the production line for their shift. Henry Ford broke production down into simple steps and created the assembly line. Like Charlie Chaplin in *Modern Times*, workers on Ford's production line performed simple, repetitive, boring tasks. Bosses and time-motion experts did all the important thinking. Everyone else merely "wielded" the screwdrivers.

But in the third wave, knowledge is required. When Toffler wrote *The Third Wave* in 1980, he predicted widespread and dramatic change. Today the evidence to support his view is all around us. Economist Nuala Beck has researched the economic growth of knowledge-based companies. As she says, the old, material-intensive economy is in decline while a new, knowledge-based economy is expanding. Some staggering facts highlight the power of the new economy:[2]

- The personal computer didn't exist in 1979. By 2005 over 200 million PCs will be sold worldwide every year!
- More North Americans make computers than cars.
- The average replacement cycle for cars lengthened tremendously between 1980 and 1997, and will probably continue to grow as automakers try to compete on better warranties and higher-quality products. By comparison, computer replacement cycles have shortened because innovation is so fast and furious.
- Young, aggressive, computer companies such as Sun Microsystems are driving the market. Sun was founded in 1982 and by 2000 its revenues topped $15.7 billion. Sun pioneered and has become the worldwide leader in "distributed computing"– the linking of powerful workstations in a network where some computing is done on the server and some on the workstation. Sun's slogan is, "The network is the computer."
- Software sales have been growing 25 percent annually for more than a decade. Microsoft's market value exceeds that of General Motors, Ford and Daimler Chrysler! While American automakers have been closing plants and laying off employees, Microsoft, which was founded in 1975, adds 35 "knowledge workers" a week to its staff of 39,000.
- Microsoft became the most valued company in the world in the late 1990's, only to later be surpassed by Cisco briefly and then finally General Electric.
- Many people think that the digital revolution is over as the NASDAQ has lost 60 per cent of its value in early 2001. But to put things into perspective, if you add the market value of all of the following companies: General Motors (GM), Ford, Daimler Chrysler, (so the entire US car

industry) add to it some aerospace sector – Boeing, and Lockheed Martin, add in some heavy equipment makers like Deere and Caterpillar, USX US Steel Group, Kodak Eastman, Marriott, Kellogg, Weyerhauser, Sears, Safeway and Union Pacific – add them all together and multiply by 1.13 you will get Microsoft value as of April 2001!

We have now entered the "fourth wave." Using Toffler's terminology, the third wave is a knowledge-based economy. But knowledge is no longer enough. Knowledge has become a commodity. Why hire a North American graduate for $30,000 a year when an equivalently educated person in China costs $1,200? And knowledge has a half-life – if you have a PhD, you know a lot about old stuff.

We have entered the fourth wave, which is a learning-based economy. In this economy the ability to learn (as an individual, team and organization) is what counts. The fourth wave is driven by organizations that focus on "meta" processes – the conscious processes of learning, thinking, innovation, working as a team and as an organization. To succeed in the fourth wave, organizations must institute processes that guarantee self-reflection and self-correction. Individuals, teams and organizations must think about how they think, learn about how they learn, become more innovative about how they innovate, as a team reflect on how they work as a team and as an organization reflect on the systems and structures that promote learning in the organization.

> All our assets have legs.
> *Louis Burgos, president,*
> *Royal LePage Commercial*

The fourth-wave economy is based on generating new knowledge, products, services and markets. The fourth wave also involves applying existing knowledge in new ways, thereby creating new value for customers. The systems and structures within organizations that promote learning at the meta level are what create success in this new era.

Innovation is this new era's most powerful force. The following story drives home the point.[3] An American company bought a British high-tech firm with a stunning track record for innovation. Six months after the takeover, the US company decided to estimate the future earnings of the new acquisition and meet with its employees, suppliers and customers. So an executive traveled to the United Kingdom.

One way to gauge a company's future success is to count its number of new patent applications, and using the company's past track record for turning patents into market winners, predict future revenue. The executive reviewed the patent applications and returned to the United States with both good news and bad news. The good news was that 22 new patents had been filed in the previous six months. The bad news was that one scientist's name appeared on more than half of them, and he had left the company six weeks after the takeover! While he appeared nowhere on the balance sheet, this scientist was the company's greatest asset.

This shift from the second wave to the third wave, and from the third wave to the fourth, turns upside down many of our assumptions about business and how to measure success:

In the old economy, the value of material assets depreciates, while in the new economy, as employees learn and develop new skills, their value to the corporation appreciates.

Such old-economy assets as buildings can be rebuilt in weeks if they burn down, but the scientist who leaves can't often be replaced as easily. It may take years of highly specialized training and/or experience for someone to reach the required level of competence in a unique field. Thus, people have time-developmental value. Employees, if they are continually learning, increase in value over time. If employees are not continually learning, the value of their static knowledge decreases over time. What I learn today about computer programming languages could have little or no value in five years.

In the old economy, protecting assets was a matter of buying insurance. In the new economy, it's a matter of treating your assets – your employees – well.

In the old economy, it was easy to protect assets with, for example, fire insurance. But what do we use in the new economy – employee retention insurance? In the old economy, installing water sprinkler systems protected assets. In the new economy, progressive and fair human resource policies as required. In the old economy, if you treated your producing assets badly, they couldn't walk out and set up shop to compete against you. But, in the new economy that certainly can happen. In the case of the US–UK high-tech firm, further research revealed that Dr. Scientist had set up his own company and had already filed three new patent applications. His track record indicated that the patents would make money, but not for the new US owners. In fact, by setting up his own company the scientist likely depressed the value of his former employer.

In the old economy, bankers made loans against such tangible assets as real estate and machinery that could be sold off in case of repayment default. But in the new economy, what's the banker's security in a new software company? Only the soundness of the company's business practices, including its ability to attract and retain the brightest people and its ability to create systems that draw out the full talents and creativity of its people.

Imagine that we were directors on the board of Microsoft in 1975 and were making a presentation to a board of bankers for a loan. Bill Gates begins by describing his vision of the future: the *MS-DOS* operating system will revolutionize computing and will make a new era of personal computers possible such that by 1995, the system will be used on 200 million PCs worldwide.

Bankers: "That's very exciting, Mr. Gates, but what are your assets?"
Gates: "I just told you. I have this revolutionary idea and incredibly talented programmers working on the project."
Bankers: "Yes, Mr. Gates, we heard that part, but what are your assets?"
Gates: "As I said, this compelling vision of the future, the incredible talent of the programmers, our ability to work together as a team and the relentless drive we have to dominate the market."
Bankers: "Sorry, Mr. Gates, we've decided to lend our money for office construction."

How do you measure drive, innovation, tenacity, knowledge and creativity? Or the ability to identify and exploit new opportunities that no one else can see yet? Have you ever seen a creativity meter?

In the old economy, there are limits to the profitability of resources. But what are the limits to innovation in a mental economy?

Physical assets are limited, the law of diminishing returns governs. In mining iron ore, the deeper the mine goes, the more expensive mining becomes. The richest veins of ore are mined first, leaving less profitable ones for later. At some point, the shafts become so deep and the ore of such a low grade that the mine is no longer profitable.

But in a mental economy, there are no limits to creativity and ingenuity. Alexander Graham Bell didn't exhaust the supply of innovation when he invented the telephone. Nor did Einstein become less creative or intelligent after he had discovered $E = mc^2$. Knowledge is a constantly expanding resource. Each innovation opens the door to new possibilities. The more creative I am, the more creative I can be. Rather than the law of diminishing returns, the new economy functions according to the law of increasing returns. Creativity breeds creativity, ingenuity fosters ingenuity, innovation drives further innovation.

The shift to the fourth wave economy challenges the theory of management on almost every front. The shifts are summarized:

Old Economy	New Economy
Material	Mental
Primarily physical value	Primarily mental value
Buildings, machinery	Ideas, people
Tangible	Intangible
Declining resources	Expanding Resources
Protect by sprinklers	Fair human resources policies
Assets depreciate	Assets appreciate
Assets have dollar value	Assets have time-development value
Assets don't compete	Assets can compete
Assets on balance sheet	Assets not on statements
Assets easy to value	Assets hard to value
Zero-sum gain	Unlimited potential
Diminishing returns	Increasing returns

INNOVATION DRIVES HIGH MARGINS

There are four ways to increase profitability. One is to increase production efficiency – for example, by installing robotics within a manufacturing environment; by implementing just-in-time (JIT) inventory systems to eliminate the warehouse and inventory carrying cost, or by implementing quality initiatives.

The second way is to increase the efficiency of distribution. When Michael Dell founded Dell Computer in his university dormitory room in 1984, the company's greatest weakness was that it had no distribution partners and no retailing presence. Dell's competitors, IBM and Compaq, dominated the distribution and retail channels. At each level of distribution – manufacturers, distributors, wholesalers and retailers – there was a mark-up. Dell sold directly to customers by advertising in magazines and newspapers, thereby eliminating overheads, distribution layers and mark-ups. As a result, Dell was able to sell higher-value products at a lower cost than his competitors.

Each additional step in a value chain adds significant cost. If a PC maker produces PCs in one location, maintains regional warehouses, deals with distributors who in turn sell to value-added resellers (VARs) who in turn deal with end customers, each layer in the distribution chain adds significant cost. If each level maintains 30 days of inventory, there are 120 days of inventory in the chain at any one time. Costs are duplicated at every stage of the value chain – inventory, warehousing, financing, shipping, administration and accounting. But the largest cost is the cost of carrying 120 days of inventory in an industry where component part prices are always falling.

When a manufacturer produces the latest, greatest, hottest new computer, should it advertise immediately? If consumers stop buying the old systems, the distribution chain is stuck with 120 days of slow-moving inventory. Discounting is usually the solution. For manufacturers who are committed to providing customers with leading-edge technology, a multiple-step value chain works against them.

Price protection is common policy in the industry. It is the manufacturer's way of shielding distributors against price drops. If a distributor maintains 30 days of inventory and the manufacturer drops prices by 20 percent, the manufacturer pays the distributor the 20 percent difference on its existing inventory. In this way the value chain creates a disincentive for manufacturers to be always lowering their prices.

Repairs and returns add significant cost within the value chain, as returned or defective products are handled at every stage. This creates delays in returning products to the ultimate customers, thereby decreasing customer satisfaction.

Finally, each distribution level puts distance between the manufacturer and the customer. By dealing directly with the customers, Dell got immediate feedback and was able to solve customers' problems quickly. Better service generated strong customer loyalty.

Traditional value chain

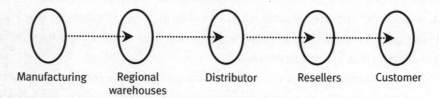

Manufacturing   Regional warehouses   Distributor   Resellers   Customer

Dell's in-bound and out-bound telemarketing sales force learned first-hand the problems and desires of customers. These sales reps became the advocates of the customer within the company. The distribution structure forced Dell to be sensitive to the needs of customers, thereby developing customer intimacy and delight.

As Dell's success grew, what was once IBM's and Compaq's greatest strength became their greatest weakness. All their distribution and retailing partners vehemently resisted their attempts to develop direct sales

Dell value chain

Dell sales

Manufacturing   Customer

programs. This allowed Dell to flourish. Finally, the paradigm shift was recognized and now everyone sells direct, even IBM. Meanwhile Dell, founded in 1984, exploded to a $25.3-billion *Fortune 500* company by 2001.

By 2000 Dell had reduced on-hand inventory to 5 days sales – down from 31 days in 1996! Dell has further compressed the value chain by allowing customers to order PCs directly over the Internet, eliminating internal salespeople from the order-taking process. Dell Direct Online gives customers up-to-the-minute real-time pricing, availability and order status, allowing Dell to provide the lowest-priced PCs in the market. These facts explain why Dell's sales grew 47 percent in 1997. As of March 1997, Dell Direct Online was selling $1 million a day of products over the Web. In March 2001, Dell was selling $50 million of product over the web everyday – 50 percent of its total sales!

Date	Sales ($m./day)	% of total sales
March 1997	1	
August 1997	2	
November 1997	3	
February 1998	4	
May 1998	5	
August 1998	6	
November 1998	10	
February 1999	14	= 25%
May 1999	18	
July 1999	30	= 40%
November 1999	35	
January 2000	40	
August 2001	50	= 50%

The third way to increase profitability is to develop a personal relationship with customers and treat them as unique individuals. Companies today are moving to develop one-to-one relationships with their customers.[4] Using the power of the Internet, Nike now offers customized athletic shoes, baseball bats and gloves. The Nike:iD program was launched in 2000, allowing customers to pick out the color, fabric, and pattern. The Michael Jordan-wannabes can even have their name stitched onto their shoes.

The fourth way to increase profitability is through innovation. Contrast the old philosophy of IBM and Intel. In the history of IBM, engineers occasionally went to the executives and said, "We have found a way to produce a mainframe that is twice as powerful as our existing systems at half the cost." The executives would respond, "That's great, but if we market these new computers, no one will buy our older, slower, more expensive ones. We would kill our existing markets." And so they held back the technology.

This strategy works as long as you're the only game in town. But if you can invent a machine that's twice as powerful as the leading model at half the cost, chances are that someone else can and will. By not making its own products obsolete, IBM allowed other companies to step in and do the job.

Intel's philosophy sharply contrasted IBM's. Intel produces central processing units (CPUs) for microcomputers. Since the introduction of Intel's first chip in 1971, processor power has doubled in power every 18 months. This exponential growth in processor power revolutionized business by enabling it to fundamentally alter information distribution, decision-making distribution, organizational systems and structures, and the way businesses relate to customers and suppliers.

Intel had two development teams working at all times, leapfrogging each other. As one team developed the CPU chip for the XT computer, a second team was developing the next generation chip, the 286. As soon as the XT was in production, the XT team began designing the 386 chip, even before the 286 chip was prototyped. As soon as the 286 chip was in production, that team began designing the 486. As soon as the 386 was released, its team began designing the 586 (known as the P5 or Pentium). Once the final version of the 486 was released, that team began designing the 686 or P6 (Pentium Pro), and then the P7 (Pentium II). This approach continued throughout the development of the PIII and the Pentium 4 chip. Intel's strategy is to always make its own products obsolete. The process is known as concurrent engineering. The result has been an explosion of the market. Radical technology breakthroughs that have allowed Intel to continue to double the power of its microprocessors every 18 months have ensured Intel's security and success.[5]

This philosophy of relentlessly obsoleting its own products has become essential for Intel because the company now has an 18- to 24-month window of opportunity in the market until its competitors copy its latest chips. Two years after the introduction of the first Pentium chip, AMD, Cyrix, IBM and Motorola had chips that perform at comparable speeds.

In 2001, Intel will invest \$4.3 billion in research and development. What is R&D but investing in people? Knowledge, innovation and creativity drive R&D and these come from people, not from financial resources or capital equipment. And training and education fuel people. [6]

Intel invests in the future (in \$billions)

Year	1992	1993	1994	1995	1996	1997	1998	1999	2000	2001 (est.)
Revenue	5.8	8.8	11.5	16.2	20.8	25.1	26.3	29.4	33.7	N/A
R&D	0.6	0.8	1.0	1.1	1.8	2.3	2.5	3.1	3.9	4.3
CA	1.2	1.9	2.4	3.6	3.0	4.5	4.0	3.4	6.7	7.5

In 2001 Intel will invest \$11.8 billion in research and development and new plant facilities, equal to 35 percent of its 2000 sales! The company's security is in its ability to reinvent itself—its products, its services, its culture.

Commodity markets are price sensitive. Market share is easily gained by lowering prices, but easily lost when a competitor lowers prices. But companies that create effective monopolies through innovation, creativity and ingenuity can charge whatever price the market will bear. This strategy is known as "price skimming." Thus Intel sustains healthy margins by allowing for heavy investment in research and development to ensure effective monopolies in the future.

The only reason that Intel can continually invest so aggressively in R&D is that it has high margins and dominates the chip market. Why? Because it always has a new chip on the market. In 2000, Intel launched the Pentium 4, a 1.5 Ghz chip. Next up, is a 1 Ghz, low-power chip for notebook computers.

The key to high margins and high profitability is innovation, which comes only from people. At the base is continual investment in the skills of people through training and education. In the new economy, training and education are to the human asset what R&D is to technological advancement. And the two are inextricably linked.

> Only the paranoid survive.
> *Andy Grove, Intel Chairman*

THE VALUE OF PEOPLE

The old economy is based on zero-sum thinking, which assumes that the pie is only so large. If you have more of it, I have less. But the new economy is built on the concept of unlimited potential. In the old mindset, companies typically opposed profit sharing because if they gave profits to the employees, there would be less for the shareholders.

The opposite attitude is a growth mentality that recognizes that the pie is not fixed in size. New thinking advocates giving away part of the pie because this way the whole pie grows larger. And while our percentage of the pie may decrease, our overall or absolute earnings will increase. After all, would you rather have 100 percent of $1-million profit or 50 percent of $10-million profit? The percentage is smaller but the absolute value is greater. Recent studies show that whatever measure you use – ROI, sales per square foot or absenteeism – profit-sharing companies outperform their competitors because employees have a sense of ownership and they benefit personally from efficiency.

LIQUID INTELLECTUAL CAPITAL

If people are the only asset of a high-tech company, how can a learning-based company retain its liquid intellectual capital? Only by rewriting the rules of business and creating an entirely new business culture.

High-tech companies have done just that. In 2000, it was estimated that 10 million American employees hold stock options, worth over $400 billion.[7] Microsoft went public in 1986 not to raise cash, but so that employees could increase value and cash in stock options. In 2000, a Giga Group analyst estimated that 7,500 of Microsoft's 39,000 employees held options worth over $1 million. Microsoft continues to grant generous options (a total of 304 million in 2000) and workers have been willing to accept low pay, keeping salaries down and earnings high.

In high-tech companies where people are the primary asset, options create the incentive that fosters a learning organization. The wealth is shared with the

> Using best available technology, we can maintain our current lifestyle using only one-quarter of the energy we currently use!
> *Amory Lovins, energy conservation expert*

people who created it. This is key to attracting and retaining the best and brightest executives, engineers and salespeople. The old mentality is that options are only for executives. In 1997, Intel expanded its option plan to include every one of its employees, which in 2001 numbered 85,000. And Intel's treasurer, Arvind Sodhani, believes that, "Eventually, every corporation in the United States will give every employee options."

In 2000, Intel issued 162.8 million of options and Microsoft issued 304 million. Options dilute the total number of shares outstanding. Gordon Moore's 16.5 percent stake when he founded Intel in 1971 has been eroded to 5.5 percent in 2000. But Moore is not complaining. In 2000, his stake was worth more than $10 billion.

Some people might think, "That's fine for high-growth, high-tech companies, but not for mature companies and industries where growth is harder to count on." Even mature industries' growth is really only limited by our perception: in the gas market for home and office heating, a company may think that it can grow only by taking market share from other gas companies. The market in the mind of executives is limited by consumer demand. Challenging the paradigm would require taking a fresh look at what business a gas company is in. Does the company exist to sell gas or meet the heating and air conditioning needs of customers? If the purpose is to meet the needs of customers in the best way possible, then the market is infinitely larger.

A gas company could sell or lease energy-efficient furnaces, or create partnerships with construction companies and offer new homeowners the option of upgrading to the highest-grade insulation. Currently, the best-insulated homes have cut their gas bill by over 75 percent! Instead of paying the construction company thousands of dollars for upgrades, the new homeowners would pay for the insulation via their heating bills over a multi-year period – in essence, leasing the upgrades. The heating bill would equal the average bill if the upgrades had not been installed, but 75 percent of the monthly heating bill would pay for insulation and 25 percent for gas.

Let's assume that the gas company does not enter these markets, and that over time furnace makers begin promoting high-efficiency furnaces that dramatically reduce consumer demand for gas. Meanwhile, construction companies begin aggressively marketing high-efficiency insulation in new homes. Won't the appliance makers and construction companies become the gas company's competition, killing the market for natural gas heating?

Of course, making significant paradigm shifts depends on people, their ingenuity, creativity and lateral thinking. But how do we value human assets? There is still much work to be done in this vital area. And yet the value of knowledge workers cannot be underestimated.[8]

The new economy has introduced many new rules, yet many established companies still measure success by old rules that are no longer relevant. It's like using a 1990 tax guide to fill out a 2002 tax return.

General Motors decides to launch a new car. The company spends millions or billions of dollars developing the prototype. Then customers can walk into any dealership, describe the options they want and preview the car on a computer screen where it's rotated three-dimensionally. The customer then presses a button to confirm the purchase, keys in a credit-card number and the car is instantly replicated at the dealership. The production of the car costs the dealership nothing. A ludicrous business model? That is exactly what software maker Microsoft does. Millions of dollars have gone into the development of the new versions of Microsoft's Web browser, Internet Explorer. Customers can download the software across the Internet! The replication of the product presents no cost to Microsoft. The physical limitations – manufacturing and distribution – of yesterday's production model disappear.

> If 25 percent of my work is not substantially different from last year, I get worried.
> *Everett Anstey, Sun Microsystems President*

In our vastly changed economy, the most successful organizations are rewriting the rules of business. Here are some questions and clues to determine whether a company is up to date:

- Are people throughout the organization empowered to use their knowledge creatively? At Sun Microsystems the philosophy is: In the absence of policy, make a decision. You will make mistakes. Worse than making a wrong decision is making no decision at all. The best organizations draw on the full talents of their people. Management philosophy and structures ensure that leaders continually challenge people but allow freedom.

- The best companies recognize that the team approach is the most effective. How a company's culture and strategic plan encourages team effort says a lot about its openness and ability to grow.

- How quickly can the organization change direction when it recognizes that the current strategic direction is wrong? What structures exist to continually challenge the senior leaders? Do the leading technologists, regardless of their age or seniority, brief the executive team on potential future opportunities or threats?

- How effective is the organization at converting R&D spending into marketable products? What percentage of the R&D budget is spent on refining existing products and what percentage is spent on making the company's core products obsolete?

- How much does the organization invest in technology? If the company's computers have been at the company longer than the average employee, then the company's days may be numbered.[9]

Organizations that place high value on the minds that produce knowledge will far surpass those that cling to physical assets. Locked out of the mental economy, old-style producers will be left in the dust of the new economy.

Companies must begin now to set up the infrastructure that will attract individuals capable of producing ideas and prosperity. Training and educational investments must be made in order to tap the full potential of people within the organization. No matter how rich the mental resources within the workforce, if they're left untapped they will produce nothing. The success of any organization depends on the degree to which it successfully releases its human potential for knowledge.

TO SUMMARIZE . . .

- While the third wave was knowledge based, the fourth is learning based.
- Individuals and organizations need to develop practices that ensure self-reflection and self-correction at all levels of the organization. The leader's role is to ensure that the systems and structures within the organization promote learning at the personal, managerial, executive and organizational levels, and within the value chain as a whole.
- People are an organization's most valuable resource.

- There are few limits to profitability in the learning-based economy.

WORKSHOP QUESTIONS AND ACTIVITIES

In the late stages of the last wave, many companies competed successfully with one or two core competencies. FedEx and UPS developed outstanding logistics management abilities through proprietary software that optimized truck routes to pick up a maximum number of packages with a minimum number of trucks. This lowered operations costs by reducing the number of trucks required per market. Both companies eventually packaged and sold this capability as software (Roadshow, for example), having dramatic impact on the direct store delivery industry. This best-practice transfer quickly became a basis for competition in the soft drink industry where bottlers bought this expertise for a few thousand dollars and instantly had world-class delivery capability.

- What are the biggest cost and information hurdles facing your company? How do people in other industries do a better job than you? How could these capabilities be transferred? What would the impact be if another company does this first?
- If these hurdles were removed, what would your company need to focus on?

Particularly for successful companies, it is difficult to find the motivation for radical innovation. However, technology has reduced the entry barriers to many industries, making industry leaders more vulnerable than ever. In the production of packaging for consumer products, for instance, one of the most lucrative steps used to be the production of film separations. Today, however, digital photography is poised to all but wipe out this step, as photographers can capture an image with a digital camera, manipulate it electronically and send it directly to press without ever creating film.

- In most companies, the people create value. In fact, in many start-ups, venture capitalists require "key-player" insurance to protect the company against the loss of key employees through death or injury. Who are your key players, and how much would you insure them for? Why?

- Where could your teams look for new learning that might change your products, provide new ways of doing business or create new business?
- How can you empower your company's employees to take more responsibility in the absence of policy or authority?
- How can the link between formal training and job performance be made stronger?
- How does your organization promote self-reflection, self-evaluation and self-correction among individuals, teams and the entire organization?

Reflection:

- What business are we really in?
- What is the key learning/insight for me in this chapter?

Action:

What one action shall I take tomorrow to move learning into action? And over time repeat, to move action into habit?

CHAPTER 8

Valuing People

A hologram is fascinating. Should one break, you could pick up any shard, hold it to the light and the entire, intact hologram will appear. The whole is revealed in the part. The way organizations treat employees – their internal customers – tends to be reflected in how employees treat external customers.

WANT TO DELIGHT YOUR CUSTOMERS? DELIGHT YOUR EMPLOYEES!

The same is true of an organization. A company cannot claim to value the customer and talk about customer service while treating employees poorly. It is essential to understand employee needs and how they can be met and exceeded.

"We'd go bankrupt paying them what they want!" is a common management refrain. If money is a sore point in the organization, then either salaries aren't competitive (by region, length of service, level or industry) or the unhappiness springs from such non-monetary sources as lack of empowerment and dated management systems that are out of sync with the lifestyle realities of today's employees.

CREATING AN EMPOWERING ENVIRONMENT

For companies wanting to draw out the full talents and resources of people, as well as attract and retain the best and brightest employees, authoritarian responses to employee challenges no longer work. Yet many companies cling to old, hierarchical systems. Companies that treat people poorly may last for a while, but eventually they destroy employee motivation, creativity and productivity.

A new model for leading people has evolved. Leaders understand that quality and productivity are directly linked to the job satisfaction of each employee, or each part of the whole organization. There will always be a need for limits, and for employees to be given a clear understanding about what is expected of them, but within this framework there is much room for creativity, decision-making – and mistakes.

Imagine a construction crew roofing your dream home. The guy next to me, Joe, is doing a sloppy job and there will be leaks in your living room during the first rainfall. Will I stick my neck out to correct this guy? And if he doesn't listen to me, would I complain to the supervisor? What if the supervisor is a friend of Joe's? Would I continue to push the issue? What if the situation got ugly and I was labeled a troublemaker on the construction crew? Would I appeal to the company president? What if the president stands behind management and management stands behind the other employee? I might even get fired. Knowing all this in advance, is it likely that I will correct Joe? And if I do, is it likely that I will have the character and determination to pursue it regardless of the consequences?

But now, imagine that you are helping the construction crew build your own dream home. What if you see the guy next to you doing a rushed job? Will you correct him? You bet! Do you care if you have a problem with the supervisor? What if it goes right up to the president? "Too bad! This company isn't getting paid until the job is done right!"

> Life is one indivisible whole. One cannot do right in one department of life whilst he is occupied in doing wrong in any other department.
> *Mahatma Gandhi, Indian spiritual leader*

Ownership creates commitment. To create ownership, organizations must put in place processes that allow employees to have creative input into their jobs. Hired hands do what they are told and expect their payment at the end of the day, owners care deeply and go the extra mile. If business sticks to the authoritarian model, will there be commitment to high standards? What will employee satisfaction and morale be like?

Disputes within organizations can be resolved by returning to the mission (why) or vision (where), which are like a blueprint (which everyone contributed to and understands). In this case the supervisor might say, "Yes, Joe is a good guy, but he isn't doing a great job and that goes against our mission to produce high-quality work."

Rather than immediately blaming Joe, a good supervisor asks some questions first. Was Joe properly trained? Do our reward systems promote undesirable behavior? Are we rewarding workers on the basis of how many shingles they lay an hour rather than the quality of the work done? Does Joe understand the mission? Focus on the problem, not the person.

Within the traditional hierarchical model, the supervisor might decide to take Joe discreetly aside and discuss how his efforts affect the entire company. Within a team environment, peers rather than a manager might correct Joe. Within a team environment, the function of leadership is to ensure that systems and structures are aligned with creating the desired behavior. The team, through the process of self-reflection and self-correction at the team level, will correct the problem.

If all efforts to correct the situation fail, the company must take a hard look at its hiring processes to reduce the odds of making such a hiring mistake again. Hewitt Associates interviews prospective candidates an average of five times before making a hiring decision, while Microsoft hires only two to three percent of the candidates it interviews.[1] Hence, a great deal of time and money is invested early in the hiring process, resulting in fewer problems downstream and a higher-caliber workforce.

In the long term, we want to create teams that are self-regulating. The team will ultimately govern performance. Each person should assume responsibility and leadership within the scope of their job descriptions. Access to the blueprints allows each person to do that.

To paraphrase Confucius:

> *Tell me and I will forget.*
> *Show me and I will remember.*
> *Involve me and I will understand.*

The final line of this saying is often interpreted as "Involve me and I will be committed"– an equally powerful insight.

QUESTION INDUSTRY "WISDOM"

At one time, the New York Fire Department's rulebook stated, "Upon arriving at the scene of a fire, immediately place a ladder against the front of the building." It was the first commandment of fire fighting in New York.

There was a fire. A brigade arrived. Its lieutenant saw that the fire was raging at the back of the building and ordered everyone around to the back without putting a ladder against the front of the building. The crew put out the blaze quickly, minimizing damage and potentially saving lives.

But one of the fire department inspectors was in the area. And what was the inspector's job? Compliance with rules and procedures. He noted the absence of the requisite ladder and began disciplinary action. Then the union got involved and a court case ensued.

In court, the defense lawyer for the lieutenant began by asking, "Why does the department have this rule?" No one knew. He even subpoenaed the chief of the fire department. The chief couldn't answer.

The defense lawyer had done his research. He brought in an 89-year-old historian who hobbled up to the witness stand and testified that nearly a century earlier in New York City there were no full-time, paid firefighters. All the brigades were voluntary, and the insurance companies paid only one brigade, the first one at the scene of a fire. How did the insurance firms determine which brigade was first? Whichever brigade had its ladder against the front of the building!

This raises several interesting points. The first is that policies, procedures or practices are usually a logical response to a problem. But if we teach a practice without the underlying principle (teach the *how to* without the *why to*) and circumstances change, people have difficulty taking decisive action. Leaders need to teach principles (the *why*) so people can adapt as circumstances change.

I ask audiences, "What is the universal mission of a fire department?" Within 30 seconds the group has come up with four key points: to put out fires, to save lives and property, prevent fires and provide education. We all intuitively know the mission of a fire department.

In the case above, what was the inspector communicating to firefighters through the disciplinary actions? That the rules should be followed without exception.

The late W. Edwards Deming, who is widely credited with founding the quality movement, said 94 percent of problems in organizations are due to bad systems and structures, not bad people. People are well intentioned and want to do well. Misaligned systems and structures create the problems.

What if the lieutenant of the brigade was fired for failing to place the

ladder against the front of the building? You are the next lieutenant arriving at the scene of a fire and you notice the fire is around the back of the
building. What will you do? You have the ladder placed against the front
of the building because you know the consequences of not following the
rules. In the extra few minutes that this takes, the fire spreads to a gas
main that explodes. Four children die in the fire. How do you feel about
the organization? The department was saying in essence, it is better to follow rules – even if it results in the incineration of children – than to use
your own judgment.

The systems and structures of organizations create misalignment. In
disciplining the lieutenant, the inspector's actions sent a clear message:
the organization's purpose is following rules, not saving lives. An organization cannot be both mission driven and rule bound. Leaders must create
the atmosphere in which employees can break the rules if they are serving
the mission.

Systems must be flexible. Principles for decision-making, rather than
etched-in-stone rules, will enable every employee to make reasonable
decisions in keeping with the mission to uphold the organization's values.
Then the organization can expect to become fast, flexible, focused and
friendly, and unleash the inherent power in people that is required to
thrive in the rapidly changing business world.

Contrast the New York Fire Department story with the following. The
Four Seasons Hotel chain is world renowned for its customer service.
How has it achieved this reputation for excellence? By allowing its
employees the freedom to make decisions within the realm of their
responsibility. Here is an example: while checking out of the Four Seasons
Hotel in New York City, you forget your briefcase at the front desk. The
bellhop grabs it, flags a cab and chases you to the airport, where he tracks
you down and gives you the briefcase before you board your flight.

Now, where in the policy manual does it say, "If a guest leaves briefcase
at front desk, flag cab, chase to airport . . . ?" No one can prescribe what
to do in every situation. Instead, employees need to treat customers the
way they themselves would want to be treated (the golden rule). Even
better, follow the platinum rule – treat the customer the way the customer
wants to be served. Because of cultural, income and age differences, the
customer will define value differently than the employees.

Empowerment has failed in many organizations. Often, people at seminars are very cynical about the principle. A man said to me, "What if a busload of senior citizens arrived at the hotel while the bellhop is away. With no bellhop to unload their luggage, empowerment has resulted in poor customer service!"

When experiencing the first problem with empowerment, some organizations retreat into the old management mode where managers go back to making arbitrary decisions. However, adjusting to new initiatives is never easy, there is always a learning curve. If returning briefcases to forgetful clientele proved to be a recurring problem, let the bellhops find a permanent solution.

Imagine you were the team of bellhops. How could you get the briefcase back to a client and maintain the same service levels so that a busload of senior citizens would not be kept waiting? Answers I have heard include: "Get the cabby to take the briefcase and chase the limousine to the airport." "Hire more bellhops." "Call the customer's office, find out his next destination and courier it to him there." "Have someone from the kitchen dress in a bellhop uniform and cover for the absent bellhop." "Call the limo company and have them radio the car."

All of these are great ideas, but as humans we tend to take the first available solution. I challenged the audience again, "How could you creatively eliminate the potential problem at no cost to the hotel?"

"Front-desk staff should ask clients if they have all their luggage," was one suggestion. The best answer was, "Make the bellhops responsible for selecting the limousine company that wins the contract for the hotel. Among the contract's conditions is the requirement that all limousines be equipped with two-way radios tuned to a base station at the bellhop desk. If, by chance, a guest leaves something behind, the bellhop can radio the driver immediately, to return to the hotel."

Here, in a ten-minute discussion, an audience with little experience in bellhop procedures came up with an elegant solution that would cost a hotel nothing to implement! Would bellhops, who know their customers and suppliers better, have been able to arrive at the same solution?

As an audience we had an unfair advantage in that we had more than 100 people brainstorming for a solution in an environment where there are no wrong answers. In other words, people felt comfortable suggesting off-the-wall ideas.

The role of leadership is to create a climate in which such a process can take place. Given enough time, the bellhops would have arrived at an equally elegant, inexpensive solution. However, organizations often do not encourage or even welcome employee input. If they do, the process of working through numerous solutions is often flawed.

Some seminar participants have argued that the bellhop problem is simple, but with complex business problems it is unrealistic to put constraints on the process – for example, challenging people to identify an elegant solution at no cost. This may be true in some cases, but if the first proposal to solve every problem is to throw more resources – money, staffing – at it, then corporations are becoming intellectually lazy. Resources are substituted for creativity as the primary means of solving problems and taking advantage of new opportunities. That is not to say that organizations should not invest resources in creating new opportunities, new products, new services or adding new value to existing products or services.

TRUST: ESSENTIAL FOR EMPOWERMENT

Technology is advancing faster than management philosophy. We can give front-line people all the information they need to make real-time decisions, but if we hold on to an old management paradigm, our efforts will fail. In essence, organizations need to create trust.

The former chairman of Matsushita Electric in Japan, Konosuke Matsushita, hit at the core of this faulty Western management paradigm when he said:

We are going to win and the industrial West is going to lose. There's nothing much to it, because the reasons for your failure are within yourselves.

With your bosses doing the thinking while the workers wield the screwdrivers, you're convinced deep down that this is the right way to run a business – getting the ideas out of the heads of the bosses and into the hands of labor.

For us, the core of management is the art of mobilizing and pulling together the intellectual resources of all employees in the service of the firm. We have measured the scope of the technological and economic challenges. We know that the intelligence of a handful of technocrats, however brilliant, is no longer enough . . .

Only by drawing on the combined brainpower of all its employees can a firm face up to the turbulence and constraints of today's environment.

This is why our large companies give their employees three to four times more training than yours. This is why they foster within the firm such intensive exchanges and communications. This is why they constantly seek everybody's suggestions and why they demand from the educational system an increasing number of graduates as well as bright and well-educated generalists – because these people are the lifeblood of industry.

New economic and social realities are forcing organizations to adopt more open and rewarding relationships with employees. Companies that remain stuck in an old, command-and-control, militaristic management paradigm will fall further and further behind in their ability to compete in the dynamic, rapidly changing business world. Organizations that hold to the notion that you can't trust people with anything more than a simple task (the thinking inherent in the production line) is doomed to fail.

INVOLVING STAFF

When researching *The 100 Best Companies to Work for in Canada*, a government agency impressed me – Canada Mortgage and Housing Corporation (CMHC). One of the goals of senior management was to be ranked in the book and the team communicated this goal to everyone in the organization. So when any decision had to be made, people at CMHC asked, "If we expect to be one of the 100 best companies to work for, what should we do in this situation?" The process of making decisions in light of this mission created a compassionate workplace.

When CMHC was ordered by the government to cut its budget by 25 percent in 1985, the executives went to the employees and said, "Look, we don't like this any more than you do, but our hands are tied. We have to cut the budget by 25 percent. You tell us how to do it."

The employees formed committees and came up with a series of recommendations:

- Institute an immediate freeze on external hiring.
- Offer all employees a voluntary leave of absence for up to two years, for any reason, with benefits and guaranteed job security. [Through the leaves of absence the organization temporarily shed staff. The intervening two years allowed normal attrition to reduce staff before those on voluntary leave returned.]
- Offer truly voluntary early retirement with a package that is more generous than required by law.
- If the first three strategies haven't reduced staff enough, offer voluntary severance with a package that is more generous than required by law.
- If, after all these efforts, CMHC had still not reduced staffing levels by 25 percent, those whose positions were eliminated would be put on a priority list. The freeze on external hiring would continue until all these people were brought back into the corporation. If no one on the list had the skills necessary for an available position, CMHC would provide training for the most suitable person on the list.

How can an organization cut staff by 25 percent (in this case, CMHC went from 4,000 to 3,000 employees) and have morale increase? Only by empowering the staff and involving them in the decisions. In times of change, ignorance breeds fear. Typically, the atmosphere of an organization undergoing downsizing is one of fear, uncertainty, confusion and stress. No one knows what is happening, rumors run rampant and everyone feels helpless. Feelings of victimization breed anger and resentment. But at CMHC employees were not only informed but also empowered. They weren't helpless, they were driving the process and were in control of their destinies.

Don't just aim to make your company one of the best companies. Expect that it will become one of the best and make all decisions based on what the best would do!

Dennis Waitley, author of *The Psychology of Winning*, tells of an experiment that highlights the importance of expectations. Three high school teachers were called in to the principal's office and told they had been specially selected to participate in a secret experiment because they were the best teachers in the school. The classes they were going to be assigned in the fall would be made up of the brightest pupils. At the end of the year, the progress of their students would be compared with that of average students in the school. But the teachers were not allowed to tell anyone else – the students, parents or other teachers.

These teachers were excited. They spent the year fostering and nurturing their students. In everything they did, their expectations shone through, "You are the best. You are the brightest. You will excel." Sure enough, at the end of the year, the progress these students had made was phenomenal. It was better than that of the students in the rest of the school, the area and the state. The teachers, who were proud, said, "Well, it's a fantastic achievement, but then our students are the best in the school."

The teachers were staggered when they found out that their students had only been average, randomly selected from the student body.

But after reflecting for a minute the three teachers perked up, "Well, that's understandable. We're the best teachers!"

"No," came the reply, "your names were randomly selected from a hat containing the names of all teachers in the school."

The teachers believed their students were the best, and so they became the best. Belief, or expectation, is a powerful force. Creating high expectations – believing in people and their inherent capacity to do well – is a powerful motivator. If you really believe you are the best, you are forced to live up to that image.

When the executive team made it their explicit goal to make CMHC one of the best companies to work for in Canada, that expectation permeated the organization.

At FedEx, a manager is a productivity enhancer or facilitator, not the "boss." A manager's job is to provide employees with the training, resources and staff support to help them do their jobs better, not tell them what to do. Managers are champions of new ideas, change and improvement.

FedEx is perhaps the best example of the inverted pyramid. If an employee is unhappy with a manager's decision, he or she can challenge it. The manager's manager is called in. If the problem is not resolved to the employee's satisfaction, the vice president of human resources becomes involved. The process ensures that managers do their best to ensure that conflicts don't escalate and that solutions are readily found. The system forces communication from the bottom up. Employees cannot be silenced by authoritarianism. Ideas cannot be stifled. Unfairness must be corrected.

The FedEx philosophy overturns the traditional view of management. In the hierarchical, top-down model, if an employee is consistently late, the manager calls him or her into the office and says, "If you're late again, you're fired."

At FedEx, the manager invites the employee to come and talk about the issue and asks if there are any problems. It may be that the employee has two toddlers who are difficult to bundle up and get to day care in the morning. Because the onus is on the manager to work out a mutually agreeable solution, he or she might suggest that the employee work another shift.

In a typical, hierarchical company, if an employee in a similar situation was disciplined or fired, his or her co-workers would undoubtedly interpret it as unjust, which would only create tension between employees and management.

Back to Deming's point that systems and structures determine performance. FedEx has created communication structures that encourage managers to get at the root cause of problems. Managers cannot act in an authoritarian way and make arbitrary decisions that could threaten livelihoods. As a result, fear can't flourish. Morale is consistently high.

THE NEW TRAINING PARADIGM

Every company provides training of some sort. Even within an organization without a formal training budget, "informal" or "unstructured" training occurs. People often start a job with little or no experience and eventually become competent at their work. They learn by trial and error, by asking questions of colleagues and bosses and through self-study. Most North American employees get their training this way. Japanese, German and French investment in on-site training and education is significantly higher. The cost of the learn-as-you-go approach is enormous, yet it is invisible and unmeasured.

Studies show that employees who develop their skills through unstructured training are half as productive, or less, during the developmental period than those with formal training. Yet staggering three-quarters of Canadian companies spend absolutely nothing on formal training! Even those with a training budget may be quick to reduce or eliminate it in times of financial stress. This is because training expenses are considered "soft" and are difficult to quantify. Companies that spend little or nothing on training may think they're saving money, but in the long run they lose a fortune in lower productivity.

> One thing worse than training employees and losing them, is not training them and keeping them.
> *Dr Ed Metcalf, professional speaker*

Here's a math problem about two new average sales representatives in a clothing store:

Sales rep "A" is put on the sales floor on Day One and takes 48 weeks to become proficient at selling $4,000 of clothes per week.

As an experiment sales rep "B" is taken off the sales floor and given an intensive, four-week, $6,000 sales course, after which she begins immediately selling $4,000 of clothes per week.

Which rep will have the highest net sales for the company? Here's how the solution is calculated:

Sales rep A's average sales are $2,000 per week. (Starts off at zero and ends up at $4,000 per week; therefore, A's total sales are 48 weeks x $2,000/week = $96,000.)

Sales rep B starts off behind because she sells no clothes for four weeks, which means she has only 44 weeks for selling clothes. But the moment she gets out on the sales floor she begins selling at a rate of $4,000 per week. So 44 weeks x $4,000/week is $176,000. But the four-week course cost $6,000. So B netted the company $170,000.

Given that $170,000 is greater than $96,000, this highlights how an HR professional can prove that formal training is more profitable for the retailer.

We can see this example in the following graphs:

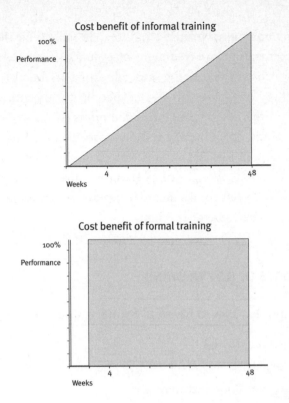

In these examples, the shaded-in area represents the dollar value. As you can see the area of the formal training is much greater than the informal.

Would we take a learn-as-you-go approach with commercial airplane pilots? Imagine boarding a plane and hearing the following announcement: "Welcome aboard Flight 907 to Miami. We'll be cruising at an altitude of 30,000 feet. Joe Henderson, one of our pilots-in-training, will be your captain today. Please fasten your seatbelt. It may be a rough ride as its Joe's first flight. We thank you for flying A Wing & A Prayer Airlines."

While the above example may appear exaggerated, it makes the point that in a highly competitive business environment, investing in employee training and education is investing in the future.

What is the lifetime value of a loyal customer? For a luxury auto dealership that delights its customers, a customer's lifetime worth can exceed $300,000! If the delighted customer convinces his or her friends to buy from the dealership, the value of that initial customer can exceed $1 million. If salespeople working at the luxury-car dealership know that anyone walking in is potentially worth $1 million, do you think that knowledge affects their perception and treatment of potential customers? If the dealership did not invest in training and educating its salespeople, it could potentially allow new sales or service people to alienate million-dollar customers! Isn't that like letting untrained pilots fly an airplane?

The onus should be on human resources professionals to assess the cost of failing to invest in formal training. For example, poorly made products or poor service can be thought of as economic losses because the customers are less likely to return. By quantifying this loss, training professionals can demonstrate the value of training.

THE TRUE COSTS OF NOT TRAINING

An organization that fails to invest in formal training will experience:

- Fewer skilled employees
- Lower-quality work
- Poor customer service
- Substandard customer satisfaction
- Higher customer turnover
- Increased marketing costs to attract new customers
- Slow corporate growth and lower corporate profitability
- Lower job satisfaction and a less motivated workforce
- Higher employee turnover and absenteeism
- Increased workload on employees in high turnover departments, leading to an increase in burnout and even higher employee turnover
- Higher recruitment costs
- Reduced ability to attract high-caliber employees (Lower-caliber applicants require more training, which, if not provided, results in a vicious cycle.)
- High "informal" training costs
- Inability to change swiftly in a dynamic business environment (When a crisis occurs, downsizing is usually seen as the answer.)

> When you buy a piece of equipment you set aside a percentage for maintenance. Shouldn't you do the same for people?
> *William Wiggenhorn, Motorola U President*

- Slow corporate turnaround for projects, proposals and bids
- Slow responsiveness to new competitors
- An inflexible organization entrenched in the way things have always been done (Employees who are not continually learning produce fewer fresh ideas and are less innovative, resulting in the organization having to compete in lower-margin "commodity" markets.)
- Employee battles over turf, politics and office size. Politics, not competency, is valued
- Decreased ability to use the latest high-productivity, high-yield tools.

In short, an organization that fails to adequately invest in training will not be focused, fast, flexible or friendly – the four characteristics that Rosabeth Moss Kanter, former editor of *Harvard Business Review*, says are essential for organizational survival. The mission will not be effectively implemented, resources will often be misallocated and internal processes will be antiquated, time-consuming and unable to adequately meet customer needs. Such an organization's chances of competing in a rapidly changing economy are poor.

EXECUTIVE DEVELOPMENT

Who needs more training and education on a 747 crew – the pilot or the flight attendant? One requires over 10,000 hours of flying education and experience to qualify, while the other requires two weeks of training.

The higher individuals are within an organization, the greater their commitment must be to lifelong learning because the consequences of error are far greater. Executives must continually be thinking "paradigmally" and strategically, reading widely, spending time with their organization's technical people, managers and project leaders who are working on the cutting edge. Executives must be leaders in learning.

SUPPORT IS EXPENSIVE TRAINING

A 1994 study of Fortune 1,000 organizations by Nolan, Norton & Co. revealed the tremendous hidden costs associated with personal computers.[2] The price of a computer is like the tip of an iceberg – it represents only a small portion of the overall cost. The average PC in 1994 cost an organization $18,000, of which:

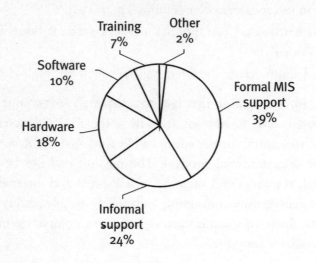

Cost of a PC

Training 7%
Other 2%
Software 10%
Formal MIS support 39%
Hardware 18%
Informal support 24%

Most of the costs associated with a PC are typically unmeasured. They are:

  7 percent training
10 percent software
18 percent hardware
24 percent informal support from colleagues
39 percent formal support from IS professionals

These last two categories are "hidden" and rarely measured, but together they total 63 percent of the cost of a personal computer – a staggering $11,340!

The corporate information systems (IS) department provides users with formal support. "Informal support" occurs when, for example, John can't paste a spreadsheet table into his word-processed document so he interrupts Sally, who takes 30 minutes from her work to teach him. Both categories represent hidden costs that go completely unmeasured and unmanaged, representing the bulk of the total cost of ownership (TCO) of a computer.

The Nolan, Norton study shows that IS support and informal training subsidize underfunded training expenditure. This is a huge waste of resources. Highly specialized, highly paid IS professionals may end up teaching end users how to turn on their computers. The IS professional will likely lack the patience required for training and get frustrated with "dumb users" asking "stupid questions." Users sense this and after an initial experience may hesitate to ask for help. They struggle along, never fully utilizing the software. Nor is an adequate solution to have a well-meaning colleague who lacks competence provide assistance. If the company increased its training commitment, end users would learn to use the systems to much better advantage as well as ensure that employee skills are continually upgraded.

If organizations doubled or tripled their formal training budgets, the hidden costs of "informal training" could be halved, resulting in a huge net saving.

Managers making computer purchases often conduct basic cost comparisons of hardware and software without considering the largest costs: ease of use and training. It's like comparing the tips of icebergs: the visible costs hardly matter!

Gartner's TCO model confirms the Nolan, Norton findings. Gartner studies show that computers' capital costs average 19 percent, operations 13 percent, downtime four percent and administration five percent, while managing the end-user accounts for 60 percent! In this final category, three percent is formal learning, six percent, file and data management, three percent application development, 20 percent casual and self-supported learning, and 28 percent peer support.[3]

COMPARATIVE TRAINING EXPENDITURES

A 2001 American Society of Training and Development (ASTD) study of its members involved in a benchmarking forum revealed average expenditures of $1,665 per employee per year, representing 1.8 percent of payroll expenses.[4] Surveys on training can be somewhat misleading as companies that fail to make training a priority rarely respond.

In 2001, the US accounts for 50 percent of expenditures. The next largest market is West Europe, with 33 percent of training expenditures.

Canada and Japan trail far behind at three percent and five percent respectively. Training and education is to people what research and development is to technological advancements.

LEARNING BY DOING

Different people learn in different ways. Some people need written material, manuals and handouts. For others, manuals never suffice. They learn by listening. People also want training that relates to their specific job situation and skills. The needs must be assessed and the training approach customized according to individual preferences.

In universities, the co-op model has shown incredible results. Microsoft hires more software engineers from Canada's University of Waterloo co-op programs than from any other university in the world. In a co-op program, students study for four months, then work for four months at a company in their field of study, then return to studying for another four months. Degrees take students a year longer than at other universities, but graduates are more qualified because what they have learned is integrated with workplace practice. It also means that professors can't teach mainframe computing theories from a 15-year-old curriculum because students know from their experience that demand for mainframe programmers is declining.[5] The whole department is market driven.

In the same way, we need to develop a new model of organizational training, one that is interactive and demand driven. The old model was to take a two-day computer course. The new model is to have 15 minutes of customized on-demand training tied specifically to the need. When I need to print labels from a database to do a mailing, I first go to the online help menu or printed manual and look up "print – labels," but it's not there, so I try "labels – print," but it's not there. In the end I find it was under "mail merge." Of course, why didn't I look there to begin with? Stupid me.

At this point I don't need a three-day course on how to use the program. All I need is 15 minutes of customized, contextualized training. Likely I will call the software company's help lines or, as discussed above, take one of my colleagues from their work to show me. In this way help lines are really providing informal training. Given that the average help call costs Microsoft between \$15 and \$30, making software easier to use in the first place is one of Microsoft's major goals.

I predict that interactive training on demand will be one of the fastest-growing segments in the training market. When I want to produce a slide presentation for the first time, I don't need to take a full-day course. I just need 15 or 20 minutes of instruction and then, time to try it myself! A rapidly growing alternative will be eLearning (see next chapter).

While training focuses on such specific skills as being able to merge computer files, education deals with conceptual development. Education must be tied to business goals, yet not so tightly that it doesn't allow room to "play." Courses should allow for interplay between theory and practice. The old model for education was to take a three-day course and then return to work. Studies show that unless new learning is applied within 48 hours, most of it will be forgotten.

> The unexamined life is not worth living.
> *Socrates, Greek philosopher*

One thing is clear: organizations significantly underestimate the amount of time, effort and expenditure involved in bringing about change. What's needed is a fresh education model that allows students to apply newly acquired knowledge immediately and for an extended period. Otherwise, the course will not prove worthwhile. One model might be to take a one-day course followed by three weeks of applied experience in the workplace, a half-day refresher for questions and problems, another two months of experience and another full-day refresher, and so on.

Perhaps there is only one valid instance in which training is not necessary and that is when a company creates a rapidly changing learning organization in a rapidly evolving industry. Learning in a "bleeding edge" environment isn't formal, it's informal and experiential. The only courses of value in this environment are ones that focus on the process of learning, the process of team facilitation, the process of creativity itself. In other words, courses on how to learn, how to be more creative and productive in teams.

Companies such as Microsoft and Sun Microsystems are always reinventing themselves. These organizations are on the bleeding edge and formal training may not exist or help them. Instead, they practice continuous team-based learning. In *Microsoft Secrets*, Michael Cusumano and Richard Selby take a look inside Microsoft:

> Rather than investing heavily in training programs, formal rules and procedures, or even detailed product documentation, Microsoft tries to hire people who can learn on their own on the job. It relies on experienced people to educate and guide new people: Team leaders, experts in certain areas, and formally appointed mentors take on the burden of teaching in addition to doing their own work.[6]

Microsoft and Sun Microsystems hire only the best and brightest programmers. Problem-solving ability, proactivity, a continual quest for the excitement of challenge and change are the key characteristics that executives search for in candidates. These companies hire only the most creative, intelligent people. The working environments always give employees more responsibility than they would get anywhere else, continually challenging them to produce results. The result is company cultures that thrive on change. On the bleeding edge, Sun and Microsoft have "excitement" capital to attract the intellectual capital they need to maintain their leadership positions.

Organizations on the bleeding edge must put in place practices that ensure self-reflection and self-correction at the individual, team, managerial, organizational and even the inter-organizational level. Individuals, teams and organizations that are venturing into uncharted waters need to be continually asking themselves, "Are we headed in the right direction? What are the perils? What are the opportunities?" And in response to these questions, they must be vigilant in correcting their course.

What would comprise formal learning courses for managers and leaders of bleeding-edge companies? Managers' courses would focus on organizational systems and structures that facilitate learning, change and creativity. For leaders, courses would focus on how to increase creativity within their organization as well as between organizations as they work to optimize relationships within the whole value chain.

PROVE THE VALUE OF TRAINING

CEOs are typically bottom-line oriented. Shareholders judge the CEO's success or failure in terms of profit, return on investment (ROI), dividends per share and market share. Facts, figures, proof and profit are the language of a CEO. Human resources (HR) and training professionals, by contrast, tend to be more concerned with people and teams in the organization.

To gain credibility with CEOs, HR and training and development professionals are increasingly tying training and education programs to corporate objectives in meaningful ways that can be measured. The American Society of Training and Development's 2001 study shows that 40 percent of US training and education initiatives are measured in terms of their bottom-line impact.

In 1979, Donald Kirkpatrick proposed four levels to evaluate the effectiveness of training. Level I diagnostics measure participants' reaction to a course, usually in the form of a survey, often called a "smile sheet." Level II measures learning. Participants complete surveys before and after the course to measure changes in self-reported attitudes and knowledge. Level III focuses on changes in behavior. This involves surveying the co-workers and supervisors of participants before and at least three months after the course to see if their behavior has changed. Finally, Level IV diagnostics seek to tie the training to business results and assess the financial impact on the bottom line. Each level is progressively more difficult and expensive. Working at Level IV is what will give HR and training departments increased respect in organizations.

The HR department, like any other department, exists to serve the overall corporate mission. HR programs must be designed to meet corporate objectives, including increasing new product innovation, team performance, creativity, sales, quality and/or customer satisfaction and decreasing costs. Creating an ROI is increasingly the aim and justification of any HR investment.

Training professionals must learn to quantify the unquantifiable. They must speak the language of the CEO. As HR professionals gain credibility with CEOs, they may begin to teach CEOs the language of HR.

THE COST OF DISRESPECT

How do you quantify the cost of disrespect? Take the case of an HR professional in a manufacturing company who knew there was a lot of tension on the production line, where workers felt they received no respect. This company manufactured new product lines every year, from prototype through to mass production. The engineers who did the design work had an arrogant manner toward the production line workers. Further, the design engineers described their designs using sophisticated, complex, academic terms that the production workers couldn't always understand. Clearly, there was a problem within the company. Pride and arrogance came ahead of the overall corporate mission.

The HR professional calculated the cost of such tension. The total wages of all the engineers and line workers involved in prototyping were $18,500 per day, and on average it took seven days to go from prototype to actual production, a total cost in wages of $130,000 per prototype. In addition, a lot of scrap was produced during prototyping as line workers tried repeatedly to create what the engineers wanted. This totaled $10,000 worth of wasted metal per prototype. Finally, there was the lost profit of having the line out of production for seven days while the machines were being retooled to accommodate the new runs. The average profit on the line for seven days of normal runs was $80,000. Adding up these three costs showed that each prototyping of seven days cost the company $220,000. The company went through prototyping seven times a year, for a total cost of about $1.5 million.

> To gain or regain our employees' loyalty we must grow their independence! This is the win–win corporate paradox. It is difficult for leaders to embrace, but embrace it we must.
> *John Kempster, former president, Hallmark Cards*

The HR professional then estimated that a custom-designed training program would heighten the engineers' awareness of the problem and its cost, increase the line staff's knowledge of engineering terms and do some team-building, halving prototyping time and saving $770,000 a year. The program would cost $200,000 to design (a one-time charge) and then $200,000 to operate every year.

If you were the CEO and saw this analysis, would you invest in the training initiative? The HR professional demonstrated the value of training in bottom-line terms. In addition, she could have argued that the company would also benefit from shorter cycle times (time it takes from concept through design, prototyping and manu-facturing), thereby enhancing the company's ability to win contracts based on speed. When presented in these terms, funding for training is seen as an investment, not as a cost.

CONTINUOUS CHALLENGE AND CHANGE

In her book *The Plateauing Trap*, Judith Bardwick examines the learning curve. She says that in the first three months of a new job, employees are inexperienced. They really don't know what they're doing and have to ask a lot of questions. The next 18 months are characterized by rapid learn-ing, in which they are also acquiring new skills. After two years, they reach a plateau where they become "expert."

Research shows that challenge and growth are the primary motivators (see Herzberg's study, discussed later in this chapter). How can we keep people continuously challenged in their work?

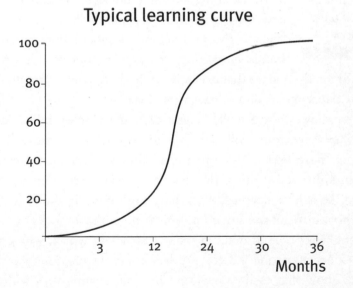

Typical learning curve

A former client of mine hires a lot of career-driven, hot-shot MBA graduates. These individuals are hungry, aggressive and driven. They thrive on challenge. Secretly, MBAs know in their heart of hearts that

"YES, some day I will be president." Given that the company hires 70 MBAs every year, the response to this is NOT. So the company has a problem. It's called "plateauing." There is little chance of promotion for these MBAs because their boss may be as young as they are and likely will not retire for 20 years. How can a company meet the needs of ambitious employees without offering upward mobility? Through lateral moves. The corporate ladder has given way to the corporate spiral. Employees move sideways three times before being eligible to move up.

Employees who have a high need for challenge and diversity are moved laterally every two years. This may seem counterproductive. Why move them right after they become fully competent or "expert"? Because the goal is to keep them excited by their work.

In the past, department heads at the company have complained about having to move good people to a different department. But the president always contended that it's more important to keep good people challenged and working for another department than to lose them to a competitor.

> We acknowledge the paradox that people must be treated differently in order to be treated fairly.
> *LEGO statement*

Lateral transfers have numerous benefits for the company, including increased internal communication and a new synergy in the workplace. Productivity increases because the product development department understands marketing, marketing understands production and so on. It also means that executives who have come through the ranks of many departments do not have tunnel vision.

For employees, there is the benefit of future employability. After eight years, they have four skill sets instead of one. Even more important, employees have learned how to learn. They know that no matter what new job is thrown at them, through study, trial, error and perseverance they will be able to succeed. They have faith in their ability to learn, no matter how difficult the situation. This is the ultimate form of security. It is essential for peace of mind in today's turbulent world, where the traditional concept of one job for life has gone. As previously mentioned, statistics show that in their working life, most employees will have ten jobs over the course of three careers.

According to psychologist Abraham Maslow, the greatest human need is to achieve self-actualization, a state in which we blossom, realizing our full potential.[7] With the "plateauing" crisis, smart companies have realized that they must find new ways to keep their employees challenged or risk losing them.

I once met a 28-year-old manager at Microsoft, who was responsible for the worldwide marketing launch of a product. Putting a 28-year-old in such a demanding position is empowering, to say the least. This sends the message, "As a company, we believe in you. We know you are capable of meeting this challenge. We have faith in your talents and your ability to continue growing."

> There is a new social contract: Job security has given way to employability security.
> *Rosabeth Moss Kanter, author*

Talk about motivation! If you had a Geiger counter to measure on-the-job satisfaction, his would be off the scale! He probably worked 80-hour weeks, partly because at 28 he could, but more importantly, because he wanted to.

"Isn't he a candidate for burnout?" I am often asked. "No, because he loves his work. He doesn't perceive it as work. It is more like the video game than writing with the other hand. He sees it as pure fun, challenge and play. His avocation has become his vocation."

Burnout, by contrast, occurs when an individual perceives that the costs of work exceed the rewards. In other words, work really is work. An employee might say, "I have to drag myself to work every day. Office politics take more of my energy than the work itself. There is little incentive to do a better job."

Don't misunderstand me, I don't want to celebrate workaholic 80-hour-a-week schedules. Balance is essential. Companies must be happy with employees who work 40 hours per week or less. Companies are finding innovative ways of evaluating the contribution people make. Corporations should be concerned by the statistic that 73 percent of North American employees feel their work is not challenging.[8] If their work allowed for passion, excitement and involvement, what would their commitment, contribution and productivity be? If employees were truly doing what they loved to do, would they consider it work? The productivity of impassioned employees is phenomenal.

> Rotating people and letting them work in different assignments is an excellent way to keep a person's work interesting. In addition, it serves to enrich and develop the employee's skills. It's a pity that it isn't practiced more widely.
> *Andy Grove, Intel Corporation CEO*

This philosophy of continuous challenge and continuous learning, which relates to our deeper desires, is growing with the demise of the traditional notion of job security. In the previous example, employees are secure in the knowledge that they have many marketable skills because they worked in a different department every two or three years.

But this new approach requires a heavy investment in training. We can't just throw employees into the deep end of a pool and expect them to know how to swim.

The smaller the company, the tougher it may be to move people laterally. In a large company of thousands, it doesn't matter whether the accounting department has 150 or 151 people. But in a company of 25 people, there is a big difference between one and two accountants. Functional divisions, however, are blurred as people pitch in to do whatever is needed. Thus, many small businesses offer even more opportunities for broader work experience than in "silo" organizations, where functions are clearly delineated and separated.

I listened to Harvey Mackay, author of *Swim with the Sharks*, talk at a conference about learning to speak Russian. Apparently, it takes 400 hours on average for an English-speaking person to learn Russian.[9]

After Harvey's talk I began to think about what it would really be like to learn Russian in a 40-hour-a-week immersion course. In the first week, nothing would make any sense. Try, try, try and nothing makes any sense. It's all Russian to me. One word sounds exactly like the next. Every time I take a drink of coffee, the instructor says the same thing. I guess she means "cup." After 40 hours in the first week I have learned only "cup," and a few other words! Big deal! In the second week, every time I take a drink the instructor says a different word. I get the impression she means the verb to drink. I learn how to conjugate drink (I drink, you drink, we drink). I learn some other words such as "beer," "another," "please," "washroom." So while I have learned some important things, I would hardly say that I can speak Russian. The experience is still characterized by frustration, like writing my name with the other hand.

The first two weeks would be characterized by pain. I would feel like a failure for 80 consecutive hours. And the pain, fear and frustration wouldn't stop at two weeks. It would continue for months. And then I only gain a little understanding here, have a little Aha! over there, but I can't understand the language. Some can plot the experience:

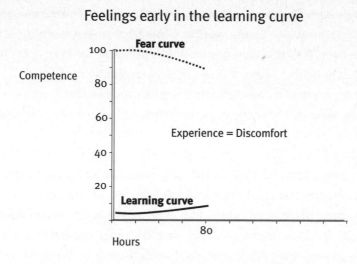

Feelings early in the learning curve

I'm in the dark. But at some point around 400 hours everything clicks into place. There is a profound Aha! And now everything makes sense. It's like a join-the-dots picture where not all the dots are joined yet, but I can see the whole picture. I even understand words that I have never heard because I can figure out what they mean from the context of the sentence. I can now say with confidence that I speak Russian. All the grammar, all the rules of construction, all the principles of the language and how to speak it make sense. I experience the YES! that kids get when they master a video game. We can plot the experience:

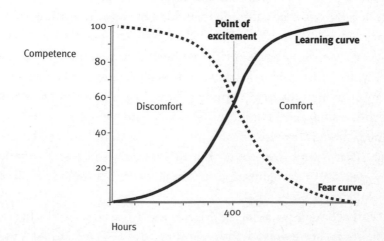

Learning and fear curves

As I approach that magical point of 400 hours my frustration, fear and anxiety have been decreasing weekly while I have been learning scattered bits of Russian. But at some point, and it is different for every person, I get the Aha! experience. I have a sense of mastery and control.

As adults we tend not to tolerate the frustration and anxiety of learning new skills. We don't have the patience required to persevere without gratification.

A child taking a first tentative step wobbles and falls over. If it takes 900 falls before the child learns balance, were the 900 scraped knees failures or necessary steps in learning the delicate art of balance?

This is how life works. Life is like a video game. There are rulebooks, such as the wisdom literature of the world's religions, but like kids with the video games, few people read the instructions first. We go through life and we make mistakes. We are doomed to make the same mistakes over and over again until we learn the underlying principles. If we learn the principles we graduate to the next level and assume more responsibility in life.

We make new mistakes because we face a higher order of challenges. Are the mistakes failures? No! Were the child's scraped knees a failure? Only by giving up the game do we stop learning.

Thus courage and tenacity are characteristics of leadership. Children will naturally continue struggling to learn to walk because the drive is innate. But adults do not naturally struggle to learn new skills. As adults we must be proactive. Only continuous effort brings success. Adults need to develop the "no fear" attitude that children show in learning to walk.

Mackay noted that most of his fellow students quit Russian class after two weeks because they didn't get it. Really, however, they had just not got it "yet." Most people learning a difficult language like Russian quit. And they can honestly say, "I tried my best. I gave it my all for two weeks of intensive study, and I still can't speak or understand Russian." We significantly underestimate the amount of time and effort required to change. That is why 75 percent of quality initiatives in North America fail and two-thirds of reengineering undertakings fail to deliver their promised results.

Think back to the story about Martin Rutte learning to dive in Chapter 2. Four stages are involved with learning how to dive. The first is when you don't know anything and your coach must tell you what you did

Confidence collapse graph

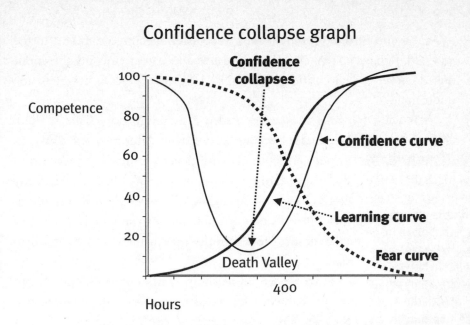

wrong or right. The second stage is when you think you have done something wrong, check with the coach and jointly figure out how to solve it. In the third stage you know when you have done something wrong. You don't have to check with the coach and you also know how to correct it. The final stage is when you know in advance what conditions lead to a mistake and prevent it before it occurs.

Confidence growth

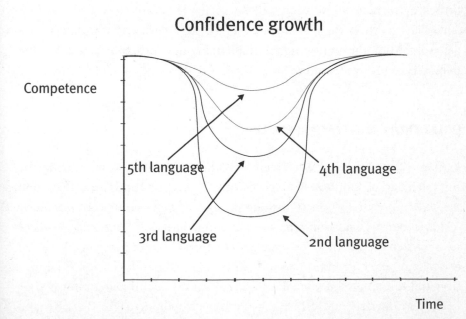

At the end of one presentation, a successful executive came up to me and said, "I have just taken a French course and you are missing the confidence curve." "The confidence curve?" I asked. "What is it? Help me understand."

"It is what happens to your confidence in this process," he replied. "When I started the course, I was very confident. After a couple of weeks of not getting it, my confidence plummeted. I wanted to quit. But I hung in there. As soon as I had the Aha!, my confidence shot up again." Salespeople call this plummet "Death Valley." If new reps can survive Death Valley in their first few months they usually will be good in sales.

> It's not so much that we're afraid of change or so in love with the old ways, but it's that place in between that we fear. It's like being in between trapezes. It's Linus when his blanket is in the dryer. There's nothing to hold on to.
> *Marilyn Ferguson, author*

How far would learners' confidence fall while learning subsequent languages? In learning a third language – Spanish, French or Italian – confidence would remain high longer, and when it did fall, it wouldn't fall as far as it did in learning the second language. Learning a fourth language would be easier because of similarities with the languages already spoken. Any dip in the confidence curve would be later and shallower. By the fifth language, learners would have complete confidence in their abilities. No matter what the language or how difficult, learners know they will succeed. They are now truly secure. They have faith in their abilities to learn. This faith can translate into a general faith in the ability to face challenging new situations and learn the necessary skills to succeed.

WHAT TRULY MOTIVATES PEOPLE?

I often ask audiences, "Who feels that their organization is utilizing the full talents of all employees?" People only raise their hands after they look around and see their boss in the audience, or if they are an entrepreneur.

How can organizations tap people's full potential? American pollster Dan Yankelovich defines "discretionary effort" as the difference between the maximum contribution an individual can make to his or her organization and the minimum contribution necessary to avoid being punished or fired. The incremental effort that employees could make, the care and concern they could demonstrate for customers and their colleagues, the creativity that they could contribute, is the discretionary effort. How can organizations elicit employees' full effort?

The goal for organizations should be to unleash the full potential of employees, to provide the training and knowledge, as well as physical, financial and human resources necessary for them to reach their full potential.

We often think that money motivates employees most. Frederick Herzberg, in what is considered a classic study, examined the nature of motivation in his 1968 *Harvard Business Review* article "One More Time: How Do You Motivate Employees?" His conclusions are both simple and powerful.

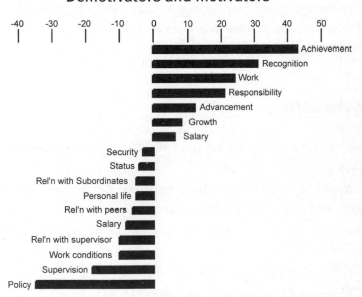

Demotivators and motivators

Herzberg argues that only challenging work and responsibility really motivate people. Money turns out to be seventh on the list of motivators.

The "dissatisfiers" are interesting as well. For instance, salary can be a bigger dissatisfier than a motivator. Underpaying employees will create more lasting unhappiness than overpaying will create lasting happiness. If a salary isn't competitive by industry, region or level within the organization, it will create dissatisfaction. But being within the highest pay range by industry, region and level will not create the satisfaction one would expect, as other factors are more important. Thus, salaries should at least equal the industry average, taking into account regional cost-of-living differences. But once the perception of fairness is addressed, other issues such as achievement, growth and advancement matter more.

For training, Herzberg's research has important messages. If achievement, growth and learning motivate people most, organizations should be continually giving employees new challenges and allowing them to direct their careers and invest in education and development. The results are a more excited and committed workforce with lower turnover, higher job satisfaction, higher productivity and higher-quality work.

Valuing people requires many businesses and organizations to look at their human resource, training and education policies in a new light. The new realities demand new approaches that will be inherently challenging for HR professionals. Few industries or professions can avoid facing up to the learning paradox.

TO SUMMARIZE...

- Informal training costs are hidden and enormous compared to formal ones.
- Investing in training and education to meet employees' growth needs is essential for survival in the new economy.
- Employee motivation and subsequent innovation produces higher profits.
- Salary is not at the top of the list of human motivators.
- Courage and tenacity overcome the fear of change.

WORKSHOP QUESTIONS AND ACTIVITIES

- Informal, on-the-job training will always play a role in organizations. How can you do it better?
- There are many ways to create ownership within an organization beyond

actually giving stock in a company. Many companies use such standard measurements as output per shift across plants, for instance, as a way of spotlighting performance and encouraging the transfer of best practices. In the best cases, pride develops among employees for the performance of their units. How can you create greater ownership for results in each area in your organization?

- What is the fundamental "industry wisdom" where you work? If you want to understand it clearly, listen to the new person. New people have not been indoctrinated in your industry's paradigms and will usually ask questions that fundamentally challenge these paradigms. How could you facilitate the implementation of the best suggestions?

- Does your organization trust its people? As a test, think about the reporting and management rules. Would you use these rules to run your family? Why or why not? Do these rules allow for innovation, or stifle it? What would you do to open the lines of communication?

- List the ways your company can enhance the working lives of employees. Rank them according to which ones will enhance satisfaction the most, which can be implemented the fastest, at the least cost, with the least amount of disruption.

- Which of these do you think will be the most important to attract and retain new people with the new skills required for your company to successfully evolve? Are these different from the ways you would enhance the work environment for existing staff? How? Why?

- List the possible benefits to your customers of increasing employee satisfaction.

- List the outdated company rules that ought to be eliminated and give your reasons. What effect would the following rule have: for each new policy introduced, the organization will eliminate two old policies.

- How much does your organization spend on training per person per year? How does this compare with national and international industry averages?

- What resources exist in your organization, community, industry or professional associations to foster continuous learning? What structures within your organization would promote continuous learning?

- Using the example on pages 171–175, create a cost/benefit analysis of how training and development in your organization would save money or increase revenue.

- Calculate cost of employee turnover in your own department and/or company.
- Develop an education plan with objectives for your organization. Provide at least one example where this would be effective. Why?
- How much of your time is spent learning? Is it enough? How would you make more time for learning?
- How much time do you spend thinking about opportunities as opposed to problem solving?
- How many meetings are open – where new ideas are welcomed and encouraged?
- On a personal note, does your job provide you with the opportunities to do things that enhance your employability? Remember, formal training is important, but what is more highly valued is actual experience performing tasks and functions that are in great demand. Does your current role allow you to do this?
- How could this happen?
- Describe your dream job. How can you create it?

Reflection:

What is the key learning/insight for me in this chapter?

Action:

What one action shall I take tomorrow to move learning into action? And over time repeat, to move action into habit?

eLearning

Strategy for Adapting Quickly in a Fast Changing World

INTRODUCTION

New technology, the exponential growth of information and knowledge, the speed of change, mergers, and the emergence of unexpected competition, all mean the business landscape is more chaotic, confusing and complex than ever before. The chances of being blindsided have never been greater.

In 1999, 18-year-old Shawn Fanning released a program called Napster that allows people to share digital music files, called MP3s, across the web for free. In its first 18 months Napster attracted over 50 million users, threatening the profitability of the $40 billion a-year music industry (all figures cited are $US). Only organizations that can quickly respond to change or new opportunities will thrive in the long term. Companies must employ new technology and strategies if they are to survive and thrive in the digital age.

> The illiterate of the 21st century will not be those who cannot read and write, but those who cannot learn, unlearn and relearn.
> *Alvin Toffler, author*

How can business leaders avoid being blindsided? What tools, techniques and strategies can help business leaders respond faster to threats or take advantage of new opportunities before competitors? eLearning is a key strategy that market leading companies are using to stay ahead of their competition.

The speed of change is accelerating. Here is a simple table of how long it took different technologies to be adopted by 25 percent of North American households:[1]

Technology	Years
Electricity	46
Car	44
Phone	35
TV	26
PC	15
Cell phone	13
Web	‹7

The web, once in place, becomes the infrastructure of the new digital economy, accelerating the rate of change to Internet speed. Because the web eliminates traditional barriers of time and distance, it accelerates commerce and the adoption of new technologies. The web is both the product and the delivery medium. Here is how long it took different technologies to reach 10 million customers:

Technology	Months
Radio	240
TV	120
Netscape	28
Hotmail	18[2]
Napster	12[3]

Because of the speed of change, companies will have to employ new strategies and tools to keep up with, let alone stay ahead of, the change in the business environment. Here's a simple fact: 80 percent of the technology we will use in our day to day lives in just 10 years hasn't been invented yet. Some people don't believe this! Netscape didn't exist prior to 1994 – and e-commerce is now estimated to grow to $6.78 trillion by 2004![4] Job security for individuals, and market share security for organizations, is now based on learning, changing, and accepting uncertainty.

> It's not the strongest of the species, who survive, nor the most intelligent, but the ones most responsive to change.
> *Charles Darwin*

"The Internet runs on dog years," the saying goes, and it's true.[5] A staggering 95 percent of Sun Microsystem's revenue comes from products that were not commercially available just 18 months ago. Bill Gates in *Business @ the Speed of Thought* writes, "In three years every product we make will be obsolete. The only question is whether we'll make them obsolete or if someone else will." If knowledge and information have a half-life of between nine months and three years, we will have to employ new ways to accelerate learning. Learning is the only sustainable competitive advantage.

How can individuals and organizations respond faster to change? For instance, Nortel Network's products have a life cycle of nine months. A traditional corporate training and development initiative takes a year to develop, pilot, refine and roll out to all employees. Nortel now rolls out new training programs in three weeks using the web. Called eLearning, the method allows the company to train all its sales reps on the features and benefits of new products and services. And the training can be extended beyond the company to third party sales reps as well as end users.

ELEARNING

eLearning is set to explode from $550 million in 1998 globally to over $11.4 billion in 2003 according to International Data Corporation (IDC) – a compounded annual growth rate of 83 percent! eLearning promises to significantly increasing the benefits and reach of learning, increasing its strategic importance, while at the same time lowering costs.

There are a number of business, technological and social factors driving the rapid adoption of eLearning. This article focuses on eLearning specifically, so the factors driving its adoption are not discussed, but are listed in Chapter 11.

eLearning is efficient and effective

eLearning is both efficient and effective. It saves organizations significant amounts of money – and while this is very attractive, it should not be the primary reason for implementing it. In 1999, IBM launched 'Basic Blue,' a 12 months training program for front line managers that was 75 percent online and 25 percent in class. IBM claims to be able to provide five times the training at one-third the cost.[6] At Dell over 70 percent of all courses are through eLearning – and the company gets double the amount of learning-per-dollar spent than its competitors. Dell is doubling the learning per dollar spent, so it is doubling the effectiveness of the training department, rather than focusing on cost cutting. This should be the aim of eLearning initiatives.

eLearning lowers costs for a number of reasons. Up to 70 percent of the cost of traditional training are travel and accommodation expenses – but these expenses are not borne by the training department – they are borne by line departments sending people on courses. As these costs are not within their budget, many training departments don't track them. eLearning eliminates them – but the benefits don't accrue to the training department, instead its to the line functions.

The second largest cost of traditional training is the opportunity cost of people being away from work. The average salary of a worker in the United States is $34,000 per year.[7] Holiday pay and other benefits increase the base wage by 27 percent to over $43,000.[8] Given an average individual works 230 days a year (excludes holidays, weekends, and statutory holidays) each day cost the company $187. We can add to this the lost revenue the company would have made had that person been working. To get that figure divide the total revenue of the company by the number of employees. In Cisco's case there are 43,000 employees and revenues of $3,081,000,000 for the 12 months ending October 31, 2000. Profit per employee, per year is $71,651; per day it's $311. So on average, the cost per day away from work is wages ($187) plus avoided profit ($311), or roughly $500 a day.

By contrast, eLearning doesn't require whole days off the job because it breaks learning down into such small increments that it becomes integrated into a normal day – just as email and voice mail. You don't take a whole day off work to answer email, you fit it in when you have time.

What is eLearning?

eLearning is technology-enabled learning. It is not just online courses. It is learning that integrates any form of technology, or uses technology to administer, track, and anticipate learning needs. It could be a sales rep listening to an MP3 file in his/her car while driving to a client's office. It could be a course that a truck driver takes on road safety while he waits a half hour for his dump truck to be filled. It could be someone at a call center taking a course while call volumes are low in the afternoon. It could be downloading a course to your notebook computer and taking a course while flying at 30,000 feet. In all these cases you would upload your test scores after connecting to the network. eLearning is anywhere, anytime, in any format, on any networkable device.

SYNCHRONOUS OR ASYNCHRONOUS Synchronous learning is when a group learns all at the same time – as in a classroom, or in a virtual classroom. Asynchronous eLearning is learning offline as in the above examples.

ELEARNING IS NETWORKED, CAPABLE OF INSTANT UPDATING, DISTRIBUTION
A core part of eLearning is a Learning Management System (LMS). An LMS performs the following functions:
- Online Course Catalogue and Registration
- Pre-course Competency Assessment
- Run and Track eLearning
- Post-course Assessment
- Management of Learner Materials
- Integration of Knowledge Management Resources
- Organization Learning Inventory
- Customized Reporting
- Systems Integration
- Encouraging Collaboration of Learning Community

What eLearning is not

ELEARNING DOES NOT MEAN THE END OF IN-CLASS LEARNING Because many people see things as polar opposites – it's either black or white – they think that eLearning means the end of all classroom learning. This is not the case. Even at Dell, one of the most advanced eLearning organizations, 30 per cent of all formal learning is in-class.

Leading edge companies that have embraced eLearning have reported significantly lower facilities costs by reducing traditional training overhead such as classrooms. The Royal Bank of Canada, the country's largest bank went from 100,000 in 1995 to only 25,000 classroom days in 2000 and saved approximately Can$4 million.

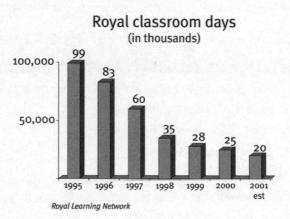

Royal classroom days
(in thousands)

Royal Learning Network

CLASSROOM VS. ELEARNING COSTS

The following cost analysis is for training 3,000 people over a three-year period (1,000 people a year). The classroom assumes a five-day course with a trainer teaching participants in groups of 25 people at a time.

Training 3,000 people in-class would take one trainer three years in groups of 25 people over five days. In the eLearning example, all 3,000 people can be trained in three days. What effect will this have on the ability of an organization to respond quickly to change in this fast-paced business environment?

Various studies show that eLearning takes 25–70 percent less time to convey the same amount of information. In part that is because there is no travel associated with it. But secondly, whenever I have taken a traditional skill-based course, part of my time has been wasted. For instance, if I were to take a *Word for Windows* course now, over 60 percent of the course would be wasted, as I know how to use most of the program's features.

I've been a *Word* user since 1993. Because most of my time would be wasted I don't take courses – and yet my performance is not optimal. With eLearning however, I can take a pre-course test, and the Learning Management System (LMS) will determine what I know and don't know and the resulting course will be tailored to my learning needs. Instead of spending a day in a class – I might only have to spend three hours online. And instead of taking it all in one day – I could spread it out over many days or weeks. Employees can learn from their desk, during slow periods of the day – rather than take the whole day off. Employees can also revisit the same lesson over and over again as a refresher. Online learning is really anywhere, anytime, and at the learner's pace.

	Classroom	**eLearning**
Program length	5 days	3 days[9]
Development[10]	100,000	140,000[11]
Maintenance[12]	60,000	84,000
Travel & accommodation	1,875,000[13]	0[14]
Delivery	3,000,000[15]	150,000[16]
Salaries while training	3,915,000[17]	2,349,000[18]
Salaries while traveling	391,500	0
Opportunity cost[19]	65,250	39,150
Total cost	9,406,750	2,762,150
eLearning saves	6,644,600	

Companies competing in Internet time, with short product life cycles, can't afford to continuously bring the sales force in for training every time a new product is launched or a new competitor identified. It's not just the cost of travel and other training overheads, it's the opportunity cost of not being with customers that is the largest expense.

INTERVIEW WITH TOM KELLY

Vice President Worldwide Training & Internet Learning Solutions, Cisco Systems

Cisco Systems is a leading provider of routers and other hardware that makes up the backbone of the Internet. Cisco has trailing 12 months revenues of $23.8 billion and employs over 43,000 people worldwide.

At Cisco, Tom Kelly, vice president of worldwide Training and Internet Learning Solutions is responsible for training Cisco's 43,000 staff, including 10,000 internal sales people, and hundreds of thousands customers and staff at partner companies.

Channel partners represent 80 percent of Cisco's revenues, so it is the training department's goal to increase technical readiness, lower partner training costs, increase productivity, provide greater accessibility to training, and reduce the amount of time spent delivering product training in person.

Cisco sells $500 million of training a year to external customers and over 80 percent of all of Cisco's courses are available internally via the web – in all some 5,000 modules. Each of these modules is tagged and the Learning Management System (LMS) points internal users to courses of greatest relevance for them. Each user creates a profile – for instance, where they work, what verticals they sell to, what products they sell. The profile also includes their training history, a development plan based on their employee evaluation and input from their manager, along with their own areas of interest. When a new course is released everyone who would benefit by taking it is informed. Cisco intends to pilot a learner centric, 'My Future,' web site. It will be the first page people will see when they log onto the training and development section on Cisco's website. 'My Future' will be customized to the individual – showing them all the courses and information they need to take based on their profile.

Training and development have to be more aligned with the corporate goals of the company instead of the training goals to become more strategic. 'Is what we are doing in training and development increasing product adoption and customer satisfaction?' asks Kelly.

Why is eLearning so critical to Cisco?

In 2000, Cisco acquired a company, on average, every 12 days. In buying these companies Cisco was really buying intellectual capital. It's essential to retain the intellectual assets, so having a smooth, quick transition for people is essential. Having an instant orientation program to make people feel comfortable is absolutely critical. Cisco's goal is to integrate employees of newly acquired companies into the Cisco culture as soon as possible – introducing them to the Cisco vision, mission, procedures and products, while at the same time informing Cisco employees about the products and services of the new company. 'If you don't integrate people well from an acquisition you end up having high turn over,' notes Kelly. Cisco's turn over rate for acquired companies is lower than that for newly hired people.

Email comes to you but with training you have to search it out on the net, find it, evaluate it, and all without knowing much about content. If you have never taken a course on a subject, how do you evaluate which one is the best one to take? If you have never read any books on the topic, which author is the best for your interests? An LMS can help cut through the information overload of the Internet by recommending to learners the best courses for their particular profile.[20]

How does eLearning compare to traditional learning methods?

"We are seeing people get higher scores on tests when they use eLearning tools. And we are experiencing higher learner satisfaction even though we use a wide variety of tools (slides, white papers, remote lab)."

How expensive is designing eLearning compared to traditional programs?

"In our experience, designing and creating an eLearning program is not two to three times greater than traditional in class training (as some have estimated). In some instances we use the 'snare and share' approach where someone goes out with a video camera and captures a subject matter expert talking about something. Nobody has to write or design anything." Kelly estimates that designing eLearning can cost from 40 percent to 80 percent more than traditional training, but Cisco programs average 20 percent more.

Why is eLearning essential for you in your industry?

"Because of the pace and complexity of the industry and because of a distributed knowledgebase, all knowledge is no longer kept in any one building. How can organizations manage and leverage the distributed human capital – across multiple organizations? eLearning is the answer.

"How do you orient the whole organization in real time? When CEO

John Chambers has an important message, everyone in the company has a link that takes them to a served video, audio or a slide show. The message is unfiltered, and can't be changed by personal agenda. All 40,000 people get the same message. Training and development replicates this information on 175 servers around the world – so that our training applications don't bottleneck the bandwidth on the whole system. The servers are LAN based.

"If the FCC requires Cisco to inform all staff about something – we can do that, or if we're having an ISO 14001 audit, all employees may go through a 15-minute instruction and at the end answer a five-question test. The system can track who hasn't completed it and managers can follow up."

What are the opportunity costs of not embracing eLearning?

"Huge. With technologies, industries and markets changing so rapidly, if an individual or company is not using eLearning tools they can miss the next shift. If you don't have email what are you missing? If your company doesn't use voicemail how many calls do you miss? It's hard to measure. We could quantify it but why? Intuitively we know all these are critical."

What are the opportunity costs of not embracing eLearning?

"Training organizations focus on training problems and costs and typically don't look at the business impact and costs. Training costs, whether borne by the training department or another department are huge. (For instance, travel and accommodation costs typically are 50–70 percent of the cost of traditional training – but this does not come out of training and development department's budget, instead it comes out of the budgets of line functions.) We have to focus on things that are much greater than training. Training people don't always get that, because typically training people are not high-level business people. That's a flaw in the industry.

"We have built a career on a set of assumption that eLearning makes invalid. It's threatening to traditional training and development professionals, but shouldn't be."

One of the criticisms of eLearning is the lack of interaction. How do you build interaction and community online?

"Where we are today is where the movie industry was 100 years ago. The first movies that were made were of plays. People took a new tool and applied it to the old medium. Now if you couldn't get to New York to see a play it was cool, but it was still a bad movie. It wasn't until the release of *Citizen Kane* that people found out how to use the camera. Until then, mostly people were making bad movies. Today in eLearning many people are making bad movies. How do you build interaction? We do a number of things. eLearning and in-class are not mutually exclusive – we are using eLearning tools in-class, and we are using classroom principles in eLearning. There can be more live interaction on the web – but ultimately we are seeing a blending of the two. Cisco is running one online course with 112 students in four countries, and eight time zones. All 112 meet once or twice a week for a live one to one-and-a-half hour class led by live instructors. Students do their homework offline, and we have created study groups based on time zone proximity not physical location, so it is encouraging interactivity with people who are not at your site. So people work in groups, either online or over the phone. And the instructor keeps office hours for ease of live contact."

If you can use the same content for internal staff, external partners' staff and customers – training immediately has three times the reach and strategic value at the same cost. Do you agree?

Cisco gets at least double the ROI on eLearning. All content developed for customers (a $500 million a year business) can be used to educate internal employees and staff of partner organizations. Content developed internally for staff can be used for partners, but sometimes would not translate for external customers. So Kelly estimates that the company automatically gets at least double the usage of every course or module developed, and in some cases triple with little or no incremental cost. As to why other companies haven't done this, Kelly comments "For the most part, people haven't done this because their online training isn't sophisticated enough and – 'customers don't want bad movies.' Customers expect good stuff."

What are the key resistors to eLearning adoption?

"Training and development professionals seem to be fearful to engage in a different business model, that obsoletes traditional design criteria, instructional approach and design methodology. But it's an old world thought process. Why should learners have to complete all 20 modules to be certified as competent? The learner might only need two modules. Some trainers think that you can't communicate something of importance in just a ten-minute module. But watching a 30-second Hallmark card commercial can make you cry. Why then do training professionals think you can't convey anything of significance in less than five days? The learner doesn't care if what they are doing is learning, training, getting information or receiving communication – they just want to get what they need, when they need it."

What is the length for eLearning Objects?

"Our upper minimum is 20-minute objects and 10–12 minutes is the average. Many are shorter."

Studies have shown that eLearning takes 25–60 percent less time to convey the same amount of information. Does your experience verify this?

"With eLearning people go through information faster. There are no distractions. They don't look at all the material anymore. Pre-testing eliminates the material they already know. This increases satisfaction, retention, and the pace of learning. All the material is new so it is more engaging. It also eliminates frustration and allows learners to achieve 'competence' faster."

LESSONS FROM CISCO

LEARNERS DON'T KNOW WHAT THEY DON'T KNOW Because of information overload, people don't always make the right choices when it comes to their own learning and development. Some are unable to identify the gaps in their own skills. An LMS may select a learning path inconsistent with the needs of the business. Even when the LMS accurately diagnoses what an individual needs, it is hard to prescribe accurately what learning will help them solve their problem. An LMS system has to help people navigate.

ELEARNING BLURS DEPARTMENTAL DISTINCTIONS Cisco makes no distinction between learning, training, informing or communicating. So when John Chambers has a video message go out to all 40,000 employees, he uses the eLearning infrastructure and LMS. So is the training and development role training or has the boundary blurred with the communications department? When there is an ISO 14001 compliance – the eLearning infrastructure is used. Does that mean the lines are blurred between training and the quality department? This raises training and development's profile and makes it far more strategic.

I was working in London, England giving a presentation on eLearning. During one of the breaks, one of the participants came up to me – John Pettigrew, the head of human resource projects at the Royal Bank of Scotland, which took over the NatWest bank – a fascinating story about the mouse eating the elephant. He wanted to implement an eLearning system at every bank branch but it wasn't until he partnered with the communications department to justify it as a communications vehicle that it went ahead quickly. Fred Goodwin, CEO of the Royal Bank, used the satellite system every morning to address all bank employees about the take-over battle.

The training department needs to make alliances with other departments and engage in new activities that in the past would have been outside the functional silo. To make maximum usage of the technology blurs departmental distinctions. These new applications increase the importance of the training department making it more strategic, and adding radically new value.

ELEARNING IS NECESSARY FOR CORPORATE SURVIVAL As technology changes at such a frenzied pace in the IT world, for companies like Cisco and Nortel, eLearning is not only an advantage, it's necessary for corporate evolution and survival.

TRAINERS MISTAKENLY BELIEVE THEIR JOBS WILL DISAPPEAR. In reinventing training at Cisco, a big problem was the misunderstanding of trainers that their jobs would become obsolete. Cisco's experience shows that this is not the case. Trainers are becoming more strategic, transitioning to new roles like online mentoring and coaching, refocusing their attention toward ensuring a high level of 'teachability' in eLearning products.

INTERVIEW WITH JOHN CONÉ

Vice President, Dell Learning

Dell is the world's leading direct computer systems company and a premier supplier of technology for the Internet infrastructure. Dell has approximately 40,000 employees and financial year 2001 revenue totaled $32 billion.

Dell's learning philosophy

Dell's eLearning initiative has grown exponentially. In 1996 only 25 percent of Dell's courses were online and in 2000, 95 percent of formal training were all or partly technology-enabled. Web technology, is the most critical component in defining learning at Dell. The company cannot afford to be *one* of the best; it feels that it must *be* the best. The Dell Learning motto is 'Just what you need to know, NOW' and the department embraces the philosophy that learning is *immediate, individual*, and *invisible* just a natural part of how we work. Dell's focus is "on-demand learning," what John Coné calls "just-in-time, just-enough" training.

"The teaching philosophy of most companies today is similar to that of schools," says Coné. "Lots of people sitting in a classroom, with an expert up front telling them things. I've always thought that if that was the natural way for people to learn, we ought to see four-year-olds on the playground spontaneously forming into rows. The natural way to learn is simply to be who we are and to do what we do. Kids learn by doing things. And they learn new things when they need to know them."

More and more of what we know today is disposable. So don't fill up your short-term or long-term memory with stuff that doesn't matter. Just know how to get it when you need it."

Corporate learning has to be based on critical issues facing the business. The alternative is individual-development based, which has a focus of

"How do we take someone from being a widget maker level 1 and develop him or her over a 30 year career to be the CEO?"

Dell begins with the individual, teaching him/her to be successful in the current and the next job – teaching exactly what they need to get ahead – but in order of the business needs. "We communicate directly with people through the web, identify the gaps and then help the individuals fill those gaps."

The ideal 'learning event' is a class size of one, lasts 5 to 10 minutes, and takes place within 10 minutes of when someone recognizes that he or she needs to know something. Our challenge is to reduce learning to its smallest, most-useful increments and to put the learner in charge of the entire process."

A staggering 95 percent of Dell's courses are available online. But Dell still offers traditional 30 person courses that last two-and-a-half days. Some 30 percent of total formal training is in-class. The other 70 percent is online, CD-based, organized in five to ten minute learning objects usually around a particular competency. Dell has 100 formal online courses and probably 9,000 to 10,000 learning objects.

Formal learning is what people receive credit for. But there is a huge amount of informal learning that occurs using many of the tools Dell has posted online. This informal learning isn't tracked by the LMS and there's no credit. Taking into account all formal and informal learning, Cone estimates that 95 percent of the learning at Dell is online.

The learning philosophy can be summed up as:

- *Learning should be synchronous with work.* Coné wants "the right people, with the right training, at the right time."
- *Less is more.* Dell's learning objects are five to 10 minute tools that enable people to "learn just enough to complete the task."
- *The best learning happens fast.* Time-to-competence is key.

What ROI case studies have you done on eLearning? How do you document ROI?

"Every year we select three or four programs to measure ROI. Before we begin training, we sit down with a business leader, develop a contract and ask, "What is the business result you expect to get? How do you measure it?" For instance, our product training for new people was creeping up from three weeks to four weeks to five weeks. One manager was very concerned about how much time new people were spending in the initial ramp up. The issue was how long does it take someone from their first day until they're achieving quota? It used to take three months and we took it down by a month. We agreed up front what was the measure of success. It was not about trying to save money. It was about reducing non-sales time.

"The orientation course for new sales reps used to be over three weeks. In 2001 it involves nine to ten hours online and four days in class.

"Another example was sales negotiations. The problem was that sales managers feared sales people were discounting too soon instead of negotiating. The goal was to decrease discounting and increase margin. We even had control groups. Some got trained, others didn't. This is outcome-based education, not even competency-based education. People may be competent at the end of training but who cares? Its the outcome that counts. Doing ROI analysis is cumbersome, so we only do it three to four times a year, just as a self-check."

Dell has focused on developing its knowledge, entry and extraction system (KEES) – to create a repository of eLearning objects that are easily retrieved and reused. It's really what I call Object Oriented Learning (OOL) but Coné prefers to call it learner controlled learning. It maximizes ROI – "because as a learner I get exactly what I need to learn when I need to learn and nothing that I don't need. I don't have to wait until 29 other people are ready to take the same course and then sit through the 70 percent that I don't need. The true value in moving to learning objects is the ability of individuals to be in complete control of their learning.

eLearning takes 25–60 percent less time to convey the same amount of information as in-class learning, according to studies. What is Dell's experience?

"eLearning only takes one-third the time (67 percent reduction!). This is because of how hard we have worked on eLearning. But the majority of eLearning out there isn't very good. Some professor takes twelve year old notes from his syllabus and gets someone who knows HTML to put it online. It's like putting a book online."

Why eLearning?

"There are three groups who embrace eLearning: the majority of people are trying eLearning – because someone is taking a group photo and I gotta be in it. They got a note from CIO saying, "We're doing this, right?"

"The second largest group is the economy of scale group – which focuses on cost reduction. And there is genuine cost reduction – but only with stable learning material and a large dispersed learning group. When people focus on reduced travel costs – this is the first indication that they are in this group. This group feels that distance learning is the same as technology enabled learning – and it isn't.

"Finally the third group is in it because of the leverage of learner control. It's Better. Faster. Available when I need it. Sheer volume of what is available. I can get virtually anything I need to know.

"Only 10–15 percent of Dell's material is stable and falls into the second category. Things like the company history, and corporate values. Each object is freshness dated. It expires after one year. A few weeks before the expiry the system automatically sends out an email to the author that if they don't review and update the material it will be taken off the web.

"The war for who is going to control learning has already been lost. Today banks can't say we don't want to let people bank online. Brokers can't say – 'we won't let people trade online.' It's too late. If you don't do it they will do it without you and you will not be a part of the equation. Training and development departments have to be a part of that equation – directing employees to the learning that will be best for your organization. If you don't, employees will do it without you."

Cisco makes no distinction between informing, communicating, training or learning. What are your thoughts?

"Someone once asked me if there was a distinction between training and education – so I answered with a question, 'Would you rather have your 15-year-old daughter taking: sex education or sex training?' The point is they are different: training is transference of skills and when you are trying to do that you do things differently than education."

In designing eLearning, Dell focuses on:

FINDING WHAT YOU NEED WHEN YOU NEED IT: "We have to make it incredibly easy for learners to access training solutions. This means putting solutions in places that are the most comfortable and natural for people to find. For example, we use 'Drive Time' audiotapes for field account executives – that they can download as an MP3; we offer multiple delivery methods for core training (classroom, CBT, CBT in the class, and self-paced)."

PERFORMANCE-BASED TRAINING "People who need training need it because they want to do something. We must always develop solutions that are relevant to the job and make that connection evident to the learner. This is simply another way to add value to the learner and the business."

VENDOR-INDEPENDENT SYSTEMS "Dell moves too fast to be dependent on vendors for updates, maintenance of Web training, administration systems, etc. We must push vendors to provide systems that are not maintenance-dependent and that work with other vendor systems. When the system is in place and the vendor is gone, Dell can manage it, change it, discard it, or whatever else is needed in the best interest of Dell."

KNOWLEDGE CREATION AND MANAGEMENT "Dell Learning doesn't create knowledge – we create access to it. We must get the knowledge connected to the groups that need it, when they need it.

"Dell Learning pursues five principles that challenge training professionals throughout the business to think globally and act locally."

Developing infrastructure

OPEN SYSTEMS "Developing, implementing, and ensuring that our administrative systems are integrated and seamless. We have got to ensure that our education systems communicate with each other, as well as with the rest of Dell's infrastructure."

LESSONS FROM DELL

CONÉ'S GOAL IS TO HAVE DELL LEARNING BECOME INVISIBLE Many people use Dell Web sites that aren't openly associated with Dell Learning. At one business meeting, one of the vice presidents asked who had attended Dell Learning classes. No one raised a hand. But when Coné asked who had visited the Dell Business Model Web site or the Manager's Online Success Tool, most raised their hands. Thousands of people a week are using the tools without going to class.

For instance, you don't say – I am going to spend two days answering the phone or sending email. It is just an integrated part of your every day work life. Cone imagines the same future with eLearning. Where eLearning is interspersed throughout the day.

85 PERCENT OF ALL ELEARNING AT DELL HAS A ONE-YEAR SHELF LIFE This is in interesting principle that all eLearning should be automatically reviewed, updated or removed from the system. The LMS does this automatically by putting the onus upon the course developer to verify that the material is current. This requires a different mentality when building courses – one focusing on rapid course design – similar to Cisco's "snare and share" philosophy.

THE GENIE IS ALREADY OUT OF THE BOTTLE The battle for who will control learning has already been lost. Any training and development organization that doesn't empower learners to control their learning experiences will be left by the wayside. Training departments can align with the trend and through an LMS direct learners to the most appropriate courses given the corporate objectives, the individual's career path, and their performance evaluations.

IT'S NOT JUST ABOUT COST REDUCTION Cost savings have been primarily associated with reduced travel costs. While this is beneficial, the really significant benefits are in the ROI from learner control. (i.e. not having to sit through the 67 percent of the traditional in-class course that you already know, or doesn't apply to you). Coné estimates that eLearning reduces time required to learn by 67 percent!

EXCLUSIVE FOCUS ON OUTCOMES Coné's focus on outcomes takes competency-based education to a higher level. Training and development professionals have to focus on business outcomes as opposed to whether someone is competent. I.e. someone could be deemed to be competent at negotiation by passing the test at the end of the course, but can they actually increase margins and reduce the amount of discounting? Along this line of thinking I came across an interesting article in the *Economist* that made this point:

Interesting uses of eLearning

The threat of terrorism is made greater because of the boredom of security guards who operate the X-ray scanning machines for travelers' luggage at airports. An average guard will work for years without ever seeing a threatening object. Because of extreme boredom there is a very real chance a dangerous object could slip by because guards are not hyper vigilant. How can airport authorities help guards remain hyper vigilant when in reality the chance of seeing a gun or knife is less than one in a million?

New computer software every so often will randomly impose a gun, knife or bomb – on the luggage contents, at which time the guard presses a threat button causing a congratulations message to flash on the screen. If the guard lets a bag pass without identifying the threatening object a warning message appears on the screen and the item is highlighted. The Threat Image Projection (TIP) software will impose a few fake images per shift and after a thousand or so bags the guard gets a score. This ensures screeners know what to look for, and their performance can be assessed. The software can be updated so that if a new threat is identified – such as a Bulgarian-made gun that resembles a key-ring is discovered, the image can be uploaded to all TIP X-ray machines.

The US Federal Aviation Authority has dozens of these machines already and plans to install 1200 more between 2000 and 2003. By 2005, TIP will probably be standard at all security check points, at which time screeners will have been exposed to five to ten million fake threat images each year.

In 2000, the US Navy started issuing student pilots with Microsoft's *Flight Simulator*, after students who had used the software in a trial had higher scores in flight training than those who had not used the software.

The Navy simply modified the aircraft panels to Navy aircraft and the scenery to resemble naval stations in Corpus Christi and elsewhere. The software package is in addition to in-flight and traditional simulator training and has been extremely effective in preparing the students for their training flights. The Navy expects that they will be able to retain anywhere from 14 to 28 more pilots each year due to the effectiveness of the additional training provided by Microsoft's *Flight Simulator*. It costs over $300,000 to train someone to fly a helicopter and over $1 million to fly a jet plane.[21]

INTERVIEW WITH JONATHAN MENON

Director of eLearning, Bell Nexxia

Bell Canada is Canada's largest communications company with 58,000 employees serving seven million residential and business customers across Canada. Bell Nexxia, its corporate services arm, provides integrated communications and e-commerce solutions to enterprises across North America. In 2001, Bell Nexxia had 2,000 employees and revenues approaching Can$3.5 billion. Nexxia owns and operates an IP Broadband network with over 100 points of presence throughout North America and has partnerships with Nortel Networks and Cisco Systems.

Bell Nexxia has reaped tremendous rewards by using eLearning; saving over $4 million in training costs in over two years (2000 and 2001), a 50 percent savings over traditional training models. This allowed Bell Nexxia to reinvest half the funds into training projects that could not previously be considered for budgetary reasons and raise the personal training allowance of each employee by 33 percent, actually making more money available to individuals at the end of the day for their personal learning needs. In 2001 Bell Nexxia's training budget served twice the number of employees than in previous years.

Despite these substantial savings, Bell Nexxia's Director of eLearning, Jonathan Menon, emphasizes that cost reduction was only a secondary goal, the real benefits of eLearning are that "it enabled us to do things we couldn't have done before" such as accelerating learning speed and enhancing job satisfaction by providing employees access to new forms of learning. As a result it increased employee retention and helped transform the sales force.

"Keeping abreast of change in this fast-paced industry is stressful. Employees feel better about their jobs when they know they are up to date. In turn, this has meant the whole organization can change faster."

To be successful, companies have to focus on implementing eLearning in areas that will "guarantee short-term wins, lead to company-wide acceptance, and long-term business impact," argues Menon. And because eLearning has to be experienced in order to fully understand its implications, Menon believes that companies should begin with a highly targeted application that will be a quick win and have a high return on investment. "Companies may only get one chance with eLearning," Menon feels, to be successful in the long-term, an eLearning program has to be socialized throughout the company to really make it work.

Bell Nexxia is continuing to enhance its eLearning implementation – and now helps its customers implement eLearning. This has become a significant portion of the company's eBusiness strategy.

The Nexxia Learning Network

The *Nexxia Learning Network* (NLN) delivers up-to-the minute training to thousands of Bell Canada employees and business partners, as well as other BCE companies such as Teleglobe, one of the world's largest international telecommunications carriers. Bell Nexxia also extends its courses to customers using the Web, positioning the company as a one-stop source of IP knowledge, emerging technologies, and the way businesses are using them to compete effectively in the global marketplace.

The Nexxia Learning Network (www.learntone.com/nexxia) is powered by *LearnTone*, the fully outsourced, ASP eLearning solution from Sun Microsystems. The NLN provides Bell with a wide range of capabilities for delivering and managing all types of training activities, including:

• Each student's personalized home page provides a single location for learners to manage their development plans, track their progress on all learning activities, and enroll in courses.

• A synchronous 'virtual classroom,' using *CentraOne* software is fully integrated into the LMS, and replaces a number of long, costly classroom courses that cut significantly into employees' work time.

- A fully integrated, threaded discussion group engine enables off-line discussions to be conducted, either as part of a course or independently.
- Classroom courses and events are handled the same way as any on-line offering, enabling user groups to plan, book, and accept registrations for conferences, "lunch and learn" sessions and important company meetings.

eLearning Content

Bell Nexxia also focuses on creating high-quality content to serve the learning needs of the fast-paced culture of a high-tech sales force on the go. Full day, in-class technology courses are repackaged into focused, two-hour learning modules that can be accessed from home, the office, or on the road.

"In 1999, when Nexxia was created, we launched new products every 45 days and we had double-digit growth targets selling technologies that many of our people had not worked with before," so Menon feels that Bell Nexxia had no choice but to move into eLearning.

The result was what Nexxia calls *Sales-on-the-Run*, a series of 15-minute modules providing core product knowledge to support a salesperson's daily sales activities. Bell Nexxia currently has 35 product lines supported through Sales-on-the-Run, in both English and French. The company has enhanced Sales-on-the-Run by making mobile learning modules available for download from the LMS to handheld devices like the Palm Pilot. This "mLearning" (mobile learning) solution enables Nexxia salespeople to take courses anywhere, such as while waiting for a meeting with a prospect. In any single month, Bell sales professionals access hundreds of Sales-on-the-Run modules. Nexxia has honed and streamlined the production process to the point where, today, most modules can be produced in three weeks, and a two-hour technology course in 45 days.

But despite the need for speed, content quality cannot be sacrificed. Menon cautions, "Many of our learners – especially our salespeople – are sophisticated users of the Internet, so they're accustomed to Web content of a very high quality. To be really successful, our asynchronous courses have to compete for their attention with everything that's now available on the Internet – at an entertainment level. Most of what passes today (in 2001) as online courses, doesn't meet our standards," says Menon. Consequently a large percentage of Nexxia's learning content is developed by a few providers who meet Bell Nexxia's standards for quality of writing, design and animation, and web savvy – meaning it embraces the potential of the new medium.

"Our whole culture has a short attention span. We sometimes don't have time to eat, but we can sit still for two hours to watch a good movie. There are a number of techniques that film-makers use to keep us riveted. We look to the art of the storyteller and the screenwriter to produce most of our training."

Off-the-shelf asynchronous and classroom courses are delivered directly to each student's home page through partnerships with industry learning providers including CDI, Northland Systems Training, and Swiss Virtual Business School, based in St Gallen, Switzerland. A similar partnership with Global Knowledge, the world's largest independent IT education integrator, enables Bell employees to pursue industry certification from product vendors such as Cisco Systems and Nortel Networks.

In a company like Bell there must be many different types of learners. How do you deal with this diversity?

"We don't believe in a one-size-fits-all philosophy, so although there's a lot of synergy, we recognize that our audiences are very different from each other. Our salespeople are so focused on driving revenue that if you take 15 minutes of their time for eLearning, it had better be the best 15 minutes that they are going to spend that day. Our Golden Rule for the salespeople is 'don't waste my time'. If you do, you'll lose them, and you won't get them back.

"This has big implications for how we develop learning for them. They don't want lots of choices – they want the one or two paths that they need to be the most effective as quickly as possible. We use a 'carrot strategy' with a lot of rewards and incentives to engage them. We gave away a trip to the 2000 Sydney Olympics as part of one campaign. You have to invest in the behavioral change.

"Our customer care client reps are different. They sit at a desk for most of the day, speak with customers constantly and process orders. The rule for them is 'Help me build my career.' We established an IP certification program for them, and now we are converting most of their process training to an eLearning form. But we are paying special attention to the changed job perceptions and cultural issues that this shift in learning could produce.

"By contrast, you can give one of our engineers a textbook and they will study it for fun on the weekend, so we give them straightforward access to the most accurate and reliable learning available – and hold the frills.

Why did you decide to use an ASP Model?

"When we created Nexxia in 1999, we had already spent Can$1 billion building a coast-to-coast IP network, so additional capital investment for an eLearning infrastructure just wasn't on the cards. Neither was hiring a large team of IT specialists to operate the system. We launched on *LearnTone* in four weeks with no up-front capital costs and started with a small team. Our costs increased only as our usage increased, so cost was easy to manage. As a true ASP service, all our back-end operations are outsourced to Sun, all hardware and software is dedicated to us and is covered by the monthly usage fee, and all software upgrades take place in the background. At the same time, we have complete control over the system and how it is used, and the application runs completely in a browser, so there is no client software to roll out."

How do you measure success?

"One of the most important ways is through our *Voice of the Client* program. We interview decision-makers and influencers throughout our client base regularly and develop a systematic action plan to improve service. One set of questions is about our customers' perceptions of how knowledgeable our account teams are. This gives us an idea of the success of our learning programs. We also use traditional assessment tests and other evaluation tools. This year, we are introducing a more comprehensive 360° assessment process related to learning.

"Because an LMS enables you to measure progress and courses taken, it forces a training organization to apply much more business rigor. This might be one reason why some training groups can feel threatened by it. Training departments can no longer say 'so many people went on courses,' but have to prove that they have a higher competency. However, it also gives you a lot of opportunities to excel.

Bell Nexxia is creating modules for handheld devices such as the Palm. Can you really learn over a handheld?

"You can, but we don't believe you can replace everything with a handheld, so we're using Palm and wireless devices in a very focused way. We want our salespeople to have product information at their fingertips when they are with a customer. We think this is an important niche where an investment in eLearning will have quick, short-term, high-impact wins. This avoids the hype in the industry.

"The Gartner Group has an interesting way of looking at hype. They call it a 'hype cycle', and it shows the effect of hype on different technologies as they mature. They have placed eLearning on this curve. In 2000 Gartner placed learning portals at the peak of inflated expectations. People thought that to create a successful learning portal you just built a website, threw a thousand courses on it and you were done. But there's so

Hype Cycle

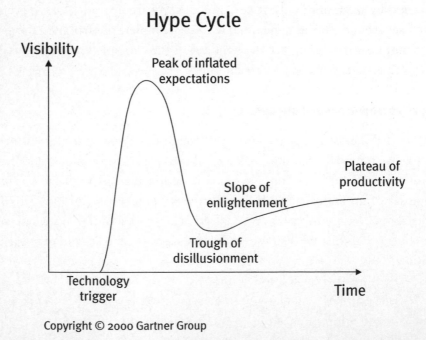

Copyright © 2000 Gartner Group

much more to it than that. We can't afford to be lured into this wasteful cycle – we put a lot of business rigor around our approach so we can be productive right away. We are not delivering on wireless just for the sake of it."

What are your predictions? Where do you think eLearning is going?

"Everyone makes predictions about eLearning, but nobody really knows what is going to happen in this industry. It's still too early. Many companies that would have claimed to be leaders two and a half years ago are nowhere to be found today. Recognizing this has shaped our eLearning approach, our technology strategy, and the advice we give our customers. So, our philosophy is to be as flexible as possible, and move quickly when things change.

"Flexibility is key to success. It is essential for the eLearning technology you select to be flexible and customizable. If the platform and software don't allow you to change your strategy, configuration, administrative options, and add new features all on short notice, you won't be able to move fast when you have to and you will be handicapped.

LESSONS FROM BELL NEXXIA

FLEXIBILITY Being ready for the unexpected is central to Bell Nexxia's thinking about eLearning. "No one really knows," where the market is going despite all the predictions about eLearning. Therefore, it is essential to ensure that whatever LMS is selected in an eLearning application, it allows for maximum flexibility.

EMBRACING AN ASP MODEL LAUNCHES YOU QUICKLY When embracing a new technology such as eLearning, you want to select an approach that will give you the most value with the least difficulty in implementation. To build corporate support for a new initiative you want to get quick wins.

FOCUS ON HIGH-VALUE NICHE APPLICATIONS Repeatedly, Menon focused on delivering niche applications that add high value. Early wins are important so that the training department gains credibility and can extend influence with eLearning across the whole organization. So, start small and when you hit a success like Sales-on-the-Run – run with it.

ELearning, as Menon calls it, is a "try and buy" solution. Nexxia started small and grew. They began by focusing on 500 salespeople and will now be providing eLearning for 7,000 BCE employees by the end of 2001.

OPEN SYSTEM   Bell Nexxia's LMS is open so that off-the-shelf courseware from other vendors such as Global Knowledge and CDI can run on it.

FOCUS ON THE WHOLE VALUE CHAIN   Bell Nexxia began by focusing internally but is now delivering eLearning systems to its customers, as well as bringing customers onto its own system. This helps customers and partners to transform their businesses, increase their success and serves as a profit center for the training and development department.

INTERVIEW WITH HEATHER MACPHERSON

Manager of Workplace Learning, Royal Bank of Canada

The Royal Bank is Canada's largest bank, serving 10 million customers in 30 countries. With $280 billion in assets in 2000, the Royal Bank has 48,000 employees.

"The case for eLearning has been built around reduced time and travel costs, consistency, just-in-time access, learner control and convenience. Other benefits include having a safe environment to practice new skills, optimal use of face time, measurement and reporting, speed and ease of updates, reach (scale), the availability of generic content, and the opportunity to integrate with Knowledge Management. But the greatest benefit in the long term will be moving beyond boundaries, the ability to keep people connected in a rapidly changing business world. As the pace of change accelerates, and face time diminishes, keeping people *connected*, not only to content but also to other people across organizational and geographic boundaries will become increasingly important."

What ROI analysis have you done on eLearning?

"I have a fundamental problem with the notion of reducing return on learning investments to a simple formula. Learning does not exist in isolation, nor do we want it to. We're going to great lengths to integrate learning with work. Learning is only one piece of the puzzle, and without looking at performance holistically, investments in learning, *e-* or otherwise, will have limited impact. If you do look at performance holistically, you can see that trying to isolate the portion of outcomes that could be directly attributed to learning would be a meaningless exercise. It's akin to trying to isolate the contribution of carrots to a good vegetable soup. What's more meaningful is to build in appropriate feedback loops to make sure you are getting to the desired outcomes, and to enable you to make in-course adjustments as appropriate. Various aspects of eLearning can contribute to this goal."

Is eLearning essential?

"Yes, we have a huge distributed workforce: some 50,000 employees, scattered among 1,400 domestic locations and 30 countries. We also have more non-traditional work arrangements than any other company in Canada, and these employees need to be just as capable as their regular full-time counterparts. We have to help our workforce learn at least as fast as the pace of change in the world around us. But doing what we've always done, only faster won't get us there. The time it takes to design, develop and deliver training using traditional methods means that messages can be obsolete by the time they reach the target audience. We have to provide access to high quality learning, where, when and as often as our employees need it."

What are the opportunity costs of not embracing eLearning?

"Companies that don't embrace eLearning will have more trouble in attracting and retaining talent. Their customer service will suffer, and they run the risk that customers will have information faster than employees. Disseminating key messages will be slow, thus limiting the organization's capacity to implement change.

"I remember in the old days, struggling to find a way to get thousands of bankers up to speed on several new mortgage products that were being launched simultaneously because the advertising campaigns were all in place. We had to train a number of trainers, who in turn had to schedule workshops that could accommodate all the personal bankers within a one week period. Each individual had to be taken away from his or her regular duties for at least a half day, without disrupting customer service. It was an enormous challenge. Today, we could reach all those personal bankers virtually at once, without anyone having to leave their desks! We could also be comfortable that they were all receiving consistent messages, and we could confirm that they understood those messages. Without eLearning, employees in remote areas could be disadvantaged in terms of their opportunities for advancement and their ability to provide excellent customer service. We want customers in rural Saskatchewan to have the same quality of service as those in downtown Toronto.

"eLearning is not just about organizations trying to do more with less, faster. Employees' expectations about workplace technology are also rising. Many, particularly those with school age children, have access to advanced technology at home, and may be frustrated if their workplace technology does not keep pace. I think organizations that resist this trend, will pay the price in terms of not being able to retain those employees."

Classroom days have fallen from 100,000 in 1995 to 20,000 in 2001. What has been substituted?

"Various forms of workplace learning, including but not limited to eLearning. We really stress coaching and informal learning, much of which doesn't include technology at all. Things like varying work assignments, learning by experimenting, weekly team meetings, project debriefs, mentoring – a number of strategies which there is no practical way to measure."

What are the resistors to eLearning?

"I think that the biggest barriers probably relate to perceptions, assumptions and experiences. People who have not tried it, or who have had a negative experience may underestimate the possibilities. Conversely, those who've had a positive experience sometimes view eLearning as a panacea. Both extremes are problematic.

"There are misconceptions about upfront costs. As long as you have web access you can jump into the game. The ASP model is relatively low cost.

"Another issue is information overload. The industry is changing so quickly that people are intimidated and they don't know where to start. To avoid making mistakes, they wait . . .

"Another barrier is the time for learning. Today's business environment is relentlessly focused on efficiency and productivity, and this is reinforced through reward systems. So, even though we understand that continuous learning is important, there's very little patience for taking time away from doing "the work". Unless learning is viewed as an integral part of the job and work, it probably won't receive sufficient attention. When you go to a traditional workshop, you are out of the office. It's protected time, and people are less likely to bother you because you're not there. But if you are sitting at our desk working on an eLearning module, customers arrive, co-workers interrupt, the phone rings. Depending on what you're working on, this may not be an effective learning environment. Notwithstanding the convenience factor of desktop learning, there may also be a role for a private area and/or protected time where employees can escape interruptions to focus on learning for longer periods, or to work on modules that require more privacy.

"In the early days traditional trainers perceived eLearning would make them redundant. However, that need not be the case. Their roles will be very different when effectively integrated with eLearning, but potentially much richer. Facilitators won't be regurgitating content, but instead focusing on the deeper learning: coaching participants and problem solving (whether it's face-to-face or virtual).

"Some have resisted eLearning because they like the social interaction during the workshop breaks and lunch. They incorrectly assume that it can't take place with eLearning. For me, taking an online MBA at Athabasca University was one of the richest learning experiences I've ever had. I was interacting with other business people who had on average 15 to 20 years experience. The richness of the dialogue was incredible. I developed enduring relationships, and still keep in touch with many of the people."

How do trainers have to change their roles?

"Rather than creating a controlled environment for learning, trainers need to help learners integrate learning with their work, as well as help them recognize opportunities to learn *from* their work and from each other. Learning needs to be treated as a process instead of a training event. Facilitators need to move from being a 'sage on the stage' during a training event, to being a 'guide on the side' throughout the learning process. This means integrating and leveraging activities, tools and opportunities that exist in an *e*-environment, as well as more traditional ones. It also means that 'facilitators' need not be training experts; sometimes the facilitator will be a manager or peer."

What mindsets do trainers have to change?

1. They need to experience the technology. Experience is the best teacher. Those who are trying to facilitate in an online environment without having experienced it may have a rude awakening.
2. Training can't be isolated – learning has to be integrated into work. Facilitation needs to go beyond one and two day courses. The class isn't over when you go back to your desk. Coaching becomes a big part of the game. Some online facilitators remark that it takes more of their time rather than less, because they get more involved with the learners.
3. Learner control is paramount. A particular course may be six hours long, but if an individual only needs one hour of it and has the option to stop, then that's an enormous savings. Those who want to learn more about a certain aspect, should have that option. Those who need to spend more time repeating a certain section should also be encouraged to do so.

LESSONS FROM THE ROYAL BANK

RICHER NOT REDUNDANT ROLES FOR FACILITATORS   In eLearning facilitators don't need to regurgitate content, but instead focus on the deeper learning: coaching participants and problem solving (whether it's face-to-face or virtual). This requires new skills for facilitators. Rather than eliminating facilitation time, eLearning may increase it, while making the role more challenging and rewarding.

SOCIAL INTERACTION CAN BE RICHER   Some have resisted eLearning because they like the social interaction during the breaks and lunch at a workshop. They incorrectly assume that it can't take place in an eLearning environment. Others who have experienced it say the level and type of interaction can actually be richer than in traditional settings. To the extent that people-to-people (and particularly learner-to-learner) interaction is supported, eLearning will be a more effective and satisfying experience.

INTERVIEW WITH OMID HODAIE

Canadian Executive Vice President, Sun Microsystems

In mid 2001, Sun Microsystems Inc. acquired ISOPIA Inc., a leading provider of open, flexible Java Beans based Learning Management Systems. Following the acquisition, Omid Hodaie, President and CEO of ISOPIA, was appointed Canadian Executive Vice President of Sun Microsystems.

Why are companies embracing eLearning?

"There are two reasons; the most significant is to advance their primary business goals – whether that is acquiring new markets or growing their market share. It's all to do with growing the top line. When eLearning started it was seen as a way to primarily reduce costs. More than 50 percent of traditional training and development costs are travel and accommodation. So when eLearning was first instituted the primary focus was to focus on the bottom line – make training and development more cost effective. Depending on whether the economic cycle is up or down – the reason switches between the two."

What differentiates Sun's LMS from those of other vendors?

"Five advantages stem from the fundamental difference that our product is based on the most advanced, open and scalable technology. When we selected the technology to base our system on, all our competition had based their products on traditional client–server architecture. The founder of ISOPIA chose to build our LMS on the latest, pure Internet architecture. So that results in the following differentiators:

1. **Our product scales significantly more than competitors' products.** This is important because the traditional training and development enterprise was limited to physical location and concerned employees. Companies are now dealing with an extended, connected enterprise that extends all the way to customers, channel and business partners. So in the past the challenge was the thousands or tens of thousands of employees that the company has – it now translates into millions of learners. Because for each employee there are thousands of partners and customers, so scalability in the Internet world, in the extended, connected enterprise world, is essential.

2. **Our product is very open and easily connects to existing corporate systems,** such as the human resource system, ERP (financial), or front office applications such as CRM (Customer Relationship Management). An LMS can't be an isolated island, it must interconnect to be successful. The Java technology we have used allows for that openness and interconnectivity.

3. **Our architecture is very flexible – introducing new features doesn't require re-architecting the product.** It's highly modular – because we use enterprise Java beans. That's very important because no LMS vendor can prophesize what the market will need 18 months from now. The challenge is not whether you have the right features at this very minute, the challenge is, "which LMS vendors have enough flexibility in their products to quickly deliver what emerging markets need?" It's not just for the features, but the ability to quickly change existing ones.

4. **Our product is based 100 percent on open standards – XML, Java.** Therefore it is much easier for the customer to make modifications themselves without having to rely on Sun. Standards-based, open products are easier for the customer to implement, update and modify.

5. **Reliability.** In contrast to all other LMS vendors, we can run our product on any platform – NT, Unix, and can scale up to IBM mainframe-class servers. We can start with a small application for a first time customer at the departmental level and scale all the way up to an enterprise wide application.

"In addition, ISOPIA pioneered the Application Service Provider (ASP) model in the eLearning market – where a company can rent or lease the application. A lot of LMS vendors are now starting to talk about their ASP offerings. But the traditional ASP model is one to many – where there is one template and everyone has to fit that template. We offer a 1:1 ASP model. Because we have such a flexible platform, each of our *LearnTone* implementations is unique and customized to their particular requirements."

What differentiates Sun's business model?

"Enterprises seeking to build a well-managed learning environment are being met by challenges posed by a highly fragmented industry.

"The different offerings available in the eLearning market have created confusion for consumers. When issuing RFPs, consumers are getting responses that completely vary from vendor to vendor – not just variation in LMS functionality, but in the level of consulting services, content compatibility and skills management. The permutations and combinations of these elements are virtually infinite in scope and daunting even to the most seasoned decision makers.

"Tired of dealing with multiple suppliers, clients are seeking clarity in this space; they are looking for an all-encompassing solution. With its acquisition of ISOPIA, Sun emerges as a leader in this space, providing the first, complete, viable end-to-end eLearning solution."

The greatest ROI isn't reduced travel it's in learner control. Dell learners access all the information they need in 67 percent less time than traditional in-class learning. Comments?

"eLearning is fantastic at personalization. There are two categories of personalization – one is the personalization of the training content – which is what Dell is talking about – the movement towards object oriented learning components. Then there is personalization in the way you administer and manage your own learning – which is the way you would personally build a curriculum for yourself. That way course catalogues are personalized for you, given your job function and that way you can close your skills gaps."

How does eLearning make training more strategic?

"The way in which business units apply eLearning to further their business goals is what makes it strategic. For instance, in the field of certification and accreditation in the field IT training, companies like Compaq, Sun, Microsoft or Cisco – one of greatest impediments to their long-term growth is lack of certified, accredited software engineers (SEs) in their products and technologies. That's why you see them investing billions in companies like Cap Gemini, Ernst and Young and KPMG. eLearning not only helps to determine who is certified, but increases the number of certified SEs. That is extremely strategic. This is just one example, it all comes down to how eLearning is applied. If a company is applying eLearning just to save travel costs that is not strategic. But if you are using eLearning to train the channel to increase market share and better serve customers, then that is strategic."

Cisco gets double and triple ROI on eLearning compared to in-class learning because what is developed for customers can also be used for the channel and employees, and what is developed for employees can also be used to train the channel. Any comments?

"This is why scalability is such a key factor. As organizations apply eLearning this way the magnitude, the scale that a single system needs to be able to grow to is multiple orders of magnitude greater than employee training. That is why scalability is our number one differentiator at Sun."

What are the key resistors to eLearning adoption?

"The largest challenge is implementation.

"Most customers underestimate the amount of time and effort for implementation. Even though we have an ASP model, we still has to integrate with other systems – such as PeopleSoft. ASP doesn't eliminate all implementation challenges – just reduces them. We may take it for granted all the business units need to be connected to the corporate network, and to have baseline browsers. And there's a lot of culture change required. Some departments refuse to come on board. These are change management issues."

Up to 70 percent of the cost of an LMS is in implementation, given that you follow the ASP model, doesn't that favor you?

"An ASP implementation takes place over a platform that's already implemented. And people doing the implementation do it for a living. Obviously that's very different than, a bank bringing in its IT department – who has never implemented an LMS before. So implementation of the ASP model is quick by comparison to buying a system."

How easy is it to modify the product without having to rely entirely on the vendor?

"We have opened up the entire learner interface in our new release – 3.0 – by publishing all the APIs (application program interfaces) – so that any partner, customer or Sun's Education Consulting Services can make modifications. This is a first of a kind where an LMS vendor has opened their product to the world."

What is the optimum eLearning course length?

"With live synchronous courses we have found the longest a course can be is 1.5–2 hours and involve 13–15 participants with lots of interactivity. With self-paced courses, half an hour is the maximum."

How do training professionals have to change their roles?

"Our experience is limited to larger companies. As opposed to centrally organizing and undertaking all the course creation, the focus should be on underlying methodologies, standards and LMS infrastructure. The business units or lines of business follow that framework but have distributed ownership of the content."

LESSONS FROM SUN MICROSYSTEMS

TIME-TO-COMPETENCE For fast growing companies like Sun, Microsoft or Cisco the greatest impediments to their long-term growth is lack of certified, accredited software engineers (SEs) in their products and technologies. ELearning is a key strategy to grow the whole category.

OPEN PRODUCT By publishing APIs Sun is letting customers or partners customize the product completely without being dependent on the vendor. By using industry standards it means the skills are more prevalent.

ELEARNING REQUIRES CHANGED ATTITUDES

eLearning offers exponentially more value to organizations than traditional training, but to achieve this value, a number of traditional mindsets, attitudes and assumptions have to change.

1. ELIMINATE BARRIERS Eliminate the mental difference between employees, partners and customers. In other words, open the Kimono. What employees are interested in learning the same subject areas as staff in partner companies, and customers? By providing internal course content externally, companies get triple the return on their investment. And more importantly it speeds up the adoption of the company's products or services. It's an expanded view of the market. It broadens the reach of training and development and raises it to a strategic role it has never had before.

2. SCALING INTELLECTUAL ASSETS Oracle has 700 instructors worldwide who are experts in teaching complex knowledge in simple ways. The company also has thousands of subject experts who have deep technical knowledge. In the past, the way Oracle scaled that knowledge was by pairing a trainer with a content expert and together the pair produced a training program, piloted it, got feedback, refined it, finalized the program, and then began training-the-trainer. Trainers would then train classes of 25 people at a time over the a week. For a company like Oracle running a new program for all 43,000 employees in 100 countries would take years and trainers would spend 30–50 weeks a year on the road. Traditional training doesn't scale quickly. The only way to do so is to add more trainers, which exponentially increase costs and reduces consistency. How do you identify key experts and then scale their knowledge across the whole organization in real time?

> Faced with the choice between changing one's mind and proving that there is no need to change . . . almost everyone gets busy on the proof.
> *John Kenneth Galbraith*

3. LEARNER CENTRIC eLearning gives learners control over how they best learn, when they learn, where they learn.

4. COMPETENCY BASED Education, especially higher education, currently focuses on inputs not outputs. Input mindset says, you have to take these courses, at this location, from these instructors, for this amount of time in order to be qualified (i.e. four years at university). But education should be based on competence, not time. What takes one individual four weeks to learn may only take another four days. Why then measure education in time? In response to the absence of competence-based education, private industry creates its own competency standards. So for instance, Microsoft created the Microsoft Certified Systems Engineer (MCSE) – defined what being competent meant, and then set up a curriculum to help people achieve it. Today professional certifications such as MCSE have as much if not more value in the market than a traditional bachelors degree. Students are given the freedom to reach that competency any way they want.

> As long as trainees are happy and do not complain, trainers feel comfortable, relaxed and secure.
> *Donald Kirkpatrick*

5. CHALLENGE THE "NOT INVENTED HERE SYNDROME" Training and development departments have to ask "What is our unique competence?" Most companies that have embraced eLearning outsource standard "off-the-shelf" training and focus on unique areas of knowledge, learning and core competence within the company.

6. MEASUREMENT Measuring the effectiveness of training has always been time consuming, expensive, and something trainers have not consistently done.[22] eLearning automates much of the process and cuts the cost of managing measurement by up to 90 percent – making ROI analysis easier and effectively proving the value of training.

I used to represent Dr Stephen R. Covey in Canada teaching *The Seven Habits of Highly Effective People* to Canadian clients. We used to sell 360-degree feedback to companies at a cost of US$175 per person. We would send eight questionnaires to the individual who would distribute one to his boss, two or three to peers, four or five to direct reports and fill out one himself. Each individual would have a pre-addressed, stamped envelope to mail them back to Provo, Utah. Frequently you had to chase people to fill in their form, forms would occasionally get lost, but eventually the data would all be keyed into the system, averaged and a report generated. It was a very labor-intensive process. Online 360 evaluations reduce costs by up to 90 percent and the whole process takes days not weeks or months.

The training department, like any other department, exists to serve the overall corporate mission. Programs must be designed to meet corporate objectives, including increasing new product innovation, team performance, creativity, sales, quality and/or customer satisfaction and decreasing costs. Creating an ROI is increasingly the aim and justification of any training investment. Given the significant drop in cost associated with measurement, trainers can increasingly prove their value to the organization, thereby graining credibility and status within the organization.

7. IT'S NOT EITHER/OR, IT'S AND People think in polar opposites. It's either black or white. It's either all classroom or all eLearning. And the answer is it's neither, it's And. Over time training organizations will move to hybrid or blended models where online tools are used in class and in-class design philosophies are used online.

In traditional training people arrive in the class with all different levels of experience. So if the trainer sets the pace for the leaders, the least experienced will be left behind. And if the trainer sets the pace for the least experienced, the most experienced will be bored. So no matter what the facilitator does, the training will not be optimal.

Over time companies will mix online learning with in-class training to create hybrid forms of learning. For instance, in order to optimize in-class training, participants could be tested online. Those who don't meet a pre-set minimum level of understanding will have online work to bring them up to speed in order to attend the in-class portion. In-class learning will be more effective as everyone taking the class will have a common basis of knowledge.

8. LEARNING IS NOT A SERIES OF EVENTS – IT'S A CONTINUOUS PROCESS.
Our current mindset is that real learning only happens in class and in three to five day events. If that were the case we would see children naturally forming into lines in the school playground. Children learn on a need to know basis – as their curiosity drives them. eLearning offers the

same promise – to granulize learning into small objects that we use seamlessly in our daily work lives.

9. "IF CONTENT IS KING, INFRASTRUCTURE IS GOD," according to Cisco. The infrastructure plays a more significant role than people may imagine. The infrastructure for running your eLearning applications should be open, non-proprietary and allow you to offer off-the-shelf courseware from a wide variety of providers.

10. ONLINE LEARNING CHANGES THE ROLE OF THE TEACHER. The teacher or trainer's new role requires a shift in mindset. Instead of being a sage on the stage, the online teacher take on more of a role as a mentor or a coach, where they challenge students and direct them to the best resources to learn. It requires giving up the illusion that one person can have all the answers or knowledge. The new role is not easier and traditional faculty doesn't want to do it.

RESISTORS TO IMPLEMENTING ELEARNING

1. **Fear of training and development experts will lose their jobs.** This has proven not to be the case – as evidence by Cisco's experience. But training professionals do have to learn new skills and change their roles. It strikes me as funny that the profession that talks so much about learning and change is perhaps the most resistant to it when it affects them personally! The need to learn and understand remains the same – but training and development professionals will have to redefine their entire role and function.

2. **Interdepartmental non-cooperation and budgeting between departments.** Large cost savings associated with eLearning are on the delivery side (50–70 percent less cost due to travel and accommodation, 25–60 percent shorter learning times and lower opportunities costs because staff can spend more time selling) and accrue to the client department not the

> We must bear in mind, then, that there is nothing more difficult and dangerous, or more doubtful of success, than an attempt to introduce a new order of things in any state. For the innovator has for enemies all those who derived advantages from the old order of things, whilst those who expect to be benefited by the new institutions will be but lukewarm defenders.
> *Nicolo Machiavelli*

training department. By contrast, development costs of eLearning has been estimated to be three times as great as classroom learning but the experience from Cisco pegs the number at 20–40 percent more. So training and development may have to increase spending while the client department experiences huge savings. To be effective, training and development professionals must reach across department silos and build the business case with counterparts in line functions.

3. **Lack of business case study/justification.** It is only by tying training to level 4 evaluation that training and development professionals will become more strategic.

4. **Not interactive enough.** eLearning has to be far more interactive than training has ever been in the past. It is a new medium. It has new rules.

5. **Immediate help.** When a learner is learning online wherever possible there should be the option for immediate help. An icon that one can click on and interact with a live trainer, or fellow student. Over time this will emerge. If this is not available, due to learning asynchronously, students should have to have the ability to go to threaded discussions, or ask questions by email.

6. **Who is closest to the future, the 65-year-old CEO who doesn't know how to turn on the computer or the 18-year-old who surfs the web every night?** Who does all the strategic planning? Who is most disenfranchised from strategic planning? Is it any wonder we only get incremental change in most organizations?

ELEARNING DESIGN

KEEP IT SHORT   While online courses can run longer, individual segments should be no longer that 20 minutes long in Cisco's opinion and 10 minutes in Dell's. Assume your audience has Attention Deficit Disorder (ADD).

BUILD AN ONLINE ORIENTATION   that new eLearners take prior to their first learning experience. The first lesson an online learner takes should be how to learn online. Studies show that if learners get through three eLearning interactions they will be eLearners for life. Different vendors have different navigation methods – therefore if a learner is taking a course from a new vendor online – it should include a brief, no more than 2-minute outline on how to navigate in this course. One eLearning professional suggested there should be a quick two minute recap at the start of every lesson. The focus is on training the learner.

ENSURE THERE ARE TOOLS TO PUT A NEW ELEARNER IN TOUCH WITH ANOTHER LIVE E- LEARNER Especially in the first use of eLearning people need to be able to reach out to others. This could be a support person who supports all eLearning that is going on continuously. One company lets eLearners see who recently in their area or building has taken the same or similar course to enable 1:1 face-to-face informal mentoring. Another company opposed doing this because those who have just taken courses may not want to be mentors. With eLearning, after a course the participants can morph the class into support clinics. There is no abrupt ending to the process as with typical in-class learning.

MIX UP THE MEDIUM Video, audio, quick quizzes, exercises, hands-on labs, chat with other students, online community.

Barriers to eLearning

1. **Some 60–70 percent of the costs of an LMS are in implementation.** That is why there has been such a rapid growth in the Application Service Provider (ASP) model, which offers a turnkey solution. Everything is browser based. There is no hardware to buy, no software to install either on the client end or the on IT department's servers. No consultants to engage. It is the ASP's responsibility to maintain the application through software upgrades, so the client doesn't have to worry if their data migrates smoothly.
2. **Savings roll up to organization: not any one department.** Training professionals have to get buy in from senior management for eLearning. And even though there are tremendous cost savings with eLearning there are nonetheless start up costs. Sometimes the department realizing the savings or the upside potential is not the same as the one making the investment, which means cross functional barriers or silos have to be broken down – and the decision has to be made at a senior level.

3. **eLearning is often criticized for not fostering collaboration** but in reality well-designed eLearning offers more collaboration between students and between students and faculty. ELearning course designers have to specifically focus on this to encourage it. In a normal class a few students will dominate the group – on the Internet, these social barriers don't exist. Shy people are just as participative. Another benefit is that knowledge is documented and captured in a threaded discussion. The learning process is self-documenting.

4. **Putting training people in charge of eLearning.** "With 40 years of training people are often put in charge of eLearning," notes Tom Kelly. "It's like having the Postal service in charge of email. Not only is it counter intuitive to what they do but shakes to the foundation how they have evaluated themselves and their work." In Kelly's opinion the ideal training and development professionals are business people doing training instead of education people trying to figure out the business world. That is a hard shift for people in the field.

5. **Learning time not respected.** When you take a traditional course you are out of the office for the day. But with eLearning you may be taking a course at your desk, and people will interrupt you. You may be reading a book, watching a video across the net – and others will think 'What's he doing?' They don't perceive it as work and you look highly interruptible. How can you stop people from interrupting the learner? Finally I hit upon the idea of distributing 2–3 feet of police crime scene tape – that said 'learning in progress.' And we taped that up across the cubicle opening. That was critical because it stopped the interruptions and made the learner focus.

eLearning's impact on society

Nuala Beck coined the phrase 'new economy' and has documented how more people work in the software industry as a whole than in the auto, auto parts, steel, mining and petroleum-refining industries combined. Even the movie industry employs more people than all of the auto industry.[23] The nations that have the highest levels of general education are the ones that will have the fastest growing economies. We really have entered the learning economy.

Is higher education capable of responding to the challenge of eLearning?

While there are a number of innovative universities and colleges, the vast majority has not embraced the new potential of eLearning. At a recent presentation on eLearning, a faculty Dean commented, 'it's easier to move a grave yard than a curriculum is true!' Higher education is not responding fast enough.

SUMMARY OF LMS VENDOR SELECTION CRITERIA

1. **Open standards**
- **Authoring tools neutral:** so that courses can run on the platform regardless of the tools they are authored in.
- **Vendor neutral:** So that courses will run on the LMS regardless the company that produced them.
- **Browser neutral:** so that it will run on either *Microsoft IE* or *Netscape Navigator.*
- **Platform neutral:** so that it will run on any operating system and hardware.
- Industry standard plug ins

2. **Scalability:** Can the system scale from one to a 1,000,000 users?
3. **ASP model:** Begin small. eLearning is a try-and-buy application.

BUSINESS CONTEXT DRIVING ELEARNING

There are a number of factors that are driving the adoption of eLearning.

Competition for talent

Currently there is a shortage of over 720,000 IT workers in North America – and this shortage is growing by 25 percent a year. Globally the shortage exceeds one million IT workers. How can companies compete in the war for talent? eLearning will explode in part because time-to-competence has become a bottleneck for most organizations. How can companies accelerate learning?

A staggering 70 percent of *Fortune 1000* CEOs say that finding and keeping qualified people was the number one barrier to sustaining growth, according to a PriceWaterhouseCoopers study! Never before has human capital been so important. Finding, developing and keeping knowledgeable workers will be the key to success and growth. Any strategies that will shorten the time-to-competence – the amount of time required to get up to speed in hot skill areas will be rapidly embraced.

Information overload

The exponential growth of information is staggering. It is now estimated that there are over 550 billion web pages![24] Information available across the web is doubling every 2.8 years.[25] There will be more books published in this decade than all books ever published prior to 1900! On an average day in 1998, three billion non-spam email messages were sent worldwide. By 2000, the figure had risen to 10 billion emails a day worldwide and by 2005 it is predicted to grow to 35 billion emails a day.[26] By the end of 2001 there will be over one billion email boxes.[27]

> The paradox of our times is that we are inundated with information yet starved for knowledge.
> *William R. Brody,*
> *President, John Hopkins University*

Even within companies information overload can be overwhelming. Oracle for instance, has over 10 million web pages on its Intranet. When you want to find something where do you start? Individuals and organizations need to have better tools for instantly finding the right information at the time it is needed.

Online explosion

International Data Corporate (IDC) estimated that there were 38 million individuals connected to the Internet in 1996.[28] By 1998, the number of users had increased to 97 million.[29] In the US alone, IDC forecasts Internet users will grow to 158 million active users by 2003 – 60 percent of the population – up from just 15 percent in 1996. Worldwide the number will grow to 320 million in 2003.

Need for speed

High-speed Internet access is a significant driver of online growth. A study conducted by MediaOne noted that in Boston, households with cable Internet connections averaged 22.5 hours of online usage per week, versus just 4.7 hours for those households with a dial-up connection.[30] Cable users connected to the Internet surf ten times more than their dial-up counterparts. A *Wall Street Journal* survey confirmed that speed is the primary factor determining time online: 65 percent of respondents said that increased speed would increase usage.[31] Broadband transmission is expected to grow from roughly one million households in North America to almost 26 million by 2003. This will enable the rich interactivity that will drive eLearning adoption.

> Learning is the only sustainable competitive advantage.
> *Arie de Geus, former head of planning, Royal Dutch Shell*

E-commerce

Revenue from business-to-consumer (B2C) e-commerce will grow to $454 billion in 2004. Business-to-business (B2B) e-commerce will expand to $6.3 trillion in 2004. Worldwide, total e-commerce will grow to $6.78 trillion by 2004, according to Forrester Research.[32]

Business challenges

Mergers and acquisitions mean that the competitive landscape can change overnight. New technologies mean whole industries can be blindsided – witness Shawn Fanning's Napster threat to decimate the profitability of the $40 billion music recording industry. With information overload, the explosion of new technologies, how can leaders cope? Clearly the old ways aren't working. Amid the confusion, chaos and complexity, what solutions will strike at the root cause of the problem as opposed to symptomatic issues?

Managing intellectual capital

Learning Management Systems (LMS) naturally lead into the whole field of Knowledge Management and Knowledge Management Systems (KMS).

A KMS is a way to inventory and track the knowledge assets within an organization.

I predict that by 2010 Wall Street will demand companies implement LMS and KMS systems in order to track the real value of new economy assets in companies.

Retooling and retraining in real time

With so much change occurring so quickly – how can individuals and organizations keep up with the speed and volume of change? In the fast-changing world of high-tech employees need 12 days of training every year just to stay current. That is predicted to grow to 32 days a year by 2010.[33] Companies like Cisco, Nortel Networks and Bell Nexxia introduce new products every 45 days – and these products have a life cycle of only nine months before they are substantially changed or re-launched. A traditional training program will take a year to develop, pilot, test, refine and roll out to thousands of people across the organization in hundreds of different locations. If your product life cycle is nine months and your training cycle is a year it's a recipe for disaster. eLearning has been able to shorten training program development, launch and completed roll-out to weeks. The need for companies to get employees up-to-speed faster, has resulted in two new concepts – and hence newly coined phrases[34] – just-in-time learning and time-to-competence. How can companies provide just the information that is needed, when it is needed, to whoever needs it? Bell Nexxia calls it sales-on-the-run.

Value of time in time based competition

My body works in real time – which means if I stick my finger in ice water I know instantly that it is cold. But few organizations work in real time. Most companies have quarterly sales reports, annual employee reviews, and training and development initiatives that take a year to roll out. Well, imagine my body worked the way an organization does! Imagine I only got biofeedback once a quarter – how well would I thrive? Or, if I could only change direction after the roll out of a yearlong training program. We don't know what we don't know. If you have never used a telephone how can you understand the benefit of phones? If you have never used email how can you appreciate its significance? If you have never worked with real time training how can you appreciate its power?

When I need to know something I am often frustrated because I don't have the time to take a course. I only need to learn one small thing – so instead I soldier through my frustration and perform sub optimally. By the time I do get around to taking a course I have forgotten the long list of little things that I need to learn. ELearning will change all this so that I can learn in real time tied to need.

Overview

Because of this context, and the benefits of eLearning, the question is not *whether* organizations will implement eLearning but *when*? Learning will become strategic. Executives and organizations will have to change a number of assumptions or 'paradigms' if they are to truly realize the full power and benefits of eLearning.

Speed is the defining characteristic of the digital world. Put simply organizations that do not embrace eLearning will no longer be able to keep up with their competitors that do. eLearning promises: Learn Anything, Anytime, Anywhere.

> The next big killer application for the Internet is going to be education. Education over the Internet is going to be so big it is going to make email usage look like a rounding error in terms of the Internet capacity it will consume.
> *John Chambers, Cisco Systems CEO*

THE LEARNING CONTEXT

Optimizing learning

How do we learn? What can be done to improve the rate of learning, the amount we retain? A fascinating study by the National Training Laboratory revealed that retention is greatly impacted by teaching method:

RETENTION BY TEACHING METHOD[35]

Lecture	5%
Reading	10
Audiovisual	20
Demonstration	30
Discussion group	50
Practice by doing	75
Teaching others	90

University based learning is predominantly by lecture – the most ineffective way to learn in terms of retention. Traditional corporate training has been largely lecture based. Good design will involve demonstration, discussion and examples – significantly increasing retention. Individuals have typically learned on their own through reading – the second most ineffective form of learning. eLearning by contrast involves streaming audio and video, as well as text, and asynchronous or synchronous interaction with other students and the teacher. By promoting far more interaction between students – eLearning can drive the highest retention. Therefore it begins with a base retention quadruple that of university, double that of self-study – and at least on par with well designed corporate training.

Challenge: the key to employee retention

Companies competing for employees in hot skill areas have learned that they must continually challenge people or risk losing them. This requires a greater commitment to training and development.

CONCLUSIONS

Companies used to embrace eLearning because of significant cost savings (up to 70 percent lower travel costs). While the savings still prevail, the reasons to embrace eLearning are far more strategic. Organizations cannot rapidly change without eLearning technology – either in responding to threats or taking advantage of opportunities.

Learning is becoming more strategic in capturing market share – by educating end users, as in the case of Cisco and Nortel's professional certification programs.

Finally by reaching out to everyone in the value chain – training departments are getting two and three times the ROI of traditional training because courses can be used for two to three different audiences once they are developed – at little or no incremental cost.

The question is not *whether* organizations will implement eLearning but *when*?

SUMMARY OF ELEARNING BENEFITS

Scalability

1. eLearning can scale from 25 to 1,000,000 learners in days instead of years with little or no incremental cost.
2. Organizations can leverage their greatest intellectual assets, taking the best teachers, visionaries, technical experts – and scale their knowledge across the whole organization instantly (Cisco's snare 'n share).
3. Learners adapt to eLearning quickly because it relies on open standards such as browser technology.

Velocity (increases speed, immediacy)

1. eLearning can take 20–67 percent less time than instructor-led, facilities based training.[36]
2. Pre course testing allows for the LMS to deliver only modules needed for learning.
3. Immediate access to information. The employee can access information and learn what they need 24/7 (Bell Nexxia 'sales on-the-run').
4. Increases organizational responsiveness. In a takeover battle, the CEO can address all employees every morning by streaming video when they log on.
5. Sales reps, within the company and at third party resellers, can learn about product features and benefits the day a new product or service launches.
6. Shortens cycle time for developing, releasing and rolling out training from years to weeks, or even days.
7. Instant updating of courses and information. So sales people can have

access to knowledge in real time. Content is more timely and more dependable so companies can compete in Internet time. Speed is an important dimension of quality.

8. Speed of finding information. Cisco makes no distinction between learning, training, informing or communicating. A good Learning Management System (LMS) and/or KMS helps people have information at their fingertips. So they can have 24/7 access to the information they need, when they need it.

9. Accelerates time-to-competence for employees.

Higher retention and educational value

1. The 48 hours 'use-it-or-lose-it' principle requires a shift from just-in-case to just-in-time education. When training is tied to deep need retention is infinitely higher.

2. Learning focused on outcomes not competence. With Bell Nexxia's Sales-on-the-Run – sales reps can access information they need when they need it, such as immediately before a sales call. This can measurably improve sales performance.

Unleashing organization capacity

The ability to learn faster than the competition is the only sustainable advantage. The most successful organizations are using LMS and KMS to connect, and unleash the power of their intellectual assets.

Learner centric, 1:1

1. Leaners control the interactions. They decide:
2. *What* to learn (objects)
3. *Where* to learn (office, home, Palm, MP3, cell phone)
4. *When* to learn (24/7)
5. *How* to learn (audio, video, text, classroom).
6. *At the pace* that is optimum for the learner.
7. Cisco has created completely customized, 1:1 learning approach using "My Future." Cisco's LMS presents course offerings to each individual based on their job, career aspirations, performance evaluation, boss' recommendations and their personal interests.

Builds community

1. Properly implemented eLearning significantly increases participant to participant interaction thus building community.
2. Documents and captures knowledge through threaded discussions – allowing for scaling of that knowledge.

Education as marketing

Corporate education has been aimed primarily at employees. But education is increasingly strategic – working to create demand among customers and in the value chain. Education becomes strategic in evangelizing new products and services within the market. Because of its scalability, eLearning doubles or triples the ROI of traditional in-class learning, allowing the training and development department to extend its reach and influence well beyond the boundaries of the traditional organization. This unleashes greater power within the value chain. What helps our partners, helps us.

Easy to document ROI

eLearning allows for instant and inexpensive evaluation of the effectiveness of learning.

Lower cost

1. Up to 70 percent of the cost of traditional training are travel and accommodation expenses. eLearning eliminates these costs.
2. The second largest cost of traditional training is the time away from work (opportunity cost). By breaking learning into the smallest possible elements – chunks or objects – learning can be interspersed throughout a business day – the same way we answer voice mail messages and emails. For example, staff at a call center could take courses when call volumes lag.
3. By using existing infrastructure – network and PCs – eLearning increases the RoIC – return on invested capital, especially the ASP model.
4. eLearning reduces training overhead – such as classrooms.
5. eLearning significantly lowers the cost of evaluation -- making ROI

analysis easier and more effectively proving the value of training and development.

CHAPTER 10

Keeping Customers; Exceeding Expectations

We've all heard about exceeding customer expectations and delighting the customer, but to really understand the importance of customer service we need to work through some basic questions: What is customer service? Why is it so important? How do we measure customer satisfaction? What proof is there that poor service has a negative impact on financial performance?

US researcher Jack Parr set out to discover how customers felt about a large, well-known American company's goods and services. He surveyed 6,000 customers. These were customers from a wide cross-section of industries and organizations.[1] His findings are typical of ratings for most companies.

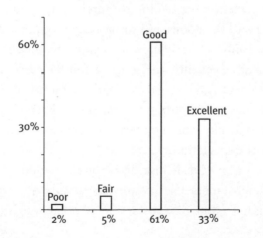

Customer satisfaction

Only 2 percent of the customers surveyed said goods and services were poor; 5 percent rated them fair; 60 percent said they were good and 33 percent reported they were excellent. Executives in most organizations would look at these results and say, "Great! A full 93 percent of our customers say our goods and services are good or excellent. Aren't we doing an amazing job? Why change anything? It's time for big executive bonuses around here!"

However, such a conclusion would have been premature. Customer responses to the next question, "How willing are you to purchase from the company again?" were staggering.

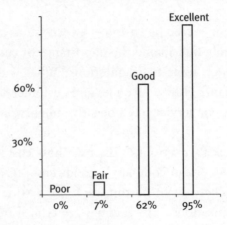

Willing to purchase again?

Of those who say they experienced poor goods and services, none wanted to be repeat customers. Of those who rated the goods and services fair, a mere 7 percent were willing to purchase from the company again. Of those who rated the goods and services as good, that is, acceptable but not impressive, only 62 percent were willing to purchase again! But of those who had an excellent experience, a full 95 percent were willing to be repeat customers. This research clearly demonstrates that the key to high-repeat business is delighting the customer. This is a typical finding in customer research. No wonder there's so much talk about the need to exceed customer expectations.

Such findings also reveal how disastrous it would be to consider the average customer satisfaction rating acceptable for any organization. Good is not good enough! Satisfaction is not enough. Delight is what we're after.

In the graph below, the first bar represents the percentage of customers who responded by rating the goods and services as poor, fair, good or excellent. The second is the number of retained customers in each category.

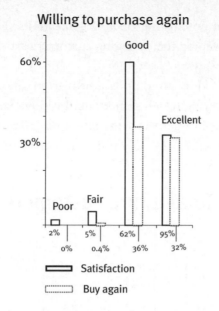

Willing to purchase again

No organization can keep all of its customers forever. The graph above shows that if an organization consistently offers excellent goods and services to its customers, it generally keeps them. However, companies that settle for average ratings will continuously lose significant numbers of customers. In fact, according to Parr's study, a company with an average customer satisfaction rating would keep only 68.8 percent of its customers after one business cycle. In the construction industry, a "cycle" may be many years, while in the grocery business, people shop every week. On the other hand, even if customer satisfaction is only "good," you may not lose customers if you have a convenient location and no competitors.

But in a fierce market where competitors are always improving, an average company must attract over 31 percent of its business from new customers every cycle just to maintain its revenue base! Good is not good enough.

> There is only one boss – the customer. And he can fire everybody in the company from the chairman on down, simply by spending his money somewhere else.
> *Sam Walton, founder, Wal-Mart*

The key to real growth in any business is customer retention. And the key to customer retention is continual improvement in products and services. This increases customer satisfaction and moves the bulk of customers from the good into the excellent category.

Studies show that it costs five times as much to attract a new customer as it does to retain an existing one. Organizations should put five times more effort into keeping their existing customers satisfied than into prospecting for new business.

But very few do. How often do you hear from salespeople? Every day I hear from people trying to sell something. I receive faxes, letters and brochures. How often do I get the same attention from the people I already do business with? Usually, the only time I hear from my suppliers is when I receive an invoice in the mail.

Total future customers

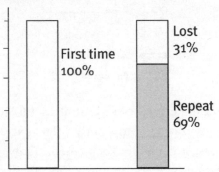

WHAT DETERMINES EXCELLENCE IN CUSTOMER SATISFACTION?

Perception is reality in the eye of the beholder. Executives need to perceive customer service as the customer does.

What is excellent service? Contrast these two examples:

Studies show that on average only one in five dissatisfied customers will complain directly, even if you provide a 1-800 telephone number. *Customer research studies*

After buying a computer and carting it home, I found that it didn't work. I called the store and was told to bring it back in. So I brought all the boxes up from the basement, repackaged everything and drove back to the store. Of course, the nearest parking spot was two and a half blocks from the store, so I lugged the boxes back into the store one at a time. The sales rep greeted me with the news:

"It has to go to the wholesaler, who will send it to the repair depot. We'll have it back for you in two to four weeks. We'll call you when it's in."

This was done with an "I'm-really-going-out-of-my-way-for-you-and-you-should-thank-me-for-this-great-service-I'm-giving-you" attitude.

"Well, what do I do for a computer in the meantime?"

"I'm sorry, sir, it's the manufacturer's fault. We aren't responsible," the salesperson said.

"But I bought it from you," I pleaded.

"Well, sir, I'm afraid it's the manufacturer's warranty. I'll see if I can get them to speed up the process."

When customers do complain, company representatives explain why things are the way they are in such a way that customers end up feeling guilty or stupid. Most people feel that it is pointless to complain. Why bother? This explains why only one in five dissatisfied customers actually do complain. Complaints offer a golden opportunity to discover new products or services that the company can offer to customers.

Now compare my experience with that of a friend who purchased a notebook computer from Dell Computer. The day after he bought it, he noticed that one of the plastic clasps that allows the screen to flip up was broken. The notebook worked fine, it was just cosmetic damage. He called Dell. The next morning a Dell representative was at his office with a brand-new notebook.

From these two examples it's easy to identify which company designed its service policies with the interests of the customer in mind and which company will get repeat business.

WHY NOT ASK?

Every quarter Dell computer hosts the Dell Platinum Council – where the company invites 100 representatives from its best customers for a multi day offsite seminar on future trends in computing. At the event Dell shares its' vision of where the market is moving – brings in industry experts and analysts, and shares with its clients its strategy for lowering the cost of ownership of computers.

At the event there is a 1:1 ratio of Dell employees to customers – and there are representatives from every Dell department – accounting, engineering design, customer service, call centers, shipping and logistics, etc.

At the meetings Dell employees listen to what it is that customers are saying.

It was at one of these Platinum Councils that Dell design engineers learned some surprising facts. Dell's biggest customer said, "The way you design computers is really pissing us off!" In complete surprise, the design engineers asked, "What do you mean?"

"Well, what you think we want is faster computers. So this quarter you ship us computers with ATI cards because they're the fastest. Next quarter there's an S3 card that's faster and the quarter after that there's a Diamond Viper card that's the fastest. And it's the same with hard disks. So after buying computers from you for four years we are supporting ten different kinds of video cards, 10 different kinds of hard disks. You are driving up our support costs exponentially and we hate it! You know we've really don't care whether a computer is five percent faster or three percent slower what we care about his consistency, backwards compatibility, stability of the network, reliability, ease of support, and lowering the total cost of ownership of PCs."

This was a stunning revelation for design engineers. If you ask an computer design engineer or a techie, "What's the best possible computer?" They'll always say, "The fastest." In fact in 2000, Dell ran a print ad in which a guy was sitting in front of his Dell computer. Underneath the image was a question, "How fast does your computer have to be?" The answer: "Faster than Bob's!" You see techies are highly competitive about their hardware. The best by definition is the latest, greatest, fastest. So while they had been working to delight the customer they had actually been pissing them off. So while they thought they were raising customer satisfaction they were in fact lowering it! It was only through the Dell Platinum Council that this was discovered. So Dell introduced a series of computers designed around stable product components and backwards compatibility.

I once was at a five-star resort. I knew it was a five-star resort the moment I walked into the lobby because there was a huge exquisite floral arrangement. There were Birds of Paradise and all sorts of rare exotic flowers. And it wasn't just in the lobby – these floral arrangements were throughout the property. I could also tell that the organization had spent millions on the decor.

Now these conferences always begin very early in the morning, usually after what has been a very good night the night before. So when I went to my room I looked for the little plastic clock radio to set the alarm. But there was no clock radio in the room – I guess the resort management felt that plastic clock radios were beneath the resort's five-star positioning. So I called the front desk and asked for a 6:00 am wake up call.

Now it is uncanny, sometimes I wake up in the morning just before the alarm is due to go off! So sure enough the next morning I woke up before the call – I stretched, got out of bed and went over to the drapes – you know the kind, the thick heavy ones that let in no light – and I threw them back to look outside – and it was really bright out! This was my first bad sign of the day. So I looked over to see the clock and see what time it was – but there wasn't one, so I rushed over to the phone to call the front desk. I found it was 8:10 am. There I was naked in my room supposedly presenting 10 minutes ago. Now that's a bad visual – so don't go there!

So what did the fresh cut flowers have to do with my customer satisfaction? Nothing. What did I care about décor. Nothing!

So we can draw a graph: on the horizontal axis we can plot "How well are we doing as a company?" On the far right we're doing exceptional job and on the far left with a terrible job. On the vertical axis we can plot "How important is to the customer?" Items at the top are very important and ones at the bottom are not important at all.

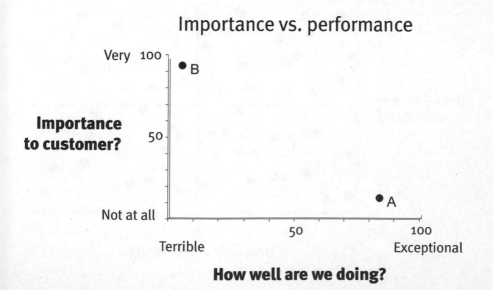

Point A would be the fresh cut flowers about the property. The organization is doing exceptional job – they are probably spending tens of thousands of dollars every month – but in terms of my satisfaction I would be just as happy if the flower in the lobby were fresh and those throughout the rest of the property were silk. Point B is the wake up call – it's very important to me and the organization is doing a terrible job.

So we can now plot 40 or 50 points of customer satisfaction that will fall all over the graph. We can then divide it into four quadrants. In the bottom right hand quadrant – QIV – the organization is doing an exceptional job at but frankly the customer doesn't care. Items falling in the bottom left hand quadrant (QIII) are ones where the organization is doing a terrible job at but thankfully the customer doesn't care. What the organization needs to do is stop investing time and energy on the products and services in these bottom two quadrant's and reinvest these resources into items falling in the top left hand quadrant (QI) – the quadrant where items are important to the customer but the organization is doing a terrible job. By reallocating resources to these products and services, the organization can drive them into the top right hand quadrant (QII) – thereby doing an excellent job at the items the customer most values.

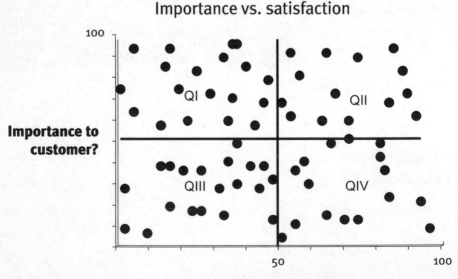

Importance vs. satisfaction

This is a very simple two-dimensional graph, but using software, teams can now add and analyze an additional six variables. Additional variables that come to mind are:

1. How much will it cost to improve this point of customer satisfaction with our product or service?
2. How much time will it take?
3. What percentage improvement is possible? For instance, if there is a point that is at 5 percent can we only get it to 10 percent or could we get it to 90 percent?
4. Competitive Analysis: are there certain points of customer satisfaction that if we were to improve would be a key differentiator from our competition – giving customers a compelling reason to switch to our product or service?
5. Input from call centers. Before Microsoft embarked on its OEM strategy of bundling Windows with hardware (such as with Dell, Compaq, IBM) it used to be the primary support for Windows. Each support call in the early 1990's cost Microsoft $12 (today it ranges up to $30 depending on the product). So before a new release of software, Microsoft software engineers would consult the call center to get the top 10 list of problems from the Call Center's perspective. When Microsoft *Office 95* was released, mail merging was very difficult. Whenever a mail merge call came in, the rep asked the customer to hold for a minute, walked over to the "mail merge couch" and took the call while laying on the couch, because everyone knew it would be a 45 minute call. So when *Office 97* was released mail merging was made far more intuitive, reducing the number and the cost of support calls to Microsoft.
6. Technical considerations: what new tools, technologies and strategies enable new features, products or services to be created? Engineers need to be consulted about what new possibilities they find most exciting.
7. Usability labs – Michael Dell tells a story about Dell's usability lab. This is where the company goes out onto the street and takes people who have never used a computer into the lab and gives them simple tasks to do. The sessions are video-taped. In one case a man was given a brand new Dell notebook in its shipping carton and was told to set up the computer. So he opened the boxed, peered inside, couldn't perceive

how to get the notebook out so he lifted the carton, and in one smooth, swift motion flipped the box upside down. From six feet up the note-book smashed onto the floor. So the usability labs showed the video footage to the guy who designed the packaging. Now the packaging guy figured he had designed the best thing since slice bread – but a dumb end user couldn't perceive how to get the notebook out of the box. So now Dell puts simple set up instructions in every shipping car-ton, and prints lift here on the cardboard packaging. Usability labs help companies understand their product and services from a dumb end user's perspective and create a top 10 list of improvements.

8. Customers' unarticulated needs. These are needs that the customer has but is unaware of. (See fuller discussion later in this chapter.)

Using software, teams can now analyze eight by eight variables. In other words, find out how do we add the most benefit from the customer perspective, in the least time, with the least cost, with the greatest improvements, with features that will give us the biggest differentiation from our competitors, have the greatest reduction in support costs, creat-ing new features that are enabled by new software and tools?

I can easily read a two-dimensional graph, and I can think three dimen-sionally – but how can I think about an eight by eight relational matrix? The new software helps me do it. The example below illustrates the rela-tionship of five variables:

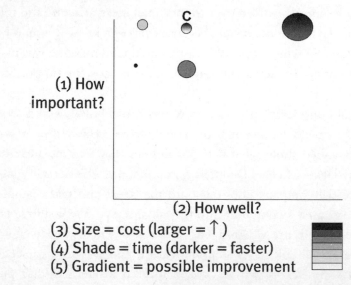

(1) How important?

(2) How well?
(3) Size = cost (larger = ↑)
(4) Shade = time (darker = faster)
(5) Gradient = possible improvement

Importance is on the vertical axis while organizational performance is on the horizontal. Cost is measured by the size of the circle (the larger the circle the greater the cost), the darkest shade in the circle represents the time, while the gradient differential with in the circle represents the possible improvement, (the greater the difference the greater the possible improvement).

So for instance, we can see point C is an issue that is important to customers, we are not doing too well, but it is an issue that will cost relatively little to improve (size of circle), we can do it relatively quickly (darkest part of the circle) and make a large relative improvement (as there is a great variation in the shading). But only by using new decision making tools can we begin to find the optimal point between all these variable. Read more about this in Cliff Saunder's reaction to *The Learning Paradox* at the back of the book (pages 400–417).

WHEN THE CHIPS ARE DOWN

When he was president of Loblaw International Merchants, Dave Nichol hired a high-powered, well-educated team of consultants to study the cookie market. They came to a startling conclusion: People who eat chocolate chip cookies like chocolate chips!

(I know the results are staggering! I was blown away myself when I read the report. But then, that's why consultants get the big bucks.)

They also found that the more chocolate chips you put in a cookie, the more customers like it!

So Nichol and his team went to the bakery that had been making the cookies and said, "We want to double, possibly triple, the number of chocolate chips in *No Name* chocolate chip cookies, and we'll reposition the new product as *President's Choice Decadent Chocolate Chip Cookies.*"

"But Dave," said the baker, "you don't understand our baking process. We bake the cookies by sending them through ovens on a conveyor belt. The chocolate actually melts during the process. If we use that many chocolate chips, there's not enough batter to keep the cookie together. There will just be a pile of cooked batter in between pools of melted chocolate when the belts emerge from the oven." In essence, the bakers were saying, "We can't change our process."

Nichol said, "Thanks, it's been great doing business with you all these years." Five bakers later, he found one who didn't know it was "impossible" to bake such cookies. The result was *President's Choice Decadent Chocolate Chip Cookies*, the top-selling cookie in Canada. But, it's only available at 20 percent of retail outlets. How do you have a number-one brand when it's only available at such a limited number of retailers? By delighting the customers and exceeding their expectations.

EXPONENTIALLY INCREASING MARGIN

The impact of treating the best customers well is awesome. In a *Harvard Business Review* article, Alan Grant and Leonard Schlesinger note:

> Given the fixed cost structure of a grocery store, the contribution margin from each additional dollar spent by a customer can earn 10 times the store's net profit margin. Thus, the company found that even small improvements in any one of the many customer behaviors led to very significant profitability gains. Expanding the customer base by two percent with primary shoppers, for example, would increase the store's profitability by more than 45 percent. Converting just 200 secondary customers into primary customers would increase profitability by more than 20 percent. Selling one more produce item to every customer would increase profitability by more than 40 percent. Persuading every customer to substitute two store-brand items for two national-brand items each time they visited the store would increase profitability by 55 percent.
>
> In other words, expanding the base of primary shoppers – the store's best customers – by a mere two percent increases the store's profits by 45 percent![2]

How do grocery stores define convenience for customers? They have special checkouts for people with 10 items or less. They treat the worst customers the best! The people who buy little or nothing get out of the store fastest. This concept probably came from supermarket executives wanting to compete against convenience stores. The average family spends $400 to $500 a month ($6,000 a year) on groceries.[3] What are supermarkets doing for their best customers? They have to wait in huge line-ups. Why not have a frequent-shopper gold card that allows the best customers to check out in special, preferential lines? First, the store would have to know who its best customers are in order to be able to treat them preferentially.

A study by the National Retail Federation in January 1996 found that nearly half the consumers surveyed feel that shopping is a hassle and try to avoid it![4] A staggering 75 percent of men and 58 percent of women said they sometimes walk out of a store because the wait is too long! If I were a retailing executive, I'd be worried. The market is ripe for companies offering alternative shopping experiences, like online grocery stores, to grow rapidly.

THE DREADED SHOPPING EXPERIENCE

Round up the children. Bundle them into snowsuits. Strap them into car seats. Search endlessly for a parking space. Try to find a quarter for a shopping cart. Fight for space at the deli counter. Take the kids to the washroom. Stand in long checkout lines. Carry out 19 bags, two of which are ripping. Dent the car with the shopping cart. These are just a few of the images that come to mind when we contemplate grocery shopping. The fact is, consumers dislike grocery shopping. According to *American Demographics*, grocery shopping is the second-least popular activity of 22 daily tasks. In fact, it only rates ahead of going to the dentist, as the activity people most hate to do.

"People spend the equivalent of two-and-a-half [work] weeks each year in the grocery store, and that's not counting driving time," says Andrew Parkinson, co-founder of Peapod, an Internet grocery shopping and delivery service. "This breaks down to a 66-minute major food shopping trip each week, with more than one 16-minute, fill-in trip."

Peapod, one of the largest interactive online grocery shopping and delivery service in the US, serves over 50,000 customers in Chicago, Boston, Southern Connecticut, Long Island and Washington DC. With a computer and modem, customers log on to Peapod's Web page at www.peapod.com Peapod offers more than over 20,000 items for sale online.

PeachTree is another leader in the online grocery business. In 2001, they delivered groceries to 16 cities in Canada and the United States. Unlike Peapod, PeachTree partners with existing physical grocery stores in each city. Customers order online through PeachTree's website (www.peachtree.com) and PeachTree picks up the groceries and delivers them at a time chosen by the customer.

ONLINE VERSUS IN-LINE SHOPPING

Customers can shop from the office or home or anywhere they have a computer and modem. With Peapod, shopping can be a 15-minute experience with a glass of wine while listening to your favorite music after the kids have gone to bed, or during your lunch hour at work. It's the beauty of online instead of "in line" shopping.

Peapod halves average shopping time. Time is one of the things that baby boomers (born between 1946 and 1966) are most pressed about. With aging parents and young children to look after, time is one thing that baby boomers who are sandwiched in midlife have very little of. As a group, boomers are computer literate, so Peapod appeals to them.

Customers can comparison shop (Coke versus Pepsi versus generic pop), easily find sale items (marked with a red tag) and check their running total of purchases at any time. Customers automatically get any in-store sales that apply to their order and can use manufacturer and electronic coupons. They can view the product picture, price, nutritional information and whether it is kosher. The computer allows the shopper to shop from their last order or to create frequently ordered items lists (i.e., weekly list, summer BBQ, dinner party, baby), reminding them of items that they might otherwise forget. By reminding customers of items they might otherwise forget, Peapod increases incremental sales, adding to profitability. Peapod offers online recipes that are educational and promote new item sales.

Enter the snacks aisle and you'll find cookies. What kind? How about chocolate chip? Click on that and get a variety of brands. They're listed alphabetically, but click again and they're listed by price and price-per-ounce. Concerned about calories? That information is there, too. Select the one you want and it goes into your virtual shopping cart.

Many new consumers may be reluctant to let someone else choose their fresh fish or strawberries, but the personal shoppers choose only the freshest and best-looking items. "Members have an option to make comments on the computer screen, instructing shoppers, for example, to buy only green bananas or to substitute sirloin if T-bone steak isn't available," says Parkinson. If the produce, meat or deli item is not up to Peapod's standards, the shopper does not fulfill the request and explains why. Groceries are delivered in temperature-controlled coolers. Peapod guarantees each order they deliver, and members can reject any items that aren't satisfactory.

Peapod charges a per-order fee that again varies by market, ranging from $1.95 to $6.95, plus five percent or less of the total order as a delivery fee. Orders are delivered to the doorstep in three hours. Specifying a half-hour time frame – such as between 3:00 and 3:30 pm – costs an extra five dollars. If a profit can be made on delivering a $10 pizza to your door within 30 minutes, why can't a profit be made on a weekly $120 grocery order for a total of $6,000 a year?

Peapod's clients are predominantly women (77 percent), a remarkable number given that only one-third of online users are women. Over 60 percent are professionals in dual-income families and 56 percent have children under 18.

INCREASE MARGIN BY PREVENTING DEFECTION OF BEST CUSTOMERS

Companies can increase customer retention and prevent customer defection by allowing the customer to build equity with their products or services over time. Microsoft *Word's* auto-correct feature is a case in point. I frequently type "beleive" instead of the proper spelling "believe." When I run the spellchecker, I can define a misspelled word to be corrected automatically. Every time I mistype the word in the future, the software will automatically correct it. The more words that I define to be automatically corrected, the less spelling I have to correct in future. The feature also allows me to create shorthand phrases. For instance, I can define "wrt" as "with respect to" or "MS" as "Microsoft" or "org" as "organization." Over the course of a year I will likely work on my word processor 1,000 hours. I am unlikely to switch to another word processor because I have built hours of equity in the product.

Similarly, airlines encourage customers to enroll in their frequent flier program to build equity. When a customer flies a certain minimum number of miles, they achieve a frequent flier status, giving them special benefits, speedy check-in at the first-class counter, use of special airport lounges with free drinks and upgrades from economy to first class.

How much does it cost the airlines to treat frequent fliers preferentially? What is the cost of allowing them to use the first-class check-in line? Or the airport lounges? Or to upgrade to first class when seats are available? These are all low cost to the airline, but have tremendous perceived value to the customer. Frequent fliers get addicted to the preferential service and are often unwilling to switch airlines for fear of losing it! For this reason, some travelers will even take a non-direct flight with "their" airline, rather than take a direct flight with a competitor.

Allowing customers to build equity with your product or service means that the more they use it, the harder it will be for a competitor to woo them away.

FEDEX: A CASE STUDY IN CUSTOMER SERVICE

Mathematical measurement of performance

At FedEx, the culture and the processes are all built on a huge investment in information technology (IT). The company measures almost everything that affects its business, and ultimately, the bottom line: service quality, customer satisfaction, employee satisfaction, employee performance and management performance. The company's extensive use of IT enables these performance measures and helps to create an environment of continuous improvement. Underlying the measurement, logistics systems and IT investment is the FedEx People-Service-Profit philosophy that dictates how the systems will be developed and implemented. This heavy IT investment has been one of the key reasons for FedEx's staggering growth. The company began operations in 1973 and as of 2001 employed 200,000 people, moving 3.2 million packages a day to and from destinations in more than 210 countries. With 650 aircraft, FedEx has the world's largest cargo fleet.

"Hard" management

When I think of FedEx' management, the word that consistently comes to mind is "hard" because it always knows what is going on. The company is able to confront problems and issues because it has gathered the necessary information. Logistics is the key to running a successful courier company. On a typical day, 3.2 million packages travel through the FedEx system, so the possibilities for errors are staggering. FedEx' goal is for 100 percent accuracy, quality and customer satisfaction on all transactions. Nothing short of the 100 percent goal is acceptable.

Most people wonder why any company would be so relentless in its pursuit of 100 percent accuracy, quality and customer satisfaction. What is wrong with 98 percent? When FedEx ships a package, many different employees handle it as it moves from its pick-up point to its destination. If 10 employees handled a package during its trip and each one performs his or her job to 98 percent accuracy before passing it off to the next person, what is the net effect?

$$98\% \times 98\% \times 98\% \times 98\% \times 98\% \times 98\% \times 98\% \times 98\% \times 98\% \times 98\% = 82\%$$

The cumulative effect is only 82 percent accuracy! This is unacceptable in terms of quality and resulting customer satisfaction. If 20 employees handle the package and each performs his or her job to 98 percent accuracy, the cumulative effect is a product with only 67 percent accuracy!

$$98\% \times 98\% \times 98\% \times 98\% \times 98\% \times 98\% \times 98\% \times 98\% \times 98\% \times 98\%\ 98\% \times 98\% \times$$
$$98\% \times 98\% \times 98\% \times 98\% \times 98\% \times 98\% \times 98\% \times 98\% = 67\%$$

Only 100 percent is acceptable.

Of the 3.2 million packages handled daily, more than 99 percent reach their destination on time, undamaged and with the right paperwork. The remaining one percent represents 32,000 potentially unhappy customers. Not all customers with a late package are unhappy but, if all 32,000 are unhappy, the company will likely hear from fewer than 10,000. How do you design a logistics system that supports 100 percent accuracy? How can a company move closer to the virtually unattainable goal of 100 percent accuracy?

FedEx Express instituted the Service Quality Indicator (SQI) in 1988 with a goal of reducing the service and quality failure by 90 percent by 1993. The company identified points of service and quality failure from the customer's viewpoint and then weighed each item according to the level of dissatisfaction it caused customers.

When a FedEx Express courier picks up a package, he or she scans the bar code on the waybill with a "supertracker." When the courier returns to the van and puts the supertracker in its holster, the information is downloaded from the hand-held unit and transmitted, by radio, to a FedEx Express station. From the station, the information is relayed to the central computer system, which tracks packages from pick-up to delivery.

A package is scanned an average of 14 times between pick-up and its final destination. So when it is delivered and given its final scan, the company knows what time it was delivered and whether it met its committed delivery time. If the package was scheduled for 10:30 a.m. delivery, but the courier dropped it off at 10:32 that would register a failure of one point in the SQI index as a Right Day/Late Delivery. If the customer requested an invoice adjustment, that would add another failure point. A single package could add many points to the SQI: if it was initially a late pick-up (3 points), if the package was not delivered on time so the customer called to ask for a trace (3 points), if the package was delivered on the wrong day (10 points) and with water damage (30 points). This one package could have potentially added 46 failure points to the SQI.

FedEx Service Failure Ratings

Item	SQI
Overnight wrong day late	10
IP inbound wrong day late	10
Other wrong day late	10
Right day late	1
International wrong day late	1
Late pick-up stops	3
Traces	3
Complaints reopened	10
Damaged packages	30
Lost packages	50
Invoice adjustments required	1
Missing proof of deliveries	1

When FedEx Express introduced the SQI in 1988, daily failures accounted for 150,000 points. The company announced its goal of reducing the SQI by 90 percent in five years. During the first year, actual service failures decreased 11 percent despite the fact that package volumes grew by 20 percent.

The graph below highlights the relationship between the SQI and package volumes. While the number of packages almost tripled between 1987 and 1995, the SQI failures fell:

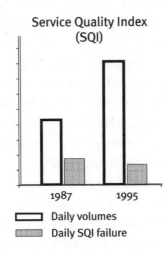

Service Quality Index (SQI)

1987   1995

☐ Daily volumes
▨ Daily SQI failure

PROACTIVE MEASUREMENT OF CUSTOMER SATISFACTION

Given that fewer than 20 percent of unhappy customers will ever call to let you know where, when or how your products or services are failing to meet their expectations, a toll-free phone number is not enough. Organizations must be proactive in getting customer feedback. Every quarter, FedEx randomly selects a new group of 2,100 customers to survey daily. During a 10-minute interview, customer satisfaction is gauged on 50 points of service on a scale of zero to 100 percent satisfaction. FedEx also conducts targeted customer satisfaction studies around such specific procedures as Saturday delivery and invoice adjustment. The company also solicits feedback via comment cards at all FedEx service centers. FedEx annually surveys its largest customers, whom the company equips with automated shipping systems. These users account for more than half of the company's total package volume.

BALANCING QUALITATIVE AND QUANTITATIVE CUSTOMER FEEDBACK

Customer surveys provide good quantitative data, allowing the organization to benchmark itself against competitors and the best businesses in other industries. Quantitative information is "left brain" (mathematical, linear, logical); it doesn't give any feedback on feelings or emotions. While a statistically significant survey such as FedEx's survey of 2,100 randomly chosen customers provides good feedback, it doesn't answer the question, "Why are customers satisfied or dissatisfied?" That is where qualitative information comes in, generally through the use of focus groups.

Focus groups provide executives with insight about how their customers relate to the company's products and services. Focus groups also allow researchers to explore customer ideas. They are "right brain" (emotional, intuitive, holistic). The research for *The 100 Best Companies to Work For in Canada* was to a large extent based on focus groups conducted with the employees of companies under consideration.

Companies focused on customer and employee satisfaction need to balance quantitative and qualitative research. Both are important. For instance, the Survey Feedback Action (SFA) program at FedEx asks all employees to rate their managers and work environment. The quantitative data will show whether employees are unhappy in a particular department. Once the problem is identified, how can it be solved? Qualitative information gives the clues. A non-threatening discussion with employees led by trained facilitators will uncover the reasons for the discontent. Both quantitative and qualitative research methods are necessary to create understanding: quantitative research gives you the hard facts and numbers, qualitative gets at the reasons behind customer or employee attitudes and preferences.

FORCE RANKING ISSUES

The researchers need to pit points of customer satisfaction against one another to create a hierarchy of needs. If the organization had only one additional dollar to spend per customer, what investment would yield the greatest delight?

Some interesting research was done by a jet manufacturer a number of years ago. Executives who bought corporate jets were asked a series of questions, "Would you like mahogany paneling in the interior?" *Yes.* "Would you like wider seats?" *Yes.* "Would you like built-in cellular phones?" *Yes.* "Would you like a faster plane?" *Yes.*

Then, when the executives were asked, "Would you be willing to pay an extra $250,000 for these added features?" their tune changed. *No way,* they said. When asked what features really mattered, their answer was, "Skip all the amenities and just make the planes as fast as possible and with the longest range." Executives who buy these jets spend a lot of time traveling. What they want is to spend less time in the air. Therefore, range is important because refueling requires landing and creates the potential for long delays. So all engineering efforts were invested in increasing the range and speed. Not surprisingly, these jets have sold extremely well.

THERE IS MORE THAN ONE CUSTOMER

Surveys show that people born before 1950 have been slow to use ATMs. These people may not be comfortable using computers. They often fear the technology because it wasn't user friendly. By contrast, people born after 1950 are rushed for time and prefer ATMs. But rather than blame older people for not using new technology, developers have to always work to make their products and services easier to use.

There is a great example of this in my neighborhood. One of the local banks has a branch located right under a seniors' residence. Seniors like human contact. In fact, they like line-ups because they can chat with other people in the line. It's a social outing. The branch only recently installed an ATM. But half a block away in a 24-hour drug store, the same bank has had an ATM for years. Baby boomers like late-night shopping. They are so pressed for time with their careers and looking after the kids that they shop based on convenience, location and speed of getting in and out of the store. If they can get cash where they buy toothpaste, they feel pleased. So within the same block the bank's marketing strategy addresses the needs of two completely different customer markets.

Organizations have more than one customer in another way. I remember a fascinating presentation by the president of a chocolate-bar manufacturer. His company's products were sold in convenience stores. So there were two customers with different needs – the chocolate-bar buyer and the convenience-store owner.

If you conduct street interviews, you'll find that no one eats chocolate bars. "No. Not me. I run five miles a day. I only eat alfalfa sprouts and granola. Chocolate bars never cross these lips. Nope. Never." If marketers could only find the one person in North America who is eating all the chocolate bars, it would be a major coup! It's interesting to note that customers will sometimes not tell us what they really feel or do because it's not fashionable, polite or politically correct.

The end customer wants a great-tasting product at a good price. The storeowner is concerned about delivery times, delivery frequency, storage, and spoilage in summer heat, attractive packaging, credit terms, display racks and whether the product is in high demand.

The food company studied the convenience-store owner's needs, force-ranking 40 separate needs. This analysis is essential because corporate resources are scarce and becoming scarcer, and executives want to make the most effective use of them. If the food company has $400,000 to spend, what would make the greatest impact? Doing more product testing with a view to changing the taste of the product? Redesigning the packaging to make it more attractive to the end customer? From the convenience-store owner's perspective, what would have the greatest impact? Better credit terms, free display racks or $400,000 of television advertising? After extensive research, the company found that redesigning the shipping carton for the candy bars so that it doubled as a marketing display when cut open, made the greatest difference to increasing sales. As a result, the company pushed two of its chocolate bars into the highly competitive top-20 bar category. This significantly increased market share, as only the top 20 bars are carried in every store in the country.

Find out who your customers are, identify their needs and then tailor your services to them.

DELL COMPUTERS: A CASE STUDY

Excellence in customer service must be defined from the customer's point of view. The truth is that many organizations have designed policies and practices from the company's point of view, policies that make it easy for the accounting department, the inventory department or the sales reps. But in a successful business, the focus must be the customer's point of view; other interests should be subordinate to that.

Dell Computers has been rated number one in terms of customer satisfaction in numerous independent computer surveys. Why have Dell's sales grown exponentially?

Dealing directly with customers allowed Dell to not only sell a higher-value product at a lower price than its competitors because of lower overheads, but it also allowed Dell to enter into a direct relationship with its customers, gaining a better understanding of their point of view and needs.

Founded in 1984, Dell became a $25.3 billion Fortune 500 company in 2001. Dell is the largest PC manufacturer in the world with 13.7 percent of the market share.[5] The secret of Dell's exponential growth is simple: listen to and understand your customers, then satisfy their needs, always exceeding their expectations. If customers can't find service or value as good as yours, they will keep coming back. The key to Dell's growth has been retention of customers.

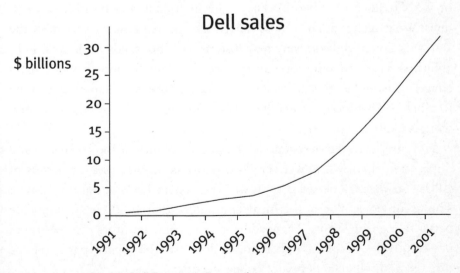

Source: Dell Computer Corporation

Techno-typing

Dell "techno-types" its customers into seven broad categories. It's a basic approach of segmenting the market.

Dell's research in 1993[6] found that 55 percent of North Americans were techno phobic to some degree – 32 percent of all adults were intimidated by computers and worried about damaging a PC if they used it without assistance. Most adults found the new technology difficult to understand (51 percent) and the rapid rate of change in technology confusing (58 percent).

Techno-typing recognizes that a "one size fits all" strategy doesn't work because large segments of the population have radically different primary needs. Each segment will create a different hierarchy of needs. Dell designs products to meet the force-ranked needs of each segment and then targets markets to each segment.

First is the Techno-Wizard. These are the computer "techies" who live on the "bleeding edge." They want the latest and greatest – machines that scream, the fastest hard disks, the fastest video graphics, the most RAM. These are the early users of technology. They are not price sensitive. They do, however, want good value and demand very little support.

Then there is the Techno-Teamer. This second type is typically an information systems professional, responsible for a LAN (local area network) or WAN (wide area network). They want high-quality, network-ready systems. What such types fear most is network failure because every hour the system is down, the company may lose tens of thousands of dollars. Reliability, service and system recovery speed are the Techno-Teamer's main concerns. Even better than recovering from failure is anticipating it in the first place. This group wants diagnostic tools to anticipate when the network is likely to fail.

Prevention strategies require a focus on reliability of the hardware and duplication (i.e., two power supplies, two sets of hard disks, two sets of CPUs), so that if one set goes down, the system itself doesn't go down. This is obvious. For non-critical computers that don't have duplicate parts, this group wants diagnostic software that monitors the LAN and pre-emptively warns of impending failure, so that spare parts can be ordered and switched in before failure occurs.

Then there is the Techno-Traveler. This third type spends a lot of time on airplanes, so the primary concern is notebook battery life. Dell has developed a series of notebooks to satisfy this group.

The Techno-Plug-and-Play group wants the computer to work the moment it is taken out of the box. No loading software, no configuring the modem or solving conflicts, just unpack the computer, plug it in and away we go. This group also wants service. When something goes wrong, this group wants someone on the other end of a 1–800 number to walk them through an easy solution.

The other market segments identified by Dell were Techno-Critical (primary concern is the network being down), Techno-Boomer (doesn't want to make a wrong buying decision) and Techno-Phobe (avoids technology whenever possible).

Dell's customer service includes setting up the network so the LAN administrator doesn't spend the day unpacking boxes, setting up systems and configuring the addresses of each computer. For an extra fee, Dell will send a technician out for a full day to set up the entire system and orient the new computer user(s).

Service is one of the key areas that differentiates Dell from many competitors. Dell offers lifetime, toll-free 24-hour, seven-days-a-week, 365-days-a-year telephone support with a guaranteed five-minute response time. There's also a 30-day money-back guarantee on all systems and a full year of next business day, on-site service for some systems.

Within the broad range of each segment, Dell is able to further customize orders according to individual needs. Techno-typing helps to zero in on a customer's expectations and also gives marketers the insights they need to develop mass advertising/marketing programs aimed at customers and potential customers in each segment.

In numerous independent surveys of the computer industry, Dell has been named best at providing service (including twice winning the J.D. Power award for customer service). In 1994, the company had a rude awakening when Hewlett Packard was awarded the top honor, which goes to show that even the best companies can't become complacent. Being the best and remaining the best requires relentless work to improve the company's product and service offerings.

The rise of Dell computers is an excellent example of the rise of the private label. IBM created the PC market. Compaq came along and offered a better product at a lower price and created the clone market by using the same off-the-shelf components as IBM but branding the PC under Compaq's name. Dell is another example of a private-label manufacturer that rose to such prominence it became a brand. When the components of the underlying computer are identical, consumers look for better value. When all else is the same, price matters most. That is why innovation is so essential. Unless a company can differentiate itself and offer higher-value goods and services in key areas that customers value most, the company will have to compete on price. Techno-typing, or market segmenting, highlights how different customers have different hierarchies of needs. Some place service first, others reliability, ease of use or price. Dell has successfully positioned its products to meet broad techno-type categories and then has customized its products within each segment.

CREATING AN "UNIMAGINABLE" FUTURE

Customer satisfaction information systems are essential, but relying solely on customers to tell you what they want is not always effective. Here is an example: German companies were once the pre-eminent camera makers. German cameras were simply the best. Imagine conducting focus groups with owners of German cameras in 1980 and asking participants, "What can we improve? What don't you like about your camera?" The owners would say: "We love everything. There's nothing you can improve. You make the best cameras in the world."

But the customers couldn't predict the invention of auto-wind cameras that allowed photographers to shoot a whole roll of film in a minute simply by holding down the shutter release, or auto-focus cameras that allowed people with no experience to shoot professional-looking pictures. Japanese firms thought of these added features and the resulting market-share loss for the German companies is history.

How many customers do you think are demanding such a feature? Companies can't rely only on customer research to understand customer needs because customers don't always know what they want or what is possible.

Customer needs exist before their discovery, just as the principles for flight existed in nature before we uncovered them. The possibility of the transistor existed before scientists "invented" it. All our needs pre-exist before we realize them. It's up to smart individuals and companies to uncover them.

Most people have a hard time articulating what they want. In fact, customer opinions can be deceiving, sometimes suggesting the opposite of what they really want. In a focus group on credit cards, participants are asked which they would prefer to have: a card with a low interest rate or one with all sorts of benefits (insurance, frequent flier air miles or 30-day purchase/return guarantees) and a high interest rate. Participants will often answer that they would rather have the featureless card with the low interest rate. But at the end of the focus group, offer them a card as a reward for participating in the group, and most will choose the card with special features. So what consumers say can be inconsistent with what they actually do. Again, researchers don't always get accurate or truthful answers from consumers, who will often give politically, correct answers when what they truly feel is embarrassing to admit. Successful organizations create systems and structures that help uncover customers' unarticulated or hidden needs.

So how can organizations uncover customers' unarticulated needs? Often, customers can't articulate what they want, but can articulate what upsets them. For instance, if I was in a focus group for a car company, the researcher would likely ask me what I do and don't like about existing cars, but this information will only help a car company refine existing features. How can a company come up with completely new features, products or services?

The researcher might ask me what upsetting experiences I have had while driving, making it clear that the answers don't have to be tied to the company's cars but just with driving in general. In response, I would relate an actual incident on a six-lane highway (three lanes each way). A truck in the far outer lane and a car on the far inner lane both moved into the center lane at the same time, colliding. Both drivers had probably checked their rearview mirrors, but neither had obviously looked opposite them.

Upon colliding, the car swerved back to the inner lane and then hit the guardrail. It bounced back into the center lane where it hit the truck again and did a complete 360 and spun out of control back into the guardrail. The truck had swerved initially and then, when hit by the car again, went careening into the ditch. All this happened only 100 yards in front of me at 60 miles per hour. I watched in horror as the whole scene played out in slow motion. Ever since, I have had a terrible fear of changing lanes, particularly into the center lane of a three-lane highway.

What I am really saying to the researcher is that I would like the car company to develop infrared or sonar-based sensors on the sides of my car that can warn me when I am about to hit something in my blind spot. Consumers may not be able to articulate what they want (positive), but they can often articulate what upsets them (negative).

Therefore, organizations must first work to uncover what upsets customers and then create solutions to these problems in the form of new features, products or services.

VISA'S NEURAL NETWORK

A neural network is a computer program that identifies patterns. The neural network can't explain why a particular pattern occurs, it only identifies that the pattern exists. In 1993, Visa was the first credit card company to use a neural network to identify fraudulent credit card transactions. The program has been so successful that Visa has been able to cut fraud from 20 cents per transaction dollar in the mid-eighties, to just 6 cents per transaction dollar in 2001. In 1999, over $1.6 trillion worth of transactions were made using a Visa card.[7]

A neural network is a program that "learns" by recognizing patterns. If a jewelry shop in Iowa requests authorization for a $5,000 purchase on my card, the computer looks at my pattern of spending and asks, "Has Jim ever been in Iowa?" *No.* "Has he ever purchased jewelry?" *No.* "Has he ever bought anything worth $5,000 using his card?" *No.* The neural net identifies that this requested transaction is outside of my usual purchasing pattern, predicts that it is a fraudulent transaction and requests that the store clerk get photo identification. If it's a thief, he runs out of the store at this point. If I am buying an engagement ring for my fiancée in Iowa, I provide the required identification.

After one seminar a participant told me that his gas card had been stolen, but that he really didn't worry about it too much. After all, how much gas can a thief steal? At the end of the day he reported it stolen and discovered that the thief had run up a $2,000 balance, going from gas station to gas station buying cartons of cigarettes! Here is a perfect case for a neural network to identify a pattern. Has this customer ever bought cigarettes? No. Well, then why is he buying 100 cartons today? It's probably fraud.

Neural nets can be used to identify overall patterns of behavior in groups of people. In analyzing stolen credit cards, neural nets came to recognize the pattern that thieves often place a long-distance phone call before going on a spending spree. Throughout the first day that the card is stolen, thieves continue making long-distance calls on the credit card before going back into stores to make more fraudulent purchases. There's a definite pattern: call, purchase, call, purchase. Today, when the neural network sees this pattern, it predicts that the transactions are fraudulent, even if the card has not yet been reported stolen.

It takes human ingenuity to find meaning in the pattern; in other words, to understand why the pattern occurs. How do thieves think? A thief wants to ensure that the credit card hasn't been reported stolen, so a long-distance call is placed to a random number. If a call is declined, the thief knows the card has been reported stolen and throws it out. The criminal hasn't risked being identified by a store clerk. If the call goes through, his spending spree begins. The thief makes more phone calls throughout the day, checking the integrity of the card.

Here's another application: car buyers in a certain age group, income bracket and geographical area buy a new car every four years, on average. After individuals in this target group buy a new home and take out a $150,000 mortgage, their behavior will change. Over time, a neural net would show that they will buy a new car every eight years as they shift priorities to pay off their mortgage. With this knowledge, a bank could save thousands of dollars in marketing costs by changing its direct marketing programs for cars loans from a four-year to an eight-year cycle for new homeowners.

PRICE IS ONLY ONE DIMENSION OF VALUE

Many organizations believe that in a recession, consumers are only price sensitive. In fact, they are value sensitive. The best goods and services with the highest value/price ratio almost always win. Certainly, price is one factor that determines customer satisfaction, especially in tough economic times, but price is not always the most important factor.

Your doctor has told you that you will die unless you have triple bypass heart surgery within a month. You find a student just out of medical school desperate for the experience, willing to perform the surgery for 50 bucks. Will you go for it?

Your only other choice in the market is a highly competent surgeon with years of experience who charges $10,000. Which of the two surgeons will you choose? How price sensitive are you?

What is your hierarchy of needs? (1) The competence of a surgeon with an excellent record of patient recovery. (2) Price. In fact, price is not really a consideration. You are completely price insensitive. You are willing to pay one surgeon 200 times more than the other, a 20,000 percent jump!

This reveals a simple principle: find your customers' pain, solve it and they become price insensitive. Similarly, find their delight and satisfy it (remember the chocolate chip cookie story).

A seminar participant once yelled, "But if the purchasing department was selecting the surgeon, they would have chosen the $50 one!" Systems create misalignment within organizations. If the purchasing manager is rewarded based on the lowest up-front cost, don't be surprised that the cheapest surgeon is hired. Organizations need to optimize the whole, not just one department. Ultimately, it is systems (in this case the compensation system) and structures that govern performance.

You do further research and find a second, equally competent surgeon. The surgeon can operate in three months for $2,000 or you can keep your appointment this month for $10,000. Remember, you will die if you don't have the surgery this month.

The hierarchy of concerns has changed. It is now (1) scheduling of the operation; (2) competence of the surgeon; (3) price. It is interesting to note how the hierarchy of needs is fluid. As more information becomes available in the market to customers, their hierarchy of needs changes. Therefore, organizations need to constantly work to understand how the market is changing and how customers' needs are shifting.

The hierarchy of needs among customers is constantly changing as they age and the world around them changes. A new breed of consumer is emerging, one who is wiser and better informed than ever before. In order to thrive in our rapidly changing world, organizations must work even harder to identify the underlying needs and motivations of their target markets.

Baby boomers are under intense pressure. In addition to both partners working, they are often balancing the demands of both young children and aging parents. Quality and service often mean more to them than the best price. To this group, quality has become more important than quantity. When boomers were in their university years they were interested in quantity – buying beer by the case. But now the concern has shifted to quality. Aging boomers, worried about their waste lines, are likely to drink only one beer, but a premium brand, likely an import or microbrewery specialty beer. So the mass-market breweries are facing new competition. Therefore, the challenge for many companies is to shift from a quantity to a quality perspective.

> You miss 100 percent of the shots you never take.
> *Wayne Gretzky,*
> *ice hockey player*

Customers make decisions based on a complex set of factors that they may be unable to articulate. Good market research uncovers hidden attitudes and needs, giving companies opportunities to delight their customers in totally new ways. The goal is to get inside customers' minds, to see and experience goods and services as customers do.

When asked, "What would excite you as a credit-card owner?" during a 1985 focus group, participants would not have answered, "Give me a frequent flier point for every dollar spent on the card."

American Airlines approached American Express in 1985 with a proposal to co-brand a credit card. Amex rejected the offer. American turned to City Bank. City Bank executives were so excited about the concept that to ensure they were first to market, they launched the card without holding focus groups to test customer response. Aimed at upscale personal and business travelers, the City Bank American AAdvantage card was introduced in 1986.

Response to the card was overwhelming. Consumers began charging items to the card that they would otherwise have paid for by cash, check or charged to another card. As a result, City Bank's AAdvantage card gained significant market share. It was the first major-scale co-branded card and was a phenomenal success, exceeding all expectations.

With the obvious success of the concept, every other airline eventually followed suit. But in 1999, City Bank's AAdvantage card was the most popular airline credit card with more than 3 million accounts. The second-place card, First USA's United Airlines card had 2.9 accounts and Amex's Delta card trailed far behind with 1.2 million accounts.

American Express eventually recognized the error of its decision and co-branded one of its cards with Delta. So it is important to recognize and correct mistakes. This case study highlights the importance of being first to market and creating the standard by which all competitors will be judged. Despite Amex's entry into the market, AAdvantage's market share is almost triple Amex's. And by being first, City Bank got to select the dominant US carrier.

Airline cardholders are significantly more affluent, with average household incomes of more than $70,000 a year as opposed to $47,000 for average classic-card households. In 2000, airline cardholders charged an average of $25,000 to 30,000 a year to their cards while the average classic cardholder charged just over $6,300 a year. Airline credit cards make up 45 percent of the total credit card market.[8]

Between 1998 and 2001, the number of credit cards in circulation in Canada rose 12 percent from 37.7 million cards to 40.1 million cards.[9] Frequent flier cards have driven most of this growth. Executives are charging expenditures to their personal cards that they never charged in the past and then are being reimbursed by their companies.

Today, $5 billion worth of expenditures are billed to the CIBC (Canadian Imperial Bank of Commerce) Aerogold card every year. Cardholders charge three to four times more than other gold cardholders. For every dollar you spend using the credit card, you receive one frequent flier point with Air Canada's frequent flier Aeroplan. Aerogold cardholders spend $20,000 a year on their cards. CIBC's strategy has literally skimmed the cream off the high end of the Canadian credit-card market. The card has also been a major win for Air Canada.

"Lateral thinking," a phrase coined by Edward de Bono, one of the world's leading thinkers on innovation and creativity, is a process to help individuals, teams and organizations be more creative. Our eyesight is perfect in hindsight. But very rarely can we see into the future with accuracy. In that sense we are all blind with respect to the future.

Our brains have right and left hemispheres. The left is linear, logical and hosts our language ability. The right brain is intuitive, holistic and emotional. Western management has come to rely predominantly on left-brain processes (facts, figures, proof). However, how could an individual "prove" the telephone would be a revolutionary invention before its introduction? How could anyone "prove" that credit cards tied to frequent flier points would radically increase credit-card usage before their invention? The ability to think laterally will increasingly determine which companies thrive. We have been educated and rewarded for left-brain thinking. Right-brain thinking is divergent, exploring solutions and possibilities.

Similarly, cross marketing will become increasingly important. Who developed American Express's front-of-the-line service? The slogan "Membership has its privileges" finds practical expression in this service. American Express cardholders get first choice for the premieres of top musicals in cities across North America, and the program has been a major hit! It's a win-win situation for Amex and the theaters.

Now, what would really motivate the under-30 crowd to get credit cards? Front-of-the-line service for rock concerts?

CREATING A FUTURE NOT EVEN CUSTOMERS CAN PREDICT

How can companies create a future when customers have trouble telling us what they want? In *Competing for the Future*, Gary Hamel and C.K. Prahalad compare applied creativity to baseball:

> The number of runs that a batter actually scores is a product of hit rate (batting average) multiplied by the number of times at bat. A player who bats 1.000,[10] but who only goes to the plate half a dozen times a season will be much less valuable to the team than a player who bats a modest .250 but gets to the plate 300 or 400 times in a year. Similarly, a company may be able to boast about its high batting average in new product introductions, but if that average is the result of a cautious, go-slow approach to creating new markets, the company may well capture less of the future than scrappier rivals with inferior batting averages but more times at bat.[11]

It is interesting to note from baseball history that Babe Ruth had the most number of home runs in his time, but he also had the most strikeouts. Creating new value for the customer requires many times at bat trying to anticipate what customers want – with many small tests – never betting the whole business on just one strategy.

Francis Vincent, former commissioner of major league baseball, said:

> Baseball teaches us, or has taught most of us, how to deal with failure. We learn at a very young age that failure is the norm in baseball and precisely because we have failed, we hold in high regard those who fail less often – those who hit safely in one out of three chances and become star players. I also find it fascinating that baseball, alone in sport, considers errors to be part of the game, part of its rigorous truth.[12]

DELIGHTING CUSTOMERS

What is the "wow" factor in your product? Use direct marketing and test, test, test. Try different offers, the same offer with different price points, and mail the same offer to different mailing lists. American Express will send 100,000 pieces of direct mail to a target audience, offering 1,000 frequent flier points for agreeing to get a second card for a spouse. Then it measures the response rate. The marketers will follow with a second mailing to another 100,000 cardholders with the same demographic background and offer 1,500 points, and measure the response again. Then they perform a cost-benefit analysis and see which is the better route.

Given that companies can buy one frequent flier point for less than a cent, 1,500 points cost less than $15. If a $15 premium generates the sale of a $60 secondary card, it's an effective incentive. Who would have thought of it 10 years ago? Look at how much business is now being generated through using points as incentive premiums!

EVERYONE NEEDS CUSTOMER FOCUS

In today's market, consumers are better informed and have greater freedom of choice. In the airline industry, I can buy tickets from a travel agent, directly from the airline, by phone or the Internet.

Jan Carlzon, former president of SAS airlines, a consortium of the national airlines of Denmark, Norway and Sweden, states in *Moments of Truth*:

Last year, each of our 10 million customers came into contact with approximately five SAS employees and this contact lasted an average of 15 seconds at a time. Thus SAS is "created" 50 million times a year, 15 seconds at a time. These 50 million "moments of truth" ultimately determine whether SAS will succeed or fail as a company. They are the moments when we must prove to our customers that SAS is their best alternative.

If we are truly dedicated to orienting our company toward each customer's individual needs, then we cannot rely on rulebooks and instructions from distant corporate offices. We have to place responsibility for ideas, decisions, and actions with the people who are SAS during those 15 seconds, ticket agents, flight attendants, baggage handlers and all the other front-line employees. If they have to go up the organizational chain of command for a decision on an individual problem, those 15 golden seconds will elapse without a response and we will have lost an opportunity to earn a loyal customer.[13]

How will employees act in that moment of truth? There is no time to check with a manager or get authorizations from three people. Employees must fully understand the value of customer service and then decide how to best meet the individual customer's needs.

WHO IS THE MOST IMPORTANT PERSON IN YOUR ORGANIZATION?

The president of a large oil and gas company asks, "Who is the most important person in this organization?" He always answers his own question saying, "The person who answers the phone!"

Providing good customer service is the corporate mission and it starts with answering the phone on the first ring.

But it's not good enough just to set goals; the entire organization must be oriented to support them. Who was on the front cover of the company newsletter after the telephone goal was instituted? The employee who answered the phone 85 percent of the time on the first ring (compared with 65 percent for the company overall).

The mission of customer responsiveness was also defined as getting back to customers within 5 minutes of a phone query and within 24 hours of written queries. Once that became the corporate goal, it forced the elimination of unnecessary bureaucracy. If an agent in the credit-card adjustment department was to call the customer back within five minutes, the company had to eliminate multiple approvals from supervisors and managers. Employees openly questioned policies and practices. Were certain meetings necessary? Were certain procedures necessary? Which approvals were unnecessary? Where should decisions be made? Authority had to be given to the front line to make decisions in order to satisfy the goal of answering customers' queries within five minutes.

The goal permeated the company. Internal departments, such as finance, service their internal clients by answering the phone on the first ring, responding to calls in less than five minutes and replying in writing in less than 24 hours so that the front-line people can fulfill their goals.

The people on the front line feel tremendously motivated when their true value to the organization is appreciated.

Treating employees as internal customers cannot guarantee high-quality customer service, but not doing so ensures that customer service will be performed without enthusiasm. If companies expect employees to "Greet each customer with a smile," they should first give employees something to smile about. At the very least, companies should ensure that internal systems are not increasing the difficulties of employees entrusted with the responsibility of delivering service.

CUSTOMER SERVICE OF THE FUTURE: MASS CUSTOMIZATION

As Alvin Toffler points out in *The Third Wave*, production of goods in the Middle Ages was by artisans. When you wanted a shirt, you went to the tailor who measured you and produced your shirt. When industrialization came along, we entered the era of mass production, creating the need for standard sizes. Goods were mass-produced.

Today we are poised to enter the era of mass customization. I went to a shoe store and stood on a device that measures the contours of the soles of my feet. The information is sent to a computer in the back of the shop and three minutes later it spits out a custom-made orthodic insole. The sales rep then takes a mass-produced shoe in your size and the style you like, and slips in the insole. It is the most comfortable shoe you have ever worn. Technology enables us to return to the days of custom crafting. It is enabling the emergence of mass customization. One-to-one customer relationships are hot among leading companies.[14]

FROM MASS CUSTOMIZATION TO CUSTOMER OWNERSHIP

In the fourth wave, knowledge is a commodity. Self-reflection and self-correction are required to take us to a higher plane. To get a 10,000-foot view of the situation I would ask, "How do we add significant new value for customers? How do we create top-of-mind position with customers? How do we create customer insistence?" Many credit-card companies provide a toll-free number for you to call to cancel your card if you lose your wallet. If you call before a thief uses the card, you are not responsible for the charges. But most people have quite a few credit cards in their wallet, perhaps a corporate American Express as well as a personal Visa and MasterCard in addition to gas cards, department store cards, debit cards and ATM access cards.

One day in the middle of the mall you start panicking because you realize that your wallet is missing. You don't remember which cards you had, let alone all the toll-free numbers you need to cancel them.

How can a credit-card company such as Visa gain mind share such that when a customer thinks "credit card," the first company that comes to mind is Visa? How could Visa create such new value for its customers that whenever they had a problem with any credit card they would call Visa? And begin to treat Visa as though it were the first point of contact for any credit-card information? How does a company build customer insistence – create a value that is so great that consumers insist on channeling their dealing through only one credit-card company? To achieve this, the thinking has to be at the meta level.

If Visa is striving for top-of-mind positioning, executives must think beyond their own credit card to all credit cards. What new value can be created for customers so that when they think of credit cards they immediately turn to Visa? Visa could record the numbers and expiry dates of all the credit cards their customers possess and provide a toll-free number, something like 1-800-I-LOST-IT.

If customers lose their wallet, they call to report the loss or theft and automatically Visa would cancel all their credit cards. The customer service agent could then ask if they would like all their cards automatically renewed, or whether some of the competing cards could be canceled and the limit increased on their Visa. By serving customers in their time of need, Visa would become the single source to turn to for help with credit cards. At times of crisis this would also offer an opportunity to convert more of customers' business to Visa. The service would also give Visa insight into consumers' total credit pattern.

Once the service had gained a dominance in the market such that everyone called this service to cancel all their cards, Visa could begin charging other credit-card companies for the service it provides to them. At that point Visa would have to drop trying to switch credit away from the other cards to Visa.

Leaders must continually venture out of their comfort zone – the familiarity of doing things the old way – and work with teams in their organizations to develop new products and services. This will ensure higher-than-average margins in the long run, but will require many attempts and tolerance for a great number of failures in the short run. This tolerance for ambiguity, acceptance of failure and comfort with not knowing all the answers are at the core of the learning paradox.

TO SUMMARIZE . . .

- It costs five times as much to develop a new customer as to keep one.
- Organizations need to perceive customer service as the customer does.
- Everyone in an organization must work from a customer focus viewpoint.
- Imagining a future of possibilities for the customer is the key to growth.
- Employees should be treated as internal customers.

WORKSHOP QUESTIONS AND ACTIVITIES

- How long ago were the current measures of performance in your organization set? Do they represent a balance of customer satisfaction variables (customer/market performance) and economic performance (internal/cost performance) variables? Do they relate your performance to the competition's performance?

- Who are your most important customers, and why? How many individual names of important customers can you name? Do the people making key decisions about the products and services that your organization offers have sufficient experience in using your products or services?

- Pretend that you are the customer of your organization or department. Describe improvements in the goods and services you provide. Use the quadrant graph on page 255 to rate your company's activities versus customer satisfaction.

- Rank all the goods and services you provide according to which ones will enhance satisfaction the most, which can be implemented fastest, at the least cost, with the least disruption. Create a quick implementation plan.

- What new product or service would keep you coming back to your company?

- Suggest online services that your company can provide to save customer time while increasing profit.

- If you were designing a neural network for your company, what information would you feed it?

- How often do your customers buy product? How do they spend their money? Create the demographic, psycho graphic and geographic profiles of your best customers.

- How could you make it easier for customers to do business with you?

- Design a cross-marketing program for your company. Explore ideas for strategic partnerships. What organization might your company form an alliance with to create more customer appeal? What would these partners bring to the partnership? How would they gain from the partnership?

- Design a new voicemail system that is easy to use and lets customers get what they need immediately.

- How can you customize your product or service for customers?

Reflection:

What is the key learning/insight for me in this chapter?

Action:

What one action shall I take tomorrow to move learning into action? And over time repeat, to move action into habit?

CHAPTER 11

Real Time Systems: The New IT Paradigm

Radical advances in information technology (IT) are fundamentally changing the way companies do business. The scope and depth of the changes wrought by IT are profoundly revolutionary. Organizations that fail to make the transition to the new IT paradigm will cease to exist.

TECHNOLOGY: THE ORGANIZATION'S NERVOUS SYSTEM

Information technology has become the central nervous system of businesses. In the human body, the central nervous system feeds information to the brain in real time, allowing the body to react almost immediately to a dynamic, changing climate. If I stick my finger in a glass of ice water, I know immediately that the water is cold. My central nervous system connects everything in my body to everything else. It allows my right hand to coordinate with my left. It allows me to react appropriately.

Many companies do not work in "real time" because separate departments have separate systems that can't communicate with one another (Chapter 4). Electronic Data Interchange (EDI) allows information to flow seamlessly through and between organizations. According to OASIS, 95 percent of Fortune 1000 companies use EDI, but only two percent of small and medium sized enterprises use EDI. There are opportunities for small and medium sized companies to get real time information by using web technology – allowing customers to access information in real time and integrating with supply chain partners. Worldwide, $15 billion a year could be saved by using EDI, eliminating time-consuming data re-entry and consequently reducing the cost of errors.[1]

WAL-MART: A RETAILING CASE STUDY

Of the top 100 US retail discounters in business in 1976, fewer than 24 remain in existence today! What happened to them? Wal-Mart! In 1983, Wal-Mart's 641 stores had sales of $4.8 billion. By 2001, Wal-Mart had grown to 2643 stores with collective sales of over $191 billion. And Wal-Mart still has lots of room for growth, as the company has captured approximately only a small percent of the $3 trillion US retailing market.

In 1994, Wal-Mart entered the Canadian market, purchasing 120 Woolco stores. By 2001, the company had become the largest discount retailer in Canada. Wal-Mart currently holds 35 percent of the Canadian discount and department store market.[2] Wal-Mart's entry spells a real shake-up for Canadian retailing.

Studies show that when Wal-Mart comes to town, sales for certain retail sectors decline significantly. Losses in hardware, jewelry, variety, shoes and discount sectors can run as high as 30 percent. How can retailers compete against the Wal-Mart onslaught? To find out, we must explore Wal-Mart's philosophy, systems and structures.

Wal-Mart works to eliminate overhead to be able to offer to customers the lowest possible prices. Wal-Mart maintains the lowest prices on 600 items that are top-of-mind items with consumers. Wal-Mart's strategic use of information technology allows it to achieve these objectives.

"Traiting"

In business today data warehousing and data mining are buzzwords. But these hot topics have little relevance unless I can understand how databases allow companies to more accurately predict what customers want.

Information technology allows Wal-Mart to "trait" its stores. Before opening a new Wal-Mart, executives study the local geographic, demographic, psychographic, financial and cultural profiles of the surrounding area. Using a relational database, the "traits" of the prospective store are compared with those of all 2,600 stores to find which are most similar. The program then predicts which 70,000 items – known as stock-keeping units (SKUs) – will be the best sellers in the new location. The choice is made from hundreds of thousands of potential SKUs.

For instance, if the target town is near a freshwater lake, the store will stock freshwater fishing gear. If it's near the ocean, it will stock saltwater fishing gear. If it's more than a given distance from any fishing area, no fishing gear may be stocked. But if a certain percentage of area residents in the catchment area own cottages where there is fishing, the store will stock fishing gear.

"Traiting" allows Wal-Mart to open a brand-new store and immediately begin selling up to $300 of merchandise per square foot, which is more than double the industry average. More importantly, "traiting" allows Wal-Mart to maximize profit per square foot from the beginning.

Wal-Mart's information network fosters continuous learning. Traiting shows how information technology has become Wal-Mart's mind, memory and central nervous system, analyzing the impact and interrelationship of a complex web of factors. The company encourages local managers to play with their product mix after the initial "traiting." They constantly fine-tune the product mix, aiming to increase profit per square foot, which is more important than sales per square foot. Managers are always asking, "What merchandise will sell well in my location and yield the highest profit margins?" When a manager discovers a hot new sales trend, this information is rapidly transmitted through the computer network, and managers of every other Wal-Mart store with similar "traits" begin experimenting with the product mix in their locations.

> Our technology helps us buy the right merchandise at the right time, and have it in the right place at the right price.
> *Wal-Mart annual report*

Imagine that a Wal-Mart manager noticed a large spike in consumption of two quite different products, Pampers diapers and Budweiser beer, at 6:00 p.m. The manager would ask, "Why?" He would think about some scenarios: hubby is working at the office and gets a call from his wife who is at home with the new baby. She says, "Honey, would you pick up some diapers on your way home?" "Of course, darling," he replies. On his way home, he would stop at Wal-Mart to buy Pampers and think, "While I'm here, what would I like? BUD!" But he would have to walk 17 aisles over and two rows down to get the beer.

The manager would ask, "Why are we making it so difficult for him?" So he would put a huge facing of Budweiser on one side of an aisle and Pampers on the opposite side of the aisle, right at the front of the store. The result is an increase in sales of both.

This imaginary case shows an interesting relationship between data, information, knowledge and wisdom. We need to "mine" data for information. We are all drowning in data. There have never been more data in the history of the earth. But data give no strategic information. From data we can extract information – Budweiser sales increase at 6:00 p.m. and Pampers sales increase at 6:00 p.m. But there are 70,000 other items in an average Wal-Mart whose sales may increase or decrease at any given time of day. The information technology sifts through millions of possible correlations in sales to highlight for the manager that these two items increase in sales at 6:00 p.m., predominantly on the same checkout bills. If this information creates a deeper understanding of customers and their behavior, then new knowledge is created.

> The people who work in corporations are not the problem; it is the systems and structures in which they work that create the problems.
> *W. Edwards Deming*

Knowledge is useless unless it is put into practice. Therefore, Wal-Mart managers must be empowered to make such local decisions as positioning the Bud opposite the Pampers. Action creates wisdom. Wisdom stems from the application of knowledge.

The expression "knowledge is power" is incorrect. Knowledge is potential power. Application of knowledge creates power. This is an example of the learning paradox at its best: organizations need to create new knowledge and then find applications to take advantage of the new understanding.

"Real Time"

Information technology allows Wal-Mart to work in "real time." Just 90 minutes after each store has closed, head office knows the day's sales figures. Analysis can be done by store, by merchandise item, by region or by any other parameter. The cost-effectiveness of regional advertising can be analyzed in relation to a specific product's performance and compared with other areas where there was no advertising. Based on this information, a decision can be made whether the promotion should be continued or altered.

Organizations that compete in real time have a tremendous advantage over those that don't. To realize how powerful an advantage, imagine my body only gave me biofeedback once a quarter!

Wal-Mart's largest suppliers manage their own inventories. This is known as vendor-managed inventory (VMI). Ninety minutes after every store closes, Wrangler knows exactly how many pairs of its jeans were sold that day. And not just how many, but what sizes and styles – straight leg, wide leg, boot fit, stonewashed or pre-bleached – and in what regions.

What happens when Wal-Mart comes to town and competes with a long-standing local retailer? The local retailer, not wanting to lose customers, wants to compete head to head with Wal-Mart. Both have 20,000 pairs of jeans in stock. Both begin an aggressive sale of jeans at $19.95 a pair. Both stores sell 5,000 pairs the first day of the sale.

Because Wal-Mart's major suppliers know every night what was sold in each store by size and style, they can go into production that night and the next morning. Since Wrangler is online with Wal-Mart, it knows how much stock different promotions will require and is prepared for the jeans onslaught, having had past experience with buying patterns and responses to promotions. Wrangler guarantees shelf replacement within 72 hours. An order for 5,000 jeans is shipped out within two days to the regional Wal-Mart warehouse. Wal-Mart guarantees daily delivery to its individual stores. The 5,000 jeans arrive on Day Four of the sale.

We work at the other store. Once a week, all the department heads give their orders to the head buyer. The buyer collates these and places the orders with head office. At head office, the orders from 120 regional stores arrive by fax. Then the lengthy process of collating and merging these orders begins. By the end of the second week, orders are placed with the manufacturers. The jeans manufacturer begins production and, by the end of the third week, ships our company-wide order to our main warehouse. This order is then sorted and broken up to fill the individual store orders and shipped off to us by the end of the fourth week (along with everything else our store ordered). By the time we get the jeans on the shelf in the clothing department, it's five weeks later. If there are any other steps in this process – for example, using a distributor instead of dealing directly with the manufacturer – the process takes even longer.

So both stores, selling jeans at the same price in the same market, are moving 5,000 pairs of jeans a day. Both stores run out after four days, but Wal-Mart receives 5,000 pairs late on Day Four. And not just 5,000 pairs of any jeans, but the "hot" stock – the sizes and styles that sold on Day One. Wal-Mart sells out again on Day Five. Since Day Two's sale of 5,000 jeans triggered alarm bells with Wrangler, 5,000 more jeans arrive late on Day Five. And so on.

Meanwhile, at our store, we know we won't see any more jeans for six weeks! We don't know how, but Wal-Mart has sold 5,000 pairs of jeans every day for the first five days. We know the store began with only 20,000 pairs. We begin to panic. All our customers are flocking across the street to Wal-Mart. We get on the phone call the manufacturer direct, eliminating the step of ordering through head office. We pull strings, and place a special, one-time volume order. At the end of Week Four, we celebrate because 120,000 pairs of jeans arrive. Hallelujah! But in the intervening four weeks, Wal-Mart has sold 5,000 pairs of jeans a day – 120,000 pairs in all – and few people in our area will buy jeans in the next three years. Now we really have a problem because we're stuck with $2,500,000 of dead inventory. The head of the clothing department is fired for incompetence.

And what happens to the jeans manufacturer that supplies our store? The manufacturer is plagued by stop/start problems created by our ordering pattern. When the manufacturer was pressed to produce 120,000 pairs of jeans in two weeks (in addition to meeting the needs of all its regular customers), the extra overtime shifts that were required cut into profits. And for the next several years, the manufacturer receives no further orders from our store as we work to flog the slow-moving jeans. Thus the manufacturer goes from boom to bust. Erratic production increases manufacturing costs. The "ordering system" does not allow the manufacturer to optimize production runs and thereby lower costs.

> Opportunity comes to pass, not pause
> *Dr Michael Smurfit,*
> *Jefferson Smurfit Group*
> *CEO*

But the failure is a systems failure: one store works in real time and the other has a five-week delay. As Peter Senge, in *Fifth Discipline: The Art & Practice of the Learning Organization*, points out, we need "systems thinking."

Increasingly organizations have to compete on speed and organizational capability not just product, price and positioning.

Lower prices

Real-time information technology helps make Wal-Mart a desirable customer to its largest suppliers. Every night, Wal-Mart pays Wrangler by electronic funds transfer (EFT) for products sold that day. Most retailers pay their suppliers in 30 days, if then. With these payment terms and its high volume of orders, Wal-Mart can negotiate very favorable deals with its suppliers.

Basing orders on up-to-the-minute information means the manufacturer produces only what the fashion market is demanding today – not last year, last quarter or even last week. And the orders are by region, so even if wide-leg, stonewashed jeans are the rage in New York and boot-cut jeans the craze in Texas, Wrangler still ships exactly what is needed to each regional Wal-Mart distribution center. Information technology allows Wal-Mart to lower its prices because it ends up with less "dead" or slow-moving inventory. Thus the technology has created an alignment between retailer and supplier interests: the retailer sells more and the supplier sells more. The retailer does more inventory turns. The supplier doesn't have to deal with erratic ordering and can therefore reduce manufacturing costs. The retailer keeps on top of current fashion trends, whereas buyers for other retailers are expected to predict the fashion trends and place orders a year in advance! The manufacturer isn't pressured to take back dead inventory. There isn't any because it produced only what was selling in the first place. For the retailer, there is little negative cash flow and dead inventory; for the manufacturer, there is payment the day the inventory sells. Both organizations know exactly what is and isn't selling.

> Computers in the future
> may weigh less than
> 1.5 tons.
> *Popular Mechanics, 1949*

Increased profitability

Once an organization uses real-time information technology, the possibilities for analysis are endless. For example, with its IT system, Wal-Mart can analyze profit per square foot of floor space. A store manager might think she should dedicate more floor space to Christmas trees in December and perhaps put on a local promotion. But Wal-Mart's system allows the store manager to analyze costs and margins. She discovers that the store makes only a $4 profit per square foot of floor space dedicated to Christmas trees. After investigating further, she finds that another hot-seller around Christmas is Nintendo game. These take up only a few inches of shelf space, can be stacked 10 shelves high and net a $38 profit margin per square foot. Rather than dedicate more floor space to Christmas trees, the store manager puts up a huge Nintendo display and launches an aggressive local flyer promotion.

The system also allows for profit maximization. Many retailers are competing blindly, they can't tell you what their true costs, margins or numbers of inventory turns are. They have an idea, a feeling about it, but IT transforms the hunch into a science.

Competing with Wal-Mart and opportunity cost

Wal-Mart's information technology analyzes which *existing* stock items *did* and *didn't* sell. But for items the company has never stocked, the system can't predict which items *would* sell if the company carried them. Wal-Mart works to offer the broadest range of merchandise possible to attract the widest segment of society. While Wal-Mart stocks over 70,000 SKUs in an average store, there are still hundreds of thousands of items the company *doesn't* stock. Items that would sell if Wal-Mart stocked them represent a lost *opportunity* for sales.

Opportunity cost is the cost of losing potential business and it is rarely measured. Opportunity costs are larger than just the lost potential sales. In the Wal-Mart example, if a retailer doesn't stock a product that a consumer wants, it drives that customer to search for the product at a competitor's store, where the consumer is likely to buy other items. If this occurs frequently, the consumer will come to think of the other store first when shopping.

Opportunity cost is difficult to measure. First, because the retailer can't analyze the sales data for items it doesn't sell. A competitor is not going to share its own analysis of which of its SKUs is the hottest-selling items. Suppliers are the sole source of information, but they only have data about their products or category, not comparative data for all SKUs.

Auditors measure what exists: existing sales, existing inventory, existing inventory turns. But how can you measure what doesn't exist? The sales you could have made if you had carried the item? The inventory turns you could have had? The profit you could have made?

How can accountants get some idea of what people would buy at, say, a

Wal-Mart but are not able to? Conduct exit interviews with shoppers to discover what they would have purchased had the store carried it.

As you recall, when Wal-Mart executives "trait" a potential site for a new store, they study the surrounding area. If fishing is nearby, the store will stock fishing gear. But Wal-Mart doesn't have the widest selection of items in any category. Instead, the company stocks only the fastest-selling items.

Wal-Mart's fishing bags may sell for $19 but have only two pockets, while in specialty fishing stores fishing bags with 16 waterproof pockets sell for $99. In its effort to offer the lowest prices, Wal-Mart may cut back too far on features that anglers want. The optimum bag may be one that has eight watertight pockets and it would sell quickly at $49.

To compete with Wal-Mart, retailers must work to find the holes in Wal-Mart's merchandising selection and meet consumers' unmet needs. Some of these niches will be highly profitable. Niche retailers can also compete on the depth of selection in a category. Wal-Mart will only carry one or two types of fishing bags, whereas a specialty retailer may carry three or four, or fishing bags from every manufacturer in the category.

All organizations need to examine the opportunity costs of not changing, not creating new products and services, not having real time capabilities.

No customer wrote to Chrysler asking them to introduce the minivan. No one asked Alexander Graham Bell to invent the telephone.

Similarly, no one at IBM was ever fired for not inventing the computer notebook. Toshiba took the honors. No one at Lotus was fired for not creating a *Windows*-based spreadsheet, until it was too late. What is the opportunity cost of not being creative, innovative and first to market? This is rarely discussed in organizations and never measured.

CAN'T MEASURE? CAN'T MANAGE!

Imagine going through school and receiving no marks on your tests, essays and final exams. At the end of the year you receive one mark. How much value would that mark have?

You would have no way of knowing which tests you did well in and which you failed, which essays were good and which were poor, what studying paid off and when going to the pub the night before really cost you. You wouldn't even know which subjects you did well in and which you didn't. How could you improve? Your mark would be totally meaningless. In business, if you can't measure your performance, you have no way of knowing how well you're doing in meeting customers' needs and company goals.

In most corporations, employee evaluations may be done annually, audits are conducted annually, inventory is taken semi-annually, projected and actual budgets are compared annually, with the real emphasis put on quarterly financial reporting. Imagine if my body gave me biofeedback only once a quarter, and I walked into the kitchen and put my hand on a red-hot burner. I'd have toast for a hand before I even knew I had a problem. It is impossible to think of our bodies working in anything but real time.

Let's say you are responsible for hiring a pay-and-benefits consultant to help your organization. You are choosing between two companies. Both have 80 staff located in your city.

I am a consultant working at Hewitt Associates. Hewitt has 80 consultants in your city and 11,000 consultants worldwide. I come to see you knowing nothing about your business. But I listen intently while you discuss your challenges and I ask a lot of questions. I return to the office, type up a case study and send an email memo to 150 Hewitt specialist consultants in nine countries who work in this field, asking what they have done in similar situations. By the next morning, I have 15 responses, each 10 pages long, detailing specific case studies. On the third day, I send you a 50-page report outlining a number of possible approaches.

Now think of a consultant at the other firm, which also has 80 consultants. When he arrives to assess your problem, he also has no knowledge of your exact industry, but neither does anyone else in his office. Which consultant will you hire? By hiring Hewitt, are you hiring 80 consultants or 11,000?

Information technology enables new working relationships within organizations. Colleagues can be anywhere in the world. But introducing new IT structures without changing management structures will not give an organization any competitive advantage. For instance, if Hewitt's promotion, recognition and compensation systems were all based on increasing revenue in local offices, why would consultants take any time from their schedules to work on a proposal from a foreign office? In other words, the management structure is just as important as the IT structure for enabling new relationships within organizations.

The information flow can be global. Some companies are outsourcing a great deal of computer programming to India and Pakistan. Former barriers to business, including national borders, time zones and even language, are now broken.

Computers have become the central nervous system of organizations, giving them the ability to respond to a changing market in real time, and become learning organizations.

I have some friends who are computer programmers. I think programmers are genetically different from the rest of us. One friend says he does his best work at 3:00 a.m. But organizations are stuck in an old paradigm of production, where workers were required to be physically present at the production line at certain times. From Alvin Toffler's perspective this bias comes out of a second wave – industrial revolution bias. Peter Senge points out that workers were actually known as "hands."[3]

INFORMATION TECHNOLOGY ENABLES NEW RELATIONSHIPS

The power of information technology isn't only in automating old processes but also in enabling new relationships. American Airlines' Sabre reservation system is a case in point. A survey of travel agents conducted by American Airlines revealed that agents had a strong tendency to book the first available flight. So American developed the Sabre reservation system and gave free terminals to a test group of travel agents. When agents made on-line inquiries about available flights, the system always listed American Airlines flights first. American experienced a 40 percent growth in bookings and a 40 percent surge in profitability from the test group. So after refining the system, Sabre launched the system throughout North America, giving all travel agents a free terminal. American's profit surged.

Sabre is the leading computer reservation system in the world and more than 40 percent of all reservations made through travel agents are processed by Sabre. The system processes more than 400 million bookings per year, which amounts to $75 billion worth of travel each year. More than 66,000 travel agents in 114 countries rely on it.

Other airlines soon caught on and began the two-year process of developing their own reservation systems. Two years later they went to travel agents offering free terminals and on-line access. But most agents said, "Thanks, but no thanks. It took us two years to get used to Sabre, and we're not going to go through that again." This example raises an important point: it's better to have a new product 80 percent right and be the first to market it than 99.9 percent right and two years late.

Sabre forged strong ties with travel agents through IT, "locking" them into a new relationship. Once this new relationship was well established, Sabre approached the other airlines and said, "Look, up until now we've been providing you with a free service by listing your flights. We're going to charge you for it now and if you don't pay we'll drop you from the listing." Today, Sabre generates more profits from American Airlines' competitors than American does from flying its own planes!

Sabre subsequently expanded. When you book a hotel with your travel agent, it's done through Sabre. When you book a car rental, it's done through Sabre. With each booking, Sabre takes a cut. At some point, American Airlines may get out of the airline business altogether.

American Airlines' use of information technology enabled the company to create a powerful new relationship with travel agents. At the time, no other airline had developed a system that enabled the agents to offer something new to their customers – the ability to instantly ascertain flight availability and offer advance-booking, discount fares.

Sabre is also a key player in the B2C online travel reservation market. Sabre owns 70 percent of Travelocity.com, the leading travel reservation website in the world, with 18 percent of the online travel purchase market.[4] Started in 1996, by 2001, Travelocity.com had sold 8 million airline tickets and had 21 million members.[5]

Some airline companies are selling directly to their customers over the web. The Luton, UK-based discount airline EasyJet sells 77 percent of its tickets across its website. The company became selling tickets over the web in 1998 and by August 2000, had sold 4 million tickets online. EasyJet cuts out travel agents all together by selling directly to its customers.

California-based computer maker Sun Microsystems touts the slogan, "The network is the computer." Taking this slogan one step further, the Sabre case study shows that, "The network is the business."

When I say "encyclopedia," what comes to mind? "Large." What else comes to mind? "Many volumes." What else? "Britannica." Yes! For over 200 years *Encyclopaedia Britannica* defined the standard for encyclopedias. First published in 1768, it is the oldest and largest English-language general encyclopedia. The 15th edition first published in 1974 consisted of 32 volumes. Updated every five years, it was sold primarily through direct mail and from door to door for $1,599 US a set. It has approximately 33,000 pages and weighs 128 pounds.

But during 1994, a company that had never published or sold encyclopedias became the number-one vendor. Microsoft. In 1994, computer retailers began giving away a free copy of Microsoft *Encarta* to customers buying a new $2,000 computer. Imagine that in your industry another company begins giving away a competing product as a premium!

Encarta integrated color illustrations with sound and video clips. Microsoft redefined what an encyclopedia was. Instead of taking up a whole shelf, you put *Encarta* in your pocket.

Production costs of *Encarta* were a fraction of those of *Encyclopaedia Britannica* and the product was updated quarterly. But it wasn't just *Encarta* that killed Britannica's markets overnight. Parents who could afford it used to buy a set of encyclopedias for their children's education. But today parents buy their kids a multimedia PC. The multimedia computer, not just the CD encyclopedia, led to the demise of the old encyclopedia market. As Don Tapscott writes in *Digital Economy:*

> In response, Britannica has taken a bold and innovative strategy. It has taken the next logical step and put its encyclopedia on the Net, charging a daily fee for those who "subscribe." The set of books has become a subscription service. The potential impact (and opportunities for the company) goes far beyond the CD-ROM model. Rather than updating every decade or every year – or even every three months as the competition does, the encyclopedia on the Net can be updated hourly! Obviously the amount of information available is much greater than can be held on a CD. In fact, the amount of information is limitless. But most important, because it is on the Net, Britannica becomes something much greater than an encyclopedia. . . . There are "hot links" enabling the reader to instantly link to related subjects contained on other Web servers around the world. It becomes a directory to all human knowledge that is electronically stored!

By embracing interactive multimedia, Britannica has been transformed from a mere publisher of books to a company providing access to all human knowledge.

Encyclopaedia Britannica is changing its customer base. Rather than selling simply to individuals, Encyclopaedia Britannica is now making licensing agreements with institutions. By September 1997, about 800 colleges and universities were subscribing to Britannica Online, and almost 40 percent of US undergraduates have access to the service through their institutions. A few dollars of each student's tuition goes to unlimited access to Britannica.

Encyclopaedia Britannica is a case of a company that changed their product (from book to subscription service, compilation of human knowledge to a digital directory); changed their distribution channels and market place (from physical to digital); and changed their customers (from families to everybody, including institutions). This kind of corporate action goes far beyond the process of reengineering. It is transformation for the digital economy.[6]

What happened to *Encyclopaedia Britannica* is frightening enough to give most people a knot in their stomach. Literally everything about the company had to change – its product, how it was delivered and sold. Ultimate security comes from changing.

In October 1999, Britannica took its strategy one step further by posting the entire contents of its highly regarded encyclopedia onto its website, www.britannica.com. The site has proved to be enormously popular. More than 10 million people visited the site each day when it was launched in October 1999. The site allows simultaneous searches of the encyclopedia, the web, and a large number of magazines. The service is available for US$5 per month or US$50 per year.

Dr Terry Paulson, a US speaker, notes:

Everyone knows the importance of lifelong learning, but how simple it is to settle for the easy learning opportunities. Anyone can quickly copy what you learn easily. As adults, we are often so afraid of being wrong that we play it safe when we need to be going for the uncertainty and the unexplored territory that will give us a sustainable strategic advantage. Relearn your childhood excitement of difficult, demanding, and challenging learning that will again require you to persevere through to skills worth learning. The difficult learning you and your team do will produce useful knowledge that others will have a harder time copying. Target your learning in the areas where you can strategically benefit you and your organization. Once you have mastered a new strategic competence, start looking for your next difficult learning opportunity. In short, the intent to seek knowledge in difficult areas may be your most important habit to ensure you and your organization's survival in the future. What difficult areas have you been avoiding that just may be the best place for you to start learning?[7]

NEW BANKING RELATIONSHIPS

Information Technology is not just more efficient, it's radically different. It enables new relationships and creates new markets. If, through ATM machines, I can get money any time, anywhere, in any currency, why do I need traveler's checks? I don't! Does that mean the ATM network enables the banks to compete with traveler's check companies such as American Express and Thomas Cook? Absolutely! The technology has allowed the banks to grow into a new market. With Interac and CIRRUS, information technology has blurred the whole concept of competition in banking. Information technology can change who your competitors are.

The Interac system is an example of "co-opetition." It requires the cooperative efforts of all banks. When I withdraw money in Florida, I'm doing it at a bank I've never even heard of. Co-opetition allows all banks to compete with traveler's check companies.

The development and spread of the inter-banking system is self-financing. When I withdraw $100 in Florida, I pay a $1 fee for the privilege of doing so. I am willing to pay the premium for the convenience, time saving and the one percent fee I avoid paying for traveler's checks.

In both the Sabre and Interac cases, the systems started small. As revenues increased, the companies reinvested in expansion. In the case of the airline industry, by the time competitors woke up, it was too late and the investment required to catch up was too great. The competitors were cooked. The same is true of Wal-Mart. Today, Wal-Mart invests millions of dollars a year in IT and the annual investment is growing. The catch-up costs are prohibitive.

So start small. Growth should come from continually reinvesting from cash flow. It's organic growth as opposed to forced growth. Paying the price, learning from small mistakes and refining and developing the corporate culture around the new IT support new relationships.

Individuals and corporations need to continually ask, "What are the 'impossible' things that are holding us back from dramatic performance improvements, both personally and organizationally? A number of processes foster creativity (Chapter 6). The goal of creativity is to make the "impossible" possible. Always question paradigms. Always think conceptually.

ALL RELATIONSHIPS MUST CHANGE

Information technology on its own does not give an organization an advantage. For instance, if I have a new computer on my desk but don't know how to use it, what advantage does it give? If everyone in the culture but the executives know how to use email, how much use will email have? To achieve a strategic advantage, the organization's culture as a whole must support the newly enabled relationships. Everything in the organization, including human resource systems and corporate training, must be oriented to the new paradigm.

As the investment in information technology grows, so must the corresponding investment in people. That is why 63 percent of the cost of maintaining a PC is hidden (Chapter 8). It is informal training and support for the end users!

The employee-employer relationship has to change as IT advancements enable new relationships. Increasingly, work requires creativity, ingenuity and thinking. As in the earlier example of the computer programmer who worked best at 3:00 a.m., some people are most productive at times other than nine to five. Organizations need to create systems and structures within the workplace (and workplace may not be the office, it may be in a client's office, in the car or at home) that support people working when it is best for them. All organizational structures and relationships need to be re-evaluated.

THE WORKPLACE OF THE FUTURE AND HOTELING

Ernst & Young International (E&Y) spearheaded an interesting program. Executives at E&Y, the second largest US accounting firm, noticed that their best consultants were spending the least amount of time in the office. Consultants with the highest billable hours were always out at their clients' offices, leaving their beautiful window and corner offices vacant. It followed that most consultants would be more effective if they were encouraged to spend more time in the field. In cities where the cost of real estate is high, large office complexes seemed an extravagant waste. As a result, the Workplace of the Future program began. Ernst & Young decided to support consultants by giving them a notebook computer, a cellular phone and cellular data fax modem. These were seen as perks by the consultants; from the company's perspective they were productivity enhancers, allowing the consultants to perform more work in the field and enabling them to communicate with support staff and customers. The company was able to reduce its total office space, realizing net savings in the millions of dollars.

This program is not to be confused with the home office. Obviously, while the home office offers gains in reducing real-estate expenses, it does not promise any significant improvement in face-to-face contact with clients. The mobile office addresses both needs.

Ernst & Young's New York and Chicago offices pioneered the practice of "hoteling." Under the "hoteling" system, a consultant in transit calls ahead to the office to reserve office space. By the time he or she arrives, his or her personal phone number will have already been transferred to the office phone and a nameplate will have been inserted in the slot beside the office door.

Executives who were initially reluctant to forsake their personal office space have been won over to the system by its financial benefits. Unnecessary office space ultimately increased overhead. As the bottom line improves, the firm can continue to invest in technology and training. Thus the firm becomes more competitive and job security is increased for all employees. Employees are less likely to defend their territory once they realize that their offices often amount to a $10,000 to $20,000 per annum luxury. The Workplace of the Future program will eliminate half of E&Y's total office space in the United States![8]

Many employees have raised concerns about the arrangement. Some believe that reduced time spent in an office complex can be detrimental to team productivity and hence achieving corporate goals. Because communication between staff members is a valuable resource, it has required some discipline on the part of employees to maintain fruitful interaction; otherwise, access to "second opinions" might decline and ultimately result in them making hasty, inappropriate decisions.

Ernst & Young continues to explore alternative means of communication to address the detrimental aspects of the Workplace of the Future initiative. These systems are encapsulated under the banner of "EY/Link." The EY/Link has four components: email, the global telephone network, database on-line discussion groups (which enable employees to work collaboratively on documents across a computer network) and desktop videoconferencing. Ernst & Young hopes that in maximizing information technology, it can maintain interpersonal cohesiveness within a more virtual corporation.

Whenever I cite a case, there is a counter case. Microsoft does not allow its programmers to work off campus, even though they are technically literate and could easily telecommute. Why does Gates demand that they be physically present on the Redmond, Washington, site? Well, first of all, because it is such a workaholic culture that programmers live in their offices, pizza boxes are stacked to the roof.[9] But second, Gates wants programmers to be physically present because of the informal synergy that occurs among programmers.

HUMAN POTENTIAL: WHAT ARE PEOPLE CAPABLE OF?

What are people capable of achieving? Outside of work, we raise families, negotiate $250,000 mortgages, decide which car to buy from a dozen competing makes, travel all over the world, deal with complex relationships and pursue many interests. But some organizations don't give employees the authority to buy $1.19 worth of paper clips. Few companies are tapping the full potential of their employees.

The goal of empowerment is to unleash the potential of employees; to provide the training, knowledge, physical, financial and human resources necessary for employees to learn, grow and thrive.

The new IT paradigm is dramatically changing information flow within organizations. The new IT enables employees to have information at their fingertips. Some companies are adopting open-book management or full disclosure, allowing employees to access any information about the business.

If we ask a construction crew to develop ideas on how to reduce construction costs, but then refuse them access to the blueprints, costs and profit margin figures, we won't get very far. We need full disclosure if we are to allow employees on the front line to make "moment-of-truth" decisions; otherwise, they could give away the store in the name of customer satisfaction.

One time I bought an inkjet printer at an electronics superstore. As you check out there's a sign above the cashier – "We only accept return of goods on the following terms. You must:

- Have the original packaging
- Have the original bill
- Return the goods with 30 days of purchase
- Provide a blood sample"

Now I am on the road so much, I didn't have time to install the printer in the 30-day period. When I did install it, I didn't like it. So I was prepared to fight with the clerk, then appeal to the manager of the computer section, then the store manager, followed by a letter writing campaign to the president of the company and then complain to an ombudsman in the city newspaper, launching a campaign for fairness in retailing. I arrived at the store; I looked at the 18-year-old clerk and boldly stated my position. She looked at me, asked for my phone number and said, "I would be happy to give you a refund."

I was actually disappointed because I had been so ready for a fight. You see, after she keyed my phone number into her terminal, the system pulled up my customer history. She could see my total cumulative purchases to date and knew that I had bought $7,000 of goods from the store in the past year. She decided on the spot to give me a full refund. Her action met the best interests of both the customer and the organization because the $50 profit from the sale of the printer was not worth losing a $7,000-a-year customer. And I am certain that she didn't have an MBA from Harvard or know how to calculate the lifetime value of a customer in net present dollars.

The clerk may or may not have received training about the importance of customer service, or have known that it costs five times as much to attract a new customer than to retain an existing one. She didn't consult a manager. The IT system gave her immediate access to the information she needed to decide how to best meet the company's and store's mission in a moment of truth.

The rapidly changing market environment demands that all participants in an organization be empowered to make these kinds of choices. No more can we afford to centralize decision-making or isolate management from the experience of workers in the field. There must be a free exchange of knowledge among all departments. New technology provides us with the means to give each member of the organization real-time access to the evolving corporate blueprint. This shows why the centralization/decentralization debate misses the point. The IT infrastructure is centralized: the company uses common hardware and software in all its locations. This is centralized – i.e. local stores couldn't make their own hardware/software decisions that would result in incompatibility and no access to real time information. But the decision making of the clerk is decentralized. In other words, she is empowered to make a decision in real time.

WHAT ARE THE TRUE COSTS OF INFORMATION TECHNOLOGY?

The real-time revolution is being driven by technology that is becoming dramatically smaller, cheaper and faster. The price-performance ratio of microprocessors is driving a shift from mainframe computing to client/server computing, based on workstation and micros. The cost per MIPS (million instructions per second) varies depending on the type of processor. Mainframe costs have only recently fallen below $100,000 per MIPS.[10]

As you will recall, Gordon Moore, co-founder of Intel, devised Moore's Law (Chapter 3, page 36). In a 1965 issue of *Electronics Magazine*, Moore speculated that the number of transistors per computer chip would double every year for 10 years while staying at the same price

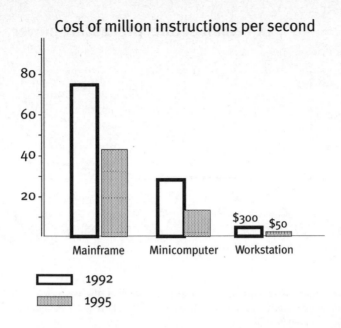

Cost of million instructions per second

	Mainframe	Minicomputer	Workstation
1992			$300
1995			$50

◻ 1992

▦ 1995

point. This became known as Moore's Law. In 1975, he revised his prediction, suggesting the pace would slow to a doubling every two years. The effect of this compounding of computing power has been phenomenal.

The explosion in computing power has been driven by the miniaturization of transistors. In the 1950s, a computer with the power of a 286 took up an entire room and consumed tremendous amounts of power. These computers were based on vacuum tubes and wires. In the 1960s, engineers learned to make these same circuits on single, small pieces of silicon. Silicon-based computers were much faster and consumed almost no power compared to their predecessors. Moore's Law has held true. The number of transistors per chip has doubled every two years since 1961; 1961 – four transistors per chip; 1971 – 2,300; 1982 – 134,000; 1991 – 1.2 million, the Pentium II 300 MHz (1997) – 7.5 million transistors and the Pentium 4, released in 2000 has just under 100 million transistors. Following this trend, Intel is expected to release a chip with one billion transistors by 2007.

The graph lists Intel's processors and their year of introduction. The 386 33 MHz chip (1989) performed at 3.7 million of theoretical operations per second (MTOPS), while the Pentium 4 1.5 GHz chip (2000) performs at 4000 MTOPS.

Chipmakers have been able to increase the number of transistors per

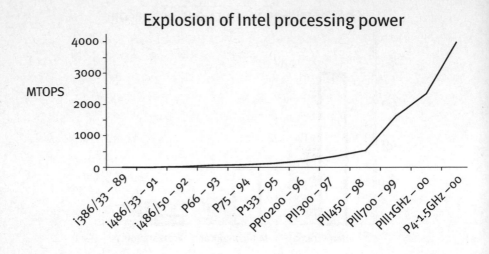

The graph lists Intel's processors and their year of introduction. The 386 33 MHz chip (1989) performed 3.7 million theoretical operations per second (MTOPS), while the Pentium 4 1.5 GHz chip (2000) performs 4,000 MTOPS.

chip by manufacturing smaller and smaller circuits. In 1961, the circuits of the 4004 chip (1971) were 10 microns wide. The Pentium II 300 (1997) line widths are 0.35 microns. In November 2000, Intel announced that it had developed a 0.13-micron manufacturing process. This process allows Intel to manufacture transistors that are approximately 1/1000th the width of a human hair! Since 1990, Intel has been able to launch a smaller manufacturing process every two years, resulting in substantial cost savings.

As the circuits get smaller they can be manufactured closer together, minimizing the distance that an electron must travel. As a result, electrons move faster through the circuits, increasing the overall processor speed. The 0.13-micron processing process will produce processor circuits that are up to 65 percent faster and use 20 percent less power than those built on the 0.18 micron processing process. Lower power consumption means longer battery life for mobile end users.

The corollary of Moore's Law is that the cost of a given amount of computer power drops 50 percent every 18 months. Whenever this happens, demand for computers increases because all sorts of new applications become economically feasible. Intel predicts that it will be able to produce chips with a 0.07-micron manufacturing process. Whatever the power and speed of today's super computers, will be the speed and power of everyday computers in just 15 years.

What applications become possible? Traditional economics assumes a stable environment. Inputs such as land, machinery and labor were assumed not to change. Labor is labor. Markets mature eventually. But the microchip industry invalidates traditional economic theory. By doubling power every 18 months at the same price point, the semiconductor industry is creating a non-linear future. If I can buy the power of today's supercomputer on a $300 chip in 10 years, what will the size of the market be for those chips?

The rapid shrinking of circuit width can't go on forever. There are fixed limits to how tiny transistors can become. But physical limits won't end computings increasing speed and falling costs.

Symmetric Multi Processing (SMP) computers harness the power of up to 30 microchips to produce mainframe-comparable performance. Microsoft's *Windows 2000* operating system allows Intel chips to work in tandem and produce mainframe-like performance. Does this mean that Sun and Microsoft have become competitors of mainframe manufacturers? Paradigm shifts redefine the very nature of competition.

In many cases, the capital costs of client/server solutions are less than the annual maintenance costs of mainframes. For instance, a company may be paying $50,000 a year to maintain a mainframe that will cost only $100,000 to replace with a new UNIX RISC-based system. While the numbers appear very attractive, they are misleading because the hardware is only a small part of the cost of a system. In the old mainframe environment, companies were locked into a dated way of doing business because the cost of changing programming was horrendous and changes took years to implement. In the new paradigm, programming development cycles are dramatically shorter and costs are much lower. But change requires hardware and software expenditures, new programming competencies and a new corporate culture to support the newly enabled relationships. Hardware savings are insignificant compared to these costs.[11]

Windows may be the dominant operating system for computers of all sizes, but upstart *Linux* is steadily creating a niche for itself. *Linux* was an unknown in 1998, but it is now on 31 percent of all Web servers. *Linux* is also being used in cutting edge devices such as pocket-sized computers and set-top boxes. IBM, Sun Microsystems, Dell, Compaq and Intel have all embraced Linux.

The lack of software that would work with *Linux* has been a major limitation. Obviously Microsoft has not created a *Microsoft Office* package for Linux. But some big software players are trying to change that – Corel sells a version of *WordPerfect* for Linux and Sun Microsystems offers *StarOffice* for Linux.

Linux began in 1990 when Finnish graduate student Linus Torvalds decided to create an Unix-like operating system that anyone could download free from the Internet and change to meet individual needs. *Linux* is non-proprietary and is open-source code.

Open-source code allows any computer programmer to access and modify the source code. Individuals can customize the operating system for personal or corporate use. *Linux* asks only that the modified code be posted to their website so that it can be used in future versions of Linux or by any other user worldwide. This means that *Linux* is improved and developed by literally millions of users worldwide. In contrast, Microsoft's Windows operating system is improved and developed by programmers. This is a fundamental paradigm shift for the software industry. Open source gives the client control over their software. They can make improvements without being dependent on the vendor.

There are other significant training questions around IT. When we know that 80 percent of the technology that we will use in 10 years has not yet been invented, how can we design training programs that will prepare people for the future? The only way is to create a learning culture. We need to enshrine lifelong learning as a corporate value.

Given that no individual or organization can accurately predict the future, the IT structure itself must be fast, flexible, focused and friendly. When determining the IT architecture, executives and IT professionals must ensure that it can be rapidly re-architected, that the selected languages allow for applications to be built and altered quickly and that the selected suppliers are forward-looking and continue to invest aggressively in research and development.

PLAN FOR A RADICALLY DIFFERENT FUTURE

The progress in computer technology is not linear, it's exponential. An incremental approach won't work when planning for the future. For instance, here is the assumption Microsoft makes when planning for the future: the size of your hard disk today will be the amount of RAM in the average new PC in seven years. By mid-2001, the average hard disk was 80 gigabytes (GB). What kinds of applications could be enabled if you had 80 gigabytes of RAM in your computer? The future is not just a linear extension of the past, it will be a radically different future. PCs will deliver 16,000 MTOPS (millions of theoretical operations per second) by 2005, and bandwidth costs will have fallen substantially, allowing for richer, two-way interactive content.[12] Using these assumptions, people at Microsoft plan for a different kind of future than the average person can "see" today.

Doom, one of the most popular computer games, is driven by a powerful graphics engine that draws pictures so quickly, you think the motion is instantaneous. The engineering behind it will eventually be the basis for virtual reality on the Internet. The software engineers who created the game, when asked which competitor they feared most didn't answer, "Microsoft, Sega or Nintendo." They replied, "Two guys in a garage, working in total obscurity. Those are the guys who are going to come up with the stuff that will blow us out of the water."[13]

INVESTING IN INFORMATION TECHNOLOGY

Technology has changed forever the retailer-supplier relationship. When making IT investments, Sam Walton, founder of Wal-Mart, always challenged IT professionals to prove the financial case for their proposed investment. IT investments were not made for the sake of investing in technology. In fact, Sam was, in his own words, "cheap." He consistently turned down requests to invest in IT. He would send the IT team back to the drawing board to find a cheaper way. And, as the old saying goes, "Necessity is the mother of invention." Having to constantly go back and work out a less expensive architecture forced the IT team to find the best and least expensive way of achieving corporate objectives. Investments were made only when the IT team could prove the technology would lower costs, raise profits, increase inventory turns, increase margins, reduce dead inventory or create better management tools. The investment was made based on business strategy, not IT strategy.

Wal-Mart's success can't be copied just by duplicating the technology. First, few organizations can afford to make a one-time investment equal to Wal-Mart's investment over the years. Few companies can even match Wal-Mart's annual IT investment. Wal-Mart has been investing heavily in IT for years. Competitors can't hope to catch up overnight. Moreover, the systems and the corporate culture have to be developed together. Information technology is only a tool. People design the systems, people implement the systems and people make the systems work.

Investing in information technology for its own sake is wasteful. What bottom-line impact will IT investments have by enabling new or better business practices? What cultural changes are required to enable new processes?

This chapter ends with an overview of the evolution of computing and the new promise of the fifth era that we are just entering. The fifth era represents a profound paradigm shift. We will have to let go of all our prior assumptions about computing. Until now EDI (electronic data interchange or inter-enterprise integration), as demonstrated in the Wal-Mart/Levi example, has only been pursued by large organizations because implementation costs run in the millions. But the fifth era of computing will make access to real time information a possibility for all organizations through the World Wide Web.

PARADIGM SHIFTS AND PUNCTUATED DISEQUILIBRIUM

Stephen Jay Gould has another way of looking at paradigm shifts. He describes biological evolution in *Wonderful Life*, calling it "punctuated equilibrium":

Over millions of years, species adapt to fill every imaginable niche. Then along comes some external force – a volcano, an asteroid, and an ice age – that changes all the niches and launches a mad scramble for survival. Evolution favors new forms of life that, through a sort of bio-logical lateral thinking, can find a whole new way to thrive. Wings, legs, lungs: all were revolutionary mutations once. Life down the ages has tended to evolve in sudden great leaps, separated by long periods of slow change. The same is true for technology, though the time scale is compressed.[14]

The computer industry has gone through a series of stable periods punctuated by disequilibrium.

FIFTH ERA OF COMPUTING

IBM created the first era of computing by introducing the mainframe. Mainframes were kept in hermetically sealed, air-conditioned rooms. Only IT professionals had access to the computer. There was only one operating system and the IT department controlled it. Programs were written in lines of code. Users worked on dumb terminals and had only periodic or batch access, which meant you ran your program and got the results hours later. The first era created the Information Technology (IT) professional. IT professionals assumed a stature comparable to the Wizard of Oz.

Digital Equipment Corporation upset the mainframe world by making mainframe-type computers, called mini-computers, available at a fraction of the price. This was the second era of computing. Competing propri-etary languages were introduced. Vendors took their clients hostage because the cost of conversion, once systems were implemented, was hor-rendous. Different operating systems would not interchange data so there was no integration among organizations.

Apple ushered in the third era of computing by introducing the per-sonal computer. This was a radical break from the mainframe mindset. Subsequently, IBM introduced the personal computer, which was based on a microchip made by Intel and an operating system from Microsoft. The personal computer took the world by storm, allowing users to work inde-pendently. Individuals gained control over computers. The PC was a democratic force, giving power to the people. But with the freedom of choice came chaos.

This department had Macintoshes, that department had IBM-compatibles. Incompatible operating systems and incompatible programs meant people couldn't share information even within the same organization. PCs couldn't communicate with the mainframe. The resulting proliferation of operating systems and applications created tremendous problems for IT professionals. The cost of ownership of computers increased tremendously as IT professionals were expected to manage the complexity of layers of incompatible software as they integrated new hardware with old.

Despite this chaos the third wave of computing brought forth tremendous innovation and wealth creation. John Doerr, a Silicon Valley venture capitalist, calculates that the introduction of the PC caused the greatest creation of wealth in the history of the planet.[15]

The personal computer was just that – a personal computer. All your applications, files and contacts were stored in one place. To gain access to your data, you could only use your computer.

The fourth wave of computing brought forth the workstation, which was based on microprocessors like those used by PCs, but with power rivaling minicomputers. Workstations introduced multiple processing where up to 64 microprocessors worked together (called symmetrical multiprocessing). Now, microprocessors working together like a 16-cylinder engine could reach performance levels rivaling minis and mainframes. Today, even some mainframes are built using small processors in an architecture called Massively Parallel Processing, where up to thousands of microprocessors work together.

The fourth era saw the rise of networked computers, where powerful workstations (clients) were connected to servers. In a client/server model some computing was done on the client and some on the server. While there was unprecedented growth in networking within organizations, a proliferation of different operating systems created challenges and meant that total cost of ownership was many times the price of the hardware (Chapter 8).

Finally, we are entering the fifth era of computing. It promises an unprecedented amount of freedom to users while significantly reducing the cost of computing.

Imagine that I could only use the telephone at my desk or that I had to carry that same telephone with me wherever I went because I could never use another telephone. Sound crazy? Well isn't that what we do with our computers?

Think about the telephone network. I can walk up to any telephone in the world, dial a sequence of numbers and reach any other telephone in the world any time of day. This is made possible by standards.

How much value would the telephone network have if each country had a different set of standards, such that telephone calls originating in one country could not be answered in another? Would telephones have become so widespread if telephones produced by one hardware manufacturer could not communicate with another's? If AT&T's network could not communicate with Sprint's or MCI's, would the value of telephones be greater or less? Or imagine that one individual in your organization bought a new telephone and it required every other person in the organization to buy the same new telephone. Sound ludicrous? Well, that is exactly what we have been experiencing in the computer world.

The fifth era of computing is based on the rise of the Internet and the World Wide Web. The Web is all about networking between organizations, regardless of their operating system. It is truly an "open" system, allowing the interchange of information between people anywhere in the world, using any operating system and any hardware. It is a revolution that will have a more profound impact than the introduction of the PC.

Netscape's Web browser will run on any computer operating system. It is platform independent. Java, a new computer language created by Sun Microsystems, is driving the new paradigm (see below).

We are in the early stages of the fifth era. Imagine you could walk up to any computer in the world, log on to the World Wide Web, key in a password or stick a smart card into the computer, and access all your files. Sound far off? Applications already exist that are proving this promise. For instance, a service called hotmail (www.hotmail.com) allows users to send and receive email using any computer in the world that can log on to the World Wide Web. As of January 2001, hotmail had 89 million users.

The Internet is going mobile. It is already becoming common to access email and the Internet from a cell phone, PDA or pager. The growth in the number of cellphones has been phenomenal. In 2001, over 300 million people worldwide were using mobile phones. In Japan, cellphones outnumber traditional land-based phones. The research firm IDC predicts that there will be half a billion Internet phones by 2004. Mobile Commerce figures are expected to rise from $3.5 million in 2000 to over $200 billion in 2005.[16]

What are the benefits of the fifth era? The value of the Internet increases with each new user. This is known as Metcalf's law. How much value did the first fax machine have? None, because it could not communicate with any other fax machine. Now that everyone has one, you would be at a business disadvantage if you didn't have one, too. The value of having a fax machine increases as the number of individuals and organizations that have fax machines grows. The same is true of the Internet and computers. With each new computer that is hooked up to the Internet, the value of the whole network increases.

Why? Don Tapscott has coined the term prosumer[17] to refer to people using the Internet who are both PROducers and conSUMERS of content. Each individual who begins to use the World Wide Web increases the total value of the Internet. The growth of the Internet is driven by such open standards as Netscape and Java.

THE PROMISE OF JAVA

Hardware represents roughly 20 percent of the total cost of a personal computer or workstation (Chapter 5). Software compatibility and training, on the other hand, eat up at least 40 percent of the costs. With the rapid changes in hardware and the continual releases of software upgrades, IT professionals are in a constant state of crisis as they attempt to manage these costs.

Software has become bloatware. *Windows 95*, for instance, has 11 million lines of code. The larger the programs, the more complex they are, the harder to develop, the more bugs they contain and the more potential conflicts they are likely to create with other programs and hardware.

Java introduces a new paradigm of computing: IT professionals have to maintain only the server applications and end users just access Java programs – called applets – across the network on a need-to-use basis. Suddenly, an employee, like a bank teller, requiring only limited functions, no longer needs to run a program like *Windows* with 11 million lines of code.

Java is platform independent, meaning it will run on an IBM-compatible or a Mac or a Unix platform. So IT professionals do not have to worry about maintaining the software for many different platforms. Similarly, developers only have to develop for one platform. One of the largest costs of software development is maintaining multiple platform versions.

Java, while still in its infancy, has ignited excitement in the software developer community. Developers know that just as Netscape created a phenomenal market for itself using the World Wide Web, Java applets are both the product and the marketing channel. Developers can sell their applets to anyone in the world using the web. Therefore, the language unleashes the get-rich hopes of developers all over the world and means that a lot of development activity will occur in this new language. It also means that developers do not have to depend on making a deal with Microsoft, which many worry will over time only extend its dominance of software development.

The fifth era brings together the best of all the other eras as information technology departments regain control of the operating systems. In large organizations, IT professionals will no longer have to spend time upgrading the software on thousands of end-user workstations (clients). They will only have to update the software on the server. By using platform-independent standards, MIS professionals will not have to spend large amounts of time solving conflicts between different layers of software.

Finally, users will have increased freedom and functionality because they will be able to access their data from any workstation in the world. Just as I can use any telephone in the world and reach anyone else. The good news for small organizations is that Web-based EDI will enable them to experience the same benefits that Wal-Mart enjoys.

KANBAN: FLEXIBLE MANUFACTURING

With retailers requiring just-in-time (JIT) delivery (as in Wal-Mart's supplier, Wrangler), manufacturers are adopting fast and flexible production processes – producing only what is needed, when it is needed, and guaranteeing delivery to where it is needed within three to five days. Kanban is the Japanese philosophy of flexible production that manufacturers are using to meet retailers' JIT demands.

Camco Inc., a 51 percent-owned subsidiary of General Electric Canada Inc. is the largest manufacturer, marketer and servicer of home appliances in Canada. Production facilities of its core products are located in Hamilton, Ontario, and Montreal, Quebec.

Camco introduced "make-to-order" production in 1990, allowing its manufacturing teams to respond rapidly to customer demand by reducing production-cycle times from months to days. This improved product availability while reducing inventory levels. Camco's closing inventory of $9 million at the end of 2000 was the lowest in the company's 24 years of operation. Prior to the implementation of "make-to-order," Camco's inventory levels reached as high as $97 million on sales over $550 million.

The Hamilton facility manufactures over 700 different styles of ranges and refrigerators under such popular brands as GE, Hotpoint, Moffat and McClary. In addition, it produces private brands for major department stores.

Camco simplified its inventory requirements. In the Hamilton plant, 95 percent of all parts used in products are the same, regardless of the model, brand or style. This allows for predictability in the ordering of parts.

Using this philosophy, manufacturers can reduce the number of suppliers to create stronger, long-term relationships where quality and guaranteed delivery is ensured.

The final five percent of unique parts are designed to be as inexpensive as possible, and the differentiation between different models and makes is made as late in the production process as possible. And it's far less expensive to keep inventory in the form of parts than finished goods.

With this modified version of Kanban, Camco maintains enough inventory of common components to manufacture and ship any customer's order within five days of receiving it.

The production line runs continuously for 16-cubic-foot and 18-cubic-foot refrigerators. The refrigerator line will produce twenty 16-cubic-foot refrigerators followed by thirty 18-cubic-foot refrigerators. The first appliance of the new batch carries an order tag alerting employees to the unique parts it requires. Production runs can be as short as a single unit!

Often in workshops executives will say, "All this theory is great, but you don't understand. We are unionized and the union is unwilling to change."

Camco's hourly employees are members of the Canadian Auto Workers (CAW). People who work on the production line are cross-trained to work at other stations. This has a number of benefits. The work is more varied and therefore more interesting. There is less risk of sustaining injuries due to repetitive motion. The line is not brought to a halt if one person is off work sick. And when demand is high, the company can put on extra shifts and run at a higher capacity.

As Camco has gone through its turnaround, workers have seen inventory levels falling. In the past when inventory was too high, work stopped as the company worked to sell existing inventory into the distribution channels. Quality has also risen. With a make-to-order philosophy, sales have been increasing. As a result, union members, who get steady and varied work, have a positive attitude toward the change.

The retailer, distributor, manufacturer and suppliers, including the metal-stamping company and steel maker, comprise the value chain. Each company adds value to the final product as it moves through production and distribution.

As the expression goes, a chain is only as strong as its weakest link. The value chain is interdependent. The whole production process is halted if one supplier fails to deliver parts that are needed for production on time. As such, Camco has established strategic relationships with selected suppliers. These suppliers are often integrated into the company's manufacturing operations and participate in decisions relating to quality, design and new materials.

Manufacturers and suppliers are going through "inter-enterprise integration," as organizations in the value chain begin to act as though they were one organization.

The human body is an example. Even though the body has separate limbs and organs that perform different functions, they are integrated. The whole body needs to work as one system in real time. The manufacturing value chain needs to work in the same way to be efficient.

Kanban shifts manufacturers from pushing products into the retail channel to allowing the end consumer to pull them. It's the difference between pushing and pulling a string.

We don't know what we don't know
We can't act on what we don't know
We won't know until we search
We won't search for what we don't question.
We won't question what we don't measure.
Hence we just don't know.[18]
Mikel Harry, author

TO SUMMARIZE...

- Real-time access to information allows individuals and organization real time analysis, which dramatically reduces cycle times, making organizations faster and more flexible, capable of responding rapidly in a dynamic, changing market.
- Fast, flexible organizations outperform their competitors by:
- bringing new products and services faster to market
- "locking" their customers into new relationships
- detecting and correcting errors faster
- enhancing individual and corporate-wide learning, and becoming "learning organizations"

WORKSHOP QUESTIONS AND EXERCISES

- If your organization implemented access to real time information over the Web, what new relationships would be enabled:
- within the organization (within teams, between departments and divisions, between different levels of the organization)?
- with customers?
- with suppliers?
- What would be the effect on cycle times?
- What new products or services might be enabled by the new paradigm?
- How would such a shift change your perception of your competitors?
- Would such a shift change your competitors' perceptions of your organization?

- What are the "impossible" things that are holding your organization back from dramatic performance improvements?

Reflection:

What is the key learning/insight for me in this chapter?

Action:

What one action shall I take tomorrow to move learning into action? And over time repeat, to move action into habit?

CHAPTER 12

The Internet Revolution

In 1997, for the first time in history, the number of email messages in the United States exceeded the total number of addressed letters carried by the US Postal Service! This fundamental shift will shake every business to its foundation.[1]

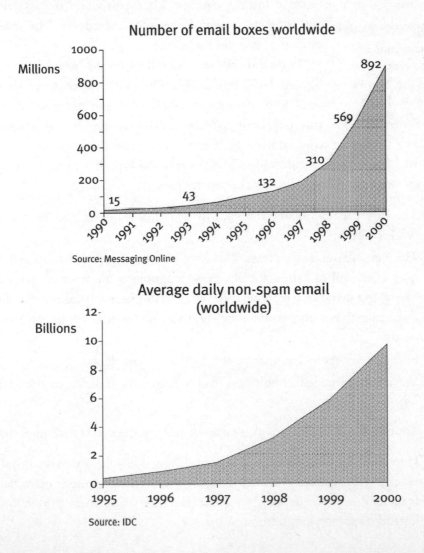

Number of email boxes worldwide

Source: Messaging Online

Average daily non-spam email (worldwide)

Source: IDC

Email-enabled corporations are radically different from traditional companies. Hierarchies fall as information is freely shared. The need-to-know philosophy of the past is crumbling. An Intel employee receives up to 300 email messages everyday. Such a high-performance culture is fast and flexible. Product development is blistering – 95 percent of Sun's revenues come from products that were not commercially available 18 months before! No wonder Sun is one of the fastest-growing companies in the history of the world.

But the Internet revolution is still in its infancy. As it matures, it will radically transform the very nature of business and many aspects of our society. Companies such as Intuit, Netscape, Microsoft, Sun Microsystems and Intel are rewriting the rules of business. The speed of change boggles the mind.

> **The Internet runs on dog years.**
> *James Gosling, Sun VP and creator of Java*

Worldwide buying and selling on the Internet, which totaled $657 billion in 2000, is projected to grow to over $6.8 trillion in 2004.[2] But the promise of the Internet is not just that it will increase sales, it will also reduce operating costs, shorten cycle times, compress the value chain and most importantly, enable radically new relationships between organizations and customers. Consider the possibilities:

- The Internet will enable the growth of online banking and electronic funds transfer.
- The Net will put heavy pressure on long-distance telephone rates, which over time will fall dramatically. New technology allows end users to make long-distance telephone calls over the Internet at local rates. Many companies have eliminated long-distance, interoffice faxing by using email.
- Email cuts costs by eliminating the need to re-key data.
- Videoconferencing technology is readily becoming available on the desktop.

Of course, this new medium also raises disturbing questions for industries:

- How will phone companies and long-distance re-sellers survive if individuals and organizations are increasingly able to make phone calls, send faxes and videoconference over the Internet using local phone calls instead of paying long-distance rates?

- If executives can videoconference, how will airlines that rely on high-margin business travelers remain profitable?
- How will travel agents survive as more and more travelers realize that they can check timetables, availability of flights and book tickets over the Internet?

THE FORCE SHAPING THE FUTURE: THE NET

The Internet was originally designed by the US Department of Defense to interconnect military and university computers so that communications networks would remain intact in the event of nuclear attack. If one computer was knocked out of the network, communication would be routed around it through the network of connections.

For decades, the Internet remained the domain of researchers and techies because of the user-vicious, cryptic commands required to communicate. This has all changed with the introduction of easy-to-use, *Windows*-like software.

In November 1990 at the European Laboratory for Particle Physics, researchers built a prototype of the World Wide Web (WWW) that linked documents located anywhere in the world on the Internet. This allowed academics to cross-reference or "hyper-link" their research to other documents on other computer servers at different locations. Just click on a word that was highlighted in a color other than the normal text and you were taken to the other document. The Web was born.

The World Wide Web is the fastest-growing part of the Internet. Netscape, Sun Microsystems, Intuit, Microsoft and Intel are competing to set the standards for the new medium. The stakes are high as the Web will become the key to commerce in the future. The company that defines this new medium will be the dominant company of the twenty-first century.

NETSCAPE: BORN OF THE WEB, MOTHER OF THE WEB

In the fall of 1995, the stock market valued Netscape, a small, one-year-old company with annual sales of $16 million, at $2 billion on the first day of its Initial Public Offering (IPO). The news stunned markets and marked a turning point. Business began to take note of the potential of the Web. The Web ushers in a new reality that will change the way all companies will work. Netscape, which has become synonymous with the Web, was a new platform, just as the personal computer spawned a revolution in 1981.

In the early 1990s, Marc Andreessen was an undergraduate at the University of Illinois, making $6.85 an hour writing computer code for the National Center for Supercomputing Applications. He and fellow student Eric Bina became intrigued by the potential of the World Wide Web. But the Web lacked a simple graphical user interface (GUI)—an intuitive way for people to unearth the vast amount of material stored on the world's interconnected computers. In a manic burst of coding in the winter of 1993, Andreessen and Bina wrote the basics of a graphical Web browser called *Mosaic*. Almost overnight, their work turned the Web into the business and pop culture phenomenon it is today.

Mosaic was the first GUI for the Web. Internet users could download the browser for free. By the fall of 1994, it had become a fundamental tool for three million Web surfers and was growing at a rate of 600,000 new users per month.

Technical merit seldom determines who wins and loses the competitive race. Being first is more important than being best. And *Mosaic* was first.

Venture capitalist and entrepreneur Jim Clark, who founded Silicon Graphics, contacted Andreessen early in 1994 and suggested that they talk. Using Clark's capital, they founded Netscape with the idea of becoming the Microsoft of the Internet.

By November 1994, *Mosaic* accounted for 60 percent of all Web traffic. In December, Netscape launched its first commercial Web browser, *Navigator*. In four months, with no advertising and no sales in retail outlets, a stunning six million copies of *Navigator* were in use. By the spring of 1995, 75 percent of Web surfers were using *Navigator*. *Mosaic's* share had plummeted to a mere 5 percent.

Netscape redefined the standard. To succeed, speed is of the essence. Netscape was a pressure-cooker, workaholic culture where brilliant, best-of-breed programmers lived in their offices, continually crunching code. Output was valued in the extreme.

"The medium is the message," said Marshall McLuhan. Netscape uses the Web to create a market for the Web. Netscape operated in a fundamentally different way than other software companies:

> If Netscape relied on standard retail distribution, the physical acts of manufacturing disks, shipping them across the country, advertising their arrival and waiting for customers to make their purchases would take months rather than minutes. If Netscape relied on traditional market surveys, the process of mailing disks to testers, following up with questionnaires and waiting for and sorting through returns would take months more. At Netscape, working off the Web translates into unthinkable delays.
>
> For most companies unthinkable delays are called business-as-usual. Consider Microsoft's August 24 [1995] launch of *Windows 95*. Microsoft had its final code on July 14. Why wait six more weeks? Because Microsoft had to organize a dozen manufacturing plants and 500 trucks to produce and deliver the software to 20,000 retail outlets. Life off the Web is awfully messy.
>
> There are, to be sure, risks to life on the Web. To an extraordinary degree, Netscape has opened itself up to the competition. Engineers from Spyglass, America Online, or any other company can log on to Netscape's user groups and see what its customers are saying, what its engineers are promising, what glitches are raising a ruckus. It's as if Pepsi published the results of its taste tests in a public forum that Coca-Cola could visit every day.[3]

MICROSOFT WAKES UP

Until December 7, 1995, it looked as if Microsoft was going to become irrelevant in the Internet age. While Microsoft dominated the PC software market, Bill Gates, who is widely seen as a visionary guru for the PC industry, was completely blind-sided by the rapid rise of Netscape and the Web.

In May 1993, Gates approved a plan to launch a proprietary online service called *Microsoft Network* (*MSN*) to compete with America Online. The plan called for developing and bundling a browser that would be bundled with *Windows 95*.

In February 1994, Steven Sinofsky, Gates' technical assistant, emailed his boss, informing him that the Internet was abuzz with *Mosaic*. On April 4, 1994, Netscape was founded. The next day, senior management at Microsoft held a retreat to debate the importance of the Internet. By this time work on *MSN* had been under way for a year. This focus prevented a shift in strategy. The decision was made to continue with *MSN*.

Throughout 1995, Microsoft was focused on the launch of *Windows 95* and *MSN*. The company was also offering to buy Intuit, and was involved in a number of inquiries with the US Department of Justice.

By October 1995, Version 2 of Netscape *Navigator* was being downloaded across the Internet for free. At yet another Microsoft retreat, Benjamin Slivka, who was in charge of *Internet Explorer*, proposed that Microsoft give away the software on the Net, just as Netscape was doing. Gates dismissed the idea saying, "What do you think we are, communists?"

On August 8, 1995, Netscape's Initial Public Offering sent a shock wave through the consciousness of the business world. On the first day, the stock offering, which was priced at $25, rose in trading to $75. Amid the subsequent blaze of publicity, no one could ignore the power of the Web. On November 16, Goldman Sachs stopped recommending Microsoft stock for purchase because of Internet concerns.

Having realized the profound importance of the Web, Gates was swift to turn Microsoft around. The Internet Platform and Tools Division, created in February 1996, by the end of 1996 employed over 2,500 people – more than Netscape, Yahoo! And the next five Net upstarts combined. In June 2000, Microsoft launched .NET – its initiative to merge its successful Windows products with the capabilities of the Internet. In 2000, .NET employed 3,700 and by the end of 2001, Microsoft anticipated that all of its 40,000 employees would be involved in .NET. Microsoft's catch-up efforts have been swift and intense. Microsoft's approach to combine *Internet Explorer* with its Windows products has led to its domination of the Web browser market. In 2000, Internet Explorer accounted for approximately 70 percent of the market, while Netscape had fallen to approximately 30 percent.

Netscape's demise is greatly exaggerated. By January 1997, Netscape sold its one-millionth Internet/intranet server. "It took Lotus *Notes* seven years to get a million seats, and in our case, it took us a year to get a million servers, not even counting the seats," said Srivats Sampath, Netscape's vice president of server marketing.

Netscape's growth is being driven by two factors. First, an "anything but Microsoft" fear that exists in the software developer community. Microsoft dominates the industry. Microsoft's 2000 profits totaled $9.4 billion. (The next nine largest PC software makers' combined profits totaled $523 million.[4]) Microsoft has used its near-monopoly practices with a ruthless competitiveness that borders on bullyboy tactics. Second, Netscape has great products and a blisteringly fast product development cycle.

This case study highlights the importance of being first and why organizations are not just competing to create a new product, but to create the market standard by which all competitors will be measured. For Microsoft, which would have been better, throwing 50 people at the opportunity early in 1994, setting the standard and creating the market, or having to pay 2,500 people to try and catch up in 1996? The leverage of time is immense.

LEADERS ARE ONLY HUMAN

Paradigm shifts can be like watching a sunrise. The black night sky sprinkled with stars slowly gives way to gray. The stars fade, the East turns pink and eventually yellow. Finally, the sun rises, breaking above the horizon. But awareness of the dawn has come long before. At what time did it dawn? Changes are subtle and incremental.

No leader is omnipotent. No leader can perfectly predict the future no matter how successful or brilliant. No one company has exclusive insight into new products or services that will excite and delight customers. Ultimately, complacency kills. Even the best and brightest individuals and organizations must continually question the way they see the world.

While this book cites examples of corporate strategies, it is important to remember that these strategies work today – not forever. At some point in the future, changes in circumstances will invalidate some of them. Therefore, it is important to think critically about all the concepts presented.

"One size fits all" solutions do not work. A strategy that works for a company at level four of business development (video game) may not work at level seven. In fact, applied at level seven it may cause the demise of the organization. What works for a manufacturer may not work for a service company. Instead, the cases and strategies cited are meant to provoke thought. Debate the issues within your organization. See how the strategies apply. For every case I cite in this book, there is a countercase.

INTERNET EXPLOSION

Before Netscape's IPO, most businesses ignored the Net. Even after Netscape's IPO, some market commentators dismissed the Web as frivolous because of the relatively small volume of commercial activity and the lack of business applications. Few businesses can ignore the Net now.

In August 2001, Dell Computers was selling $50 million of products over its website every day – 50 percent of Dell's daily sales take place on the Internet. In 2001, 45 percent of Dell's revenue was earned from sales to government and corporate customers, 40 percent from small and medium-sized businesses and 15 percent from consumers.[5] In August 1997, Dell went live with corporate intranet sales.[6] Dell will put a custom store directly on its customers' intranet, with custom corporate configurations and pricing.

> Business on the Net is "a zero-variable cost transaction. The only thing better would be mental telepathy."
> *Michael Dell, Dell Computer Corporation CEO*

An intranet is a computer network within an organization that uses Internet protocols. The benefit to the company is that it can cut software costs by using the same software for external communications (Internet) and internal communications (Intranet). Similarly, employees only have to learn how to use a single piece of software, the browser, to access information inside or outside the company.

Internet sales not only cost less, but they also save time as customers can answer their own pricing queries and create their own configurations, saving Dell money. People on the phone who visit the website before calling are 1.5 times more likely to buy than those who cold-call the toll-free number.

Cisco is selling $40 million a day of network products across its website. That's $14.6 billion a year and accounts for 82 percent of all sales. According to Cisco Chief Information Officer Peter Solvik, Internet sales saved the company $330 million in 2000. Thus, companies can reach more customers with fewer staff while raising the quality of service to 24 hours a day, 365 days a year with relative ease, not to mention the huge savings on the phone bills.[7]

Companies are using the Web in very creative ways.

PC Flowers

PC Flowers, launched in January 1990, allowed users of online services such as Prodigy to order flowers. At that time the company ranked last among the 25,000 Florists' Transworld Delivery (FTD) Association's US members.

FTD is the largest retail trade association of florists in North America. Founded in 1910 to facilitate the exchange of floral orders among florists, it has grown to an affiliation of more than 52,000 florists in 154 countries.

By May 15, 1990, PC Flowers had become the tenth-largest FTD florist in America and by 1997, it was the second largest.

In December 1994, the company launched its PC Flowers & Gifts service on the Internet (www.pcflowers.com). One year later, the company launched its "Internet Consumer Incentive Traffic Program," linking major websites and online services to the PC Flowers & Gifts website. The consumer traffic is tracked and PC Flowers pays the online services and websites a percentage of each sale. Orders placed with PC Flowers are transmitted directly into the FTD order processing.

Email reminder

PC Flowers' website features an email reminder service. Customers can enter important dates – wedding anniversary, family members' birthdays, Mother's Day – and the service will send you an email to alert you well in advance of the event. Of course, this gives you plenty of time to choose the flowers or gift you want to send from PC Flowers.

Loans online

Bank of America is just one of a growing list of banks in the United States and around the world that are offering their customers the opportunity to apply for a loan online. Their customers don't have to take time off and go see the dreaded loan officer at their local branch. They can now apply for a loan from Bank of America's website at any time of the day or night in the comfort of their own home. Customers can choose the type of loan they need – mortgage, car, home improvement, or education.

Applying for a loan online is easy and fast. Bank of America has put its entire loan application form online. Customers simply enter their data (name, address, amount applying for, collateral information) into the boxes and click on the "Submit Application" button. The whole process takes less than 10 minutes.

The web also makes it easy for customers to shop around for the right loan or mortgage. The website LendingTree.com allows customers to compare loan offers from different institutions and accept the one that is best for them. The customer fills out one online form and can get up to four offers. A customer doesn't have to go from bank to bank to get the best deal and doesn't even have to go from website to website!

Bank of America and LendingTree provide extra value to their customers by providing tools and resources such as mortgage calculators, glossaries, and articles on credit related topics. A satisfied customer is one who is empowered with knowledge and understands the process.

Free phone calls across the Net

Less than 1 percent of long distance phone traffic went across the web in 1999 using a standard called Voice over Internet Protocol (VoIP). But this will explode to 17 percent in 2003 and to 30 percent by 2005, according to a study by US Bancorp Piper Jaffray. VoIP can reduce long distance phone bills up to 90 percent.

Here is how it works. VoIP digitizes voice which is then broken up into packets. These packets are sent across the Internet – and re-assembled at the target site and turned back into audio. Across the Internet packets can use many different routes, whereas in a traditional telephone call a single dedicated circuit is required for each call. The digital routers that direct traffic on the Internet are a fraction of cost of switches on traditional long distance phone networks. All this means cheaper phone calls.

There are two main ways to place calls over the Internet. First, there

Worldwide VoIP market share

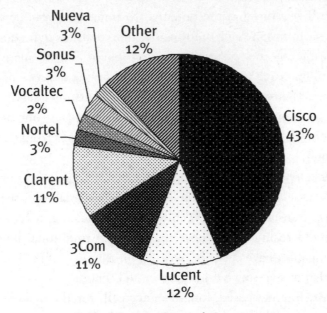

Nueva 3%
Sonus 3%
Vocaltec 2%
Nortel 3%
Clarent 11%
3Com 11%
Lucent 12%
Cisco 43%
Other 12%

Source: Synergy Research Group, 2000

are software applications, such as *HotTelephone* and *Net2Phone*. These systems are cheap and relatively easy to use. In fact, HotTelephone is free! It only requires that the computer you are using have a microphone, speakers and sound card. *HotTelephone* is like *Hotmail* – you can access it from any PC anywhere in the world, and make a call to some 30 countries. However, in 2001, these systems weren't quite as reliable as business people demand for their calls. For more information, visit www.hottelephone.com.

The second way to place calls over the Internet is to use a hardware-based system, such as those by Cisco and Lucent. These are card-based systems that offload telephony tasks from the computer's processor, which allows for greater reliability and better sound quality than software-based systems. Many of these systems allow a standard telephone to be connected to the computer and the call is sent over the Internet instead of the phone line.

Internet software providers have been able to offer traditional telephone features, including call waiting, caller ID, conferencing and hold. Valuable business applications such as whiteboard teleconferencing and the ability to upload and download files while speaking are making Internet telephony attractive to corporations.

Internet Telephony has the potential to improve e-commerce returns. Companies can install "call" buttons on their websites that allow customers to talk directly to a customer service reps. In North America e-tailers lose $58 million each month in uncompleted online orders – because purchasers have unanswered questions. Improved customer service will help solve this problem. NetworkMCI's *Clic'nConnect* is just one of a number of systems available that allow a company to route calls from its website to its call center.

Internet telephony has enormous potential. Huge savings on long-distance calls, its e-commerce customer service potential, and the ability to merge voice transmission with Web-video conferencing, text and graphics will become a reality in the near future. Even traditional long distance phone companies have seen the writing on the wall. AT&T is leading a coalition that is investing $1.4 billion in Net2Phone.

Low-cost, Internet-based, long-distance calls for the masses are frightening the telcos. The phone companies are feeling so threatened that in March 1995, over 130 of them acting through the American Carriers Telecommunication Association (ACTA) petitioned the Federal Communications Commission (FCC) to define VocalTec and other software vendors as telecom carriers. This would subject them to tariffs, and ACTA further argued that until the FCC decides the case, VocalTec and other companies

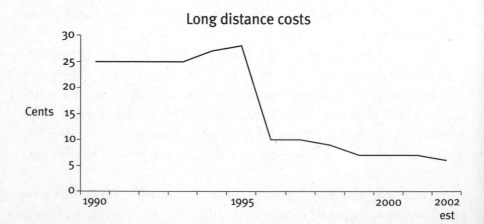

should be prevented from selling their products. In March 1996, the FCC rejected ACTA's petition, recognizing that it would be impossible to subject VoIP service providers to the same rules as conventional circuit-switched voice carriers. On the Internet, it is impossible to separate voice packets from data packets to impose tariffs.

It is easy to see why the telcos are upset. Internet Service Providers buy data lines from the telcos and resell them to end users for a monthly hook-up fee, typically $20. In the end, the telephone traffic is going across the phone companies' lines, but as data, not voice, at a fraction of the revenue to the telco.

In October 2000, telecom leader C & W signed a $1.4 billion, 10-year deal with Nortel Networks to implement a VoIP network throughout North America and Europe. C & W expects to migrate all of its voice customers to the VoIP network by 2004. This deal represented the first major deployment of VoIP for a public network. Clearly, C & W saw the writing on the wall and decided to lead the change to VoIP instead of being left behind. C & W sees VoIP as a way of providing new value to its customers. The new IP network will allow the company to provide video conferencing, integrating call centers with company websites, unified messaging as well as low-cost long distance calling.

The demand for IP telephone services is expected to explode by 2002.

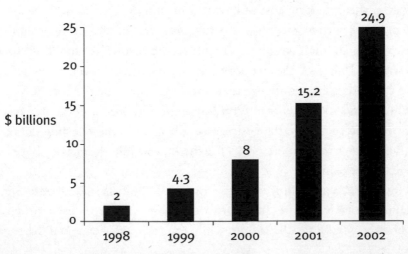

IP telephony services revenue forecast

$ billions

Source: International Data Corporation, 1998

IDC predicts that IP telephone revenues will grow to $24.9 billion in 2002, up from $8 billion in 2000. As more and more customers begin using Internet Phones or sign up with services that digitize their normal phone calls and send them over the Internet, companies will save money on toll-free numbers. Companies can already integrate call centers with the Internet. For example, a national catalog sales company accepting orders via a toll-free voice line can also accept voice and email orders from buyers browsing its interactive Web-based catalog, capturing sales more quickly and cost effectively.

> In the future, reality will be too expensive for businesses.
> *Wayne Seifreid, multimedia manager, Nortel*

Virtual meetings replace real ones

Wayne Seifreid, a Nortel manager, pointed out to me that he can have a virtual meeting with someone 30 miles from his office for free using the Internet. To have a real meeting requires him to have a car or take a taxi, go on the highway for 45 minutes, pay for parking, have the meeting, then take 45 minutes to get back to the office. The real meeting costs at least $50. If he was "meeting" someone in Hong Kong, a virtual meeting would still be free while the real meeting would cost more than $5,000. Eventually, most meetings will be virtual. The virtual meeting isn't actually free because Nortel had to make a capital investment in its computer network and videoconferencing software. Once this investment is made, however, the operating cost of having a meeting is next to nothing.

Currently, virtual meetings are the privilege of the elite. Companies must invest in their systems, create secure firewalls that link to the Internet and manage the network. At the individual level, users have to have the patience to configure their modem, work out the conflicts in the hardware and software, deal with logging on or hire a computer technician to do it, and have the courage to go through the learning curve. So for now, the virtual experience is for the elite, while the masses have only the real experience.

However, in the future, as the price of desktop videoconferencing plummets and hardware and software become easier to use, the virtual experience will be for the masses while the real experience will be for the elite.

Andy Grove, chairman of Intel, addressed the 1995 National Speakers Association conference in Minneapolis. Andy was very polite to speak to us for 15 minutes. I say polite because in 1995 Intel revenues were $16.2 billion. Assuming Andy works 50 hours a week – or 2,500 hours a year – the company revenue divided by his number of hours ($16.2 billion divided by 2,500 hours) gives a figure of $6.5 million per hour. Thus Andy should be focusing each hour of his time on activities that are of significant enough importance to generate $6.5 million over the long term. (In 2000, Intel's revenue was $33.7 billion and Andy would have focused on activities that would generate $13.5 million per hour.) So why would Andy Grove fly to Minneapolis, take a taxi to the hotel and address 2,000 professional speakers who have little to do with his industry? The answer is that he won't. The real experience would take at least eight hours of his time for 15 minutes of speaking. So instead, Andy addressed us from his desk using Intel's videoconferencing system. The total experience took 20 minutes out of his day. He still was generous with us and did it for the public relations opportunity.

When will Andy Grove conduct a face-to-face meeting? When he is working on high-leverage activities that have a profound effect on the future of Intel, meeting with Intel's senior design engineers, scientists and executive team, meeting with industry partners and talking to a software developers conference or Wall Street analysts. For senior executives whose limiting factor is time, the virtual experience is already the way they communicate with most people.

Charles Schwab revolutionizes stock trading

Charles Schwab allows its clients to buy and sell stocks, options, mutual funds and bonds 24 hours a day. Clients can also short stocks, place limits or stop orders, good 'til and cancel orders. They can get real-time quotes, independent analysts' picks, choose from 6,700 company reports, create a personalized news clipping service, check their order status, review and download transactions, trace interest and dividend payments, and organize tax schedule information – all from the comfort of their home or office. Clients also have the freedom to choose how to access this information: Web-based trading, automated phone trading or talking to a broker.

Schwab was the first brokerage to offer online trading, introducing a *DOS*-based software in 1984, and *Windows*-based software in 1993. In 1995, the company introduced an "all electric account" called *e.Schwab*, giving investors real-time quotes, news and research, and trading at Schwab's lowest commission rates. Customers pay just $29.95 for stock trades up to 1,000 shares and $.03 a share for trades over 1,000 shares. *e.Schwab* clients do all their business electronically and have almost no interaction with people at Schwab. In 1996, the firm introduced its Web-based *SchwabNOW!* Any customer can use the site to place trades and access account data and investment information. Clients who normally place trades over the phone with brokers at Schwab receive 20 percent off Web trades. In 1996, the company also introduced the industry's first speech recognition quotation service, providing real-time quotes on over 13,000 stocks, mutual funds and market indicators. It complements Schwab's automated phone system, which allows clients to access account balances and make trades.

Schwab's aggressive and strategic investments in new technology have given its customers the widest range of choice on how to access information and trade. Schwab has grown quickly:

Charles Schwab Online trading volumes

Year	# of customer accounts (millions)	Assets (US$b.)
1997	1.2	80
1998	2.2	174.1
1999	3.3	348.7
2000	4.3	364.9

Schwab's PC-based electronic services (excluding phone-based) accounted for 30 percent of Schwab's 21 million trades in 1996 and over half of the company's 97 million calls. In March 2001, 81 percent of all trades at Schwab occurred online, up from 36 percent in June 1997.

As of April 2001, Schwab had over 4.3 million active online users with over $328 billion in customer assets. Schwab has become a leader in the online trading industry with 21 percent of the market share.

By comparison, e*Trade in 2001 reported 3.2 million accounts and $41 billion in assets. While e*Trade has experienced incredible growth, Schwab still leads this rapidly growing market. Schwab offers "multi-

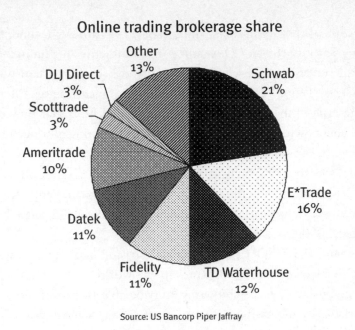

Online trading brokerage share

Other 13%
DLJ Direct 3%
Scotttrade 3%
Ameritrade 10%
Datek 11%
Fidelity 11%
TD Waterhouse 12%
E*Trade 16%
Schwab 21%

Source: US Bancorp Piper Jaffray

ple-channel" capabilities for investors, including 250 branches, Internet, telephone, and round-the-clock service.

"Our online growth is directly related to investors' comfort with being able to get through to us many different ways, regardless of market volatility," notes Tom Taggart of Schwab. "This is something that Internet-only brokers just can't deliver. The chat-rooms are littered with disgruntled investors who have tried to get through to their Internet broker on a busy market day."

Schwab's heavy investment in IT has lowered the cost of transactions, allowing the company to deal profitability with small investors who were unprofitable for other brokerages and therefore considered a nuisance.

"In the traditional brokerage, clients are controlled through a commission broker," comments Taggart. "But we empower clients with a lot of tools without trying to control the relationship. What used to be the exclusive domain of brokers is now available online to Schwab clients: Dow Jones News Retrieval, S&P Market Scope, Reuters Money Network, company reports, analysts' reports and independent research."

Schwab has added features with each release of its software. "Our clients wanted more mutual fund information," notes Taggart. So Schwab introduced *FundMap for Windows*, allowing clients to compare, select and track 1,300 different mutual funds from 194 different fund families, including 750 of Schwab's *OneSource* (no-transaction-fee mutual funds).

Schwab wants to give clients a compelling reason to consolidate all their assets. "People don't want the hassle," Taggart states. "Instead of receiving a monthly statement from each mutual fund that they own, we provide clients with one consolidated statement listing all their funds and access points 24 hours a day."

From 1994 to 1999, Schwab's revenue grew at a compounded annual rate of 30 percent while the average commission per revenue trade actually decreased by 9 percent. Customers' assets exceeded $364 billion in December 2000.

Chairman and CEO Charles Schwab's vision is to build one of the greatest financial services companies in the world. In the highly dynamic brokerage business, successful firms must be able to prosper in good and bad markets. By increasing operational efficiency, Schwab ensures its cost structure will be far lower than traditional brokers', giving it the capital required to further invest in technology and offer investors better investment tools and greater choice. Despite record trading volumes, Schwab's high-tech, high-touch philosophy kept customer satisfaction levels up at 95 percent.

"With all this technology you may wonder why we need branches," notes Taggart. "While many customers enjoy doing business over the phone or PC, most customers bring us new assets in person at our office, where they can get personal service and convenience you simply cannot match with a machine. Most investors want both high-tech and high-touch service, depending on their needs at the moment. This requires a difficult balancing act."

Schwab maintains 300 branch offices in the United States, Puerto Rico, Britain, the Cayman Islands and Hong Kong. Schwab shatters paradigms on more than just the technological level. Who would have thought you could get a Visa card or checking account from a broker?

Schwab's strategy is attracting a new generation of investors. Some of the estimated 75 million baby boomers who are entering their wealth-building years are more concerned than ever about their financial future, paying for their children's education, managing their parents' health care and planning for their own retirement. This group doesn't want a traditional relationship with their broker. Many are Net-literate and know how to access the same information. A traditional broker sending annual reports to them by snail mail insults their intelligence. They can read corporate reports online, have stock prices running across their computer screen at the office or home continuously, and read the same Reuters and Bloomberg news service announcements as fast as traders can.

Baby boomers, a large number of whom are new to investing, are turning to Schwab in record numbers. In 1996, Schwab opened nearly one million new accounts.

Schwab has also developed a strategy for first-time investors who may be overwhelmed. There are now more funds to choose from than there are stocks on the New York Stock Exchange. Investors want guidance. For investors who do not want or are unable to hire a personal financial advisor for ongoing investment management, Schwab's investment specialists evaluate a customer's investment profile using computer-based tools and then recommend several simple approaches to mutual fund investing.

In 1996, Schwab, for the first time in its history, began offering customers advice, but not the way traditional brokerages do. Traditional, commissioned brokers are in a conflict of interest, because their companies often expect them to sell stock placements that the firm is underwriting. Clients can't be sure whether a broker recommends a stock because it truly is a good investment and fits with their investment strategy or because the firm expects the broker to sell a certain amount of the stock. Second, traditional brokers are only paid upon the buying or selling of stocks. This creates an incentive to "churn" accounts – buy and sell stocks just to make commissions. Therefore many investors don't trust advice to buy or sell. They wonder, "Is it based truly on my interest or the broker's interest in a commission?" Schwab investment advisors are paid for their advice, regardless of the client's action. Therefore the advisor, not seeking to make money, does not bias the advice.

TECHNOLOGY IS ACCELERATING THE RATE OF ORGANIZATIONAL LEARNING

A number of technology trends have been discussed. As the cost of technology falls, more organizations can afford to deploy IT to accelerate the distribution of information and decision-making.

> Look at what it is doing. It is reducing the cost of disseminating information by over 99 percent; replacing face to face contact, with lonely, silent scanning; allowing bright students to break free from their teacher's grasp. Its invention and increased use has many workers worried about their jobs. It has the potential to widen the gap between the more knowledgeable and wealthier citizens and those who are less so. It is allowing for the uncontrolled dissemination of inaccurate information and pornography. It's the most rapidly accepted technological advance in history ... or at least close. But it isn't the Internet. It is the printing press, more accurately movable type – circa 1450 – and it changed the way we read, write, think and govern ourselves. It even changed our religions.
> *Alan Parisse – On the impact of the printing press*

Four million years ago in Africa, humans first stood up on two limbs. Two million years ago, they began making tools. Only 35,000 years ago, cave paintings appeared. Just 12,000 years ago, humans began domesticating plants and animals. Starting only 10,000 years ago, most languages and vocabulary were developed.[8] So it took humanity almost four million years to create language. These days most children can speak by age two. If children were isolated from any contact with people, they would not develop language on their own. Language learning comes through interaction with others.

The oldest written language is Sumerian, which emerged around 3100 BC. As written language spread, only an elite group could read and write. It wasn't until the invention of the Gutenberg press in 1450 – just 550 years ago – that reading and writing became more widespread. In Western society we consider reading and writing to be essential skills, and most children have learned these by age five. Children today stand on the shoulders of millions of years of human development by the time they are six. And we take it all for granted.

While learning occurs best through interaction with others, accelerated learning results from increasing interaction.

As more and more organizations adopt leading-edge technology – email, computer networks, the Internet, intranets, videoconferencing and Electronic Data Interchange – employees are able to learn faster and make better-informed decisions, through access to more information, than ever before.

FACTORS THAT WILL PROPEL THE WEB EXPLOSION AT HIGHER VELOCITY

The Web will grow even faster as certain restraining forces are removed. Six factors slowing the Internet's explosive growth are: (1) competing hardware/software standards; (2) ease of use; (3) bandwidth; (4) perceptions about security; (5) tools to exchange cash; (6) copyright. As these are removed, the Web's impact on organizations will increase.

Standards

The phrase "competing standards" is an oxymoron. But in any new industry, until standards emerge the industry can't reach its full potential. As an example, in the early 1800s there were dozens of different gauges of railway. (The gauge is the distance between the rails.) A train traveling on a narrow-gauge railway track could not travel on a wide-gauge track. Eventually, a standard gauge emerged.

The absence of standards will always be a problem for the Internet until competing companies cooperate and set common ones, or until one company dominates a market segment and creates the de facto standard. Internet standards need to be established in dozens of technical areas and applications.

Ease of use

The user-vicious computer industry is its own worst enemy. The combination of configuring a modem, installing and getting the software working with the hardware, the challenges of logging on to an online service for the first time are still too much of a challenge for most users. In 2001, half of all American households have a computer and 42 percent have Internet access. Just over 116 million Americans are online.[9] (The population of the US is 284 million.) The untapped market is huge. To develop mass markets, user-friendliness has to be the most important dimension not just for using software, but for the whole process of getting online – purchasing and installing the modem, configuring and operating the system, trouble-shooting hardware-software conflicts and logging on to the Internet.

Bandwidth

To get on the Internet you must have a connection to it, and the speed of your connection will determine the speed at which you will get information and the kind of applications you can run. Bandwidth is currently a challenge, but there is such an intense focus on the solution to this limiting factor that by 2002 it will not be an issue.

Bandwidth is like a plumbing pipe that carries water. A one-inch pipe with a steady flow of water passing through it will have a certain amount of water flow through it over a period of time. A pipe four inches wide at the same pressure and over the same period will transfer sixteen times greater volume (volume increase by the square of the diameter). The principle is the same when transferring data across the Internet. The faster the connection to the Internet (the wider the pipe) the more data you can get instantly and the richer the applications.

> In real estate the axiom used to be location, location, location . . . perhaps now it should be location, bandwidth, location.
> *Real estate broker attending a conference*

Regular phone lines called POTS (plain old telephone service) are like a narrow pipe. The standard modem speed for 2001 – 56.6 kps (kilobytes per second) – is great for transferring text. However, pictures and audio are slow, and video is unacceptably slow. Modem technology is pushing the limits of what it is possible to transfer by standard phone lines.

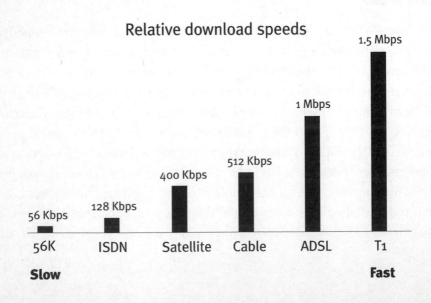

Relative download speeds

56 Kbps	128 Kbps	400 Kbps	512 Kbps	1 Mbps	1.5 Mbps
56K	ISDN	Satellite	Cable	ADSL	T1

Slow   **Fast**

A T3 Internet connection is so fast, it soars off the chart at a blistering 44.7 Mbps!

Telecom companies also offer ISDN (Integrated Services Dedicated Network), which is like having four phone lines rolled into one, and there is an even faster connection called a T1. Only companies can afford to install and pay monthly charges for this type of bandwidth. Unless the price falls substantially, the market will find other ways to increase bandwidth.

Cable television companies are beginning to convert their one-way systems (delivering TV programming from the cable company to your home) into interactive, two-way systems. Using a cable modem in your PC, you will then be able to transfer data at rates that are 50–100 times faster than 33.6 kps modems. All of a sudden, new applications become possible. These speeds are fantastic for transferring photographs and audio, but still slow with video.

Finally, satellites can provide broadband, two-way communication, but are prohibitively expensive. All these mediums are racing to provide more bandwidth. One thing is certain: as the cost of bandwidth plummets, demand will increase exponentially.

Security

In 1997, Visa and Mastercard joined together to form SET Secure Electronic Transaction, a joint standard for processing secure payments across the Net. The companies participating in developing the standard include Intuit, Netscape, IBM, Microsoft, VeriSign, and American Express.

The process works by involves security checks performed using digital certificates, which are issued to purchasers, merchants, banks and credit card companies. The consumer uses a wallet, a piece of software, to initiates the payment and contains their credit card information. The merchant also uses SET compliant software to verify the payment. All SET compliant software programs use encryption to ensure that credit card information is safe and secure.[10]

The purchasing of goods and services on the Internet has been stalled by the *perception* that Internet transactions are insecure. Many people have been unwilling to type their credit-card number into their terminal and email it out into cyberspace. But the problem is perceptual, not technical. As the figures of commerce across the Net already indicate, people are becoming more comfortable in their perception of how secure this new medium is.

When I go to a restaurant, have a meal, and give the waiter my credit card to pay the bill, it is far less secure than using the web. Browsers in North America use 128-bit encryption – which is very secure.

Cash Transferring Tools

Ultimately what will explode e-commerce is the proliferation of tools allowing consumers to send and receive money across the Internet. Currently, I can buy across the Internet by typing in my credit-card number when I am on a secure server, but as a consumer I have no way to receive money from someone else across the Internet.

Receiving money across the Internet could be achieved if the credit-card companies changed the way they saw their product. Imagine that credit cards really lived up to their name, allowing cardholders to receive money and have their accounts credited. This way, at month's end, Visa or MasterCard might owe you money and pay you interest for the time the money sat in your account! Now that's a paradigm shift!

COPYRIGHT

The Internet is the world's largest printing press. Anyone hooked up to the Net can distribute information globally to millions of online users at no cost. Digital information can be sent instantly to any number of online users. The Net is also the world's largest photocopier. Hundreds or millions of users on the Internet can choose to make copies of a file that is posted on a public site.

At the heart of copyright issues is the question of who should control the expression of ideas. Since we can't physically restrain or control thought, companies making money from copyrighted materials have worked to control the containers that thoughts come in: compact disks, books, videotapes and software diskettes. Essentially, companies have sought to control the packaging.[11]

The purchasing of goods and services on the Internet has rendered this process obsolete, because no physical container is required when information is digitized.

For the explosion of commerce in copyrighted materials, new methods need to be developed that pay a royalty to the author and publishing company every time a document is accessed, a song played or a piece of software downloaded. The ability to transfer small increments of cash will be available by the year 2004.

PROPRIETARY WALLS ARE FALLING TO OPEN SYSTEMS

In 2001, America Online had 28 million people using its AOL Internet access service, along with 2.8 million CompuServe members making it the largest Internet service provider in the world.

Meanwhile, the Internet has been growing exponentially. From 2000 to 2001, the number of Internet hosts exploded by 45 percent to 100 million, according to Telecordia Technologies. Although no one knows for sure, conservative estimates put the number of Internet users at 407.1 million worldwide.

Microsoft has a huge, installed base of more than 160 million users worldwide. Imagine that Microsoft decides to bypass retailers and sell its own software directly to end-users across the Internet. Eliminating the intermediary, Microsoft could sell its software at current retail prices, while doubling or tripling the profitability of each transaction for the company, and simplifying the entire purchasing process for the customer.

Imagine logging on to the Internet, surfing to Microsoft's Web site, browsing through various menus of software, making a selection, keying in your Visa number, confirming the selection and then watching as the software immediately downloads onto your system and automatically configures itself on your hard disk. You wouldn't even have to leave your desk!

Over time, Microsoft could include remote access software in its operating system. Under such a system, an online Microsoft technician could take control of your PC across the Internet and solve configuration problems. Microsoft could either include free support for the first 90 days in the price of the software or charge a support fee. For the customer, it would be better service and less hassle at the same price as retail. Within the first year of selling software directly to end users, Microsoft would likely become the world's largest retail vendor of software and experience a corresponding surge in profit.

With the launch of *Windows 95*, Microsoft had planned to include *Office 95*, its product suite –*Word* (word processor), *Excel* (spreadsheet), *PowerPoint* (graphics), *Mail* (mail client) and *Access* (database) – on the CD-ROM version of *Windows 95*. CD-ROMs have about 650 megabytes (MB) of storage space and *Windows 95* only takes up about 100 MB. Customers would have gone to the retailer, paid roughly $100 to buy a copy of *Windows 95* on CD and installed it on their system. The software then would have asked them, "Would you like to install *Office 95?*" Users wanting to purchase it would have been prompted to call a toll-free number, whereupon a Microsoft representative would have taken their credit-card number and given them a unique numeric key to unlock and install *Office 95*. Under the plan, Microsoft would have received the secondary sale without any portion going to the software retailer. Rumors of this plan so frightened a group of US software vendors that a number of them banded together to bring anti-trust action against Microsoft.

Online software sales are on the verge of becoming a major market. In 1999, the worldwide market was $3.5 billion and is expected to reach $32.9 billion in 2003.[12]

Netscape, when it launched, bypassed the retail channel by allowing anyone to download *Navigator* for free from its Web side. However, to get support, users must purchase a copy by keying in their credit-card number. Netscape has produced the software on diskette for purchase in retail stores. But why bother when you can get it for free?

In the software business, sales are one-off, with upgrades every year or two. By contrast, utilities such as the telephone carriers and electrical utilities receive monthly payments that generate huge cash flow. Utilities experience ongoing and ever-increasing revenues as more and more individuals and organizations subscribe. Microsoft, Netscape and Sun Microsystems want to become utility companies.

Online Flight Reservations

American Airlines has its own Web page that allows travelers to compare flights from different airlines, select flights by schedule, or price or look at existing reservations (www.americanair.com).

The Sabre reservation case (Chapter 10) highlighted how redefining the relationship between the company and customers shifted the very nature of competition. American Airlines, by offering a free reservation system to travel agents, created a new business: real-time, online reservation systems for travel agents. But the explosion of the Net now threatens travel agents, as American and other airlines can make bookings directly with customers. Sabre is also threatened, as the reservation market is once again open to competition. In response, Sabre launched its own online reservation system at www.travelocity.com.

If you are interested in online information and reservations for airline travel, visit www.flyaow.com. The site lists every airline in the world, along with information on frequent flier programs.

Online Commerce

In 1994, Microsoft announced its intention to buy Intuit. Intuit's *Quicken for Windows* is one of the most user-friendly pieces of software on the market today. It is a simple program that allows individuals and small home/home office businesses to perform accounting easily and painlessly. Microsoft's plan to buy Intuit was stalled by the US Justice Department, and Microsoft eventually withdrew the offer. Microsoft's own product, *Money*, has not matched *Quicken's* ease of use, functionality or popularity, despite years of Microsoft's marketing effort.

In 2001, Intuit launched the latest version of *QuickBooks*, its extremely popular accounting software. This new version takes advantage of the Internet by offering its users the ability to bill clients and receive payments online. A company can now send an online invoice that allows the client to make payment with a credit card or account transfer. No paper invoices or checks need to be sent through the mail. The online payment option is fully integrated with the accounting software, which means that the financial records are automatically updated. This will minimize the time needed to deal with the accounting and the inevitable errors.

Microsoft, Intuit's nearest competitor, offers a similar software program called *Money*. However, *Money* isn't yet as sophisticated at QuickBooks, but does allow an individual to integrate the program with their online bank account and online investments. It will only be a matter of time before Intuit, Microsoft and the banks make sending money across the Web a common practice.

WHAT ABOUT THE BANKS?

Some banks have been building branches – although banking in the future will have more to do with keystrokes, mouse clicks and phone lines than visiting buildings. What is really driving the adoption of the Internet in general is the cost of transactions. As you can see, the cost of transactions to the bank varies greatly:

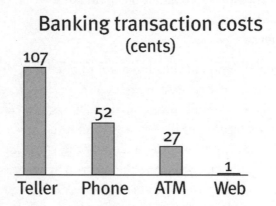

Banking transaction costs
(cents)

Source: Booz, Allen & Hamilton

It costs US$1.07 to do a face-to-face transaction at a teller; 52¢ by phone; 27¢ at the ATM, but less than 1¢ using the Web. Here is the principle at work – water runs down hill. Overtime, I can tell you which way the market will move based on the cost structure.

Why then have few banks been active in this field? Online banking will change the industry more fundamentally than ATMs did.

The explosion of the Net won't be driven by current applications. What will explode the Net are real-world, commercial applications that make life significantly easier for people.

This leads me to conclude that banking is essential but banks are not. We need to separate form from function. The form that banking takes in the future will not be the same form as it is today.

Now in my presentations some people say – "but the vision you are presenting of banking in the future – there is no valuable human interaction." I find that an interesting statement because I never defined standing in a bank line-up for 20 minutes over my lunch hour to be a valuable human interaction.

And it's not an either/or – it's an and. In our company we use electronic banking wherever possible, but we still use a teller for complex transactions. It's not about restricting customers choice, it's about increasing it. Customers will choose to automate routine, simple transactions to save themselves time and money.

Banks of the future

In 1998, seven million American households were accessing their bank accounts via the Internet and that number is expected to explode to 24 million by 2004. Over half of the households surveyed used the Internet to pay bills. In Europe the number of online bank accounts is expected to rise to 66.2 million in 2003, from 26.1 million in 2000.[13]

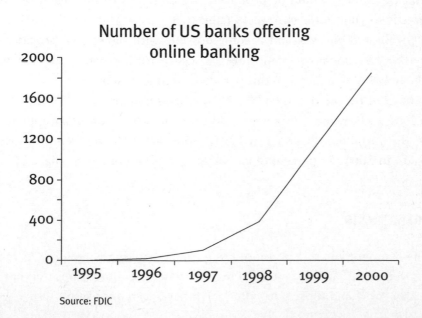

Number of US banks offering online banking

Source: FDIC

There are 9,905 banks in the US and in 2001, 1850 of them offered transaction online banking (conduct transactions such as checking account balance or bill payments as opposed to just providing information).

In 1998, the US Treasury began using eChecks to issue approximately 857 million payments each year on behalf of government agencies such as the Social Security Administration and the Department of Veterans Affairs.[14] An eCheque program has also been launched in Singapore, allowing consumers to pay bills with their email.

IMAGINE SOME OF THESE POSSIBILITIES

Imagine visiting a car dealership, test-driving a new General Motors model, then going home, logging on to a Web site and viewing the custom features of your choice online. You could choose the color, air conditioning, sunroof, stereo, leather or fabric seats, five-speed or automatic transmission, with or without cruise control – and watch how each option affects the price and see the car rotate three-dimensionally. You could then punch the purchase button using your mouse. After a series of confirmations, your selection would be automatically conveyed to the assembly plant, where, through flexible manufacturing processes (see Chapter 11), your custom car would be produced and delivered to the dealer or even directly to your home two weeks later.

All these services would become possible with the service provider or credit-card company guaranteeing the security of payment across the Net. The only limiting factor in this paradigm shift is imagination.

In 1994 for the first time North Americans bought more PCs than televisions. In fact, more PCs were sold than any other consumer appliance. Of the 40 million PCs sold in 1995, more than half were sold to households. In 2001, 51 percent of all North American households have PCs.

PREDICTIONS

The demographic shift to those using online banking will closely parallel the usage of ATMs. People born before 1950 have a predisposition not to use an ATM and those born after 1950 have a predisposition to use one.

Likewise, consumers born after 1960 will be more likely to use online systems.

Given demographic and technological trends, a large shake-up in banking systems and market share is inevitable. Only time will tell which banks will survive. One or two companies – a credit-card company and/or software company – could emerge as major winners in defining new banking standards.

TO SUMMARIZE . . .

- The Internet is the fastest-growing social and business phenomenon of this century. Its impact will be more significant than the invention of the Gutenberg press.
- Barriers to the explosion of commerce across the Internet will fall as consumers adapt to the new medium.
- Companies that thrive in this new medium will create the tools of commerce of the future.

WORKSHOP QUESTIONS AND ACTIVITIES

- If you were starting a company today to serve your customers, what technologies would you use to simplify the industry? What advantages would these give you versus your current practices? Why isn't someone doing this?
- One of the characteristics of the Internet is that it eliminates the physical distance between buyer and seller. A search for drill bits may yield suppliers from Taiwan, Canada, Germany, and the United States. While this effectively brings new competitors into your markets, it also opens the world to you. How will your business deal with the implications of global market access by all competitors, including the small start-ups on other continents?
- What will be the role of your Internet presence? Many shoppers use the Internet solely for gathering product information, but many observers feel that this is because of nervousness using the Internet for transac-

tions. Should your role on the Net be that of information provider, or will you use the Net as a completely new channel of distribution for your company?

- Remembering that everyone, including your competition, has access to your site, how much information should you make available?
- Many grocers are treating companies such as Peapod with the same indifference that local drugstores treated the entry of Wal-Mart into small towns during the 1980s. Not many small drugstores are left. What new technologies or new players are likely to hurt your business over the next few years? How can you offset these effects?
- Suggest ways your company teams can understand the problems that prevent the organization from increasing its operational efficiency.

Reflection:

What is the key learning/insight for me in this chapter?

Action:

What one action shall I take tomorrow to move learning into action? And over time repeat, to move action into habit?

CHAPTER 13

Business and the Environment

As we enter the next century, nothing will have a greater impact on business than the environment. While the media's focus on the environment appears to have waned since the 1980s, researchers note it has become a core issue, a non-negotiable concern. The public expects corporations and governments to protect the environment.

Green is not a new product line or a new sector, it is a new way of doing business. It is not something to do as a legal obligation, as a contribution to society or the planet.

The shifts that individuals, organizations and society as a whole will have to make as a result of the environmental imperative are more confounding than any other changes discussed so far.

At the core of most organizational problems are faulty paradigms. One of these is the concept of control and power. Paradoxically, the more leaders cling to power, the less powerful their organizations are. The more they control, the more out-of-control their organization. Hierarchical, top-down companies can no longer compete in this rapidly changing environment. The loss of market share, increased competition and the speed of change are causing a great deal of pain for individuals in organizations. Out of this pain comes the search for new ways of working.

This book is written to help people understand the forces that are driving change and to bring about greater freedom of action for individuals within organizations. Once individuals can more freely interact to shape the mission and vision of their organization, companies and society will be in a better position to address the environmental problems we currently face.

Politicians often say it's an issue of jobs or the environment. This is a false dichotomy. We can't have one or the other, it must be both. We need a new way of thinking.

GOOD FOR THE ENVIRONMENT; GOOD FOR THE BOTTOM LINE

On March 25, 1989, the Exxon *Valdez* – an oil tanker three-football fields in length – ran aground in Prince William Sound, a sensitive marine area off the coast of Alaska. The tanker spilled 200,000 barrels of crude oil.

What was the true cost of the disaster to the company? Not only did the clean-up cost Exxon $2 billion, the bad publicity resulted in the loss of thousands of customers, many of whom wrote to the company, saying they would never again buy gasoline from Exxon.

> Not everything that counts can be counted and not everything that can be counted counts.
> Albert Einstein, physicist

Research shows that for every customer who complains, four or five feel the same way but won't take the time to call or write to complain. The loss of market share for Exxon was huge. Being a corporate polluter cost the company billions of dollars.

THE END OF WORK

Jeremy Rifkin in *The End of Work* argues that new technology is ushering in an era of workerless production. Rifkin predicts that by 2020, blue-collar work will have been completely eliminated and that three-quarters of all current white-collar work will be lost to automation. If Rifkin's predictions come true, society as a whole will have to redefine the concept of work. Workweeks will be significantly shorter, allowing for more quality of life. Participation in the volunteer sector will rise steeply. With fewer people making money at work, there will be less disposable income for the purchase of discretionary goods. GNP may begin an annual descent.

With three-quarters of all North Americans out of work, how will individuals be able to maintain a sense of self-worth when society and individuals currently place so much value on jobs? How will companies stay in business if 75 percent of former consumers are unemployed and have little or no income? How will society hold together? If Rifkin's predictions transpire, it will shake the very foundations of our faith in organizations and government. It will force us to question the purpose of the individual in society and business, and the role of government. It will require a complete rethinking of what it means to be "successful." If

Rifkin's predictions prove correct, the consequences could be the most disastrous or the most liberating shift in the world's history.

NEW ECONOMIC MEASURES OF WHAT COUNTS

Gross National Product (GNP) measures monetary transactions, not value. For instance, when the Exxon *Valdez* sinks and spills oil all over the Alaskan coast, GNP goes up. Why? Because the company has to spend $2 billion on clean up. Similarly, wars are great stimulators of GNP. But never would people argue that these events were good for society, people or the environment.

We need a new economic measure. We need to start looking at what Thomas Berry, co-author of *The Universe Story*, calls GEP – Gross Earth Product. It's a genuine progress indicator. When we clear-cut a forest, GEP decreases because we encroach on the natural habitat of plants and animals. Animal and plant populations decrease, sometimes to the point of extinction. When the Japanese and other whaling nations hunt certain species of whales to extinction, GEP decreases as the diversity of life on earth is decreased and the food chain is imperiled.

As Berry says, "The earth economy is primary, the human economy derivative. Anything that hurts the earth economy will eventually hurt the human economy. We need to be wary, because the earth economy is showing signs of bankruptcy."

The Canadian government shocked the world when it banned cod fishing off the Atlantic Grand Banks in 1994. An area once teeming with fish, the stock was so depleted by over-fishing that the government took this unprecedented measure. As a result, East Coast fisheries shut down and thousands of people were thrown out of work in a region dependent on fishing. The costs to the government – make-work programs, grants and social assistance – ran into the hundreds of millions of dollars.

Economic growth can only continue if our material impact on the earth is dramatically reduced. Fortunately, the new economy offers hope (Chapter 7), as our economy shifts from being materially based to mentally based. Computer hardware and software, entertainment and the arts generate far more jobs and have little negative impact on the environment, while strip mining and clear-cut logging generate few jobs and have very negative environmental impact.

Our economy may grow, but our material consumption must decrease. In other words, GNP can increase, but only if GEP is stable or preferably increasing. If we think of the world as a one-time capital endowment, we can live off the interest, but never the capital. There is enough for our need but not our greed. To behave responsibly is far from limiting. It offers exciting possibilities for the enterprising mind.

For example, the dominant belief within most North American electric utilities is, "We exist to produce electricity. Increased economic growth is good. Increased economic growth requires increased electricity production. So increased electricity consumption is good."

However, North Americans consume more energy per person than any other people in the world. If everyone else in the world consumed as much electricity as we do, the resulting environmental damage would be catastrophic. The production-oriented mindset is dangerous. We can't have infinite material-based economic growth on a finite planet.

Consumers don't want electricity or gas, they want cold beer and warm showers. How they get cold beer and warm showers is relatively unimportant to them. Why couldn't a utility lease the best available energy-efficiency equipment – hot-water heaters, refrigerators – to consumers that use 80 percent less electricity? The average electricity bill would remain the same, but 80 percent of the payment would be for leasing appliances and the remaining 20 percent for electricity.

Unless the utilities can adopt such a mindset, their competitors will be energy-efficient appliance companies. How can a company make more money by selling less of its product or service? Only by dramatically changing the way it looks at its business. Such shifts, however, would be good for the environment and good for business.

Green is gold

Loblaw, one of Canada's largest food retailers has embraced environmentalism because it adds to the bottom line. For instance, energy efficiency has become a major profit center for the grocery chain. Every $100,000 a year that Loblaw saves by retrofitting its stores with energy-efficient lighting has the same bottom-line impact as increasing grocery sales by $10 million! This is because in the grocery business margins are only one percent (for every $100 worth of groceries sold, the company makes a profit of one dollar). Once retrofitting is done it will continue adding to the bottom line every year to come. So $100,000 of energy savings over 10 years has the same impact as increasing sales by $100 million over the same period! A one-time expenditure produces a lifetime saving.

Ben & Jerry's Ice Cream

Ice cream maker Ben & Jerry's generated tremendous publicity in 1994 when the state of Illinois prevented it from selling anti-rBGH labeled products. Recombinant bovine growth hormone, known as rBGH, is a bioengineered hormone that stimulates a cow's natural body processes to "trick" it into producing more milk than is natural. Environmentalist and organic farmers argue that rBGH increases the risk of dairy cows contracting a variety of diseases including udder infections, which require increased amounts of antibiotics to treat. Opponents argue that milk from rBGH-treated cows has not been proven unsafe for human consumption.

Despite objections, the FDA approved rBGH for use in November 1993, but the agency did not require foods containing rBGH to be labeled.

The State of Illinois and the City of Chicago forbade Ben & Jerry's from anti-rBGH labeling under threat of seizing all the company's product. Vermont-based Ben & Jerry's, along with natural food manufacturers, producers and retailers, launched a court case. The suit, filed in May of 1996 against the State of Illinois and the City of Chicago, charged that prohibiting anti-rBGH labeling was a violation of the company's First Amendment right to honestly inform customers about the contents of their products amid a controversial political issue. The case was settled out of court in August 1997. Ben & Jerry's packages now say, "We oppose the use of recombinant bovine growth hormone (rGBH). The family farmers who supply our milk and cream pledge not to treat their cows with rBGH. The FDA has concluded that no significant difference has been shown, and no test can now distinguish between milk from rBGH and untreated cows."

"The use of bio-engineered growth hormones in dairy cows is inconsistent with everything we stand for," said Perry Odak, the CEO of Ben & Jerry's. "Consumers should have a right to information that allows them to make an informed choice."

Ben and Jerry's got tremendous publicity from the initiative. The news stories about the issue gave the company tremendous name recognition, which had a far greater impact than any advertising campaign could ever have had.

The Body Shop

The international skin care and cosmetics chain has become one of the most vocal and active store chains to promote environmentally friendly products and packaging. The majority of the Body Shop's products are available in refillable containers. When lip balm containers or shampoo bottles have been emptied, the containers can be brought back to the store. This extends the life of the packaging, lowers costs for the Body Shop (they don't have to buy new packaging) and reduces waste. As an incentive, The Body Shop offers a 10 percent discount to customers who return packaging. Since 1992, over 407,000 bottles have been refilled and 591,000 have been recycled.

The Body Shop uses sustainable resources at all levels of its operation and urges all of its suppliers to do the same.

SOCIAL MARKETING: COST EFFECTIVE AND ELEGANT

Loblaw's energy efficiency, The Body Shop and Ben & Jerry's Ice Cream are all examples of social marketing.

Markets are fragmenting as highly focused niche players carve out high-margin business, while large warehouse/discount chains carve out price-sensitive mass markets.

Similarly, advertising media are increasingly fragmenting. As we move to 500 TV channels and then thousands of channels with the rise of the Internet, advertisers can no longer reach consumers with one message advertised in one media.

Social marketing creates products that are in alignment with the consciousness of consumers. It offers no-cost advertising in the form of consumer support and media coverage, and creates consumer insistence. In other words, consumers insist on buying your products or services.

For instance, The Body Shop does not spend one cent on advertising yet receives millions of dollars' worth of publicity every year. The company sends out executives, store managers and franchisees to organizations to talk about social responsibility. The Body Shop products are not tested on animals and the company works to return part of the profits to the communities in which its products are made.

Being responsible about the environment doesn't cost these companies anything, and the publicity far exceeds the reach of buying advertising. The only costs are the product development expenses, which are a necessary investment anyway.

CFCS AND LILY PONDS

The ozone layer prevents most of the sun's ultraviolet (UV) radiation from penetrating the earth's atmosphere. Chlorofluorocarbons (CFCs) are used in refrigerators, aerosol cans and in many manufacturing processes. Their release into the atmosphere is destroying ozone, resulting in the thinning of the ozone layer. The "holes" in the ozone layer, as they are known in the media, are allowing increased levels of UV radiation to reach Earth.

A CFC molecule that is released into the atmosphere rises 30 miles to the stratosphere where the ultraviolet rays will shatter it, releasing a chlorine atom. Each free-floating chlorine atom will destroy 100,000 ozone molecules over a 25-year period. The destruction of the ozone layer will continue for 25 years from the day the last CFC is released into the atmosphere.

As the ozone layer thins, the increasing levels of UV radiation are causing increases in incidents of sunburn, eye cataracts and skin cancer (melanoma). Increased UV levels also affect the food chain, reducing the amount of plankton in the seas, which in turn reduces the number of fish that feed upon it, and so on.

The United Nation's Montreal Protocol on Substances That Deplete the Ozone Layer (known as the Montreal Protocol), signed on September 16, 1987, calls for the elimination of all CFCs in industrial processes by 2003.

"Environmental crisis" may appear to be a misnomer. "Sure, there are problems," some say, "but there is still a great deal of time to prevent them from growing to the crisis point." Recall the lesson of the lilies and the pond. Today, a few people are running around shouting warnings of impending doom, that our pond is about to be covered over by lilies. When so much of the water is still open, the casual observer can be easily forgiven for dismissing these warnings and thinking, "These people are crazy."

When not addressed, exponentially growing problems become enormous very quickly. That is why it is so important for individuals, organizations and governments to pay attention to the early warnings. Environmental security can only come from a willingness to question the wisdom of current ways of working and to change our personal lifestyles and business practices based on a new understanding of our interdependence with nature.

Thankfully, more and more corporations are making decisions based on long-term ecological viability, not just short-term profitability. Nortel used to be one of the largest industrial users of CFCs. The Montreal Protocol calls for the elimination of CFCs from industrial processes by 2003. When it was signed, the company could have spent millions of dollars hiring lobbyists and public relations firms to oppose it. Arguments could have been advanced that the agreement was unfair and that thousands of people would have to be laid off as the company was forced to shut down plants that used CFCs in the manufacturing process. Veiled threats could have been made to politicians that their parties and campaigns would no longer receive financial support. Politicians could have been told that the company would blame them, their parties and the government when the plants in their ridings closed down unless they worked to repeal the protocol.

Instead, Nortel chose to be proactive. Rather than fighting the agreement, the company decided to embrace it. And rather than waiting until 2003, the company decided to do something immediately. Three task forces were struck.

The first task force asked, "How can we immediately reduce our CFC use through better conservation techniques, better CFC-recapture methods and slight modifications to the process so that the need for CFCs is reduced?"

In the telecommunications industry, CFCs were used to "clean" circuit boards. After the boards had been soldered, CFC solvents were sprayed on the boards to dissolve the excess flux. This first task force was able to reduce CFC usage by 50 percent within a year, through simple conservation techniques and modifications to the production processes.

The second task force looked at redesigning the industrial process by asking such questions as, "Are CFCs necessary at all? Can some other substance remove excess flux? Do we have to use solder at all or can we electronically join points without soldering? If we have to solder, could it be done in such a way that no flux is left over at the end? Is there a way to solder that does not require cleaning?" Every assumption of the process was questioned.

The third task force looked at partnering, asking, "How can we partner with our customers, our suppliers, the government and even our competitors to help us in this process?" Nortel shared its challenge with suppliers, including the solder supplier. They asked customers if they could accept greater amounts of flux left on the board as long as it did not compromise the performance of the board. They even asked competitors what solutions they had come up with.

In the end, Nortel, working with its material and equipment suppliers, developed an entirely new manufacturing method. The process uses low-solid flux while soldering in a nitrogen atmosphere, leaving little residue on the board and therefore requiring no cleaning, which eliminates the need to use CFCs. In the process, Nortel has saved $50 million a year since it no longer has to purchase or pay to dispose of CFCs. Over a decade this translates into a $500-million saving – half a billion dollars! Rather than a threat, environmental sensitivity has been a bottom-line blessing!

The engineers in Nortel were excited, galvanized by the challenge. There is nothing an engineer likes more than a really formidable problem. The task forces were excited by the process of questioning the manufacturing process.

Nortel did not rest on its laurels. The company recognized its corporate responsibility and immediately began transferring the technology to its competitors around the world. The company made all the technical information available to anyone and any company worldwide interested in learning the details of the redesigned industrial process.

In addition to saving $500 million over 10 years, Nortel's actions increased the pride that employees feel in working for a company that is a world leader in social responsibility. It is difficult to estimate how much pride, trust and loyalty the company's actions created for Nortel employees when the corporate policies were aligned with their personal values. The company won wide praise for meeting the Montreal Protocol ten years ahead of schedule. If the company had failed to act, it is difficult to estimate how much resentment, anger and fear it would have generated from employees, customers and suppliers, environmental groups and the public had it continued to participate in the destruction of the ozone layer.

PERCEPTION IS PRIMARY

How individuals or organizations perceive problems determines the solutions that they will propose. Because of the billions of dollars that change hands every day in the stock and money markets, that industry attracts the best and brightest minds. In his book *Market Wizards*, Jack Schwager quotes one broker saying, "We have been thinking about this problem for a long time [10 years]. Half the work in solving a problem is finding the right way to conceptualize it. It took us years before we figured out the right questions to ask."[1]

This is powerful and instructive. How much time do we spend thinking about how we perceive the problem, compared to the time spent trying to solve it? Most people tend to jump in and try to solve it.

SEVEN ENVIRONMENTAL/BUSINESS OPERATING PRINCIPLES

Businesses can save the planet while bettering the bottom line. Environmental principles are simple, elegant and can be implemented immediately. Here are the operating principles:

1. Do more with fewer natural resources

Businesses need to do more with fewer material resources. Decreasing raw inputs is good for business. Low raw-material costs actually promote inefficiency because material resources are not identified as a limiting factor.

Therefore, an organization's intellectual capital is not focused on reducing or eliminating certain material inputs (as in the case of the CFCs with Nortel).

Doing more with less does not mean doing more with fewer people. People are the engines of the new economy. In a downturn, few companies sell off their capital equipment. But many companies lay off people, their only producing asset in the new economy. People alone add value by redesigning production processes. Creativity, ingenuity and innovation come from people alone. They are the producing capital assets in new economy companies.

The three R's (Reduce, Reuse, Recycle) need to include Rethink and Repair: Rethink, Repair, Reduce, Reuse, Recycle. The order is important. A tremendous emphasis has been placed on recycling, but in the order of the five Rs, it is last. We first need to rethink. Do we need to use this product at all? If we do have to use it, how can we reduce its use, then reuse, then repair, and finally, recycle? There is an imperative that business can no longer ignore: we have to decrease our material consumption per person because the earth cannot sustain growing levels of demand. Two thousand years ago, there were only 250 million people on earth. The number has grown steadily to 500 million in 1640, one billion in 1850, six billion today and is expected to level off in 2200 at just over 10 billion, according to the United Nations. The greater the earth's population, the greater the pressure on the natural ecosystems as humans clear more land for farming, catch more fish and mine more minerals. The individual actions of six billion people have a powerful collective impact on the earth's ecosystems.

The earth appears to be such a vast place from our individual perception that it is very difficult to understand the severity of our human impact. Here is a simple but significant fact: more people are alive at this moment than all humans who have died throughout history combined.

Emerging nations aspire to our lifestyles in the developed world. Explosive population growth coupled with exponential per capita material consumption is a recipe for disaster. We need to significantly decrease our per capita consumption of resources in developed nations.

Fortunately there is hope. Amory Lovins, the world's leading energy-efficiency expert at the Rocky Mountain Institute, has proven how North Americans could reduce their energy consumption by three-quarters and still maintain their current standard of living! All it would take is using the best available technology.[2]

Amory Lovins and William Browning prove that energy savings of 75 to 80 percent are possible from the use of efficient lighting, advanced window glazing, better heating, ventilation and air-conditioning system (HVAC) design for buildings even less than five years old![3]

Lovins cites the case study of retrofitting Boeing Aircraft's office-building lighting, reducing lighting costs by 90 percent with a less than two-year payback! The goal was achieved by redesigning the building, increasing the number of skylights and windows, and by using special window glazing, which allow in 75 percent of visible light but keep out 50 percent of the heat. Lighting levels were increased, and overheating, which occurs even in winter, was reduced. The 90 percent cost savings from lighting came not just from the lighting cost reduction, but also the large savings in the reduced capital and operating costs of significantly lower air-conditioning requirements.

Lovins promotes life cycle costing, where lifetime capital and operating costs are taken into account. For instance, baseboard heating is cheap to install, hence it is used in public housing projects for people with low income, but it has the highest operating costs. When capital and operating costs are added together, it is the most expensive home-heating option.

2. Align systems with environmental principles

An organization is nothing more than a collection of individuals. And yet individuals within organizations often behave differently than they would in their personal affairs. Within some organizations, decisions are made based on values that are contrary to the values that govern employees' personal lives.

Deming believed that systems and structures determine behaviors. If companies are not performing in the best interests of all stakeholders—and the health of the environment affects us all—it is not due to bad people, it is due to bad systems and structures. But we must remember that people create systems and structures in the first place.

In many jurisdictions non-returnable pop bottles and cans are cheaper than returnable ones. So most consumers buy the cheaper ones. But if landfill and garbage-hauling costs were added into the equation, in other words, if full-cost accounting was performed, it would be cheaper to use refillable bottles.

It is the responsibility of all individuals in an organization or in society to work to change the systems and structures to create greater alignment with their values and environmental principles.

3. The learning-based economy has arrived

The new economy gives the world hope because it is not as intensive in its use of raw materials as the old economy. Value is added principally through knowledge, creativity and innovation. Physical commerce will not disappear as humans will always have physical needs such as shelter, food and clothing. But an ever-increasing percentage of rapidly expanding and high-value companies are learning-based. The stock market values software companies in the billions of dollars, but these firms work exclusively to produce non-physical products and services.

The new economy is not limited to western nations and does not recognize national boundaries. India and Pakistan have large communities of computer programmers, working remotely for western corporations.

4. Be proactive

While environmental activism may have seemed more prevalent in the 1980s, it is not an issue that will ever go away. The environment will remain a priority as long as it is under serious threat. The problems are getting worse, not better.

Occurrences of cancer and other diseases are rising at an alarming rate. Many researchers are pointing to increased chemical contamination of our environment as the source. And the impacts are greater than just cancer.

As the baby boomers (people born from 1947 to 1963) become more conscious of their own mortality, they are questioning their values and searching for meaning in their lives. They are concerned about such issues as fertility. Studies now show that sperm count in men has been falling by 2.1 percent a year between 1976 and 1996 in industrialized countries. This trend is blamed largely on chemical pollution.[4] The boomers are concerned about the health and welfare of their children. As the boomers' values shift, putting the environment on the business agenda is good business.

We tend not to appreciate how quickly paradigms can shift. If in 1980 I had said, "An imprisoned black revolutionary leader will become the president of South Africa and that apartheid will end; the Berlin Wall will crumble when people tear it apart with their bare hands; the Soviet Union will dissolve," you would have thought I was crazy. The future is not a linear extension of the past.

5. Resource poverty forces innovation richness

Resource-poor companies and countries, if they are to succeed, must be more creative than their competitors. Many environmentalists have tremendous, simple and financially sound solutions to problems.

Challenge, as in Nortel's case, can help an organization. Higher resource prices force companies to be creative. Resource-rich companies often experience an ingenuity void.

One of the benefits of having high raw-material costs is that companies are forced to become efficient very quickly. Japanese steel manufacturers became energy-efficient in the 1980s because electricity costs were higher than those of North American steel makers.

6. Leveraged partnerships and creating synergy

Ecosystems work together in symbiotic relationships. The challenges we face in business and the environment are so large that no one company can solve all the problems or create all the opportunities. Leveraged partnerships will be key in the future and they will not necessarily involve cash. We need to be more resourceful, not more gluttonous, with resources.

When intellectual capital replaces financial or physical capital as the primary means of generating wealth, a whole new series of laws come into place. Synergy is achieved through attraction. To attract intellectual capital, people must have a stake in the project emotionally, mentally and spiritually.

This is the age of emerging spirituality. People want to know, why? What is the meaning of life? Why am I here? What is my contribution? One of the significant benefits that Nortel's employees experienced was the increased pride in working for an environmentally responsible company, and avoiding negative feelings of guilt in working for a polluting company. Employees want to make a difference.

There are numerous examples of employee-driven, environmental programs saving thousands of dollars while increasing morale. Many actions are simple things, like eliminating disposable cups in the cafeteria and using mugs. North Americans use and discard enough disposable cups every year to circle the Earth 40 times! Employees want to make a difference, and they will if allowed and encouraged by the corporate structure.

7. Leadership

At times, leadership requires tremendous courage. We have reached a point in human history where environmentalists can now say, "The emperor has no clothes." Our current business system is leading the world to the brink of collapse. To stand up among business peers and deliver such a message requires tremendous courage—the kind of courage and conviction Columbus had to display when everyone believed the world was flat.

Given the depth of their concern over the seriousness of the crisis, some environmentalists come across as shrill and alarmist. But what do you do if you are watching the lily pond? We need the courage to hear the truth about the environmental crisis we face, and then speak out within organizations. We also need creativity to address these challenges in a positive way that brings environmentalists and business leaders together. Blame, guilt, finger pointing and anger will not bring about a better world. Environmentalists actually need entrepreneurs to create market demand and sell new concepts to consumers. Likewise, business leaders need environmentalists because of the low-cost, simple, elegant solutions that they devise, which can significantly improve the bottom line and win market share.

THE FUTURE OF BUSINESS

Business will not be able to operate if the earth's economy is bankrupt. The earth economy is primary, the human economy a derivative. Business leaders and environmentalists must work together to find creative and practical solutions to the environmental challenge. Business leaders and environmentalists, by assuming leadership roles and forming partnerships, can forge a new society.

TO SUMMARIZE . . .

- An irresponsible environmental record is a public relations death knell.
- Companies that are good to the environment are winning market share.
- By acting in an environmentally responsible manner, businesses can attract top-quality professionals and consumer support.

WORKSHOP QUESTIONS AND ACTIVITIES

- How important are environmental issues to your employees?
- What is your "worst nightmare" in terms of your company's potential impact on the environment? What would the newspapers look like the next day? How would you feel about this personally? What can be done now to prevent this?

Reflection:

What is the key learning/insight for me in this chapter?

Action:

What one action shall I take tomorrow to move learning into action? And over time repeat, to move action into habit?

REACTIONS

Following are three reactions to The Learning Paradox *from thought leaders.*

Hunter and Amory Lovins *are the leading energy efficiency experts worldwide. They argue that businesses need to create a business model that can sustain the needs of human and the environment, and that these goals are not contradictory.*

Lou Pritchett *was the vice-president of Proctor and Gamble who initiated the supply chain integration with Wal-Mart. As the first major project of its kind, it sparked in its wake a host of new buzz words: partnering, value chain integration, inter-enterprise integration and vendor managed inventory.*

Cliff Saunders *is a design engineer and consultant who speaks and writes about complexity. He has developed software that helps teams in organizations resolve complex problems. As the world grows more complex this will be an increasingly important area of study.*

HUNTER AND AMORY LOVINS

The Next Industrial Revolution

In our newest book, *Natural Capitalism: Creating the Next Industrial Revolution* we argue that capitalism – as it is currently practiced – is an aberration. It is violating its own logic by not valuing all forms of capital. Capitalism now only counts two of the four forms of capital, the financial and manufactured capital. It ignores and is liquidating the other two forms of capital: natural and human capital. True capitalism would be based on the productive use and reinvestment in all four forms of capital.

Capitalism grew out of the first industrial revolution. In the late 1700s English textile mills introduced technology that enabled one Lancashire weaver to do the work previously done by 200. The mills were only one of many technologies that exponentially increased the productivity of workers. Before this it was inconceivable that people could work more productively: if you needed two horse power you needed two horses, and the same with people. The first industrial revolution increased labor productivity 100-fold at a time when skilled labor was scarce and natural resources were plentiful and cheap. Profit-maximizing capitalists substituted the use of the plentiful resource and economized on their scarce resource.

Now, the relative scarcities have shifted. With 10,000 more people arriving on earth every hour, people are no longer the scarce resource. But economists still believe that increasing labor productivity is the basis of prosperity, as if one person on earth should produce all goods with the rest of us out of work. At the same time, in large measure because of the success of this industrial system, every known ecosystem on earth is in decline. Therefore, profit-maximizing capitalists will economize on the scarce resources, the natural capital, using more people and more brains to wring 4, 10, or even 100 times as much benefit from each unit of energy, water, materials, or anything else borrowed from the planet. Success at this will be the basis of competitiveness in the decades to come and will be the hallmark of the next industrial revolution. It is also the first principle of a new form of economics that we call *natural capitalism*.

Part of the problem, noted in *The Learning Paradox*, is that our measures of economic success are seriously flawed. Our mental model of the economy is a linear flow from extraction to disposal. It does not take into account the natural environment, which, as Herman Daly points out, surrounds and provisions the entire economy. This environment is not linear, but cyclical. It is delivers tens of trillions of dollars worth of benefits annually – more than the combined economic output of all nations' economies. But none of this is reflected on company balance sheets or in any economic measure.

Deficient logic of this sort cannot be corrected simply by placing a monetary value on natural capital. Many key ecosystem services have no known substitutes at any price. For example, the $200 million Biosphere II project, despite a great deal of impressive science, was unable to provide breathable air for eight people. Biosphere I, our home, performs this task daily at no charge for six billion of us.

The best technologies cannot substitute for water and nutrient cycling, atmospheric and ecological stability, pollination and biodiversity, topsoil and biological productivity, and the process of assimilating and detoxifying society's wastes. The limits to economic growth will increasingly be set by scarcities of natural capital.

This is not to say we are running out of such commodities as copper and oil. Even with recent fluctuations, prices for almost all commodities are near record lows and will fall for some time, in part because of improvements in extraction technologies. But these technologies impose environmental costs that further degrade the ability of living systems to sustain a growing human population.

The first of four principles of natural capitalism, radically increasing resource efficiency, is the best way to deal with this challenge. Increasing resource productivity is profitable, and it also solves most of the environmental dilemmas facing the world today. It greatly slows resource depletion at one end of the economic process and discharge of pollution (resources out of place) at the other end. It creates profits by reducing the costs of both resources and pollution. And it also buys time, forestalling the threatened collapse of natural systems.

This time should then be used to implement the other three principles of natural capitalism. These are: (2) biomimicry: eliminate the concept of waste by redesigning the economy based on closed-loop materials flow models; (3) shift the focus of the economy from processing materials and making things to creating service and flow; and (4) reverse the destruction of the planet now under way by instituting restorative programs of that invest in natural capital.

By applying the four principles of natural capitalism, businesses can behave as if ecosystem services were properly valued and begin to reverse the loss of such services even as they increase profits.

1. Increase resource productivity

We all use resources incredibly wastefully. As noted in *The Learning Paradox*, Progressive Insurance was able to cut insurance claim pay outs from eight weeks to eight hours on average by eliminating, "time-intensive, paperbound, linear process." The material inputs for the US economy are one million pounds per person per year. Globally, this amounts to half a trillion tons per year. But only one percent of all the materials mobilized in the economy are ever embodied in a product and is still there six months after sale. Cutting such waste offers a vast business opportunity.

Nowhere are the opportunities for savings easier to see than in energy. The United States has already cut its annual energy bills by $200 billion relative to what they would have been if savings had not been implemented since the first oil shock in 1973. However, we still waste $300 billion worth of energy each year. Just the energy lost as waste heat at US power stations equals the total energy used by Japan.

Fortunately, many companies have shown how to improve energy efficiency (i.e. reduce waste) and increase profits.

Southwire Corporation – an energy-intensive maker of cable, rod, and wire – halved its energy per pound of product in six years. The savings roughly equaled the company's profits during that period, and company officials estimated that the energy-efficiency effort probably saved 4,000 jobs at ten plants in six states that were jeopardized by competitive market forces. The company then went on to save even more energy, achieving two-year paybacks despite all the earlier energy-efficiency improvements.

Dow's Louisiana division implemented over 900 worker-suggested energy-saving projects during the period 1981–1993. Average annual returns on investment were over 200 percent, with annual savings of $100 million. Both returns and savings rose in later years, because the engineers were learning faster than they were using up the cheapest opportunities.

How are such savings achieved? An international company recently redesigned a standard industrial pumping loop. The original, supposedly optimized, design needed 95 horsepower for pumping. Dutch engineer Jan Schilham made two simple design changes that cut that 95 hp to only 7 hp – a 92 percent reduction. The redesigned system cost less to build and worked better in all respects. How did he do it? As *The Learning Paradox* emphasizes, he "optimized the whole."

First, Schilham chose big pipes and small pumps rather than small pipes and big pumps. The friction in a pipe falls as the pipe gets bigger. In considering how big to make the pipes, normal engineers balance the capital cost of bigger pipe against the savings in energy costs of pumping fluid through the pipe. But this ignores the capital cost of the pumping equipment – the pump, motor, variable-speed electronic control, and electrical supply – that must all be big enough to fight the pipe friction. Ignoring the potential equipment saving, and optimizing one component (the pipe) in isolation, "pessimizes" the larger system. Optimizing the whole system instead, and counting savings in total capital cost as well as in energy cost, makes it clear that, as pipe size increases the capital cost falls more rapidly for equipment than it rises for the much fatter pipe. This much more efficient whole system therefore costs less and works better.

Schilham's second innovation was to lay out the pipes first, then the equipment. The normal sequence used to be the opposite: install the equipment in traditional positions (far apart, at the wrong height, facing the wrong way, with other stuff in between), then tell the pipe fitter to hook it all up. The resulting long, crooked pipes have about three to six times as much friction as short, straight pipes. Using short, straight pipes to minimize friction cuts both capital and operating costs. In this case, it also saved 70 kilowatts of heat loss, because straight pipes are easier to insulate.

This matters because pumping is a major user of electricity worldwide. Optimizing a pumping system, at the level of a whole building or factory, can typically yield energy savings of 3- to 10-fold and cost less to operate. But more importantly, the thought process of whole systems thinking should be applied to almost every technical system that uses resources. The ability to achieve such savings mean that many of the actions needed to protect, for example, the climate can be taken not at a cost but profitably. Saving fuel costs less than buying fuel. This is why DuPont recently announced that it will reduce its CO_2 emissions by 65% from 1990 levels, by 2010, while increasing output revenues 6 percent a year. Using energy in a way that saves money strengthens the bottom line and the whole economy, while also resolving the climate problem.

2. Biomimicry: eliminate the concept of waste

The Learning Paradox also argues that the most successful companies will be the ones that foster creativity and ingenuity among their employees. Such creativity is fostered by the second principle of natural capitalism: eliminating the entire concept of waste by adopting biological patterns, processes, and often materials, by asking, "how would nature solve this problem?" In nature there is no waste. The output from any process is food for some other process. Nature does not make any persistent toxins. This implies eliminating any industrial output that represents a disposal cost rather than a salable product.

Architect Bill McDonough tells the story of being asked by the Steelcase subsidiary DesignTex to design a "green" textile for upholstering office chairs. The fabric it was to replace used such toxic chemicals to dye the cloth that the Swiss government had declared its edge trimmings a hazardous waste.

McDonough's team screened more than 8,000 chemicals, rejecting any that were toxic, built up in food chains, or caused cancer, mutations, birth defects, or endocrine disruption. The 38 that passed could make all colors. The cloth looked better, felt better and lasted longer, because the natural fibers weren't damaged by harsh chemicals. The new fabric was beautiful and won numerous design awards. It was also cheaper to produce, requiring fewer and more ordinary materials. The workers didn't need protection from the process.

The Swiss environmental inspectors who tested the new plant thought their equipment was malfunctioning when the effluent water proved cleaner than the Swiss drinking water: the cloth itself was acting as a filter. But the real point is that this is a product that is clean by design: instead of having to filter toxins out of the effluent, the redesigned process put the filters "where they belong, in the designers' heads."

Or consider the Films division of DuPont. Once failing, it now leads its 59-firm market because it makes its films thinner, stronger, and better matched to customers' needs. This enables it to produce higher-value products using fewer materials. It also recycles used film, closing the materials loops, getting it back from customers with a process now coming to be known as "reverse logistics," a new topic of study in business schools. Jack Krol, past chairman of DuPont, has remarked that he sees no end to DuPont's ability to profit in this way.

Some of the most exciting industrial developments are modeled on nature's low-temperature, low-pressure assembly techniques, whose products rival anything man-made. Janine Benyus' book *Biomimicry* points out that spiders make silk as strong as Kevlar – but much tougher – from digested crickets and flies, without needing boiling sulfuric acid and high-pressure extruders.

The abalone makes an inner shell twice as tough as ceramics, and diatoms make seawater into glass; neither need furnaces. Trees turn air, sunlight, and soil into cellulose, a sugar stiffer and stronger than nylon. We may never be as skillful as spiders, abalone, diatoms, or trees, but such benign natural chemistry may be a better model than the approach of "heat, beat, and treat."

This is an archetype for the emerging world where environmental regulation will be an anachronism. In that biological world, the design lessons of nature will improve business – as well as health, housing, mobility, community, and national security. Such a world emerges from the cybernetics of not inflicting on others any emission to which you wouldn't expose yourself: How clean a car would you buy if its exhaust pipe, instead of being aimed at pedestrians, fed directly into the passenger compartment? How clean would a city or factory make the water it discharges if its intake pipes were downstream of its outlets? We all live downwind, downstream.

3. Create service and flow

The Learning Paradox argues that companies should not exist to sell their products or services; instead they exist to meet the underlying need of the customer. Most organizations see themselves as tied to their product or service. The third principle of natural capitalism stresses that businesses should shift from focusing on making and selling things to providing service and flow; from material production to selling the customer a continual flow of value and performance.

Dow Chemical prefers not to sell solvent, but to lease dissolving services. This way the user is never tempted to pour the solvent down the drain, but returns it to the owner, who repurifies it, puts it through perhaps 50 trips, makes more money, reduces waste and closes the loops of this industrial process.

Interface prefers to lease floor-covering services rather than sell carpet. People want to walk on and look at industrial carpet, not own it. They can obtain these services better if Interface owns the carpet and remains responsible for keeping it clean and fresh. For a service fee, Interface periodically replaces the 10–20 percent of the carpet tiles that show 80–90 percent of the wear. This reduces the mass flow of carpet to landfill by about 80 percent and provides better service at lower cost. It increases net employment, eliminates the disruption (worn tiles are seldom under furniture), and turns a capital expenditure into an operating lease.

4. Invest in natural capital

In *The Learning Paradox*, Jim Harris states that, "Economic growth can only continue if our material impact on the earth is dramatically reduced." The fourth principle of natural capitalism points out that any good capitalist reinvests in the productive capital that is in short supply, to be better able to produce even more wealth. If natural capital is the most important, valuable, and indispensable form of capital, a true capitalist will restore it where degraded and sustain it where healthy. It is hard now for most businesses to see how behaving in ways that are restorative is profitable.

However, the industries that are most dependent on natural capital –

ranching forestry, farming – are starting to find ways in to do this. It will become more widely true as the inputs to industry come to be grown, not mined. This approach is also beginning to interest the large institutional investors such as pension funds who own most of the large companies. They are realizing that spectacular performance by any one company does not help their portfolios over the several decade time period of concern to them, especially if these short-term profits come at the expense of the health of the living systems that underlie the health of the whole economy,

Catching up with centuries of deferred but unbooked planetary maintenance might sound expensive. But whole-system solutions create more life, more value, and ultimately more profits. In this exciting sphere of innovation lie such opportunities as these:

The California Rice Industry Association partnered with environmental groups to switch from burning rice straw to flooding the rice fields after harvest and inviting in the wildfowl to decompose the straw and fertilize the fields. They now flood 30 percent of California's rice acreage, from which they harvest a more profitable mix of wildfowl, high-silica straw, groundwater recharge credits, and other benefits, with rice as a byproduct.

Dr John Todd of the New Alchemy Institute in East Falmouth, Massachusetts, builds biological "Living Machines" that turn sewage into clean water – plus valuable flowers, a tourist venue, and other by-products – with no toxicity, no odor, and reduced capital costs. Such "bioneers'" are using living organisms to "bioremediate" toxic pollutants into forms that are harmless or salable or both.

Allan Savory, founder of the Albuquerque-based Center for Holistic Management, has demonstrated how ranching managed to mimic the migration of large herds of native grazers that co-evolved with grasslands can double the carrying capacity of even degraded rangelands, while improving the health of the range.

These practices adopt the design experience of nearly four billion years of evolutionary testing in which products that failed were recalled by the Manufacturer. Though many details of such nature-mimicking practices are still evolving, the broad contours of the lessons they teach are already clear.

PUTTING IT ALL TOGETHER

A striking example of how a natural capitalist company can perform is emerging at the Atlanta based multinational interiors company, Interface. Made from fossil fuels, most carpet is replaced every decade because it develops worn areas. An office is shut down, furniture removed, and carpet torn up and sent to landfill. (The millions of tons deposited each year will last up to 20,000 years.) New carpet is laid down, the office restored, operations resumed, and workers get sick from the carpet-glue fumes.

Interface's visionary chair, Ray Anderson, realized that if his company was to become sustainable, he first had to eliminate waste. Since making this commitment in 1996, Interface has eliminated about half of its smokestacks, outfall pipes, and trips to the dump. This program has added $157 million to the company's bottom line and now provides 27 percent of its operating profits.

Other manufacturers say that they recycle carpet. Actually they downcycle it – reusing it in lower-grade products. In contrast, Interface's new Solenium product provides floor covering that is almost completely re-manufacturable into identical carpet. This will cut their net flow of materials and energy it takes to make them by 97 percent. It provides a superior product, and is cheaper to make.

Interface's Evergreen Service Contract, described above, implements principle three in a way that increases the savings in resources needed to provide the service by 99 percent, by using modular carpet tiles that are made of recycled content, recyclable, and leased not sold. Part of the rationale is that Interface wants the carpet back after its useful life: it's their supply of molecules from which to make more carpet, if they are to eliminate petroleum from their supply chain.

Finally, to really break its dependence on the oil well, Interface has figured how to make carpet from a non-food component of corn. But this means that the company also has to be sure that its corn polymers come from sustainably sourced corn. This puts the company into the role of promoting restorative practices throughout its supply chain.

So how is the company doing? Interface's first four years on this systematic quest produced doubled revenues, tripled operating profits, and nearly doubled employment. Its latest $250 million revenue came with no increase in energy or materials inputs, from mining internal waste.

BEYOND PROFITS: WHAT'S IN IT FOR US?

Companies that commit to the principles of natural capitalism find an extraordinary outpouring of energy, initiative, and enthusiasm at all levels. But many companies lack the organizational learning atmosphere necessary to adopt the principles. *The Learning Paradox* offers powerful ways that organizations can create an environment where people will want to work and become problem-solvers, rather than impediments to progress. Together, these approaches remove the contradiction between what people do at work and what they want for their families when they go home. This makes natural capitalist firms some of the most exciting places in the world to work.

Firms that pursue these ideas will gain a commanding competitive advantage. They'll be behaving as if natural and human capital were properly valued. And as Edgar Wollard, former Chairman of DuPont once remarked, "companies that don't take these principles seriously won't be a problem, because they won't be around."

Hunter and Amory Lovins founded the Rocky Mountain Institute (RMI) in 1982. RMI is a nonprofit research and educational organization whose mission is to foster the efficient and sustainable use of resources as a path to global security. RMI has 45 full-time staff and a $4 million annual operating budget. For more information visit www.rmi.org or www.natcap.org from which you can download the book or a Harvard Business School article on natural capitalism.

LOU PRITCHETT

Load 'em and Leave 'em

As Vice President of Sales at Procter & Gamble, Lou Pritchett, approached Sam Walton, the founder of Wal-Mart, with a proposal to partner by integrating their operations. In 1997 Wal-Mart sold almost $6 billion of P&G goods, well beyond the $400 million when Pritchett became Vice President in 1985. This is the story of how P&G, the 23rd largest Fortune 500 company, and Wal-Mart, the largest retailer in the world with 1.24 million employees and sales of $223 billion in 2000, created a partnership that changed retailing forever.

Procter & Gamble is one of the most successful companies of the 20th century. Founded in 1837, the company has steadily grown to become a $40 billion global empire. Decades of success resulted in the codification about the way to market and manage brands. Historically we would bring extensive, comprehensive research on consumers to retailers and use it to argue for more volume, more newspaper ads, and more shelf space. We sales reps lived and died on the number of cases of product we could sell to the retail customer. Our goal was to ensure that the retailer had more of our product than of our competitors, both in his store room and displayed in the selling area. We believed that if we tied up the retailer's cash, we would prevent him from buying competitive brands.

There has always been a certain selfishness in the selling game and it manifested itself in the consumer products business, particularly in the soft drink and soap categories. What it amounted to was, "If I can swap more of my product for more of your dollars, I will 'control' the store." Known as "load 'em and leave 'em," it was exactly opposite partnering. But industry wisdom was that a "loaded customer is a loyal customer." All

> If you want to increase the speed of a train by 10 percent, you work on engines and horsepower. But if you want to double the speed you throw away the existing designs, assemble a group of talented people and start over with a clean sheet of paper.

manufacturers followed this 'push–pull' strategy. Their sales reps would 'push' the product into the distribution channel and then radio and television commercials would influence the end-using consumer to 'pull' it out of the stores.

MY EXPERIENCE

In my first managerial job, in 1955, I developed a special relationship with Malone & Hyde, the largest Southern wholesaler. I convinced the buyer to let me come in every week, count inventory and write my own orders. I asked, "Why don't you let me be a part of your company?" I was convinced that if we could build a relationship on trust, I would never violate that trust and as a result the customer would get a P&G expert working on his business at no cost to him. This was my first taste of partnering.

In 1981, I became president of P&G's Philippine operations. Studies showed that Philippine consumers preferred P&G toilet soaps, Camay and Safeguard, 70 to 30 over competing brands. Yet these two brands ranked last in the market. I discovered that the "load 'em and leave 'em" strategy was alive and well in the Philippines. Being volume driven, our sales reps had loaded up to 30 weeks inventory in the supply chain. Since the Philippines is just a few degrees north of the equator, and few buildings were air conditioned, temperatures of 140 degrees weren't unusual in warehouses. Sitting in warehouses for 30 weeks in this heat, our toilet soaps lost their properties. Not only did they lose their lather, the coconut oil and fat ingredients lost their perfume and began to smell like rancid tallow. I called an immediate moratorium on selling to reduce retail inventories. Although we missed our sales targets by over 40 percent the first year, retail inventories fell to an acceptable four weeks.

Eighteen months later Safeguard and Camay were the top two selling toilet soaps in the Philippines. Volume and profits rose to record levels, substantially higher dividends were paid to the parent company, working capital was reduced by 70 percent, receivables were reduced by 33 percent, and company morale soared. These experiences prepared me for my next post.

CREATING CHANGE

When I became Corporate Vice President of Sales in 1985, I quickly learned that Wal-Mart was our largest customer, but I could find no record of where a P&G corporate officer had ever contacted Wal-Mart's top executives. So I called Sam Walton and invited him on a two-day "let's get to know each other" canoe trip in Arkansas.

On the trip, we discussed Sam's concerns. "Your products are very important to my stores," said Sam, "but in total, your brands are just a small portion of what I sell. And yet, every month, your sales people call on me and want me to change my product mix to conform to your sales plan."

> When the rate of external change exceeds the rate of internal change – disaster is imminent!
> *Lou Pritchett*

"You've got a formula for making Tide," continued Sam, "so many tons of chemical A, and so many tons of chemical B, and so many tons of chemical C, whatever. Suppose a chemical salesman called on you every 30 days and said, 'I've got $200 a ton off chemical A this month. Why don't you change your Tide formula? Why don't you put more chemical A in the product this month?'"

This was a powerful, fresh insight for me as to how retailers felt when we called on them 12 times a year asking them to change their product mix to sell more of our brands.

Sam said, "Your guys are always trying to sell me more Tide. I really don't care if I sell Tide or Fab. I just want to sell what the consumer wants. Your efforts should be to help me sell more of the detergent category, to help me bring more customers into the store, and to help me increase total revenue per check out transaction."

I am not criticizing my old *alma mater*; this is the way all manufacturers sold to retailers. This was the way business was done and we at P&G had perfected it. In fact, P&G was used at Harvard and other business schools as the textbook model for brand management. However, after lengthy discussions with Sam and other retail executives, I became convinced that volume follows consumption and that our volume driven strategy was not necessarily the best approach. We need to work closely with retailers to help drive consumption. We should modify from push–pull to pull.

> Bottlenecks are always near the top of the bottle.
> *Pritchett's Law*

Sam continued, "I'm absolutely convinced that this dual system that we've got, this almost adversarial system where we've created our independent system and you've created yours, we're not planning together, were barely talking to each other. Both of us focus on end-user, the consumer, but we do it independently, without consulting each other. What we need to do is revolutionize the way we do business and away from the 'you-ship-product-and-we-do-whatever-we-do-with-it mentality.' We need to become partners."

We realized there was no sharing of information, no joint planning, no systems of coordination – there were simply two entities going their own way burdened and oblivious to the excess costs created by this dual and obsolete system. Our two very large, complex, sophisticated companies' communicating with each other was equivalent of passing notes under the door.

> As the Jesuits teach, caring always precedes sharing. In other words if you don't care for a person or organization, you most likely won't share.

The only contact between our two multi-billion dollar systems were six to eight sales representatives from P&G and buyers from Wal-Mart. These were well trained, honest, intelligent, dedicated people but none were equipped to represent these total corporate systems. Additionally, both our sales reps and Wal-Mart's buyers were influenced by conflicting internal reward and recognition systems.

Sam and I had an idea of what we wanted the new relationship to look like, but we had no idea of how to make it work. We knew that we had to start working on the system as opposed to working in it so within three months of the canoe trip, P&G's top 10 officers traveled to Bentonville to discuss 'how to" ideas with Wal-Mart's top executives. Within six months, we had created a joint working group – a multi-functional team – representing most major departments in both companies. This team of very bright and very creative people who designed this special partnership, worked out all the details, created the systems and structures, implemented, tested and solved the problems. I have the deepest respect for all the original team members who, often under duress, had the courage and vision to become a part of this major change effort at P&G. Three of the key players were Bill Burns, Tom Muccio and Mike Szymanczyk.[1]

Through electronic data interchange (EDI) P&G began directly monitoring Wal-Mart's sales and inventory, and using the data to make its own production and shipping schedules. The order, shipping, billing processes were restructured, thus dramatically reducing costs and virtually eliminating stock outs. The partnering team created a concept called "I for an I" which meant substitute information for inventory. Today, if you go into a Wal-Mart and buy a tube of Crest, the inventory people at both Wal-Mart and P&G know it instantly and a replacement is on the way. In 1998, over 80 Procter & Gamble employees and their families live in Bentonville, Arkansas, servicing this major customer which represents over 10 percent of P&G's total sales.

> It's not who's right, it's what's right. You have to be issue focused not position focused.

SHIFTING POWER

When I started in the business in 1953, there were thousands of retailers, the majority of them independent "mom & pop" stores. The supermarket industry was in its infancy. But since 1950, technology and consolidation have dramatically changed the grocery industry landscape.

In the 1950s, all consumer products manufacturers could dictate to the small mom and pop stores, not only because of the power of their brands, but because of the strength of their consumer advertising. P&G, for example, spent millions advertising directly to the end consumer using radio and the new medium, television, in order to pull the product through the stores.

In the 1960s, retailers began adding scanners at check out counters to lower front-end costs. This, in hindsight, turned out to be the least important benefit. The real benefit was the valuable information the scanners provided. Retailers began keeping track of their own inventory, to know where it was going, what was selling and what wasn't. Retailers suddenly knew more about what was selling than the suppliers and they often knew it faster.

> If you don't know where you are going, any road will get you there.
> *The Koran*

In the 1980s and 1990s, there was a massive consolidation in the retail industry and as a result the top 10 retailers today control 80 percent of the total market and hold the upper hand in power and control over the manufacturers. This power shift coupled with the influence of the three major TV networks waning in a 500-channel universe and with consumers starved for time, is causing manufacturers to rethink their dependence on the media and to learn how to create collaborative marketing relationships with retailers in the retail stores. Today, the retailer, once considered a necessary evil in the supply chain, is becoming a collaborative marketing partner with the manufacturer in the quest for consumer loyalty.

> Things do not change, we do.
> *Henry David Thoreau*

P&G, like most consumer product manufacturers, was product focused. But with the shift in retail power there was a need to completely revamp the sales role. Historically, our training focus was on product knowledge. Today that is no longer enough. Today's reps must become experts in customer systems, processes, logistics and finances. They must know as much about the retail business as retailers. Additionally, the sales rep today must represent the customer to the company, not the other way around.

CHANGE AGENTS AND RESISTANCE TO CHANGE

Corporate functional fiefdoms tend to develop bad habits in a traditionally structured organization. Functional managers protect their turf. Quite often the structure and the reward systems cause the members of each function to view those in other units, and sometimes even the company itself, as the enemy. At one time P&G had so many different organizations, that CEO Artzt complained, "it's like trying to get a bill though Congress."[2]

> People change not because they see the light, rather because they feel the heat. So my question is how do we get them to change before they feel the heat.

Recognizing this problem is one thing but changing it is another. My decision to try to change it was influenced by one of the most successful change agents ever – Thomas Edison. Someone said to me once that Edison did not invent the light bulb by tinkering with the candle. I took this to heart and as a self-styled change agent, I was impatient with tinkering with the system, I thought we should completely reinvent it.

From focus group interviews with key retailers, I knew our customers wanted to have only one P&G sales rep calling on them. However, each of our eight divisions had its own sales force. So when I proposed we test a unified sale force I ran into a firestorm from the division Vice Presidents.

My situation reminded me of the quote from *The Prince* by Nicolo Machiavelli:

> There is nothing more difficult to take in hand, more perilous to conduct, or more uncertain in its success, than to take the lead in the introduction of a new order of things, because the innovator has for enemies all those who have done well under the old condition, and lukewarm defenders in those who may do well under the new.

Unfortunately, I learned too late the change agent's creed, "Never sacrifice yourself on the field of battle, rather live to fight another day."

It's important to point out that I genuinely cared for P&G. Had I not, I would not have put my career at risk. I believed there was a better way, and I committed myself to find it.

A team approach is essential in implementing change, because, as Sam Walton used to say, "People tend to support best that which they help create." Sam called these the ten most powerful words in American business. Involving people in the vision and the process is critical because an organization requires committed individuals who deeply believe there is a better way, are emotionally committed to finding it, and are willing to suffer the pain of leading change.

> The future will not be the big eating the little – it will be the fast eating the slow.

SYSTEMS AND STRUCTURES

To paraphrase Winston Churchill, we shape our buildings then they shape us: corporate structures, internal reward/recognition systems over time shape the company and the people. People hear what management says, but they do what they are rewarded for doing and avoid what they are punished for doing.

If workers have been taught and required to do certain jobs certain ways and have been rewarded by management for doing so, who should bear responsibility when technology or other changes in the market render the traditional methods obsolete?

In the past, information went first to the top. The CEO would get the information and decide what to disseminate. Executives born before 1945 still tend to believe that information is something to be controlled and parceled out sparingly. This old school operates on a "need to know" basis. But today everybody obtains information at the same time. The people at the bottom of the organization often know what's going on as quickly as those at the top – in fact they may even know sooner.

> The difficulty in reinventing any organization lies not in developing new ideas, but in escaping from old ones.

We all accept that a sports team is no better than the people who make it up. Why then do we think a company or a business enterprise is any different? Until management understands and embraces the fact that the ultimate success of the enterprise depends upon skilled and committed people, working together in a positive and enlightened environment, they will continue to get mediocre results.

Younger companies have a major advantage, because they are not yet culture-bound. The PC industry began in 1976, and the software industry that has grown up around it is in its infancy. I believe these companies, led by very young people, not bound by old rules, will totally outmaneuver old inflexible companies.

DRIVE OUT FEAR

One of the most stimulating learning experiences of my career was taking a week-long course from Dr W. Edwards Deming. The eighth of his fourteen points is "drive out fear." Fear dissuades people from speaking out and telling what they see as the truth.

To me, if you can't argue with your boss or suggest ideas then he or she isn't worth working for. I believe that hundreds, if not thousands of employees at IBM, GM, and Sears knew they were headed for trouble several years ago. They knew that their organizations had taken its eyes off the customer and become more focused internally than externally. They also knew that you're not supposed to speak up unless spoken to. So no one spoke up.

> You cannot see the field from the field.
> *Ralph Waldo Emerson*

Boat rockers and plain old employees who tell executives what they don't want to hear – are rarely welcome within the corporation. This is understandable, because it is human nature to want to maintain the status quo, avoid discomfort, and keep doing what you've always done, take the safe road, avoid risks, and follow the proven formula for success. But if employees fear speaking out, if the organization shoots the messenger, does that enhance or retard the organization's chance of thriving and surviving?

> The command and control management is the top telling the middle to do it to the bottom.

GM also failed to ask consumers what they really liked and disliked about its cars. GM, not the Japanese, hurt GM. Internal lack of vigilance has ruined more companies than any other single factor.

Complacency kills. By the mid to late 1980s I was predicting that Sears Roebuck was on its way down because the company appeared to be operating on the basis of simply doing better what they had always done. In my judgement, that is a prescription for failure. What Sears should have done is to have done things differently. Wal-Mart was the perfect role model for doing things differently.

LEADERSHIP: HUMILITY AND EMPOWERING

All of us have tremendous resources available to us – superiors, peers and subordinates. But few of us use all of them. Why? Because some executives stop learning because they assume they know it all. During my years as vice president, I felt I could learn a lot more by eating lunch with six, eight, twelve different employees every day in the employee cafeteria than I could by sitting down five times a week with the same group of officers.

Similarly there are tremendous resources outside the organization – suppliers, customers and even competitors. Go to suppliers and ask them, "How do you like how we run our business? If it were not for _____ (fill in the blank) we would be your favorite customer. What would you change?"

> Nothing will ever be attempted if all possible objections must first be overcome.
> *Nathan Cummings, industrial philanthropist*

Managers need to have the humility to continually ask others how to improve the business. Until his company got too big, Sam Walton prided himself on visiting every Wal-Mart store at least once a year. Right up to the end of his life, the thing he enjoyed most was visiting his stores. He would go into those stores and talk to as many employees as he could, from the stock clerks all the way up to the manager; he certainly did not confine himself to the top brass. He always said that most of his best ideas came from store clerks. He would ride with truckers and ask them how to improve delivery times to stores. He was a mind-picker.

> Give them any color they want as long as it's black.
> *Henry Ford*

If I had to single out one thing about Sam Walton that accounted for his success, it was that he truly understood that people are the most important factor in the business equation. He knew that he couldn't run all the stores or drive all the trucks. Sam knew that all leadership is about leading people, not managing things. He was a marvelous people person and delegator.

Allowing people to input is paying them the supreme compliment, because you're asking for their judgement, their opinion, and you're valuing it. It critical to solicit input because I have never seen one person who is smart as ten.

People are most objective during their first six to ten months on the job because they have not yet become part of the system. I challenged every new hire to question all the basic premises, before they too, became indoctrinated in "the way." Before they began to act, talk and walk like the rest of us. Unfortunately, most corporations today try to homogenize their people.

> Yesterday's tools won't solve tomorrow's problems.

The leader's role is to create an environment where people feel free to experiment, to speak up, to try new things. Most importantly the leaders role is to run interference in the organization for people – to do the downfield blocking, remove the roadblocks and allow employees to do their jobs. A leader's primary goal should be to unleash the talents of each individual worker for the good of the employee and the good of the enterprise as a whole.

Real leaders have a relentless approach to continuous improvement and the humility to continually seek input.

THE HIGHER YOU GO, THE HARDER THE FALL

The higher you go in an organization the more you have to lose – salary, stock options, company plane, company car, and prestige. As an a manager climbs the ladder he typically becomes more conservative and more risk adverse and works to maintaining the status quo, as opposed to rocking the boat. Rarely is one criticized for keeping things the same. Conversely, people are often criticized for trying new ways of doing things. If you play to win you will dramatically increase your chances of winning. If you play not to lose, you will dramatically increase your chances of losing. My experience is that the owners of private companies are much less fearful of creativity and boat rockers.

> In organizations, as with nature, if something is not growing it is dying. There is no status quo.

LESSONS LEARNED

Reflecting on my career, there were few guideposts or maps, and practically no correctional warnings along the way. It was a period of trial and error, of profiting from mistakes and growing in the process. You might call it learning by osmosis. The better you were at absorbing everything you experienced the greater your chance of moving up the corporate ladder. Those who absorbed the most the fastest while learning from their mistakes succeeded. Those who did not fare well in an osmosis learning environment repeated the same mistakes and fell by the way side.

To advance you had to pay the price. Paying the price means learning, learning, learning all the time, zeroing in on your weaknesses and trying to correct them and most important, capitalizing on your strengths.

> If we are to achieve result never before accomplished, we must expect to employ methods never before attempted.
> *Francis Bacon*

My scoutmaster, Buddy Irwin told me, "In most sports, like football or baseball, you play to beat the competition. But in golf it's a different – you pit your skills and strengths against the course. It make no difference how good or bad the competition is. You're playing against a fixed set of circumstances. And that's the way you ought to play life." The name of the game in both business and life is the same: it isn't to get ahead of others, it is to get ahead of yourself

– to improve. This means to play the course not the competition. Do your best; don't worry about how others are doing.

DOING IT ALL OVER AGAIN

If I were to do it all over again what would I do differently? I saw that the world was changing – the balance of power was shifting more to retailers, and we had to change the way we worked. I knew something bad was going to happen, and it was going to happen to us at P&G. I felt an urgency to be first to create this partnering relationship before any of our competitors. I was blinded by my passion and the sense of urgency – and was too far out in front – I didn't spend enough time to get the Division Vice Presidents on my side – and to help fellow executives to see the same thing that I saw on my radar screen.

> The fact that we are a multidivisional, multifunctional, multiregional, multiplant, multiproduct company is not the customer's problem.

Peter Senge argues that individual and collective learning is essential for success. A theme echoed by *The Learning Paradox*. Senge and Harris are lucky because they have seen "the other side" but their challenge and the challenge of any change agent is to help others see it – and that is a very difficult assignment. I would imagine it is not unlike a "born again Christian" attempting to tell an atheist about their experience and the glories of it. Most of the "unborn agains" – are like me and have an attitude of thank you very much, but no thanks!" Most managers hear the need to become a learning organization – but it simply does not fit their field of reason or experience. They don't appreciate the fundamental change it involves in attitude, approach, systems and structures.

CHECKPOINTS

In creating partnerships, here are some checkpoints:

- What do you want to do for your customer in three years that you cannot do for them today?

- How badly would your business be affected if your top five customers formed partnerships today with your competitors? Would it make any difference?
- If a holding company bought your organization and your largest customer, would you continue to do business the same way?
- If you don't have the capability or are unwilling to measure results don't partner.

THE NEW RULES

Over the years I have learned from many outstanding, people – my mother, scout master, teachers, bosses, customers, peers, employees, writers, thinkers, lecturers and friends. I want to share what I have learned from them:

- Big was what made companies successful in the old economy. Today being big is often a liability. Innovation, agility, and organization learning are the key variables for success.
- Leaders can no longer learn for the organization. Rather, leaders must become the designers, stewards and teachers responsible for creating the environment in which people learn.
- The new rules, new ways of going things will always be written at the lonely, fragile, dangerous, frightening edge – never in the comfort of the center.
- Trust is a resource, like capital, that is mandatory in optimizing the system. Without trust there can be no cooperation between teams, departments, divisions, management-labor, or between organizations.
- The key for management in this new environment is how to create a "curious" organization. Having a highly developed sense of curiosity will be the key determinant of success for managers.
- The organizations that dominate the future will be "learning organizations."
- One of the best kept secrets is the people at the bottom of the organization know precisely where the problems are.
- The worst problem for a manager is not to know he or she has a problem.

- In the new global economy raw materials and technology will be available to all. Only people will make a unique difference.

- You can only reach 100 percent customer satisfaction when you have reached 100 percent employee satisfaction.

- When pupils become your teachers, you have reached management maturity

- All corporations must make room for dreamers and poets, because an idea is a thousand times more powerful than a fact. Ideas will be the new currency in the 21st century.

- In partnering, information technology will drive change in the 21st century. Therefore access to information, not access to capital will determine success in the future.

- I've been around for a long time, and I've yet to come across one person who's as smart as 10.

- The greatest training program in the world is trial and error.

- The first lesson in selling is, make it easy for the buyer to buy. Always give them a choice between something and something else, not between something and nothing.

- Deadly sin: Being product driven (internally focused), not customer focused (externally focused).

- The traditional mass market has been replaced by a new liberated one composed of hundreds of mini markets. Vendors and retailers must align, share technology and work together as never before.

- No company can get close to the customer with a six or eight tiered corporate structure or with a big brother bureaucracy (designed to help but actually encumbers).

LITMUS TEST FOR MANAGERS

1. Nothing will work as well without me as it will with me.
   ( ) true ( ) false
2. I capitalize on all my resources – superiors, peers, subordinates.
   ( ) true ( ) false
3. I find change easy and rapidly embrace it.
   ( ) true ( ) false

4. I assume the future will be an extension of the present and past.
( ) true ( ) false

5. Our systems and structures, really recognize that people are our main resource.
( ) true ( ) false

6. I attempt to overcome all objections before trying something new.
( ) true ( ) false

7. I provide feedback in a way that is helpful to others.
( ) true ( ) false

8. I recognize that trust, like capital is a resource, mandatory for system optimization.
( ) true ( ) false

9. I never shoot the messenger – thereby always encouraging people to tell the truth.
( ) true ( ) false

10. I believe that for me to win, others must lose.
( ) true ( ) false

11. I am willing to admit that what I said yesterday was wrong.
( ) true ( ) false

12. I am excited and open to listening and learning from people many levels below me in the organization.
( ) true ( ) false

Lou Pritchett is a leading business author and speaker. His book Stop Paddling and Start Rocking the Boat *is a bestseller. Lou speaks on the issues of change management and partnering. He can be reached at www.loupritchett.com or boatrock@aol.com.*

DR CLIFFORD SAUNDERS AND JIM HARRIS

Simplifying Complexity: Without Being Simplistic

Dr Clifford Saunders is a consultant and speaker and the Principal consultant Too Serious! Limited. He served as a senior engineer for Bell Northern Research (BNR) in Ottawa, and the Director of BNR's Innovation Center. He is the creator of Resolver®, Resolver*Ballot®, The Resolver* Response®, and VoteStream® that allow large groups of people to make decisions efficiently. His clients include Arthur Andersen, BBC, Bell Canada, Ernst & Young, Ford, KPMG, NorTel, Royal Bank, and Xerox.

In 1977 Cliff began working for Bell Northern Research (BNR) as a designing engineer. Design projects typically had five engineers and lasted a year. In 1979 Cliff went to work in Saudi Arabia for five years. When he returned he began working on design teams again – but he noticed a number of differences that had escaped others. By 1983 design teams had

mushroomed to 50 engineers. The complexity of the systems had grown exponentially – but the tools that the teams were using to make product design decisions had remained constant. Essentially, decisions were made in discussion groups and using flip charts and markers.

Between 1985 and 1988 Cliff participated in three design projects. The first, involved over 250 engineers, and the architectural team alone was over 50 engineers, cost over $100 million to develop – and was a commercial failure. So Cliff was "re-vectored," the HR buzzword at the time for reassigned, to another design team.

This new design team spent $100 million trying to achieve 40 percent of the goals of the failed project while incorporating 60 percent new goals. It too failed. Reflecting on it, Cliff notes, "It was just like the English when they travel abroad and want to be understood – they simply speak louder and slower." Only ten systems were sold and the company didn't even recover its development costs.

So Cliff was re-vectored to a *third* project that was different than the other two and attempted to take on IBM – head to head – at the peak of its power. The project was an attempt to design a new type of computer that was networked and would compete directly with IBM mainframes. Another $100 million project and 50 person team. One client bought one on spec but returned it to the company.

Cliff had misgivings about the decision making, but felt uncomfortable questioning the process – after all, he was only recently back from overseas, and as the "new kid on the block" he didn't have the political clout to question the way things worked. In fact, people who continually questioned and challenged the project leader were considered troublemakers and re-vectored.

Cliff often didn't air his reservations and discounted his own ideas, in the face of certain individuals who spun glorious stories of future success. Others on the design teams likely did the same.

"Further, I didn't have evidence to support my views, while those in the cheerleading section had snazzy presentations and 'estimated sales' numbers on spreadsheets to support their claims."

Cliff began to reflect on the dismal product development projects and a number of shortcomings of group dynamics and the way groups make decisions.

The creative process is fraught with problems – who can accurately predict the future? If there is bias in the organization – people don't want to be critical for fear of alienating their colleagues – do large groups make the best decision. When design teams are creating new products or services that have never been created before, who can prove whether they will be a success or failure? By definition no one. Today the problems are so complex, the future so uncertain that the only way to go is with teams. But teams without the tools are awful. And the solution isn't moving backwards to solving problems with only a few "experts."

> We can't use the same level of thinking as did when we created the problem in the first place.
> *Albert Einstein*

FAILURES OF GROUP PLANNING

Humans aren't wired properly to deal with complexity and complex issues. Psychologist George Miller discovered in the 1950s that the maximum number of items which the human brain can retain in short-term memory is seven, plus or minus two. Given this limitation of our brains we need new tools to help us deal with complexity.[3]

GroupThink

GroupThink is the concept that individuals disagree with the group when discussing an issue on their own, but in the group will concur.

In other words, individuals moderate or censor their opinions because of some social pressure within the group. This is a powerful reason for using technology that allows individuals to vote anonymously – this moderates these social forces. A classic case of groupthink is the Bay of Pigs invasion. While individually the many of the decision makers had serious reservations about the invasion, as a group they supported the decision to go ahead.

> Insanity is doing the same thing over and over again and expecting different results.
> *Alcoholics Anonymous*

Spreadthink

Most of us think that we see things objectively. However, within any group there will be "spreadthink." Often we think that there is just one root cause to a problem – and hence just one solution. So we search for the simple solution, the magic bullet. The panacea. But spreadthink proves that everyone sees the problem a different way.

DYNAMICS OF LARGE GROUPS

Think of a design team of 50 engineers – how many ideas can they discuss at once? How efficiently do these groups operate? Think about your own experience in large group meetings – I personally find them boring. Most of the time people aren't talking about issues that interest me.

Usually the personality of the leader or a few people will dominate the group. And the answer is not fewer meetings – it is changing the *kind* of meetings that we have.

STAKEHOLDER ANALYSIS

Different stakeholders often see issues in very different ways – sales departments see things different than marketing, finance has different perceptions than shipping, the IT department has a different agenda than the executive team, and the HR department has a different orientation than manufacturing.

When debating issues there is no easy way to keep track of the degree of feeling different stakeholders have on different issues.

UNDISCUSSABLES

Certain issues become "undiscussable" in groups as Chris Argyris' work highlights. And the fact that there are undiscussables is in fact undiscussable. Organizations and design teams are really then caught in a double bind. You can't solve a problem until you can see it – or admit to it.

Jim really believes the challenge of the 21st century is not problem solving – it's problem seeing. Managers have honed the practice of problem solving, what we need to do is develop our problem seeing capacity.

Individual Style

As Myers–Briggs and other personality indicators have shown we all have different decision making styles and personality traits. Some individuals are shy or reserved and are nervous speaking in front of large groups. Some are unwilling to air their thoughts until they are fully thought through. And different cultures have different cultural styles. For instance, Asian people in general will not contradict their boss in a group setting. These two factors – individual style and cultural differences – ensure that in an average meeting not everyone will contribute. Instead, outgoing individuals will tend to dominate the group discussion and decision making. Those individuals holding back may have important information for the rest of the group. Any process that is to improve decision making will have to have methodologies to draw out these types of people.

Mental Limitations

Psychological studies have shown that we have a short-term memory limitation of 7 ± 2 items.[4] This means that most people can only remember seven items that they are introduced to without aid. This is very important in the area of complexity – because complexity overwhelms this human limitation. As you will see later, the greatest number of problems ever facilitated out of an interactive management (IM) session was 678.[5] This is an overwhelming number. Faced with that many problems, where do you start? Where are the high leverage items? How can we get to root cause? Where is the trim tab factor? Pareto's law holds for complexity – 20 percent of the factors will cause 80 percent of the headaches. What process can be used to identify these high leverage items?

SEARCH FOR A SOLUTION

Cliff realized that to be more effective in solving complicated problems groups needed new tools and processes. Just as our individual capacity to solve problems increases with new tools, so does a group's ability. Groups can handle so much hard stuff unaided, but soon reach a limit. Using a skilled facilitator and pens and flipcharts the groups capacity is greatly increased. But Cliff realized that if a group is given a powerful, computer-based *thinkware* tool – software that increases the group's ability to think about complex problems, along with a skilled facilitator they can often solve "insoluble" problems.

So Cliff began searching for solutions and discovered Professor John Warfield's work on Interpretive Structural Modeling (ISM) – a qualitative, computer-assisted way to structure complex situations. Most problems can be analyzed in terms of elements, sets and relations. From these models can be built. Cliff studies with Warfield and learned about his pioneering work in the field of complexity.

In 1988 Cliff began to create software that teams could use to address the chronic problems in group decision making.

The first problem is that we cannot evaluate or keep track of more than seven issues at a time in our mind. So how can we keep track of dozens of issues and rank them? Cliff designed software that will keep track of up to 200 issues at a time.

BIAS FOR ACTION

Western managers have a "bias for action." But most people are unaware that in dealing with complexity this is part of the problem. Warfield was talking with a prospective client who wanted to resolve a complex situation. Ford Motor Company had been working to develop "Analytical Power Train" and some 200 engineers had been wrestling with the project for seven months without any success. So John proposed a three-day IM session with 15–20 key people. The manager's response was, "We don't have three days to spare."

So we are now using my words not John's – "So let me understand, you have just told me that 700 people have been working without success for seven months. Is that correct? Yes. But you don't have three days? So if you go another seven months without success will you have three days then?" The manager got it and planned for the three-day workshop – in fact the IM sessions were so successful that Ford established permanent on staff IM experts and eventually spent over one million dollars on complexity consulting services.

> Every organization is perfectly aligned to get the results it gets.
> *Stephen Covey*

LAW OF ENFORCED SUBSTITUTION

Warfield coined a law – the Law of Enforced Substitution. Organizations – in their bias for action will quickly study a complex situation – make a decision how to solve it and move on to the next problem. In their haste the group will never get to the heart of the complex situation and resolve it at a root cause level. In the haste for a solution, any solution will do but it will not get to root causes. In fact, the solution will cause a seeming unrelated problem in another area.

Few individuals, groups and organizations have studied complexity and therefore don't understand the difficulty there is in conceptually coping with complex situations. We are condemned to go round and round the merry go round without even knowing it.

LAW OF INHERENT CONFLICT

The law of inherent conflict states that resolving complex situations without the proper tools will always result in conflict. Often it will be an open battle of the egos – as individuals strive to have their position adopted by the group. Or the conflict may simmer under the surface as those individuals who lose this time engage in rear guard action in subsequent meetings raising the same problem again and again – because their perspective was not considered by the group in its haste to adopt a "solution." Groups adopt one approach because they had no other way of dealing with the complexity.

Individuals cannot realize or get at another root of the situation – (1) Spreadthink – each individual in the group is arguing to advance their understanding of the hierarchy of contributing factors; (2) these contributing factors or problems may interact in ways which create other problems; (3) with no effective way of resolving complexity, the group's solution will not get at the root of the situation. Thus the law of enforced substitution will prevail.

Interactive Management, which is outlined below, effectively resolves complex situations. The time is spent productively because it "harmonizes" each individual's perceptions – drawing out the collective wisdom of the group.

Harmonize is an appropriate word – because traditional problem solving methodologies homogenize perception – that is, only one perspective typically is taken. But IM takes into account all the perceptions of individuals in the group. This not only increases buy-in and reduces fighting, but also makes the end strategy far more effective.

We too often look for simplistic answers that do not adequately address the complexity of the situation at hand. Yet how can we maintain diversity without being overwhelmed by conflicting ideas, trends and information? The processes outlined here do just that – respect and maintain the diversity of opinion and perception while at the same time creating a shared and collective understanding.

FRUSTRATION

Maier studied frustration by training rats to solve a simple maze. There was a standing platform and the rat could jump to the left or the right. On one side was a red card and the other was a blue card. Behind one of the cards was a piece of food. The rats quickly learned it was behind the red card. Maier then moved the cards so the red was on the left instead of the right. And the rats learned it was behind the red card regardless of its position. Then Maier changed the rules again, by putting the food behind the blue card. It didn't take the rats long to figure it out. Then he began changing the rules often. And finally he stopped putting any food behind the cards at all. So that no matter how hard they tried, the rats could never win. The rats got frustrated, so they stopped playing the game.

> The eye cannot see itself.
> *Proverb*

Maier then began to electrocute the rats to force them to jump from the platform. The rats went crazy – because they were forced to play a game they knew they could not win. They rolled themselves up into a ball, bit themselves, bit their handlers.

This is exactly what happens in organizations when people are forced to participate in a system that they know makes no sense or could be improved, but they feel powerless. The result is frustration and cynicism – and it is this sentiment that gives rise to the Dilbert phenomenon. In organizations certain issues become undiscussable. They do not realize that their frustration is often a function to trying to resolve complex situation with tools that are incapable of getting at the root causes.

MISTAKING SUBJECTIVE FEELING FOR OBJECTIVE REALITY

When we confront a complex situation we confuse our own subjective feeling of frustration, being perplexed, as being objective characteristics of the problem itself. Like a child being frustrated at not yet being able to ride a bike – the true deficiency is the child's lack of skill – not the impossibility of the bike riding itself. By labeling a situation as being "complex" we take no responsibility for looking at our own deficiencies. Have we individually studied the science of complexity? Have we taken time to understand how our perceptions limit us individually, in groups and in organizations? What corrective actions are we taking? What new ways of working are we employing on all three levels to take remedial action.

INTERPRETIVE STRUCTURAL MODELING (ISM)

Interpretive Structural Modeling consists of five stages: preparation, brainstorming, voting, model construction and model interpretation.

The preparation phase consists of formulating trigger questions to stimulate the generation of issues and criteria to study the relationship between these issues. In the brainstorming phase issues are generated. The voting phase ranks the issues. We will discuss the last two phases later in the article.

Cliff designed software that helps groups make better decisions. Each participant in the group receives a wireless numeric keypad, which sends signals to a radio receiver. Once everyone has voted, the results are tabulated instantly and are displayed on a screen.

So the problem of the number of people is solved by using the wireless keypads. Our short term memory limitation is solved by the fact that the computer remembers. And the difference in language and mental models is solved by the facilitation of the trained professional.

Data gathering sounds simple, but how for instance, can you swiftly and accurately find out how 1,700 people at a conference feel about a number of issues? In past, you could vote by show of hands with all its inherent limitations, or you had to use a time-intensive, cumbersome paper-based voting system. But with the new system you can vote on up to 200 issues, with up to 10 answers per question, and segment the group by up to 10 stakeholders. And the data is collected, analyzed and displayed instantly!

THREE LEVELS OF PROBLEMS

There are three distinct levels of complexity of problems:

Level 3 problems

Level three problems are messy. These are difficult to describe, have undefined boundaries and are very confusing. Complex problems involve many issues, are influenced by existing and emerging trends which may conflict, and the data is confusing. Solving a messy problem requires a team. The more complex the problem, the more people with technical expertise have to be involved in solving it. This further complicates the problems because each individual has different mental models or paradigms of the problem, interprets the data and trends differently, and evaluates importance by different criteria. Manufacturing will see the problem differently than Engineering, Accounting or the Information Technology group. And each group will put forward what it perceives to be the best solution to the perceived problem.

> Our age of anxiety is, in great part, the result of trying to do today's jobs with yesterday's tools.
> *Marshall McLuhan,*
> *On Technology*

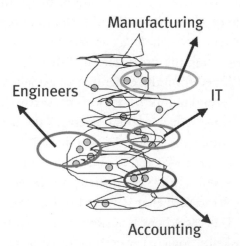

How can a group solve complex problems? Cliff's thinkware clumps issues together, and then isolating each clump the group makes judgements, and builds models of solutions together. It's the salami approach – the problem is solved one slice at a time. When a group solves a level 3 problem it really feels like magic.

Level 2 problems

Level two problems are still complex but operate within a defined area. For instance, a CEO sets the goal for the organization of increasing market share by 3 percent and profitability by 5 percent. How will the management team execute? Or how can the organization improve customer satisfaction? The challenge is clearly defined – we need to figure out how to accomplish it. In a level three problem the problem itself has not yet been defined, nor the strategies.

Level 1 problems

Level 1 problems are the simplest of all – involving collecting data. It could be impressions from a focus group, an executive team or delegates at a conference. There are also real time applications.

HIGHLIGHTING HOT SPOTS

Cliff and Jim were working with a management team. They broke the group up into the executive team – a group of five, and the general management – a group of about 40 – and had each group register separately as different stakeholders. The whole group was then asked a series of questions about issues facing the organization. When the perceptions of the executive team differed from the general management Cliff asked for different points of view. The software highlights with whisker hairs around averages the degree of agreement within the group. So, for instance, on the question of access to capital – one person on the executive team voted it was very difficult while the other four executives voted that it was very easy. So while the average was easy there was significant disagreement within the group. So Cliff asked, "Someone who voted that access to capital is easy please explain your point of view." And one of the executives replied, "We've been doing it for years, it's not a problem."

> For every one individual hacking at the root of evil there are thousands hacking at the leaves.
> *Henry David Thoreau*

Okay, replied Cliff, "now who voted that it was hard?"

The reply took us by surprise, "It's not hard to raise capital – it is hard to distribute it. To make the decision which operating unit to invest it in, where it will be most beneficial – that's the hard part."

So for the executive team raising capital wasn't an issue but distributing it was.

The general management perceived raising capital as a difficult issue. From the voting it clearly showed that senior executives were not concerned about capital – further discussion may have highlighted the need for managers to prepare better cost/benefit analysis cases to present to executives.

SEARCH FOR SIMPLE SOLUTIONS

We find that there is a deep yearning for the simpler times. Executives are under incredible pressure and yearn for stability, security, peace and tranquility – for simpler lives and jobs. We have experienced this strong desire ourselves. They are fatigued. They want the magic bullet, simple solution, the panacea.

Our perception is also flawed because we often think – "If we could just get to the root problem – if we could just get the answer." It is this thinking that plays into the latest management fad of the day – or the law of enforced substitution.

But with a complex situation by definition there is not just one root cause. (Unless you argued that the root cause of complex situations perpetuating is our lack of a systematic, scientific approach to resolve them).

Again the problem rests in our perception – it is the interplay of a number of factors that cause complex situations. In other words – our problem is that we think there is only one problem! This reductionistic approach dooms many individuals and organizations to stay stuck in their problems indefinitely as stated by the Law of Enforced Substitution.

Instead of thinking about a problem – we need to think of a "problem set." A cloud of problems that surrounds the issue or situation. The greatest number of problems facilitated out by an IM facilitator was 678 – in dealing with a group redesigning the US military acquisition process.

In IM it is important to identify all the problems and clarify them. This process is expansive, opening the minds of the participants to the scope and inter-relatedness of the factors. However IM doesn't just stop there. The process also sorts out which are the most significant problems.

Problems of Groups

Many people consider meetings unproductive. To begin with in a meeting of 20 people one person is speaking and 19 are listening. It is like having a 20-cylinder engine but using only one cylinder at a time. How can more creativity and power be released through the meeting? How can an organization generate more commitment to change in its employees? The IM workshop uses a number of parallel processes so that all people are thinking and working at the same time. And their reactions to issues are being captured simultaneously.

As discussed above, departments often plan independently but are operating in an interdependent reality. As in the cases above where marketing launches a new product and production is overwhelmed. While marketing executives are getting bonuses, customer satisfaction with the organization is plummeting. This ties into the concept of spreadthink that we all have a different perspective on issues. Whatever process we use to resolve complex situations must address spreadthink.

> Fish discover water last.
> *Zen saying*

Decision making in most organizations has not fundamentally changed in decades. But the problems organizations face have grown infinitely more complex. As Einstein said, "we can't be at the same level of thinking as when we got ourselves into the problem in the first place." We have to employ new tools.

Interactive Management

IM should only be used when a situation is complex. A complex situation is by definition one in which no one individual has all the information, knowledge, intuition, anticipation of trends, or perspective to be able to resolve it. IM should only be employed after normal problem solving methods have failed.

IM will bring together a cross section of individuals from different departments who are involved in the complex situation. The assembled individuals should have a good understanding of their department and perspective on the complex situation from their departmental perspective.

At the start of an IM session the individuals are given a triggering question – for instance what are the problems that are preventing us from resolving this problematic situation?

Each participant is asked to silently generate answers to the triggering question. Every five or 10 minutes the facilitator can collect these sheets and have the typist key them into the computer so that they are projected on the wall so everyone can see them, when participants see other people's ideas it triggers more responses. After 30 minutes of silent generation the next phase can begin.

The process moves then into clarification – where in a round robin format individuals talk about their ideas. So the first person would talk about their first idea. Others in the group could ask questions. A statement should contain only one idea so there should be no "and" statements or any "and/or" statements.

The second person would then talk about their first idea. This process continues until everyone has clarified all their ideas. This process can take up to three days – as in the case when groups identify 200 problems that they are facing. There is tremendous learning at this stage as people from different departments begin to appreciate how other people in other departments see the situation.

During the clarification process ideas can be added or modified. Some statements will be broken up into two statements, while often ideas from different individuals will be combined.

As each statement is clarified, it is numbered and printed out on the laser printer and hung on the wall surrounding the group. In the process of clarification as ideas are clarified and modified by the group as a whole, ownership of the ideas shifts from the individual to the group. In this spirit, ideas are numbered as opposed to attributed to the original author.

So at the end of the clarification process – which may take up to three days – the group will have literally hundreds of ideas surrounding them on the walls of the work space.

At this point each individual is asked to vote for the top five ideas that they feel are contributing to the complex situation. Here the concept of spreadthink is most evident. You might think that after three days of idea clarification and discussion the group would be all thinking alike – but if you have 15 people in the group you will likely get 60 different answers when each individual votes for only five issues. While some items will receive multiple votes, the majority of issues raised receive only one vote!

What this does do is winnow down the number of issues. As mentioned earlier, Pareto's law applies to complexity: 20 percent of the issues will cause 80 percent of the problem.

Still it is overwhelming for a group to sort through even 60 issues because of our short-term memory limitation (7 ± 2), and spreadthink. So these issues have to be structured.

Spreadthink is Always Operating

Once you have taken a group of 20 individuals from different departments who are each intimately involved in a complex situation, and have spent three days in an Interactive Management (IM) session to identify all the contributing problems, you will have a list of hundreds of problems. Each problem has been discussed and clarified so that there is a deep shared understanding of all of them in the group.

To know and not to do . . .
is not to know
Proverb

Ask each of these 20 individuals to vote on the top five problems and you will end up with over 50 different answers. This is spreadthink – each of us has a different perception of what the situation is – and we will each rank factors in different hierarchies of importance in our efforts to resolve a complex situation. If traditional problem solving methodologies are used to resolve complex situations – most of the group's time will be unproductive – spent arguing over which strategy to employ. First of all because people have not sought to understand the situation – and without understanding each other's points of view they will never understand the complexity and never resolve it effectively.

After three days of clarification and discussion which promotes mutual understanding, everyone in the group votes for the top five issues. If there was perfect alignment of thought in the group – everyone would vote for the same five issues. Spreadthink guarantees that members of the group will still perceive the problem fundamentally differently. The following equation predicts the number that will be raised with the following formula:

$$\text{Items} = \frac{\text{participants} \times \text{votes per participant}}{2}$$

For instance, if there are 20 participants and each gets to vote on which are the top five issues, the number of issues to be structured will be:

$$\text{\# of items} = \frac{20 \times 5}{2} = \frac{100}{2} = 50$$

Structuring

While our minds cannot sort through all relationships implied by 50 variables we can easily compare two. So for instance you could ask "Does problem 211 – the fact that we do not grant stock options" significantly aggravate problem 47 "attracting and retaining the best computer programmers?" If the majority of people in the group answer yes there is a positive correlation between 211 > 47.

Most relationships are transitive. That is if A > B and B > C and C > D then A > D. Now there are exceptions to every rule, for instance if Liz loves Tom and Tom loves Mary, does Liz love Mary? This example may not be transitive – but it deals with emotions as opposed to facts.

The relationships in an IM session are transitive. Because of this the computer software can eliminate 80 percent of the questions required to sift through all the relationships of 50 variables. Because of this fact, IM offers organizations incredible leverage.

At the end of the paired rankings the software produces a "structure" of the problems as seen below:

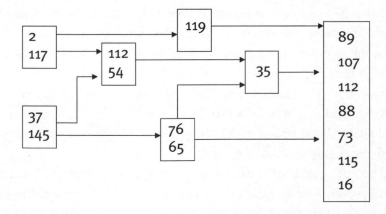

The "structures" show the inter-relatedness of the problems. So for instance, problem 2 and 117 are in the same box which means they are self reinforcing. If an organization tackles problem 117 but does not tackle two at the same time once the organization has "beaten" 117 and stops inventing time, money and other resources in solving it, problem 117 will re-emerge – because the organization did not eliminate problem 2 at the same time as 117. The structural model also shows the hierarchy of problems. Problem 88 is a downstream problem – imagine it could be bad morale in the organization. This is a byproduct or a symptom of the upstream problems.

An human resource department might try to solve this by giving everyone motivational posters or putting on a company picnic – unaware that the real problems – say lack of real time information systems and better strategic planning – remain unaddressed.

Having the problems structured allows the team to get at the root and find the high leverage items. In this case items 2, 117, 37 and 145 – and to focus on solving the most important problems in this complex situation.

So the group might have begun by identifying 200 problems – which is overwhelming, then narrowing the list to 50 – which is still too many (remember our short term memory limitation of 7 ± 2) and finally the structuring. This now gives us a clear map of the inter relatedness of the problems.

THE POWER OF IM

Interactive Management software is able to eliminate 80 percent of the required questions. To ascertain all the relationships in a group of variables would require creating and filling a matrix with $N(N-1)$ cells where N is the number of items that is to finally be structured by the group. So if the group had 60 items that have to be structured, the number of matrix cells to be filled would be $50 \times (50-1) = 50 \times 49 = 2,450$. In other words, the facilitator would have to ask the group 2,450 questions. This would take an incredible amount of time.

But because of the software, the group only has to answer 20 percent of these questions – or 490 questions. This still seems to be a lot. But to put it into perspective, remember that the group was originally dealing with a far larger universe of questions, before each individual voted for the top five.

To structure them would require asking 200 (200–1) = 39,800 questions. Assuming each question took only two minutes to ask and have the group think about and answer, it would take 165 hours – over 20 eight-hour days. However because after the issues are clarified, group participants can only select the top five problems – the group has only to structure 50 problems. Or in other words, you could say to a leader give us three days of your time with a group of 15 people from departments across your organization and the process will give you back the equivalent of 20 days of this group's decisions making.

What higher leverage activity can there be?

Dr Clifford Saunders is a consultant and speaker and the Principal consultant of Too Serious! Limited. For more information go to www.tooserious.com. He can be reached at (416) 481–0006 or by email at cliff@tooserious.com.

Hope and Optimism

I would like to convey hope and optimism. Thriving in the future (for individuals, organizations and society as a whole) requires a willingness to being flexible and adaptable, and constantly questioning, learning and meeting new challenges. We can change ourselves, examine our paradigms, assume leadership and strengthen our relationships with others. By becoming comfortable with the fear and discomfort that we experience when learning new skills, questioning assumptions, developing new products and services, we develop a greater tolerance for ambiguity, uncertainty and paradox. As we gain experience by repeatedly passing through the learning paradox, the greater the faith we develop in our talents and abilities. Security and self-esteem develop. The more this occurs, the more power and knowledge an individual can share with others.

> What lies behind us and what lies before us are tiny matters compared to what lies within us.
> *Ralph Waldo Emerson, philosopher*

I would like to write a book about personal growth and call it *Being and Becoming*. I envision the cover having an acorn on it. The central question of the book will be: Is an acorn just an acorn or is it a potential oak tree? Who am I? Am I all I am today, or am I who I could potentially be? What is the purpose of my life? Why am I here? As I wrestle with these questions, I get a sense of who I could become. If I revel in this potential, if I continue to develop the sense of whom I am and the commitment to live out of my potential rather than my past or present, I become who I am meant to be. I hope that this book serves as a catalyst for personal and organizational growth and success.

> If you treat a man as he is, he will stay that way, but if you treat him as if he were what he ought to be and could be, he will become that bigger and better man.
> *Johann Wolfgang von Goethe, philosopher*

Notes

1. I am grateful to Janice McNally, an editor on an earlier edition of the book, for suggesting that readers rip out the first page.

Notes to Chapter 1

1. Matthew R. Sanders with Bruce D. Temkin, "Global ecommerce approaches hypergrowth," Forrester Research Inc., 18 April 2000.
2. Since 1995, IBM's employment ranks have consistently grown. In 1995, IBM employed 225,247 people and by 1999, had grown to 307,401.
3. *Fortune*, "Brands rule," 4 Mar. 1996.
4. Figure provided by Cott Corporation.
5. Judith Bardwick, *Danger in the Comfort Zone*. American Management Association: New York, 1991.
6. George Hartman uses this analogy to make the point that an investment strategy needs to be custom tailored for a client in *Risk is a Four Letter Word: The Asset Allocation Approach to Investing* (Stoddart : Toronto, 1994), p. 9.
7. See Chapter 12: The Internet Revolution.
8. IDC, "Email usage forecast and analysis, 2000–2005," Mark Levitt, September 2000.
9. Robert Levering, *A Great Place to Work: What Makes Some Employers So Good (and Most So Bad)* (Random House: New York, 1985). Based on the polling work of Daniel Yankelovich who found that in the US, only 27 percent of employees report that their work turns them on. Despite these figures, Yankelovich found most American workers still want to do a good job.
10. US News Online annually ranks the 325 accredited MBA programs, as well as other graduate programs offered in the US. Check out the rankings on their website at www.usnews.com.
11. National Center for Educational Statistics. *Digest of Educational Statistics*, 1999.
12. Stephen R. Covey, *How to Succeed with People* (Deseret Book Company: Salt Lake City, 1971), p. 23.
13. *Information Week 500*. The complete rankings from 1995 to 2000 can be found on their website at www.informationweek.com.
14. All figures cited are in US dollars unless otherwise noted.

Notes to Chapter 2

1. This expression is from Kelly Smith, a former colleague, who now works with Franklin Covey in Calgary, Alberta.
2. The diving story is told by professional speaker Martin Rutte, who discusses spirituality in the workplace. He is co-author of *Chicken Soup for the Soul at Work*. Check out his website at www.martinrutte.com. Martin is based in Santa Fe, New Mexico and can be contacted at (505) 466–1510.
3. Michael Hammer, "Reengineering work: don't automate, obliterate," *Harvard Business Review*, Jul.–Aug. 1990.
4. Michael Hammer quoted in *Fortune* magazine, 17 Apr. 1995.
5. M. Scott Peck, *The Road Less Traveled* (Simon & Schuster: New York, 1978), p. 15.
6. Don Tapscott, *The Digital Economy: Promise and Peril in the Age of Networked Intelligence* (McGraw-Hill: New York, 1996), p. 3.

Notes to Chapter 3

1. Adapted from a story in *The More Than Complete Hitchhiker's Guide to the Galaxy* by Douglas Adams.
2. Joel Arthur Barker, *Paradigms: The Business of Discovering the Future* (Harper Business: New York, 1993), pp. 15–17.
3. For more information about the Swatch Group, visit their website at www.swatchgroup.com. The Swatch Group produces Longines, Omega and Breguet watches as well as the Swatch.
4. "Whither Moore's Law," *Forbes*, 11 Sep. 1995, pp. 167–168.
5. Sun Microsystems press release, Nov. 1994.
6. Don Tapscott uses this term in *The Digital Economy: Promise and Peril in the Age of Networked Intelligence* (McGraw-Hill: New York, 1996).
7. Most people remember visual and spatial relationships easily. For instance, you always know that your letter opener is in the top right drawer of your desk. Using this principle, Macintosh computers kept files and programs as pictures on the screen of your computer. Apple did not invent this graphical user interface. Steven Jobs was exposed to the concept at a demonstration at the Xerox PARC research facility in Palo Alto.
8. Michael A. Cusumano and Richard W. Selby, *Microsoft Secrets: How the World's Most Powerful Software Company Creates Technology, Shapes Markets and Manages People* (Free Press: New York, 1995), p. 169.
9. Egil Juliussen, "Worldwide PC sales will surpass 200m units in 2005," *ETForecasts*, 25 Feb 2000 (www.etforecasts.com).
10. Figures provided by Jim Sanders, Director of Research at the Software Publishers Association (SPA). Figures are total shipments for North American retail market in millions of dollars. For more updated information visit SPA's website at www.spa.org.
11. The SPA does not provide information on individual title sales. These figures are for total DOS vs. total Windows sales of spreadsheets. However, given that in the DOS paradigm Lotus 1-2-3 enjoyed 75 percent of market share, while now in the Windows environment, Microsoft's Excel sold through the Office suite enjoys almost 90 percent market share of current spreadsheet sales, these figures provided by Jim Sanders, Director of Research at the Software Publishers Association (SPA) for the whole category can be taken to apply to 1-2-3 and Excel. Figures are based on total shipments for North American retail market in millions of dollars. For information on software sales, visit the SPA's website at www.spa.org
12. *Smart Computing*, Nov. 1999,vol.10 issue 11.
13. Cusumano and Selby, *Microsoft Secrets*, p. 146.

Notes to Chapter 4

1. For more information about Larry Wilson, go to www.larrywilson.com.
2. FedEx Corporation.
3. Interview with Dennis Jones, FedEx's former CIO.
4. "Service is everybody's business," *Fortune*, 27 June 1994.
5. Lincoln Continental advertisement in *Forbes*, 17 June 1996, pp. 256–257.
6. John F. Smith, Jr, "Hands on the wheel: mind on the task. The OnStar approach to in-vehicle communication and safety," Keynote Address, Convergence 2000 Conference, 20 Oct. 2000.
7. US Bancorp Piper Jaffray, press release.
8. Gary Hamel and C.K. Prahalad, *Competing for the Future: Breakthrough Strategies for Seizing Control of Your Industry and Creating the Markets of Tomorrow* (Harvard Business School Press: Boston, MA, 1994), pp. 8–9.
9. Christopher Cerf and Victor Navasky, *The Experts Speak* (Pantheon: New York, 1984).
10. Stephen R. Covey, *The 7 Habits of Highly Effective People* (Fireside: New York, 1989), p. 101.

Notes to Chapter 5

1. The origin of the Serenity Prayer is obscure. It may date back to Boethius, a philosopher who lived about AD 500 and was martyred by Christians. It is usually credited to Reinhold Niebuhr, a 20th-century theologian who in turn credited an 18th-century theologian, Friedrich Oetinger.
2. Wilfredo Pareto (1848–1923) was an Italian economist and political sociologist who devised Pareto's Law. Known as the 80:20 rule, it is the law of the trivial many and the critical few. The rule states that in any activity 80 percent of potential value can be achieved from just 20 percent of effort, and that one can spend the remaining 80 percent of effort for relatively little return.
3. Robert Levering, *A Great Place to Work: What Makes Some Employers So Good (and Most So Bad)* (Random House: New York, 1985). Based on the polling work of Daniel Yankelovich, who found that in the US only 27 percent of employees report that their work turns them on. Despite these figures, Yankelovich found most American workers want to do a good job.

Notes to Chapter 6

1. David Osborne and Ted Gaebler, *Reinventing Government: How the Entrepreneurial Spirit is Transforming the Public Sector* (Addison-Wesley: Toronto, 1992), p. 110.
2. Robyn Allan is President of CYF Consulting Limited. When Ms Allan became President of the Insurance Corporation of British Columbia, ICBC had a projected $200 million annual deficit. Within 10 months, without downsizing, the corporation had a $150 million profit. She can be reached at (604) 685–4160.
3. Contrary to popular myth, Edison was not the first to develop the light bulb. The patent was awarded to British inventor Sir Joseph Swan. However, Edison designed the first practical light bulb that could burn brightly for many hours.
4. Other fun oxymorons include: airline cuisine, fresh frozen, criminal justice, military intelligence, pretty ugly, strategic planning, jumbo shrimp, air traffic control, great depression, competing standards, fresh frozen jumbo shrimp, gourmet pizza, mandatory option, first annual, relatively simple, unofficial record. Most of these come from Don Tapscott.
5. Ravi Vijh of Moval International can be reached at (416) 730–8811.
6. A tree grows by adding to its outer layer. Information is added to your hard disk in the same way. When you edit an existing document, the new text cannot be physically stored next to the original text on the hard disk. Over time the data on the hard disk become fragmented. For instance, your hard disk may have to access ten different spots to open a single document. Defragmenting your hard disk eliminates all the fragments, reconfiguring the data on your hard disk so that all the data for a single document reside at the same physical location on your hard disk.
7. Gary Hamel, "Killer strategies," *Fortune*, 23 June 1997, p. 72.
8. Ibid., p. 74.
9. Ibid., p. 73.
10. Center for Research in Electronic Commerce, Graduate School of Business, University of Texas at Austin, © 1999.
11. US Business Reporter (www.activemedia-guide.com).
12. Francis Aguilar and Arvind Bhambri, "Johnson & Johnson," *Harvard Business Case Studies*, 1983, p. 5.

Notes to Chapter 7

1. Alvin Toffler, *The Third Wave* (Bantam Books: New York, 1981), pp. 1–25.
2. Nuala Beck, *Shifting Gears: Thriving in the New Economy* (HarperCollins: Toronto, 1992).

3. Bruce Little, "Tilting at smokestacks," *The Globe and Mail's Report on Business*, 20 July 1991.
4. Don Peppers and Martha Rogers, *The One to One Future* (Currency Doubleday: New York, 1993).
5. For the most recent figures visit www.intel.com.
6. Figures from Howard High at Intel's investor and media relations department.
7. United States Security and Exchange Commission.
8. An interesting case highlights the value of employee experience. In Europe, General Motor's head of purchasing, Jose Ignacio Lopez, after saving the company $1 billion in just a few years, left to join Volkswagen. What was Lopez' value? GM successfully sued Volkswagen, after it proved that some of Lopez' lieutenants (known as "warriors") had stolen GM documents. The documents in question were lists of GM parts and suppliers, which have little value to Volkswagen. Why was this case so hotly contested? On a personal level, GM executives felt betrayed by a former colleague. From a competitive standpoint it is even more upsetting that Lopez and a number of his team took their considerable knowledge to a competitor's camp. No book or course could replace the practical experience and inside information that the managers took with them.
9. Beck, *Shifting Gears*, p. 90.

Notes to Chapter 8

1. Michael A. Cusumano and Richard W. Selby, *Microsoft Secrets: How the World's Most Powerful Software Company Creates Technology, Shapes Markets and Manages People* (Free Press: New York, 1995), p. 92.
2. "Managing end user computing," Multi-Client Research Study, Nolan, Norton & Co, 1992.
3. Gartner, TCO Manager for Distributed Computing Software. Data provided by analyst Mike Silver.
4. The 2001 ASTD *State of the Industry Report*.
5. The exception to this statement was the demand for Cobol programmers to deal with the year 2000 crisis. Old mainframe systems were designed with only two digits for the year – instead of 1997, the program reads 97. In 2000, the year read 00 and some programs did not generate proper results. Companies spent an estimated one trillion dollars between 1995 and the year 2000 fixing this problem! Estimates range from $600 billion (Gartner) to $1.6 trillion (Capers Jones). Peter de Jager, a world authority on the Y2K crisis estimates the cost at $1 trillion! To learn more visit his site at www.year2000.com/.
6. Cusumano and Selby, *Microsoft Secrets*, p. 10.
7. On his deathbed Maslow actually refuted this claim, suggesting that the highest need is self-transcendence, working for some larger, worthier goal than just our own interests. Paradoxically, the only way an individual can achieve self-fulfillment is through service to others.
8. Robert Levering, *A Great Place to Work: What Makes Some Employers So Good (and Most So Bad)* (Random House: New York, 1985), p. xx.
9. National Speakers Association 1995 Convention, Minneapolis, 15–18 July 1995.

Notes to Chapter 9

1. Milken Institute.
2. Microsoft Network press releases.
3. Napster Public Relations Department.
4. Worldwide Ecommerce Growth, Forrester Research Inc.
5. This phrase was coined by James Gosling, the creator of Java and a Vice President at Sun Microsystems.
6. Morgan Keenan, "Elearning: the engine of the knowledge economy," Industry Report, p. 71.
7. United States Department of Labor, based on average weekly salary of $659.06, as of June 2000.

8. United States Bureau of Labor Statistics, based on a survey conducted in March 2000.

9. eLearning can take 25–70 percent less time to convey the same amount of information or instruction than that in traditional classroom designed programs, according to studies.

10. While some analysis have estimated that eLearning can cost up to three times as much as traditional learning to develop, Tom Kelly's experience as Vice President for Internet Learning at Cisco is that it cost no more than 40 percent more than traditional programs to develop, and in many cases costs less. On average he feels it costs 20 percent more. I have taken the 40 percent figure here.

11. The cost of infrastructure for both types of learning is not included – i.e. for classroom the cost of classroom facilities and computer labs, for eLearning the cost of the LMS – because in both cases they are sunk costs.

12. These are typically 20–40 percent of the develop costs per year in years 2 and 3 (in this example they are assumed to be 30 percent of development cost).

13. Hotels estimated at $140/night with Saturday night stay (total $840) plus cheaper airfares (estimated at $400) = $1240 per person. Assume only 50 percent of people travel for the course.

14. Assumes everyone uses their desktop at work or home

15. Based on an assumption of $200 per student per day. This accounts for meals, manuals, etc.

16. Assumes an administrative cost of $50 per user

17. Assumes average salary of $45,000 which when grossed up to include cost of benefits is $57,150 (holidays, sick time, Workers' Compensation). The typical work-year is 230 days – (deducting for weekends, holiday, vacations, etc.) giving a daily figure of $261.

18. Salaries for eLearning are only two-thirds because of the shorter time required to convey the same information.

19. This is the avoided profit while away from work. This figure was obtained by taking the average profit and dividing by number of employees and to give an average profit per employee. For instance, Oracle has revenues of $10 million and I am guessing here has 10,000 employees. This gives $1,000 per employee per year in profit. Divided by 230 days a year you get a figure of $4.35 per day avoided profit.

20. Over time I predict that the training and development department will add value by having learner comments and rating systems, which the LMS will track, much as Amazon.com has book ratings by readers. And readers then rate the reviewers. The same will happen for education and the LMS.

21. Commander Cooper, Chief of Navy Education and Training and LTJG Barbara Kelly at Chief of Naval Air Training office. The flight simulator software became "standard issue" in January 2000. It is an optional part of the students' training and not required. Those who choose to use the software can use it on their home computers or at computer labs on the bases. As a point of comparison, the home version of Microsoft's *Flight Simulator 2000 Pro* retails for $80 US and a traditional flight simulator at a Navy base can cost anywhere from $8,000 to $30 million depending on the tasks being performed and the level of realism required.

22. In 1979, Donald Kirkpatrick proposed four levels to evaluate the effectiveness of training. Level I diagnostics measure participants' reaction to a course, usually in the form of a survey, often called a "smile sheet." Level II measures learning. Participants complete surveys before and after the course to measure changes in self-reported attitudes and knowledge. Level III focuses on changes in behavior. This involves surveying the co-workers and supervisors of participants before and at least three months after the course to see if their behavior has changed. Finally, Level IV diagnostics seek to tie the training to business results and assess the financial impact on the bottom line. Each level is progressively more difficult and expensive. Working at Level IV is what will give HR and training departments increased respect in organizations.

23. Nuala Beck, *Shifting Gears: Thriving in the New Economy* (HarperCollins: Toronto, 1992).

24. "The deep Web: surfacing hidden value," white paper by Bright Planet.com LLC.

25. Morgan Keenan, "ELearning: the engine of the knowledge economy," Industry Report, p. 12.

26. "Email usage forecast and analysis, 2000–2005", study by IDC.

27. Year-end 1999 Mailbox Report, Messaging Online, www.messagingonline.com.

28. "ELearning and knowledge technology," SunTrust Equitable Securities White Paper, p. 9.
29. Ibid., p. 5.
30. Ibid., p. 7.
31. Ibid., p. 8.
32. "Global ecommerce approaches hypergrowth," Research Brief, Forrester Research Inc
33. "E-learning featuring ISOPIA: leading strategies for executive education and corporate training," *Fortune*, Special Advertising Section, 27 Nov. 2000.
34. I have always found the key to success in consulting is to coin a new phrase. Any consultant worth his or her salt has to have a new cutting-edge buzzword. And the pinnacle of success is to have your new buzzword quoted in Dilbert of course.
35. National Training Laboratory study.
36. "ELearning and knowledge technology," SunTrust Equitable Securities White Paper p. 12.

Notes to Chapter 10

1. Jack Parr researches customer satisfaction. Contact Jack Parr and Associates, (913) 827–0404 or on the web at www.jackparr.com.
2. "Realize your customers' full profit potential," *Harvard Business Review*, Sep.–Oct. 1995.
3. *Strategies for Seizing Control of Your Industry and Creating the Markets of Tomorrow* (Harvard Business School Press: Boston, MA, 1994), p. 97.
4. For more information about the National Retail Federation, call (202) 783–7971 or surf www.nrf.com.
5. Compaq is the largest PC manufacturer in the world with 13.7 percent market share, according to a survey by Gartner, August 2001.
6. "Fear of technology is phobia of the 90's; computer habits, attitudes determine 'techno-type'," Dell Computer Corporation, 26 July 1993.
7. For more information about Visa's neural network, check out their website at www.visa.com.
8. Scott Strumello of Auriemma Consulting Group. Contact (516) 333–4800.
9. Figures from Canadian Bankers Association Fast Statistics.
10. A 1.000 batter – pronounced one thousand – will hit the ball 1,000 times out of 1,000 times at bat. A .250 batter will hit the ball 250 times out of 1,000 times at bat.
11. Gary Hamel and C.K. Prahalad, *Competing for the Future: Breakthrough Strategies for Seizing Control of Your Industry and Creating the Markets of Tomorrow* (Harvard Business School Press: Boston, MA, 1994), p. 238.
12. Francis Vincent's speech at Fairfield University, "Education and baseball" reported in *America*, 6 April 1991, pp. 372–373.
13. Jan Carlzon, *Moments of Truth* (Harper & Row: New York, 1987), p. 3.
14. For an excellent study of this trend, read Don Peppers and Martha Rogers, *The One to One Future* (Currency Doubleday: New York, 1993).

Notes to Chapter 11

1. Don Tapscott and Art Caston, *Paradigm Shift: The New Promise of Information Technology* (McGraw-Hill: New York, 1993), p. 97.
2. Wal-Mart Annual Report 2000.
3. Peter Senge, *The Fifth Discipline: The Art and Practice of the Learning Organization* (Doubleday Currency: New York, 1990).
4. Nielson/Netratings, "Online travel industry captures $1.2 billion in January, led by Travelocity," 20 Mar. 2001.
5. For more information about Sabre, check out their website at www.sabre.com.
6. Don Tapscott, *The Digital Economy: Promise and Peril in the Digital Economy* (McGraw-Hill: New York, 1996), p. 77.

7. Other processes that foster creativity and innovation include Edward de Bono's *Six Thinking Hats or Lateral Thinking*. For information call MICA at (416) 366-6422 or 1-800-668-8298.
8. *Time* Special Issue, "Age of the road warrior," Spring 1995, p. 39.
9. Douglas Coupland's *Microserfs* is a great read.
10. Tapscott and Caston, *Paradigm Shift*, p. 129.
11. Ibid.
12. Interview with Ken Nickerson, Director of Technical Services, Microsoft.
13. Christos Cotsakos, President and CEO of e*Trade, "Chaos and uncertainty please . . .," *Entrepriser*, vol. 4, Fall 1996.
14. "The birth of a new species," *The Economist*, Software Industry Survey, 25 May 1996, p. 1.
15. Ibid., p. 4.
16. OVUM Research Group.
17. Don Tapscott, *Digital Economy*, p. 62.
18. Mikel Harry, *The Vision of Six Sigma*.

Chapter 12

1. Between September 1999 and September 2000, the US Post Service Office delivered 103.5 billion first-class letters, 10.4 billion pieces of periodical mail and 1 billion international pieces of mail, for a total of 200 billion letters. According Messaging Online, the number of email boxes exceeded 440 million in the United States alone. According to Thomas Staffing of California, an average of 300 million email messages are sent each day in the US. These means that email volumes exceed postal volumes. Internal use of email is booming in Sun Microsystems, Intel, Microsoft and Netscape, where it runs as high as 300 per person per day. This creates fundamental changes in the way organizations work.
2. Matthew R. Sanders with Bruce D. Temkin. "Global ecommerce approaches hypergrowth," Forrester, 18 April 2000 (www.forrester.com).
3. "Are you fast enough? Are you hungry enough? Are you tough enough to work, live, compete in Netscape time?" *Fast Company*, Premier issue, p. 96.
4. Steve Hamm, "The long shadow of Bill Gates," *Business Week*, 18 Aug. 1997, p. 85.
5. Steve M. Fortuna, Michael Hillmeyer and Melanie Hollands, "Dell field trip highlights and company strengths," Merrill Lynch, 5 Mar. 2001.
6. Blane, Modahl and Johnson, *Business*, vol. 1, no. 1.
7. "Could," *Fortune*, p. 26.
8. Figures by US Bancorp Piper Jaffray. Third quarter 2000.
9. Brian Swimme and Thomas Berry, *The Universe Story* (Harper Collins: New York, 1992), pp. 11-12.
10. US Department of Commerce, "Falling through the Net: toward digital inclusion," October 2000.
11. For more information about SET, check out their website at www.setco.org.
12. K.K. Campbell, "A question of copyright," *Toronto Star*, 18 Jan. 1996, pp. H1, H5.
13. International Data Corporation, press release.
14. Datamonitor, press release.
15. For more information about the eCheck Project, check out their website at www.eheck.org.

Notes to Chapter 13

1. Richard Dennis, quoted by Jack D Schwager, *Market Wizards* (Harper Business: New York, 1993), p. 110.
2. Contact the Rocky Mountain Institute at (970) 927-3851.
3. Amory Lovins and William Browning, "Negawatts for buildings," *Urban Land*, July 1992.
4. *MacLean's*, Apr. 1996, p. 41.

Notes on Reactions to The Learning Paradox

1. Tom Muccio is now Vice President at P&G, Mike Szymanczyk, is president of Phillip Morris and Bill Burns founded TPG – the Partnering Group, a consulting firm on partnering.
2. Alecia Swasy, *Soap Opera: The Inside Story of Procter & Gamble*, p. 60.
3. George A. Miller, "The magical number seven, plus or minus two: some limits on our capacity for processing information," *Psychological Review*, vol. 63 no. 2 (March 1956). A psychologist studies human short term memory.
4. Ibid.
5. Henry Albert's work in helping to redesign the US Defense Acquisition System.

Bibliography

Allan, Robyn. *Quest for Prosperity: The Dance of Success*. Vancouver: Blue Feather Publishing (A Division of CYF Consulting), 1995.

American Management Association. *Blueprints for Service Quality: The FedEx Approach*. AMA Briefing, 1991.

Argyris, Chris. *Overcoming Defensive Routines*.

Bandler, Richard and John Grinder. *Frogs into Princes*, 1981.

Bardwick, Judith, *The Plateauing Trap*. New York: Bantam, 1988.

Bardwick, Judith. *Danger in the Comfort Zone*. New York: American Management Association, 1991.

Barker, Joel Arthur. *Paradigms: The Business of Discovering the Future*. New York: HarperBusiness, 1993.

Beck, Nuala. *Shifting Gears: Thriving in the New Economy*. Toronto: HarperCollins, 1992.

Canaccord Capital. *eLearning: Special Industry Report*, June 2000.

Carlzon, Jan. *Moments of Truth*. New York: Harper & Row, 1987.

Carnegie, Dale. *How to Win Friends and Influence People*. New York: Pocket Books, 1936.

Carson, Patrick and Julia Moulden. *Green Is Gold*. Toronto: HarperBusiness, 1991.

Cerf, Christopher and Victor Navasky. *The Experts Speak*. New York: Pantheon, 1984

Champy, James. *Reengineering Management: The Mandate for New Leadership*. New York: HarperBusiness, 1995.

Churchland, Paul, *The Engine of Reason, the Seat of the Soul*

Close, Richard C., Rob Humphreys and Brian W. Ruttenbur. *E-Learning and Knowledge Technology*. SunTrust Equitable Securities. March, 2000.

Covey, Stephen. *How to Succeed with People*. Salt Lake City: Deseret Book Company, 1971.

Covey, Stephen. *The 7 Habits of Highly Effective People*. New York: Fireside, 1989.

Covey, Stephen. *Principle Centered Leadership*. New York: Summit Books, 1990.

Csikszentmihalyi, Mihaly. *Flow: The Psychology of Optimal Experience*. New York: Harper & Row, 1990.

Cusumano, Michael A. and Richard W. Selby *Microsoft Secrets: How the World's Most Powerful Software Company Creates Technology, Shapes Markets and Manages People*. New York: Free Press (Simon & Schuster), 1995.

De Geus, Arie. "Planning as Learning." *Harvard Business Review*, 66, no. 2 (1988), 70–74

De Geus, Arie. *The Living Company*. Boston, MA: Harvard Business School Press, 1997.

Delphi Group. *Need to Know: Integrating e-Learning with High Velocity Value Chains*. White Paper. December 2000.

Deming, W. Edwards. *Out of Crisis*. Cambridge, MA: MIT Center for Advanced Engineering Study, 1982.

Eden, Colin, Sue Jones and David Sims. *Messing About in Problems: An Informal Structured Approach to their Identification and Management*. Oxford: Pergamon Press, 1983.

Fisher, Roger and William Ury. *Getting to Yes: Negotiating Agreement Without Giving In*. New York: Penguin, 1981.

Fitz-Enz, Jac. *Benchmarking Staff Performance*. San Francisco: Jossey-Bass, 1993.

Fitz-Enz, Jac. *Human Value Management*. San Francisco: Jossey-Bass, 1990.

Many times I realize how much of my own outer and inner life is built upon the labors of my fellowmen, both living and dead and how earnestly I must exert myself in order to give in return as much as I have received.
Albert Einstein

Foot, David with Daniel Stoffman. *Boom, Bust & Echo*. Toronto: Macfarlane Walter & Ross, 1996.

Frappaolo, Carl. *Ushering In the Knowledge-Based Economy*. The Delphi Group (Forbes Magazine Special Advertising Section) April, 1998.

Friend, John and Allen Hickling, *Planning Under Pressure: The Strategic Choice Approach*

Gerlach, Charles. "The ASP revolution: why hosting applications will transform business." *Mainspring*. Jan. 2000.

Gleick James, *Chaos: Making a New Science Canada*,.Penguin Books, New York, 1988.

Graff, James. "Left behind: Europe's labor force is out of date . . . and out of work," *Time Magazine*, May 8, 2000.

Grove, Andrew. *Only the Paranoid Survive*. New York: Bantam Doubleday Dell, 1996.

Hamel, Gary and C.K. Prahalad. *Competing for the Future: Breakthrough Strategies for Seizing Control of Your Industry and Creating the Markets of Tomorrow*. Boston, MA: Harvard Business School Press, 1994.

Hammer, Michael. "Reengineering work: don't automate, obliterate." *Harvard Business Review*, July/Aug. 1990.

Hammer, Michael and James Champy. *Reengineering the Corporation: A Manifesto for Business Revolution*. New York: HarperBusiness, 1993.

Harris, Jim. *The Learning Paradox*, Toronto: Macmillan Canada, 1998

Herzberg, Frederick. "One more time: how do you motivate employees?" *Harvard Business Review*, Jan./Feb. 1968.

Innes, Eva, Jim Lyon and Jim Harris. *The 100 Best Companies to Work for in Canada*. Toronto: HarperCollins, 1990.

ISOPIA. "E-Learning: leading strategies for executive education and corporate training." Special Advertising Section, *Fortune*, 27 Nov. 2000.

Janes, F.R. "Interpretive structural modeling: a methodology for structuring complex issues." *Trans Inst Mech. Engrs* C, 10, no. 3, August 1988

Kanter, Rosabeth Moss. *When Giants Learn to Dance*. New York: Simon & Schuster, 1989.

Kerry, Senator Bob and Rep Johnny Isakson. *The Power of the Internet for Learning*. Report of the Web-based Education Commission to the President and the Congress of the United States, Dec. 2000.

Kirkpatrick, Donald L. *Evaluating Training Programs: The Four Levels*, 2nd edn. San Francisco: Berrett-Koehler, 1998.

Kuhn, Thomas S. *The Structure of Scientific Revolutions*. Chicago: University of Chicago Press, 1970.

Levering, Robert. *A Great Place to Work: What Makes Some Employers So Good (and Most So Bad)*. New York: Random House, 1985.

Levering, Robert. and Milton Moskowitz. *The 100 Best Companies to Work for in America*. New York: Doubleday/Currency, 1993.

Lynch, Dudley and Paul L. Kordis. *Strategy of the Dolphin*. New York: Ballantine, 1988.

McMurrer, Daniel P., Mark E. Van Buren and William H. Woodwell, Jr. *The 2000 ASTD State of the Industry Report*. The American Society for Training and Development, 2000.

Mintzberg, Henry "That's not turbulence, Chicken Little, that's real opportunity." *Planning Review*, 22, no.6 (1994), 7–9.

Moe, Michael T. and Henry Blodget. *The Knowledge Web: People Power – Fuel for the New Economy*. Merrill Lynch & Co. May 2000.

Negroponte, Nicholas. *Being Digital*. New York: Alfred A. Knopf, 1995.

O'Toole, James. *Leading Change: The Argument for Values-Based Leadership*. New York: Random House, 1995.

Osborne, David and Ted Gaebler. *Reinventing Government*. Reading, MA: Addison-Wesley, 1992.

Peck, M. Scott. *The Road Less Traveled*. New York: Simon & Schuster, 1978.

Peppers, Don and Martha Rogers. *The One to One Future*. New York: Currency Doubleday, 1993.

Personal Selling Power. 'E-Train: how sales training takes on new life through internet connections.' May 2000.

Personal Selling Power. "E-Train: how sales training takes on new life through internet connections." May 2000.

Porter, Michael *Competitive Advantage: Creating and Sustaining Superior Performance* (June 1998).

Pritchett, Lou. *Stop Paddling and Start Rocking the Boat*. EastWest Books, 1999.

Pugh, Stuart. *Concept Selection – A Method that Works*. Paper delivered to the International Conference on Engineering Design, 9–13 March 1981

Rebello, Kathy. "Inside Microsoft: the untold story of how the Internet forced Bill Gates to reverse his corporate strategy." *Business Week*, 15 Jul. 1996, 56–67.

Reichheld, Frederick F. *The Loyalty Effect: The Hidden Force Behind Growth, Profits, and Lasting Value*. Boston, MA: Harvard Business School Press, 1996.

Reynolds, Bob. *The 100 Best Companies to Work for in the UK*. London: Fontana, 1989.

Roberts, Wayne and Susan Brandum. "Get a life: how to make a good buck, dance around the dinosaurs and save the world while you're at it." *Publishing House*, October 1995.

Rosenberg, Marc J. *e-Learning: Strategies for Delivering Knowledge in the Digital Age*. New York: McGraw-Hill, 2001.

Ruttenbur, Brian W., Ginger Spickler and Sebastian Lurie. *ELearning: The Engine of the Knowledge Economy*. Morgan Keegan. July 2000.

Schwartz, Peter *The Art of the Long View: Planning for the Future in an Uncertain World*, 1996.

Semler, Ricardo. *Maverick*. New York: Warner Books, 1993.

Senge, P. *The Fifth Discipline: The Art and Practice of the Learning Organization*. New York: Doubleday/Currency, 1990.

Souque, Jean-Pascal. *Training & Development Practices, Expenditures and Trends*. Conference Board of Canada, 1996.

Stein, Daniel. "All systems slow: how everything from glass to the economy takes shape." *The Sciences*, Sep./Oct. 1988

Swanson, Richard A. and Deane B. Gradous. *Forecasting Financial Benefits of Human Resource Development*. San Francisco: Jossey-Bass, 1988.

Tapscott, Don and Art Caston. *Paradigm Shift: The New Promise of Information Technology*. New York: McGraw-Hill, 1993.

Tapscott, Don and Art Caston. *The Digital Economy: Promise and Peril in the Age of Networked Intelligence*. New York: McGraw-Hill, 1996.

Thomas, Gilovich. *How We Know What Isn't So: The Fallibility of Human Reason in Everyday Life*.

Toffler, Alvin. *The Third Wave*. New York: Bantam Books, 1981.

Treacy, Michael and Fred Wiersema. *The Discipline of Market Leaders*. Reading, MA: Addison-Wesley, 1995.

Tsai Chih Chung, *Zen Speaks* (translated by Grian Bruya). Anchor Books, Doubleday, New York, 1994.

Urdan, Trace A. *Corporate E-Learning: Exploring a New Frontier*. W.R. Hambrecht. Apr 2000.

Wack, Pierre. "Scenarios: shooting the rapids." *Harvard Business Review*, 63, no. 6 (1985), 139–150.

Wack, Pierre. "Scenarios: the gentle art of reperceiving." Harvard Business School working paper. Cambridge MA: Harvard College, 1984.

Wack, Pierre. "Scenarios: uncharted waters ahead." *Harvard Business Review*, 63, no. 5 (1985): 72–9

Waldrop, M. Mitchell. *Complexity: The Emerging Science at the Edge of Order and Chaos*. Touchstone (Simon & Schuster), New York, 1992.

Wallace, James and Jim Erickson. *Hard Drive: Bill Gates and the Making of the Microsoft Empire*. New York: HarperBusiness, 1992.

Warfield, John N. and A. Roxana Cárdenas, *A Handbook of Interactive Management*. Ames, IA: Iowa State University Press, 1994.

Warfield, John N. *Societal Systems: Planning, Policy, and Complexity*. New York: Wiley Interscience, 1976.

Warfield, John N. *A Science of Generic Design: Managing Complexity through Systems Design*, in Salinas, C.A: *Intersystems, 1990*, 2nd edn, 2 vols. Ames, IA: Iowa State University Press, 1994.

Wheatley, Margaret J. *Leadership and the New Science: Learning About Organization from an Orderly Universe*. San Francisco: Berrett-Koehler, 1992.

Wilson, Larry and Hersch Wilson. *Play to Win!: Choosing Growth over Fear in Work and Life*. Bard Press, 1998.

Wilson, Larry and Hersch Wilson. *Stop Selling and Start Partnering: The New Thinking about Finding and Keeping Customers*. New York: John Wiley, 1996.

Acknowledgments

Writing *The Learning Paradox* began in response to the question, "How can individuals and organizations create greater security?" This material evolved in working with clients over eight years. It has been tested by thousands of executives, managers, front-line staff, parents and community group volunteers who participated in seminars around the world. Their insights, questions, critiques and feedback have shaped the material. I am grateful to them for their wisdom.

I am really excited to be working with Capstone: Mark Allin and Richard Burton the founders of Capstone and co-publishers, and Katherine Hieronymus and Sue McCormick who are responsible for marketing and promotion, Nick Allen for editing and his attention to details, Mark Essen for text design and Darren Hayball for the elegant, fun and provocative cover design. Capstone is an imprint of John Wiley & Sons, a global publisher of print and electronic products. In addition to offices in the US, Wiley has operations in Europe (England and Germany), Canada, Asia and Australia. It is exciting that *The Learning Paradox* will be released in all these markets simultaneously.

I am especially grateful to my literary agents, Robert Mackwood and Perry Goldsmith of Contemporary Communications, who are diligent, professional, skilled and delightful to work with.

I want to thank the team at Strategic Advantage – especially Victoria Musgrave for all her hard work in researching and updating this edition of *The Learning Paradox*, to Shawnessy Johnson who served as the office manager during this period.

I am grateful to the four authors and consultants for their reactions to *The Learning Paradox*. As the global thought leaders in energy conservation, Hunter and Amory Lovins' groundbreaking work gives me tremendous hope for the future. I feel lucky to call Lou Pritchett a friend – his pioneering work in integrating the operations of Procter and Gamble and Wal-Mart is the definitive case study for supply chain management. Lou is an inspiration for me – he has such a positive uplifting and friendly spirit. He is a joy to be around. Finally to my colleague Cliff Saunders whose work I greatly admire – he and I plan to write a book on complexity.

I wish to thank my clients. They are my best teachers. Their encouragement and feedback on this journey has been the ultimate reward. So many individuals have enthusiastically embraced this work. Seeing the principles applied has given me tremendous satisfaction. Over 40,000 copies of *The Learning Paradox* are now in print. Thanks to my friends, colleagues and clients who have greatly enriched the text through their insights: Robyn Allan, Everett Anstey, Christopher Ash, Colum Bastable, Judy Bell, Ralph Beslin, Alison Besse, Jeremy Boudreau, Rick Broadhead, Meghan Brousseau, Eli Bay, Ruth Brothers, Donna Burn, Peter Buchanan, Tom Burney, Jim Carroll, Ken Clarke, Jim Clubine, Fredrik Carlberg, Patrick Carson, Charles S. Coffey, Carol Cox, David Cox, Phyllis Downing, Diane Eisele, Jim Evans, Catherine Fels-Smith, Brian Foley, Wayne Fiander, Bill Foster, Barbara Frances, Theresa Gill, Margo Gordon, Arlynn Greenbaum, David Hardy, Sharon Harvey-Smith, Pat Henderson, Chuck Hoffman, Richard Jensen, Bill Johnston, Susan Jurow, Paddy Kamen, John Kempster, Wayne Kempton, Debra Kerby, Marla Krisko, Andrea Kuch, Jill Lambert, Ray Lancashire, Donald Languedoc, Daphne Lavers, Irene Lum, D'Arcy Mackenzie, Alison Maclean, Ginette Maklo, Stephen Marks, Barbara Marshall, Fraser McAllan, Brian McConnell, Sheree McGarrity, Suzanne McGee, David McIntyre, Susan McLarty, Andrew McMurtry, Janice McNally, David McWhirter, Ian Melanson, Eric Mills, Catherine Middleton, Nancy Myers, John Mowat, James Mitchell, Gail Palkovich, Randy Parkin, Ian Percy, Farah Perelmuter, Jim Poirier, Shannon Potts, David Power, Wayne Roberts, Lionel Robins, Glori Rosato-Sararus, Richard Searns, Kathleen Seaver, Kelly Smith, Rick Spence, Arthur Soler, JoAnne Sommers, Anna Stancer, Jody Stevens, Chris Stoate, Nat Stoddard, Meg Taylor, Anthony Thomas, Nick Truyens, Ravi Vijh, Pat Vincent, Chantal Vlachos, Jonathan Wellum, Debi Whistlecraft, Bob Willard, Bill Wilson, Warner Woodley, Hugh Zochling and Ken Zoschke.

Chapter 5, "Creating Sustainable Enterprises," is a collaborative effort. The primary contributor is Don Beeken of Key Consulting in Calgary, Alberta, with input from Randy Parkin, Robert Craddock, Ron Koper.

I am *truly grateful* to my global agents at Can*Speak: Linda Davidson, Tina Boudreau, Sheree McGarrity, Belinda Miller-Foey, Lesley Rizvi, Laurie Peck, Andrea Linsley, and Christine Christianson. Life is short so it had better be fun, and the team certainly has made it fun. They are a joy to work with!

Jim Harris

Jim Harris is a one of North America's foremost authors and thinkers on change and leadership. As a management consultant and best-selling author he is much sought after. *Association* magazine ranked him as one of Canada's top ten speakers. As a management consultant, Jim speaks internationally at over 50 conferences a year on the issues of most concern to executives:

- Leadership
- Change, Creativity & Innovation
- Future Trends
- Information Technology's Impact
- Customer Retention & Intimacy
- Creating Learning Organizations

He gives workshops on:
- Strategic planning
- Creating Common Mission/Vision
- Teamwork

His intensive, hands-on seminars range from an hour to three days. For information visit www.jimharris.com.

Mr Harris' clients include Agilent Technologies, Arthur Andersen, Association of Research Libraries, Barclays Bank, Centra, Certified Management Accountants, Columbia Tristar Pictures, Deloitte & Touche, European Snack Food Association, General Motors, Glaxo Wellcome, IABC, IEEE, International Council of Shopping Centers, JD Edwards, Johnson & Johnson, Mastercard, Munich Reassurance, Nortel Networks, Novartis, Pasteur Mérieux Connaught, Saba, Society of Professional Engineers, Sun Microsystems, Sybase, TNT Worldwide Express, and Zurich.

The Learning Paradox was nominated for the Canadian National Business Book Award, and has appeared on numerous bestseller lists. Books for Business has ranked it as one of the top 10 business books in all of North America. There are now over 40,000 copies in print.

Mr Harris coauthored the national bestseller *The 100 Best Companies to Work for in Canada* – which sold 50,000 copies. As a management consultant Mr Harris, works with leading businesses, *Fortune 500* companies, and organizations aspiring to join these ranks. Between 1992 and 1996 he represented the Covey Leadership Center in Canada – teaching Dr Stephen Covey's work, *The Seven Habits of Highly Effective People* to clients.

Jim Harris' presentations have a powerful impact. Here's what clients say:

Your workshop was the most highly rated by our partners and managers.
– Megan Frigon, Specialty Consulting, Arthur Andersen & Co.

The audience's attention was riveted. Wow, what thought-provoking material!
– Gilbert Cordell, International Conference on Horizontal Well Drilling

Your presentation initiated a shift in strategic thinking within our plant management.
– Richard Jensen, P.Eng, General Manager, Manufacturing, CXY Chemicals

The content was applicable to everyone's professional and personal lives. Your immense popularity was indicative of the audience's positive response, as were the results of our Symposium survey. We can unequivocally recommend Jim Harris as a speaker.
– Pete Peters, Chair, Continuous Improvement Symposium, General Motors

Your thought provoking presentation brought the demands of the future into sharp focus. In the course of my work with CEO's of growth oriented companies, I have experienced many first-class presentations. Without a doubt, yours ranks among the most insightful.
– Peter Buchanan, CEO Network, 50 Best Managed Private Companies

The median rating for your workshops was 10/10.
– Delmarie Scherloski, Director, Certified General Accountants

THANK YOU for a simply fantastic keynote presentation. Weeks later I am still hearing my colleagues referring to your talk.
– Al Doran, Past President, CHRSP (now IHRIM)

As if the enthusiastic response of our audience wasn't enough, the results of our post conference survey are conclusive: you were a major hit! In fact, the response of 2,000 delegates closely paralleled my own assessment: the content was on target, the presentation superlative. You are at the top of our list as a speaker for future events.
– Phil Cunningham, President, Mackenzie Financial

Having attended countless motivational seminars over the years, I am very selective. One of the best training messages I've heard at MPI was delivered by Jim Harris.

– Marjorie Hamilton, Past International President, Meeting Professionals Int'l

Thank you for kicking off our Executive Teambuilding workshop in such an inspiring way. You wove together up-to-date business case information, inspiring thoughts from significant business leaders and your own personal thoughts on leadership in such an entertaining and thought provoking manner.

– Kathleen Seaver, Director, Worldwide Business Process Improvement, Pasteur Mérieux Connaught

What's particularly noteworthy is that you went beyond the standard 'shelf talk' and were able to link your ideas to the interests and experiences of the audience. The overwhelming favorable reviews give me reason to invite you back.

– Marvin Morrison, Senior VP, International Council of Shopping Centers

You are an extremely charismatic presenter who totally involves your audience. You allow participants to internalize your points and understand completely through the use of meaningful real-world anecdotes.

– Nick Truyens, General Manager, LEGO Canada

Thank you for the extraordinary success of our technology showcase series. We hit a home run! . . . delivering a fresh topic to over 550 participants in four markets. The strength and freshness of your presentation and delivery skills kept the whole program on track.

– Jessica McMahon, Marketing Director, Northeast Region, Sybase

Congratulations on completely captivating your audience! Your session got an outstanding response! Thanks for a *superb* job. It was well noted that you took the time to get to know the crowd. They loved you, Jim, as I'm sure you could tell by the crush of attention following the session. You won this year's 'most fun speaker to work with' vote.

– Julie Charles, Editor, Meetings & Incentive Travel

Index

Volume Discount Schedule: International Audio Tape and CD Orders

Many organizations have purchased *The Learning Paradox* in bulk, giving a copy of the single audio (tape or CD) or audio set (three tapes or two CDs) to every executive, manager and employee. Some companies are giving these to clients as marketing and promotion premiums. The aggressive discount schedule below makes this possible. *The Learning Paradox* was nominated for the Canadian National Business Book Award in 1999, and Books for Business has ranked it as one of the top 10 business books in all of North America. There are now over 40,000 copies in print!

# Items ordered together	% Discount	Price per item $US	
		Single audio	Audio set
Cost	–	11.95	32.50
25+	20	9.60	26.00
50+	30	8.40	22.75
100+	40	7.20	19.50
200+	46	6.45	17.55
500+	50	6.00	16.25
1,500+	56	5.30	14.30
2,500+	61	4.70	12.70
5,000+	65	4.20	11.40
10,000+	70	3.60	9.75

AUDIO   75 minutes of live presentation.

THREE-TAPE SET   3½ hours of live presentation.

Prices quoted in $US. Taxes & shipping are extra. You can mix and match – i.e. when buying 500 units – 300 single audios and 200 of the three tape sets – you get the 50 percent discount on all items. *Minimum order is 25 units.*

Four ways to order

speakers'
spotlight

179 John St., Suite 201
Toronto, Ontario M5T 1X4

1 800 333-4453
t: 416 345-1559
f: 416 345-9589
e: info@speakers.ca
www.speakers.ca